RETHINKING JUDICIAL JURISDICTION IN PRIVATE INTERNATIONAL LAW

This book explores the theory and practice of judicial jurisdiction within the field of private international law. It offers a revised look at values justifying the power of courts to hear and decide cross-border disputes, and demonstrates that a re-conceptualisation of jurisdiction is needed. Rather than deriving from territorial power of states, jurisdiction in civil and commercial cross-border matters ought to be driven by party autonomy. This autonomy can be limited by certain considerations of equality and critical state sovereign interests.

The book applies this normative view to the existing rules of jurisdiction in the European Union and the Russian Federation. These regimes are chosen due to their unique positions towards values in private international law and contrasting societal norms that generate and accommodate these values. Notwithstanding disparate cultural and political ideas, these regimes reveal a surprising level of consistency when it comes to enforcement of party autonomy. There is, nevertheless, room for improvement. The book demonstrates to scholars, policy makers and lawmakers that jurisdiction should be re-centred around the interests of private actors, and proposes ways to improve the current rules.

Volume 24 in the series Studies in Private International Law

Studies in Private International Law

Recent titles in the series

Child Abduction within the European Union
Katarina Trimmings

International Surrogacy Arrangements: Legal Regulation at the International Level
Edited by Katarina Trimmings and Paul Beaumont

The Hague Child Abduction Convention: A Critical Analysis
Rhona Schuz

Interregional Recognition and Enforcement of Civil and Commercial Judgments: Lessons for China from the US and EU Law
Jie Huang

The Recovery of Maintenance in the EU and Worldwide
Paul Beaumont, Burkhard Hess, Lara Walker and Stefanie Spancken

Australian Private International Law for the 21st Century: Facing Outwards
Edited by Andrew Dickinson, Thomas John and Mary Keyes

Maintenance and Child Support in Private International Law
Lara Walker

The Choice of Law Contract
Maria Hook

The Nature and Enforcement of Choice of Court Agreements: A Comparative Study
Mukarrum Ahmed

Cross-Border Litigation in Europe
Edited by Paul Beaumont, Mihail Danov, Katarina Trimmings and Burcu Yuksel

Forum (Non) Conveniens in England: Past, Present, and Future
Ardavan Arzandeh

Commercial Issues in Private International Law: A Common Law Perspective
Edited by Vivienne Bath, Andrew Dickinson, Michael Douglas and Mary Keyes

Jurisdiction and Cross-Border Collective Redress: A European Private International Law Perspective
Alexia Pato

Rethinking Judicial Jurisdiction in Private International Law

Party Autonomy, Categorical Equality and Sovereignty

Milana Karayanidi

• HART •
OXFORD • LONDON • NEW YORK • NEW DELHI • SYDNEY

HART PUBLISHING
Bloomsbury Publishing Plc
Kemp House, Chawley Park, Cumnor Hill, Oxford, OX2 9PH, UK
1385 Broadway, New York, NY 10018, USA

First published in Great Britain 2020

A catalogue record for this book is available from the British Library.

Library of Congress Cataloging-in-Publication data

Names: Karayanidi, Milana, author.

Title: Rethinking judicial jurisdiction in private international law : party autonomy, categorical equality and sovereignty / Milana Karayanidi.

Description: Oxford ; New York : Hart, 2020. | Series: Studies in private international law; volume 24 | Based on author's thesis (doctoral – Trinity College (Dublin, Ireland), 2016) issued under title: Reassessing the approach to jurisdiction in civil and commercial matters : party autonomy, categorical equality and sovereignty. | Includes bibliographical references and index.

Identifiers: LCCN 2019039855 (print) | LCCN 2019039856 (ebook) | ISBN 9781509924776 (hardback) | ISBN 9781509924783 (Epub)

Subjects: LCSH: Conflict of laws—Jurisdiction. | Conflict of laws—Jurisdiction—European Union countries. | Conflict of laws—Jurisdiction—Russia (Federation) | Conflict of laws—Jurisdiction—English-speaking countries.

Classification: LCC K7625 .K37 2020 (print) | LCC K7625 (ebook) | DDC 340.9—dc23

LC record available at https://lccn.loc.gov/2019039855

LC ebook record available at https://lccn.loc.gov/2019039856

ISBN: HB: 978-1-50992-477-6
ePDF: 978-1-50992-479-0
ePub: 978-1-50992-478-3

Typeset by Compuscript Ltd, Shannon

To my loved ones and my mentors

SERIES EDITOR'S PREFACE

This book advocates a theory of private international law of jurisdiction based primarily on private interests rather than State sovereignty or territoriality. Karayanidi argues that private interests are best promoted through party autonomy – with appropriate restrictions for categories of weaker parties and a few bases of exclusive jurisdiction – which should only be restricted in the public interest which in turn largely reflects collective private interests.

The author focuses on the jurisdiction regimes in the EU and Russia. She proposes a number of changes to both regimes based on her normative, private interests dominated theory of jurisdiction. The author's ideas for law reform are always interesting. Whilst her analysis of the existing EU regime will contain few surprises for most readers the explanation of the Russian law on jurisdiction based on the provisions in the codes, academic writings and case law will be new to many readers including me. Karayanidi does a significant service to non-Russian speakers by this work. The analysis of Russian jurisdiction is completely new to the Hart Studies in Private International Law Series.

I commend this book to readers as a serious attempt to advance the theory of private international law of jurisdiction and to apply that theory to the specific contexts of the EU and Russia.

Paul Beaumont
(University of Stirling)

PREFACE

The subject of conflict of laws and the topic of judicial jurisdiction in particular are not often theorised about. This work aims to contribute to the scholarship in the area by offering a revised look on values behind a jurisdiction regime. The findings demonstrate that reconceptualisation of justification for judicial jurisdiction is needed. Rather than deriving from the territorial power of the states, determination of jurisdiction in international matters ought to be driven by party autonomy. The general rule of party autonomy can be limited by considerations of categorical equality (in view of protecting certain categories of private parties) and sovereignty (limited state sovereign interests essential to preserve the integrity of the international system).

This book developed from observing the existing rules on judicial jurisdiction and case law in the EU and Russia, and evaluating the hypotheses and theories justifying those rules. This book evolved on an analysis of relevant primary sources, the legal principles behind the rules, and the theoretical background of jurisdiction in private international law. To construct the argument, a comparison[1] of legal traditions in private international law of these two regimes was studied: the Brussels jurisdiction regime applicable across the European Union, and Russian rules on international jurisdiction in civil and commercial matters. Since the EU constitutes a unique merger of many differing legal principles, the interpretation of the EU rules was derived both from the case law of the European Court of Justice (ECJ) and some national case law. The choice of these jurisdictions was predicated by their unique positions towards values in private international law and by contrasting the societal norms that accommodate those values. Legal training in English common law and EU law, and emergence in the Russian language and culture by origin of the author, provided the necessary fluency in the target jurisdiction regimes. The comparative assessment of the values and rules prevailing in these legal systems aimed 'to bring about a certain sense of relativity'[2] to the prevailing views. By discussing the similarities and

[1] For more discourse on comparative law being viewed as a method or as a discipline, see, eg, S Glanert, 'Method?' in P Monateri (ed), *Methods of Comparative Law* (Edward Elgar Publishing, 2012), citing Frederick Pollock's speech at the international conference on comparative law in Paris at the beginning of the twentieth century.

[2] P Legrand, 'Beyond Method: Comparative Law as a Perspective' (1988) 36 *American Journal of Comparative Law* 788, 789.

differences, and the merits of national solutions, ways were sought to improve the existing rules.

Finally, it covers the history behind the legal concepts and certain unusual rules, so as to 'obtain the mastery over them by a thorough grounding in history'.[3]

Thus, this book proposes a fresh view on jurisdiction that can fit the rules of jurisdiction in the EU and Russia in their current form, with certain adjustments.

[3] FK von Savigny, *Of the Vocation of Our Age for Legislation and Jurisprudence* (Abraham Hayward tr, Littlewood & Co Old Bailey, 1831) 132.

CONTENTS

PART II
PARTY EQUALITY

LIST OF ABBREVIATIONS

ASIL	American Society of International Law
BGB	Bürgerliches Gesetzbuch, German Civil Code
CAP	Arbitrazhno-Protsessual'nyĭ Kodeks Rossiĭskoĭ Federatsii, Russian Code of *Arbitrazh* (Commercial) Procedure
CCP	Grazhdanskiĭ Protsessual'nyĭ Kodeks Rossiĭskoĭ Federatsii, Russian Code of Civil Procedure
ECJ	European Court of Justice
EU	European Union
PCIJ	Permanent Court of International Justice
RF	Russian Federation
RSFSR	Russian Soviet Federative Socialist Republic
UK	United Kingdom
US	United States
ZPO	Zivilprozessordnung, German Code of Civil Procedure

TABLE OF CASES

The EU

Russia

UK

Other

TABLE OF LEGISLATION

EU

Russia

UK

Other

1

Introduction

The fundamental question I explore in this book concerns reconceptualisation of values in judicial jurisdiction based on party autonomy. Judicial jurisdiction is best defined as the authority of a given court over a particular dispute. As a subject of study, jurisdiction is fascinating and mysterious, similar to the conundrum of Schrödinger's cat.[1] The mystery is whether the court shall or shall not have the authority to handle a dispute. In many cases, the answer could be yes and no simultaneously. At any rate, the question presents a challenge and a topic for an engaging intellectual discussion. Complexity and diversity of private international law regimes across the world, and each of them offering their own unique solution to different questions, make the discussion even more interesting. The recent reform of the Brussels I Regulation on jurisdiction in 2012–15[2] and the ongoing judicial reform in Russia[3] shows the subject matter of this research to be at the heart of legislative discussions. Moreover, the Judgments Project by the Hague Conference on Private International Law brings renewed global attention to the question of jurisdiction.[4]

This book challenges the traditional approach to jurisdiction that understands jurisdiction in terms of power, territoriality and sovereignty and contends that states set conditions for allocating personal jurisdiction based on their sovereignty. However, placing state sovereignty as the foundation for jurisdiction fails to account for the individual interests of private parties. It appears inadequate in light of the rise of private interests in the liberalised world economy. It lacks

[1] For comparison of the Conflict of Laws to Schrödinger's cat, see Lord Mance, 'In a Manner of Speaking: How Do Common, Civil and European Law Compare? (2014) 78 *Rabel Zeitschrift für Ausländisches und Internationales Privatrecht* 231.

[2] Regulation (EU) 1215/2012 of 12 December 2012 on Jurisdiction and the Recognition and Enforcement of Judgments in Civil and Commercial Matters (Recast) [2012] OJ L351/1 (the Brussels I Recast), which substantially revised Regulation (EC) 44/2001 of 22 December 2000 on Jurisdiction and the Recognition and Enforcement of Judgments in Civil and Commercial Matters [2001] OJ L12/1 (the Brussels I Regulation).

[3] In 2014, the Supreme *Arbitrazh* (Commercial) Court was abolished and its functions and authority were transferred to the Supreme Court of the Russian Federation. Since then (and projected for the next few years), the rules of civil and *arbitrazh* procedure are to be consolidated in the forthcoming unified Civil Procedural Code. See text to n 65 of ch 2.

[4] The Hague Conference on Private International Law (HCCH), 'The Judgments Project' (Overview by the HCCH), available at: www.hcch.net/en/projects/legislative-projects/judgments.

necessary personification of individuals and legal entities as autonomous actors in international law. That is why I am proposing an alternative and novel way to analyse the rules of jurisdiction in private international law.

The main idea of this book is that an ideal jurisdiction system should give full effect to the parties' will, limited by considerations of equality and fairness and some state original interests. I construct a normative argument regarding the values in private international law that justify and determine judicial jurisdiction. My purpose is to offer a better perspective on these values. I aim to persuade scholars, policymakers and lawmakers that as a normative standard, an ideal jurisdiction system shall take the interests of private actors as a primary building block and define the rest of the rules from there. I argue that private international law rules should aim to enforce the will of private parties. Rather than the states, I show that private actors (natural and legal persons) should drive and shape the order of prescribing adjudicative jurisdiction of courts in international matters. Their autonomous choice of forum, as the ultimate expression of private interests, should constitute the basis of determining judicial jurisdiction. Where parties explicitly express their choice of jurisdiction (via jurisdiction agreements and by voluntary submission), it would be upheld by the courts.

However, although party autonomy should be an essential element in the hierarchy of values behind civil jurisdiction, it cannot be unlimited. Unlimited party autonomy to choose a forum might result in opportunism and advantage being taken by a party better positioned to negotiate jurisdiction. With no governmental interference, unrestricted private power to allocate jurisdiction would inevitably lean in the direction beneficial to the actors with stronger bargaining positions. In view of protecting the equality and rights of all market players, including those with weaker bargaining power, some constraints should be placed on party autonomy to choose a forum. Having learned from the nineteenth century's economic liberalism and the reasons that led to the decline of the pure laissez-faire policy, our society should be cautious about unlimited freedom to designate a forum for dispute resolution. So, for example, forum selection clauses inserted unilaterally in contracts of adhesion should only be given effect where they do not abrogate the weaker party's access to justice.

I concede to further limitations on private party autonomy to choose jurisdiction. In exceptional cases, party autonomy may be overridden by state exclusive jurisdiction rules, if protecting state interests is of crucial importance. These exceptions should not extend further than absolutely necessity. They manifest themselves in a few uniformly accepted exclusive jurisdiction rules, such as jurisdiction at the location of real property in cases regarding titles to real property, etc. By conceding to certain exceptions to party autonomy, I advance a reconstructed liberal view. Unlike a classical view (unchanged by the development of academic thought throughout the last century), I engage with many traditional and contemporary views and use them to help refine my argument. In the end, I propose an argument, aware of the critique, and defend it against inconsistent approaches.

My argument relies on the rules of jurisdiction as they exist today in two legal systems: the EU and Russia. My choice of the EU and Russia is predicated by their unique positions towards values in private international law and contrasting societal norms that generate and accommodate these values. It is also supported by my knowledge of these two regimes acquired during educational training in a post-Soviet (civil) legal system, the UK common law and EU law, as well as my cultural immersion in these societies. I compare jurisdiction rules in these regimes and analyse the problems arising in practice. I discern and revisit the broader values of private international law. I reveal a surprising consistency when it comes to recognition and enforcement of party autonomy in both targeted regimes, notwithstanding disparate cultural and political ideas. By engaging with the Russian and the EU regimes (and English common law), I show ways to improve the existing rules.

There are many other connected questions that could have been included in this study, such as choice of law, enforcement of judgments, or rules in other jurisdictions. However, in this book, I focus only on allocating an appropriate forum to settle disputes (judicial jurisdiction) and only in relation to the common EU regime and the Russian system. I focus only on the disputes of international character, ie, relationships falling outside the range of one state (as opposed to purely national jurisdiction rules). At some junctions, my analysis delves into national jurisdiction doctrine and law, but only to apply the results of the findings to the private international law sphere. Finally, I concentrate on the regulation of jurisdiction in civil and commercial matters. I exclude disputes of an administrative nature, the matters of antitrust and other areas traditionally classified as public law. Furthermore, I exclude matters of family law, since the subject of family law constitutes an autonomous category within private international law, and is guided by principles slightly different from those organising civil and commercial relationships. Moreover, international jurisdiction of courts in family matters (matrimonial matters, divorce proceedings, maintenance, wills and succession, etc) in the EU is regulated by a number of instruments,[5] all of which could not be comprehensively analysed within this book.

The following chapters are organised as follows:

- The first chapter presents the main argument.
- The three parts elaborate on the details of the overall argument.
- An overall conclusion follows.

[5] Council Regulation (EC) No 2201/2003 of 27 November 2003 Concerning Jurisdiction and the Recognition and Judgments in Matrimonial Matters and the Matters of Parental Responsibility [2003] OJ L338/1 (the Brussels II-bis Regulation); Council Regulation (EC) No 4/2009 of 18 December 2008 on Jurisdiction, Applicable Law, Recognition and Enforcement of Decisions and Cooperation in Matters Relating to Maintenance Obligation [2009] OJ L7/1 (the Maintenance Regulation); Regulation (EU) No 650/2012 of the European Parliament and of the Council of 4 July 2012 on Jurisdiction, Applicable Law, Recognition and Enforcement of Decisions and Acceptance and Enforcement of Authentic Instruments in Matters of Succession and on the Creation of a European Certificate of Succession [2012] OJ L201/107 (the Succession Regulation) etc.

In the first chapter, I summarise my main argument. I argue that jurisdiction in civil and commercial matters should be based on a framework of values different from the status quo. I present an approach based on party autonomy limited by considerations of categorical equality and sovereignty. I set out the correlation of these values in relation to each other. I also introduce general features of the existing EU and Russian jurisdictional regimes.

Further, this book consists of three parts. In part I (chapters three and four), I delve into the details on justification of the general rule in an ideal jurisdiction regime – party autonomy. I justify the notion of party autonomy as the grounding rule of an ideal jurisdiction system that caters to the interests of private parties. I argue that state sovereignty should play only an auxiliary role. In an attempt to demonstrate the shift of priorities in judicial jurisdiction, I seek support in the philosophical and legal arguments offered by Western and Russian scholars. On that basis, I demonstrate how my proposed approach can fit the existing jurisdictional systems in the EU and Russia. I analyse the rules and the case law, showing the degree of recognition of party autonomy in these regimes, and comment on ways to improve the existing rules to better reflect private interests.

In Part II (chapters five and six), I revisit and re-evaluate the case law and scholarship, explaining why party autonomy cannot be unlimited. I show how the notion of party equality should safeguard enforcement of meaningful consent in jurisdiction. I demonstrate the degree of consistency of the existing legal rules in the EU and Russia with this view in my analysis of the rules of protective jurisdiction. I further theorise how balancing private interests should guide allocating jurisdiction in the absence of a clear choice of forum by the parties.

In Part III (chapters seven and eight), I continue my argument against sovereignty, being traditionally placed at the foundation of a jurisdiction system. In light of the decline of the importance of state sovereignty and territoriality, I propose to reconsider the traditional position. I agree, however, that there is some limited place for sovereignty in the hierarchy of values behind jurisdiction rules. I specify why and in which exceptional cases state sovereign interests may override party autonomy. Again, I measure this approach against the existing general and exclusive jurisdiction rules in the EU and Russia.

In conclusion, I bring all threads of my argument together and summarise my findings (chapter nine). I also propose some recommendations for improving the existing EU and Russian jurisdiction regimes.

2

Reconciliation of Values in Jurisdiction

I. The Big Picture

A major part of this book is devoted to weighing various objectives and values of private international law. One of the main objectives of this book is to align this plurality of values into an ideal balance. The best way to find this balance is to set priorities and to propose an acceptable course of action in cases where these values conflict. In this section, I do exactly that: I set out the framework of values and their correlation with each other for the entire book.

A. General Rule: Party Autonomy

At the foundation of an ideal jurisdiction system, party autonomy should determine the appropriate forum to handle private disputes. Party autonomy represents the primary expression of private interests in jurisdiction. Enforcing the parties' will is what conflict of laws rules should strive to achieve.

Evidently, some problems with this approach may be connected with variations in the understanding of party autonomy in light of differing cultural, social, economic and moral values in different states. I address these issues by focusing on two actual jurisdiction regimes (the EU and Russia). I appeal to their theoretical and doctrinal thought to find what party autonomy ultimately means and should mean in the context of their corresponding private international law systems.

I first examine the evolution of party autonomy in the national jurisdictional mechanisms. I chose Germany – as one of the founding Members of the EU and an influential actor during the formation of the Brussels jurisdiction regime. Based on my enquiry into German legal history, I discover that party autonomy to choose forum was already recognised in the Code of Civil Procedure Rules of Germany enacted in 1877. Prior to that, no uniform legislation on civil law and civil procedure existed in Germany. Over 30 different legal systems in the German state featured various rules. In some of these territories (eg, Bavaria), the French civil law traditions influenced local codification efforts. Furthermore, the French Revolution, in proclaiming men free and equal in their rights, and upholding the principle of fair trial and due process of law, had its share of influence on the public officials and scholars in the neighbouring European states, including the German states.

Similarly, Russian civil procedure already envisaged party autonomy to choose a forum in the nineteenth century. This happened first in the commercial context: the Statute of Commercial Procedure of 1832 recognised parties' choice of (civil) court. It facilitated the option for merchants to utilise local civil courts to settle disputes instead of travelling to commercial courts in distant locations. Later, the Code of Civil Procedure, enacted during the great judicial reform of 1864, recognised party autonomy in choosing jurisdiction in civil matters as well. The drafters of these provisions built on their familiarity with both the Russian and Western (French and German) traditions.

Having traced the origins of recognition of private parties' choice of jurisdiction in the selected national systems, I conclude that judicial enforcement of forum selection agreements was predicated by (i) practical convenience sought in commercial disputes, (ii) the French Revolution and the values that it proclaimed, and (iii) the enlightened liberal thought and utilitarianism. Similar rationales, I argue, may be carried over and applied today, in order to justify party autonomy in disputes beyond national borders.

My further search into the meaning of party autonomy inevitably engages with the Western intellectual thought of liberalism. I rely on certain philosophical arguments that justify enforcing the parties' choice of a competent forum to settle their private disputes. My understanding of autonomy is consistent with the Kantian idea of individual autonomy, a fundamental moral compass of a rational individual, who makes individual rational choices. Kant describes autonomy as that which empowers the individual, liberating him (her) of the constraints placed on them by society. Autonomous agents are moral agents; they do what is right because it is right. This Kantian categorical imperative is relevant for defining autonomy in private international law. Private international law actors should be empowered with individual autonomy. An ideal jurisdiction regime would remove the constraints of rigid predetermined rules. Rather than allocating a limited role to autonomy in the big scheme of jurisdiction, an ideal regime would build on it, granting it the place of a general rule. It would trust liberated autonomous agents to make rational (and moral) choices of jurisdiction. To a certain extent, I supplement the Kantian concept of autonomous moral agents with consequentialist argument, that justifies party autonomy in the context of corporate entities acting to the benefit of their shareholders and not out of moral motives.

In this sense, this book advocates a liberal approach to jurisdiction. By liberal, I mean focusing on the demands and interests of the private actors in international law. In international relations theory, liberalism represents the main alternative to realism, differing from the latter by fundamental assumptions about the international system. Realists (from Thucydides to Machiavelli to Morgenthau) view the states as primary actors in the international system. They believe that states' fixed interests range from survival to aggrandisement, and they see the world in an actual conflict or perceived uncertainly, that states must constantly prepare for the possibility of war. In contrast, liberalism offers an alternative view, where individuals and groups of individuals are the main actors in the international system.

In this world, voluntary norms are set by individuals and groups in transnational society and are facilitated by states. I offer a variation of the law on jurisdiction that fits into this world-view.

It is important to draw a border and clarify what is not meant by 'liberal' in the context of this book. First, the term is not understood in the sense of domestic politics. There, 'liberal' is often seen as and equated with 'progressive' and perceived as 'left-wing'. It opposes governmental interference into various social spheres of life, while allowing governmental regulation of the economy. My argument is limited to international civil jurisdiction only, it does not venture onto the broad political discussion of 'who governs' and how much the government should or should not interfere in private lives overall. It attempts to narrowly discuss the normative basis for jurisdiction, balancing the notions of 'private' and 'public' in cross-border civil suits.

The liberal approach in this book should also be distinguished from the pure enlightened liberalism in political philosophy associated with Hobbes, Locke, Rousseau, etc. Their teachings concerned liberty, equality and social fraternity leading to equal distribution of resources. I do not delve into the theory of social organisation in general and attempt to circumvent the political argument, because the scope of this book is limited to private international law. My argument only echoes the enlightenment liberal thought by focusing on the interests of individuals. In this sense – by catering to the interests of individuals and opposing the traditional values – this book may be classified as liberal.

In practical terms, adopting my approach would translate into unequivocal enforcement of the parties' choice of forum. Party autonomy to choose a forum may manifest in two ways: *ex ante* and *ex post*. *Ex ante* jurisdiction agreements specify a forum for potential future disputes, while *ex post* parties appearing in court and arguing on the merits solidifies the parties' choice of jurisdiction by submission (silent acceptance).

Both analysed regimes (the EU and Russia) recognise party autonomy to confer jurisdiction via a choice-of-forum agreement. Parties possess the autonomy to designate a particular court or courts to bring their disputes to and to choose a body of law to govern their relationships. In case of absence of a choice-of-court agreement, an existing choice of law would influence (but not necessarily determine) that the court should retain jurisdiction. Problems appear in practice in relation to interpreting the validity of choice-of-forum agreements and their enforcement.

On the other hand, analysis of the EU and Russian international jurisdiction rules and case law shows differing levels of recognition of voluntary submission. In the EU, the submission to jurisdiction rule is clearly embedded in cross-border practice and explicitly established in Article 26 of the Brussels I Recast[1] and is an integral part of EU judicial practice. Further recognition

[1] Regulation (EU) 1215/2012 of 12 December 2012 on Jurisdiction and the Recognition and Enforcement of Judgments in Civil and Commercial Matters (Recast) [2012] OJ L 351/1 (the Brussels I Recast).

of the submission rule with no reservation may be found in national jurisdiction regimes across the EU.

In Russia, however, the civil procedure rules do not foresee a mechanism analogous to Article 26 of the Brussels I Recast. Court practice abounds with examples where parties complain about the jurisdiction after having taken part in the proceedings and argued the case on its merits. The case in point can be demonstrated by the dispute of a bank against the Administration of Chukotka autonomous area (Chukotskiĭ avtonomnyĭ okrug) and the non-profit Foundation of Economics of Chukotka. The parties had a jurisdiction agreement in favour of an *arbitrazh* court in Moscow city. The bank sued the administration to recover the debt in another court, an *arbitrazh* court of the Chukotka autonomous area (Chukotskiy avtonomniy okrug), at the location of the defendant.[2] The parties took part in the proceedings. The Court ruled to satisfy the plaintiff's claim for the recovery of the debt, to be paid by the defendants. Then, the ruling was appealed by one of the defendants in an *arbitrazh* court of appeal.[3] The court of appeal cancelled the original decision of the court of first instance. It decided that appearance by the parties did not constitute a change to the original jurisdiction agreement in a proper written form; therefore, the original claim was filed in violation of jurisdiction rules. On further appeal, the Federal *Arbitrazh* Court (cassation) finally confirmed that the agreement on jurisdiction had been changed, since

> the plaintiff, having sued at the location of the defendants, thus proposed such a change in the agreement (offer), and the defendant, having responded on the merits of the claim without objecting to the amended jurisdiction, accepted the change of jurisdiction (acceptance).[4]

Thus, the silent acceptance by the parties was enough to have changed the agreement on jurisdiction, and the reasoning of the original court of first instance was sound. The party did not object to jurisdiction and argued the case on its merits, so it was assumed that the party accepted the jurisdiction. The decision by the Russian court resembled the submission as embedded in the Brussels I Regulation (Recast), Article 26.

A similar situation recently occurred in a Russian tort case involving a foreign party. In its Informational Letter reviewing the lower courts' practice, the Presidium of the Supreme *Arbitrazh* Court described a case where a Russian party

[2] Reshenie Arbitrazhnogo Suda Chukotskogo Avtonomnogo Okruga ot 13 marta 2002 g (Decision of the *Arbitrazh* Court of the Chukotka Autonomous Area) of 13 March 2002 no A80-05/2002. All the codes and laws of the Russian Federation are cited from the Russian electronic source *ConsultantPlus*, available at: www.consultant.ru.

[3] Postanovlenie Shestogo Arbitrazhnogo Appelliatsionnogo suda ot 30 maia 2002 g (Decision of the Sixth *Arbitrazh* Court of Appeal) of 30 May 2002 no A80-05/2002 (A80-21/2002-а/ж).

[4] Postanovlenie Federal'nogo Arbitrazhnogo Suda Dal'nevostochnogo Okruga ot 3 sentiabria 2002 g (Resolution of the Federal *Arbitrazh* Court of the Far East Area) of 3 September 2002 no Ф03-А80/02-1/1755.

filed a claim against a foreign party in Russia for compensation for damages for a road traffic accident. Both parties took part in the proceedings and argued the case on the merits. The Court ruled in favour of the plaintiff. On appeal, the defendant argued that the *arbitrazh* court did not have the authority to hear the case, since the accident occurred in the territory of a foreign state. The court of appeal rightfully dismissed the appeal, because the fact that the foreign company took part in the judicial proceedings with no objections towards the competence of the court entailed the loss (or a waiver) of their right to challenge the competence of court *post factum*. The Supreme Court summarised this rule as a principle of the loss of entitlement for objection (*princip utrati prava na vozrazhenie*), whereas absence of objections by a party confirms the will of the party to have the dispute resolved by the court.[5] Although this should now serve as guidance for lower courts, the discussion on silent acceptance and its advantages and disadvantages in Russia continues.[6]

B. Exception One: Categorical Equality

While pre-eminently enforcing party autonomy, the rules of private international law must embody the principle of equal treatment of parties. The principle originates from civil procedure and civil law, and it is also prevalent in private law. All parties should have a chance to present and establish their contention, to defend their interests, to voice their beliefs, etc. Also, equality is one of the principles ensuring impartiality of the judicial process. Judicial systems administer justice, and they ought to balance out the private interests at hand because parties are unambiguously and unequivocally equal in the eyes of the law.

In the context of jurisdiction rules, equality matters where one of the parties lacks bargaining power at the outset of negotiations. Inequality of bargaining power is understood as disparity in access to resources, lack of sophistication in business transactions or informational imbalance between parties. The gap between the negotiating powers of the parties in such transactions may raise concerns regarding an unfair imposition of jurisdiction choice upon the subordinate, the disadvantaged, or otherwise perceived 'weaker' party.

[5] Informatsionnoe Pismo Presidiuma Vysshego Arbitrazhnogo Suda RF ot 9 iiulia 2013 g no 158 'Obzor Praktiki Rassmotreniia Arbitrazhnymi Sudami Del s Uchastiem Inostrannykh Lits' (Information Letter of the Presidium of the Supreme *Arbitrazh* Court of the RF 'Review of Judicial Practice on Certain Issues Connected with Deciding Cases by Russian *Arbitrazh* Courts with Participation of Foreign Entities') of 9 July 2013 no 158, para 7.

[6] Interview with Symeon Dergachev, Assistant Professor, Chair of Civil, *Arbitrazh* and Administrative Procedural Law, Russian Academy of Justice (Dublin, Ireland–Moscow, Russia (skype) 20 April 2015).

To reconcile party autonomy with party equality where they conflict is to conceive of party autonomy as a general rule and party equality[7] as an exception. Since equality pertains to balance of power between private parties, I will refer to it as an exception of 'private dimension'. Upholding the equality of parties should safeguard against unlimited party autonomy swaying in favour of one or other party. The best-suited court to decide a case is the court best situated to hear both sides. Excessive favouritism towards one party would upset the balance of rights that private international law aims to achieve. Are the rules pro-defendant or, rather, are they stretched too far to protect the plaintiff? Neither should be happening.

In practice, the role of the judiciary becomes to enforce choice-of-forum clauses while protecting the parties against potential subjugation of the will. In some cases, it translates into providing the weaker party with an alternative to sue or be sued in a forum different from the one specified in the choice-of-forum clause. This means restriction of recognition of some unilateral or asymmetric jurisdiction clauses. These terms are rarely meaningfully negotiated. Parties with weaker bargaining power simply agree to jurisdiction together with the rest of the boilerplate (adhesion) contract terms that come with the transaction. In such situations, where the agreement on forum could not have possibly reflected the will of autonomous subjects and was based not on fully free and informed consent, such 'pseudo' party autonomy can be limited. Then, unilateral (also called optional) jurisdiction clauses may be declared void by the courts. This may be relevant in contractual relationships involving consumers, employees or insured persons. In such situations, state jurisdiction rules can provide an alternative for the weaker parties to gain access to justice. A right to access to justice means that there is no gap where a person is left without access to court. It is encompassed within the broader human right to a fair trial. The task of ensuring respect towards the parties' access to justice should belong to a state court and legal system. Thus, it is up to courts to determine where unilateral forum selection clauses cut the weaker parties' access to court. If so, weaker parties might require an alternative to sue at their domicile, in order to compensate for the imbalance incurred by the difference in bargaining power.

In the absence of the parties' agreement, the principle of equality requires the same: both parties' interests should be equally taken into account. For instance, given the unpredictable nature of tort claims, where parties usually have no predetermined consent on jurisdiction, the consideration of equality transpires through (or is almost synonymous to) fairness requirement. In such cases, the imbalance is corrected by providing the victims of civil wrongs (the plaintiffs) an

[7] I speak of categorical equality (rather than equality overall, or equal treatment) in order to underscore that equality should interfere and limit party autonomy only in relation to certain categories of actors in private international law. Equality of such categories of individuals and entities should be backed by the power of the state, through enforcement in the state courts.

opportunity to sue at their location (classical corrective justice justification). At the same time, where a plaintiff wishes to bring a suit at his location, the interests of the defendant must be considered and protected as well.

Thus, for jurisdictional conflicts, categorical party equality should be conceived as a way of bringing the actors to the same level playing field in cases involving certain disadvantaged categories of actors. A claimant makes a choice where to bring an action, and such choice may disadvantage the defendant. The defendant has the right to contest the jurisdiction, if he believes there is a forum more appropriate for the dispute. His right to contest, then, would constitute the first limitation on the rule of jurisdiction by submission. However, where the defendant appears and argues the case on its merits, he can hardly complain about the jurisdiction. By participating in the case, he expresses his consent, and, therefore, is not treated unfairly or at a disadvantage.

Based on the analysis of the EU and Russian jurisdictional regimes, usually, the parties' access to justice and enforcement of party autonomy to choose a forum do not conflict. It happens, however, when they do.

By virtue of sections 3, 4 and 5 of the Brussels I Recast, weaker parties domiciled in the EU (consumers, insured individuals, and employees) are given special protection through jurisdiction. They are guaranteed the predictability and convenience of being sued at the place of their domicile and suing at their domicile or at the location of the other party. The weaker parties domiciled in the EU enjoy this jurisdictional protection, no matter whether the dispute involves an EU or a foreign entrepreneur represented in the EU through a branch or an agency, or by directing its activity towards the particular EU Member State (thus, 'deemed' to have domicile in the EU).

The protective jurisdiction rights granted to EU weaker parties are reasonably limited, as evidenced by European Court of Justice (ECJ) case law. In most cases, consumers are afforded protection if they act as passive consumers.[8] When actively pursuing the transaction with a foreign supplier carrying out his business activity beyond the country of the consumer's domicile, such an 'active' consumer is deprived of jurisdictional protection. According to this interpretation, the weaker parties will not have the privilege of being sued at the convenience of their location if they sought the transaction with the stronger party outside their state of abode. With these limitations, the rule is properly interpreted in a way that a party must not rely on protective jurisdiction if it purposefully avails itself to foreign litigation by crossing the borders of its country, including the 'virtual' borders. At the same time, it must be considered whether the supplier actively pursues conducting business at the location of potential consumers. In *Gabriel v Schlank & Schick GmbH*,[9]

[8] P Nielsen, 'Jurisdiction over Consumer Contracts' in U Magnus and P Mankowski (eds), *European Commentaries on Private International Law: Brussels I Regulation*, 2nd edn (Sellier European Law Publishers, 2012) 333.

[9] Case C96/00 *Gabriel v Schlank & Schick GmbH* [2002] ECR I-6367.

the Court decided that the action of a professional vendor having contacted a consumer at his home by one or more letters, which led the consumer to buy goods to obtain a prize, could be interpreted as a specific invitation addressed to the consumer or advertising within the meaning of the Brussels jurisdiction regime.

As the existing jurisdictional rules stand in the EU, the protective jurisdictional rules transcend party autonomy in jurisdiction. In particular, Articles 15, 19 and 23 only give effect to jurisdiction agreements with the weaker parties *ex post* where such agreement expands the choice of available fora for the weaker party. Also, parties can agree to confer jurisdiction to courts of a Member State where they are both domiciled, if the law of that state permits it.[10] The reasoning behind the prevalence of protective jurisdiction over party autonomy is:

> [W]here the position of the parties is clearly unequal, as one party is strong and the other is weak, fully accepting freedom of choice [of forum] could prejudice the weak party insofar as the strong party would tend to impose his solutions on the weaker one.[11]

Similarly, consumers are afforded protection through special jurisdiction rules in Russia. In addition to suing at the location of the defendant, claims on protecting the rights of consumers in Russia can be brought at the plaintiff's place of residence, or at the place of entering into or execution of a corresponding contract, or at the defendant's location. The choice between these places belongs to the plaintiff, ie, consumer in such cases.[12] A slight difference between Russia and the EU is that the Russian law allows for protective jurisdiction in relation to consumers' rights in general, both arising out of and independent of contractual relationships. In addition, the rule currently presupposes that a consumer himself or herself has the right to sue the other party (business, seller, provider, etc) at the place of their residence although a proposal for a European directive on representative actions for the protection of collective interests of consumers is being considered by the European legislators. In Russia, claims may be also brought pursuant to this jurisdictional provision by third persons, state authorities or organisations protecting the interests of consumers at their location, and not necessarily where breach of contracts is involved. In this regard, the Russian approach provides an even wider protection of consumers' interests than the EU.

Thus, I argue that individual actors have the right and power to make rational choices with respect to jurisdiction, but they should act against the backdrop of equality. Parties shall have the right to choose a forum to decide disputes. However, such a choice should be enforced in a way mindful of both parties' will, intentions

[10] ibid 345.

[11] U Magnus and P Mankowski (eds), *European Commentaries on Private International Law: Brussels I Regulation*, 2nd edn (Sellier European Law Publishers, 2012) 411, citing P Moreno, *Derecho Internacional y de la Integración 2* (*International Law and Integration 2*) (2003) 7, 27.

[12] Grazhdanskiĭ Protsessual'nyĭ Kodeks Rossiĭskoĭ Federatsii (Code of Civil Procedure of the RF) of 14 November 2002 no 138-ФЗ (Russia) (the CCP) art 29(7); Zakon RF o Zashchite Prav Potrebiteleĭ ot 7 fevralia 1992 g (Law of the RF on Protection of the Rights of the Consumers) art 17.

and interests. Further analysis of practice in the EU and Russia demonstrates that protective jurisdiction rules are consistent with this view; perhaps even to a greater degree than I see minimally required.

C. Exception Two: Maintaining Sovereignty

The principal tension in the bundle of values in private international law and jurisdiction in particular is between party autonomy and state sovereignty. Sovereignty is that without which the global system of states would collapse. It is the core of the states' integrity – their territorial borders, and the power 'to protect the interests of the community and [their] general welfare'.[13] In jurisdiction, state sovereignty manifests itself in asserting state power over the subjects by adjudicating their disputes. Sovereignty has provided the foundation for rules of jurisdiction for centuries in many jurisdictional systems. A substantial number of private international law scholars as well as judges see territoriality and state sovereignty as the undisputable and unshakable foundation of jurisdiction.

Nevertheless, I see sovereignty rather as an exception to the general rule of party autonomy in an ideal hierarchy of values.[14] It should transcend party autonomy only where crucial state interests are at stake. Only some considerations of state sovereignty may limit party autonomy to choose a forum to settle disputes. Essentially, when it comes to sovereignty, I approach the power relationships between the state and private parties as follows: rather than conceiving party autonomy in dispute resolution as a power granted by the state to private parties, I reverse the understanding and propose to base jurisdiction on party autonomy, with some room allocated for exceptions based on sovereignty.

To understand sovereignty, one must grapple with what exact state interests are at stake when (if) asserting jurisdiction over private matters. First, there is the crucial interest of society of the state to maintain state territorial integrity and sovereignty in the public international law sense (international sovereignty). This includes, in addition to the obvious desire not to be invaded and attacked, a 'common interest in ensuring that the [members' of society] affairs is not infringed upon by those outside the community'.[15] This also includes the state interest to ensure certain resources are protected from outsiders.[16] States are careful in asserting jurisdiction over the subjects of other states, because of the principle

[13] P Babie, 'Sovereignty as Governance: An Organising Theme for Australian Property Law' (2013) 36 *University of New South Wales (UNSW) Law Journal* 1075, 1078.

[14] In contrast to Exception One: party equality, this is an exception of public character, as it concerns the relationship between private parties and the state.

[15] S Burchill, *The National Interest in International Relations Theory* (Palgrave MacMillan, 2005) 27.

[16] In addition to the considerations of national security and the protection of the state borders by the military, states may be interested to advance their spheres of influence across the world. This area, however, is better left for the international relations realm and only needs to be mentioned in passing in relation to private international law controversies.

of non-interference in the affairs of the foreign state. Such non-interference is a principle respected both in public and private international law. Jurisdiction over nationals of a foreign state may raise 'red flags' regarding sovereignty of the foreign state.

Moreover, states pursue integrity of their internal structure and institutions – ie, their home sovereignty. I recognise its importance, because it secures a state's internal political and economic stability. Such stability helps maintain integrity of the international legal order. An ideal jurisdiction system would strive for such stability. Therefore, it is conceivable to accept some limitation to party autonomy in jurisdiction for the sake of maintaining the integrity of the state as sovereign. For instance, the Russian Constitution proclaims the necessity to limit the rights and freedoms of the individual to protect the foundations of the constitutional system, morals, health, rights and legitimate interests of other persons, maintenance of defence of the country and safety of the state.[17] Where the question of legitimate threat to these core legal values is at stake, it is feasible to limit private party autonomy to choose jurisdiction.

In addition, another important interest of some states may be in making themselves viewed as an attractive forum for dispute resolution. From a pragmatic or economic point of view, it may bring, in some cases, substantial revenue for the justice system in the form of court fees and remuneration for service of state lawyers. Moreover, accepting and exercising jurisdiction by state courts may bring such benefits for the state as the development and enrichment of case law and establishment of 'an implicit contract' with other jurisdictions leading to a broader choice of fora.[18] At the same time, some states' interest in asserting jurisdiction might be the opposite: instead of an 'open forum' approach, states may want to reject jurisdiction. One such example would be the unwillingness of states to retain jurisdiction ensuing from state sovereign interests in cases raised under the Acts of State doctrine.

Furthermore, states aim to protect the general interests of their citizens and corporations. These interests can be united under the umbrella of collective public interest. This national public interest represents the combined private interests of persons domiciled in a particular state. In terms of jurisdiction over private international matters, examples of such public interest can include keeping the administration of justice costs low for taxpayers, ascertaining jurisdiction over matters with potential public implication (such as disputes having an effect on pharmaceuticals distributed in that state), etc. Adjusting absolute party autonomy with respect to such public interest helps balance the individual private parties' interests in relation to the private interests of a larger union (a nation, or a state). Consistent with this argument, states may still provide an independent 'residual

[17] Konstitutsiia Rossiĭskoĭ Federatsii (Constitution of the RF) art 55(3) (Russia).

[18] M Whincop and M Keyes, *Policy and Pragmatism in the Conflict of Laws* (Ashgate, 2001) 160–61, fn 2, referring to *James Hardie Industries Pty Ltd v Grigor* (1998) 45 NSWLR 20, 40–41.

judicial control'[19] to issues that are more and more regulated by powerful non-state stakeholders, to provide a counterbalance and take into account general interests and the rights of third parties.

In harmony with these multidimensional state interests, the sovereignty exception to party autonomy would take multidimensional shape. The simplest application of this approach transpires in cases relating to titles to real property in a state. A careful individual approach is required in such cases; not every case mentioning land may qualify. Thus, in disputes relating to property *in rem*, a given state proprietary interest of maintaining its territorial integrity may be the reason to limit private parties to choose a foreign sovereign's court to make judgments against the state's land. Other cases where state sovereign interests may trump private power to allocate jurisdiction in civil and commercial matters can include disputes relating to changes in state registers (on titles to land or registers of companies) and a few other cases (as outlined in later chapters). In jurisdictional terms, this is expressed in the state's mandatory (or exclusive) jurisdiction rules.

The mandatory (or exclusive) jurisdiction rules perform the function of maintaining the integrity of the state and its institutions. The problem is that the public policy justifying the mandatory rules is affected by constant societal change. As once stated by an English judge, 'the law relating to public policy cannot remain immutable. It must change with the passage of time. The wind of change blows upon it'.[20] Hence, it is necessary to review and adjust what states might consider as their basic policies in need of protection. Another problem is that these mandatory rules vary greatly from one state to another, and there is no one universally recognised standard. This creates the need to determine the minimum number of acceptable exceptions that may override private parties' consensual choice of jurisdiction.

As the laws in Russia and the EU are now, the main reflection of the principle of territoriality in substantive jurisdiction rules becomes apparent when examining, for instance, the domicile rule of jurisdiction (suing at the location of the defendant). From the states' perspective, the rule reflects the power of the state over its subjects. If a plaintiff wants to sue a state domiciliary, he must bear the cost and inconvenience of travelling to and suing at the location of the defendant, because jurisdiction was initially understood strictly in a territorial sense. In the world of blurred territorial borders, high mobility of people and assets, a person or an event may no longer be regarded strictly as belonging to or occurring in a certain physical place. Domicile of the defendant becomes harder to determine. The significance of the rule, then, diminishes within the hierarchy of jurisdiction rules. Rather than providing a fundamental basis for general jurisdiction, its role

[19] See, eg, this argument articulated by Burkhard Hess: B Hess, *Private–Public Divide in International Dispute Resolution* (Recueil des cours, 2017).

[20] S Waddams, 'Private Right and Public Interest' in M Bryan (ed), *Private Law in Theory and Practice* (Routledge-Cavendish, 2007) 14, referring to *Nagle v Fielden* [1966] 2 QB 633, 650 (CA) (Danckwerts LJ).

should become auxiliary. In addition, the rationale for the domicile rule should be reconsidered. Instead of the state's power over its territory, the ground for a court to have jurisdiction over defendants in its territory may be that of catering for the interests of the defendant. Thus, the rule may still be adequate, but the reasoning behind it has changed since its inception. Rather than acting based on a state's power at its territory, the focus should shift to the interests of the parties, convenience and practicality.

Another expression of state territoriality and sovereignty that needs to be revised may be found in the rules of special (or specific) jurisdiction. For instance, where a court jurisdiction is based on close and substantial connection between the suit and forum, it reflects the sovereign and territorial power of the state over affairs taking place in its territory.[21] Perhaps, such rationale was previously acceptable. In the present day, it appears that the reason behind the fact that the court at the location of the delict shall have jurisdiction should rather derive from practicality. A court at the place of a negligence tort would have the best access to the evidence needed to make such a decision. Such a court would be the most familiar with local laws and customs, according to which it may be easier to understand whether the act in question constituted a tort. This being so, however, other factors may outweigh these reasons, and it may be more feasible for a situation to be considered at the location of the plaintiff, for instance. Because tort situations are of unplanned character, and one side may be classified as a 'victim' of an allegedly committed wrong, it may be just to allow the plaintiff to bring suit at the victim's location. Again, state territorial hegemony should not overpower the interests of the private parties. Considerations of restoring justice and satisfying private interests should prevail over the perceived 'battle' over jurisdiction based on the place of committing the civil wrong.

Therefore, in situations that occur without any predetermined jurisdiction agreement (for instance, in negligence torts), the order of values remains the same. Party autonomy seems less applicable to negligence cases than other civil wrongs. Nevertheless, parties may agree on a forum: by mutual agreement right before the suit, or by silent acceptance by the defendant of the forum choice. Where parties have a pre-existing relationship and choice-of-forum agreement in relation to contractual but not tort matters, or where no choice-of-forum agreement exists, choice of court may still later be adjusted or coordinated according to the parties' wishes. Party equality may further guide the choice of forum. A party disadvantaged by a civil wrong may have leverage to bring the suit at its location. Finally, the court at the location of evidence may be properly authorised to hear and decide a claim. In this dichotomy of values, state sovereignty (ie, regulation of tortious behaviour on state territory) plays the last possible valuable role. After all, as van

[21] Such as found, eg, in *OAO Neftyanaya Kompaniya Yukos v Russia*, ECHR judgment of 20 September 2011. Also, A von Mehren and D Trautman, 'Jurisdiction to Adjudicate: A Suggested Analysis' (1966) 79 *Harvard Law Review* 1121.

Calster noted, one barely bases his choice of not moving to a country on that county's regulation of tort liability.[22] State's regulation of tort liability is the last thing on the person's mind when engaging in activity in a forum, and it should be the last in the hierarchy of values helping determine the appropriate forum.

In addition, practicality may replace sovereignty in justifying a court's jurisdiction in certain cases. For instance, in cases relating to real property in the state, a state court shall assume jurisdiction at the location of the real property, not on a whim of a sovereign but rather for practical reasons. The local court possesses the fastest and easiest access to some evidence that may be crucial to a case (public register of the immovable property, etc). Furthermore, presumably, a local court order can be enforced in a more speedy and efficient manner than a foreign judgment. Thus, a local court at the location of the real property will be best placed to decide the case. Similar rationale fuelled general jurisdiction at the location of the defendant in the history of English law. A court's judgments could not personally bind the defendant, unless the defendant appeared in response to one of the devices compelling him to do so (such as summons and attachment to *capias* (arrest) and outlawry). The plaintiff, thus, had 'little incentive to bring before the court disputes arising outside the forum unless the defendant was readily available'.[23] For similar reasons, filing at the location of the defendant makes practical sense for the claimant nowadays, for he hopes the defendant will appear in court and a court order will be enforced smoothly afterwards. Further discussion of practicality ensues.

D. Additional Rule: Correcting Choices for Practical Reasons

Having several jurisdictional options is desirable from a liberal standpoint. It is acceptable for a system to implement a set of rules that confer jurisdiction on multiple courts. Frequently, multiple courts in the same state or courts of different states may be equally competent to determine a case.

However, it is not desirable to have a system where any court in any state shall have potential jurisdiction to hear a civil case to ensure unlimited access to a fair and effective trial anywhere. To ensure the sound administration of justice, a system would (ideally) direct a dispute towards a single court. Then, the chance of concurrent proceedings would be minimised. Also, no irreconcilable judgments would be given in the same dispute between the same parties, on the same grounds, and regarding the same subject matter.

To eliminate concurrent proceedings, the principle of practicality can be the key to breaking the tie between several competent courts determined by the

[22] G van Calster, *European Private International Law* (Hart Publishing, 2013) 153.

[23] M Twitchell, 'The Myth of General Jurisdiction' (1988) 101 *Harvard Law Review* 610, 615, fn 20, referring to W Blume, 'Place of Trial of Civil Cases: Early English and Modern Federal' (1949) 48 *Michigan Law Review* 11 citing F Pollock and FW Maitland, *The History of English Law*, 2nd edn (Cambridge University Press, 1911) 594.

general rule of party autonomy and the exceptions outlined above. Considerations of practicality may help reach the simplest solution for conflict of jurisdiction, by narrowing down the choice between several potentially competent venues to hear and decide a case.

Thus, a clear choice-of-court agreement overrides all other possible choices of court. In the absence of a jurisdiction agreement, party equality may guide the choice of court by allowing the disadvantaged (eg, wronged) party to bring suit at its location. Simultaneously, the same party equality may direct claims to the location of the defendant, since the defendant is a party disadvantaged by default, by not having the advantage of choosing where to bring suit. To break the tie, for practical reasons, an ideally suited court would be the one best situated to obtain necessary evidence. Considerations on proximity of evidence (where relevant) may help narrow down the selection of jurisdictional options for the parties.

Additional values to guide finding an appropriate forum include clarity and predictability. Without legal clarity, the rules would be a bundle of complicated, ambiguous and confusing information thrown together. To achieve legal clarity, definitions in law need to be sharpened; and the wording of the rules must precisely reflect the intent of the legislator and the underlying policies. The structure of the legislative act must also be straightforward, logical and easy to navigate. Legal clarity and predictability ensure finding a univocal answer to controversial questions, secure ease in understanding of the law, and uniformity in interpreting the law.

II. Summary of Jurisdiction Rules in the EU and Russia

The main argument of this book flows from analysis of the rules of jurisdiction and case law in the EU and Russia. These two different approaches are studied through a liberal prism and measured against the hierarchy of values outlined above. Particularities of application of the rules in practice reveal nuances of these legal systems. In this section, I describe the main features of these regimes, focusing on their international dimensions. At times, the discussion inevitably delves into the national rules on jurisdiction, which supplement or constitute a part of private international law regulation of international jurisdiction.

A. The EU

The EU legal system presents a unique case when it comes to jurisdiction. Regulation of jurisdiction in civil and commercial matters in the EU is multifaceted. The Brussels I Recast lays out the rules of jurisdiction for commercial and civil disputes involving parties domiciled in the EU Member States, including Denmark. The Brussels I Recast came into force in January 2015. The revision of the Brussels I Regulation aimed to further develop the European area of justice by removing the obstacles for the free movement of judgments; enhance the access to justice for EU companies in transactions with partners from third countries and extend the jurisdiction rules to third state defendants; improve the legal certainty and predictability of dispute resolution when parties conclude choice-of-court agreements; and enhance the interaction between litigation and arbitration. Many shortcomings of the Brussels I jurisdiction regime were fixed, including those relating to correlation between the *lis pendens* rule and jurisdiction agreements, and clarification in relation to transactions with the weaker parties. In addition to the Brussels I Recast, the Lugano Convention 2007[24] applies to the EU Member States and Iceland, Switzerland and Norway. Together, these sources comprise the 'Brussels jurisdiction regime'.

The Brussels jurisdiction regime is based on the principle of domicile. According to this principle, natural and legal persons domiciled in a Member State shall, whatever their nationality, be sued in the courts of that Member State governed by the rules of jurisdiction applicable to nationals of that state.[25] The Brussels I Recast foresees exceptions to this general rule: special, exclusive jurisdiction and prorogation of jurisdiction by choice-of-court agreements. Under special jurisdiction rules, persons domiciled in a Member State may be sued in a different Member State. Special jurisdiction applies in matters relating to insurance, consumer contracts, individual contracts of employment, matters relating to obligation arising out of a contract, torts, counterclaims, etc.[26] Prorogation of jurisdiction enforces choice-of-court agreements entered into by parties.[27] Such jurisdiction agreements override the general and special rules of jurisdiction (except for claims involving 'weaker' parties: consumers, insured individuals and employees), but can be superseded by the rules of exclusive jurisdiction. Exclusive jurisdiction applies in Europe when a strong connection exists with a Member State's jurisdiction, notwithstanding the domicile of the defendant. Then, a certain court or courts can adjudicate a case to the exclusion of all other courts. Examples include proceedings which have as their object rights *in rem* in immovable property, cases concerning the validity of the constitution, the nullity or the dissolution of legal persons, or the validity of the decisions of their organs, registration or validity of patents, etc.[28] In addition, the Brussels regime recognises voluntary submission to jurisdiction,[29] the *lis pendens* rule (all courts but the court first seized shall stay its proceedings until jurisdiction of the court first seized is established), and allows for protective measures.[30]

[24] Convention on Jurisdiction and the Recognition and Enforcement of Judgments in Civil and Commercial Matters [2007] OJ L339/3-91.

[25] Brussels I Recast art 4.

[26] ibid ss 2–5.

[27] ibid art 25.

[28] ibid art 24.

[29] ibid art 26.

[30] ibid ss 9, 10.

At the same time, Article 4(2) of the Brussels I Recast defers to the rules of the EU Member States when it comes to cases involving non-EU domiciliary defendants. These 'residual' national jurisdiction rules continue to apply outside the scope of the Brussels I Recast. These rules differ from one EU Member State to another.

The most interesting approach is taken by the English courts which follow the common law tradition. The common law rules – the body of law consisting of court cases – contain jurisdictional provisions for claims over persons (*in personam*) and property (*in rem*). Dicey's *Conflict of Laws* defines a claim *in personam* as any civil claim, except for divorce and separation proceedings, claims for declaration of nullity or legitimacy of marriage, bankruptcy proceedings, claims for custody of children, and claims to set aside arbitral awards.[31] Under English law, almost all civil and commercial claims, excluding the abovementioned exceptions, are subject to personal jurisdiction rules.

General personal jurisdiction is established over a person consenting to the English court's jurisdiction or serviced with process while physically present in England. Briggs explains that historically, the rules of jurisdiction in England have been defined by rules about the service of process, with considerations of nationality, domicile and property being irrelevant.[32] It does not matter whether the defendant has assets in England, or whether there is any substantive connection with England, in order for English courts to seize jurisdiction.[33] In practice, even the transient physical presence of an individual in England can be found satisfactory for the purpose of service of process (such as staying in a hotel in London for one night,[34] coming for a short visit to attend horse races,[35] etc). However, there are limits to this far-reaching jurisdiction of English courts. First, the court can refuse the proceedings if doing so might lead to injustice. Also, where the defendant is tricked or kidnapped to come to England for the purpose of serving a claim on him, such service would be considered invalid. Notably, serving a defendant who is not ordinarily resident or domiciled in England with a claim form posted to an address which has been used by him occasionally in England cannot be valid, since the address cannot be described as 'his last known residence', and at the time of service, he was out of England.[36] Part 6 of the English Civil Procedure Rules (CPR) outlines the proper methods of serving claims to individuals, companies and limited liability partnerships in England.

[31] L Collins et al (eds), *Dicey, Morris & Collins on the Conflict of Laws*, 14th edn (Sweet & Maxwell, 2006) 306, para 11-002.

[32] A Briggs, 'The Impact of Recent Judgments of the European Court on English Procedural Law and Practice' (2006) University of Oxford, Faculty of Law Legal Studies Research Paper Series, Working Paper No 11/2006.

[33] R Smith, *Conflict of Laws* (Cavendish Publishing Limited, 1993) 53. Rule 22 of 1998 Civil Procedure Rules (CPR) reads: '[T]he court has jurisdiction to entertain a claim *in personam* if, and only if, the defendant is served with process in England or abroad in the circumstances authorised by, and in the manner prescribed by, statute or statutory order' (Collins et al (n 31) 305).

[34] *Colt Industries v Sarlie* [1966] 1 WLR 440.

[35] *Maharanee of Baroda v Wildenstein* [1972] 2 QB 283 (CA).

[36] J Sorabji, 'Service where the Defendant is Outside the Jurisdiction' (2007) 26 *Civil Justice Quarterly* 279.

In addition to general personal jurisdiction, in specific cases, an English court shall have jurisdiction even if the defendant has been properly served in accordance with a court order for alternative (substituted) service outside England. A court may authorise the alternative method to serve process (eg, serving a foreign defendant by alternative service on its UK branch), if it has a good reason to do so. The tests for courts to determine whether alternative service of process is permissible have been outlined by Lord Reading in *Porter v Freudenberg*,[37] recommending that courts should consider in what circumstances substituted service can be ordered.[38] The substituted service may be permitted, where there is some kind of practical impossibility of actual service, and the alternative method should guarantee that the writ of summons would be brought to the knowledge of the defendant 'in reasonable probability, if not certainty'.[39]

In some cases, a claim may be served out of the jurisdiction – with or without the court's permission. If certain conditions are met, a court's permission is not required for a claim form to be served on a defendant in Scotland or Northern Ireland,[40] or on a defendant in a territory within Europe of an EU Member State or a territory outside the EU (where jurisdiction is established pursuant to the Brussels regime or the Hague Choice of Court Agreements Convention or otherwise).[41] Outside the Brussels I Recast, such cases of serving out of the jurisdiction without the need to obtain permission in advance are relatively rare.[42] When filing and serving such a claim, it should be accompanied by a practice form containing a statement of the grounds on which the claimant is entitled to serve the claim form out of the jurisdiction.[43] Notably, a court has a discretion to permit service of the claim form in the absence of such form.[44]

In cases other than the above-mentioned, a claim form may be served out of the jurisdiction with a court's order if certain grounds apply.[45] In such cases, service effected under such order gives the court jurisdiction over the defendant. A court shall not give permission unless satisfied that England is *forum conveniens* for the case. For instance, in *MRG (Japan) Ltd v Engelhard Metals Japan Ltd*,[46] service out of the jurisdiction (in Japan) was permitted for the claim relating to a contract governed by English law and containing an English jurisdiction clause. Where the court gives permission to service a claim form out of the jurisdiction, it may give directions about the method of service.[47] There have been divergent judicial

[37] *Porter v Freudenberg* [1915] 1 KB 857 (CA).
[38] ibid 887–88.
[39] 'Service by Alternative Method' (2000) 19 *Civil Justice Quarterly* 211.
[40] CPR r 6.32.
[41] CPR r 6.33.
[42] A Briggs and P Rees (eds), *Civil Jurisdiction and Judgments*, 6th edn (Proforma, 2015) 382, para 4.04.
[43] CPR r 6.34.
[44] eg, in *DSG International Sourcing Ltd v Universal Media Corporation* (Slovakia) SRO [2011] EWHC 1116 (Comm), the Applicant has sustained no prejudice as a result of the defective form.
[45] CPR r 6.36; CPR para 3.1 of Practice Direction 6B.
[46] *MRG (Japan) Ltd v Engelhard Metals Japan Ltd* [2003] EWHC 3418 (Comm).
[47] CPR r 6.37.

views whether service of process out of the jurisdiction may be effected by alternative methods.[48] In *Abela and others v Baadarani*,[49] where the claim related to a contract governed by English law and containing a non-exclusive English jurisdiction clause, the Supreme Court confirmed that the court may retrospectively validate alternative service in a service out of the jurisdiction case. The proceedings, however, must have been properly brought to the attention of the defendant and the method should not be expressly contrary to the law of the defendant's jurisdiction.[50]

English *in rem* jurisdiction applies to actions relating to property, including ships and aircraft. Statutory law[51] describes the mode of exercise of admiralty jurisdiction in actions *in rem*. It provides the High Court with the power to adjudicate actions against the ship or property in connection with which the claim arises.

These traditional common law rules of jurisdiction *in personam* and *in rem* have existed in England for a long time, and after the accession of the UK to the Brussels jurisdiction regime, they have only fulfilled the function of filling in the gaps, when EU legislation directed them to do so. In addition to the common law, some rules on English jurisdiction can be found in the Civil Jurisdiction and Judgments Act 1982 and Order 2001, and the CPR 1998 (former Rules of the Supreme Court Order 11). Moreover, all the English jurisdictional rules are interpreted in accordance with the principles outlined in the European Convention on Human Rights, enacted in the UK through the Human Rights Act 1998. Also, some international conventions that the UK is a party to contain additional jurisdiction rules relevant to this discussion, such as carriage of passengers and goods by air, sea or rail (the Warsaw Convention 1929, the Guadalajara Convention 1961, the Berne Convention 1980, and the Geneva Convention 1956, etc) or jurisdiction based on choice-of-court agreements (the Hague Convention 2005).

Notably, I look at the example of the British courts applying the rules on jurisdiction, as it is at the moment, without the complications associated with the British impending exit from the EU (Brexit). I focus on the current situation, leaving out the obscurity of the future application of the Brussels jurisdiction regime in the UK. Since the Brussels jurisdiction regime is incomplete by itself without national courts implementing it, I examine the Brussels jurisdiction regime rules as applied and interpreted by English courts to date.

B. Russia

Conversely, the Russian legal system belongs to the legal family of civil law. It originates from the Roman legal tradition. It resembles the European continental

[48] *Bacon v Automattic Inc & Ors* [2011] EWHC 1072 (QB) (06 May 2011) [28].
[49] *Abela and others v Baadarani* [2013] UKSC 44.
[50] ibid [21].
[51] Supreme Court Act 1981 (renamed as Senior Courts Act 1981) s 21 (UK).

approach towards jurisdiction, but is specific in its own way. First, rules of jurisdiction are heavily codified. The regulation of civil and commercial litigation appears in a few legislative acts in Russia. The main federal laws include the Civil Code,[52] the Code of Civil Procedure, and the Code of *Arbitrazh* Procedure, the federal laws on the judicial system, on legal status of foreign individuals, etc. In addition, secondary statutory legislation (presidential decrees, resolutions issued by the government, resolutions by the Supreme Court)[53] contain some clarifications regarding jurisdiction rules.

Some international agreements, to which Russia is a contracting state, also outline some rules on jurisdiction. Provisions of international treaties to which Russia is a party prevail over Russian domestic law in case of a conflict.[54] The main regional treaties related to civil and commercial litigation include the 1992 Kiev Treaty[55] and the 1993 Minsk Convention.[56] These treaties establish mechanisms for providing mutual assistance among the courts in civil and commercial cases and the recognition and enforcement of judgments across the former USSR (now, the Commonwealth of Independent States, the CIS). These treaties emphasise the principles of respect for sovereignty of the State Parties, equality (*ravnopravie*) of commercial parties, and of reciprocity (*vzaimnost*) in the recognition and enforcement of judgments in the State Parties. In addition to these regional treaties, Russia has signed bilateral international agreements on mutual legal and judicial assistance in civil procedure with a number of countries.

[52] Grazhdanskiĭ Kodeks Rossiĭskoĭ Federatsii (Civil Code of the RF) (the Russian Civil Code) pt 3 (2001).

[53] Ukaz Prezidenta RF ot 7 maia 2012 g ob Osnovnykh Napravleniiakh Sovershenstvovaniia Sistemy Gosudarstvennogo Upravleniia (Decree of the President of the RF on General Direction for Improvement of the System of State Administration) of 7 May 2012 no 601; and, eg, Postanovlenie Plenuma Vyshchego Arbitrazhnogo Suda o Deistvii Mezhdunarodnykh Dogovorov RF Primenitel' no k Voprosam Arbitrazhnogo Protsessa (Resolution of the Highest *Arbitrazh* Court on the Operation of International Agreements of the Russian Federation Relating to Matters of Arbitrazh Procedure) of 11 June 1999 no 8.

[54] Konstitutsiia Rossiĭskoĭ Federatsii, art 15.4.

[55] Soglashenie o Poriadke Razresheniia Sporov, Sviazannykh s Osushestvleniem Khoziaĭstvennoĭ Deiatelnosti (Agreement of the Commonwealth of Independent States (CIS) on the Procedure for Resolving Disputes Related to Commercial Matters) of 20 March 1992, Kiev (the Kiev Treaty). The Treaty has been signed by and applies among the following countries: Armenia, Belarus, Kazakhstan, Kyrgyzstan, Moldova, Russia, Tajikistan, Turkmenistan, Uzbekistan and Ukraine. Azerbaijan acceded to the Treaty but has not ratified it yet.

[56] Konventsiia o Pravovoĭ Pomoshchi i Pravovykh Otnosheniiakh po Grazhdanskim, Semeĭnym i Ugolovnym Delam (Convention on Judicial Cooperation and Legal Relations in Civil, Family, and Criminal Matters) of 22 January 1993, Minsk, amended by Protocol of 28 March 1997 (the Minsk Treaty). The Minsk Treaty has been ratified and enforced in the following states (in chronological order): Belarus, Uzbekistan, Kazakhstan, Russia, Tajikistan, Armenia, Ukraine, Kyrgyzstan, Moldova, Azerbaijan, Georgia and Turkmenistan. The Convention ceased to be effective from 2002 for its few signatories who adopted the revised version of the treaty in Kishinev (Konventsiia o Pravovoĭ Pomoshchi i Pravovykh Otnosheniiakh po Grazhdanskim, Semeĭnym i Ugolovnym Delam (Convention on Judicial Cooperation in Civil, Family and Criminal Matters) of 7 October 2002, Kishinev, Moldova (the Kishinev Treaty). The Kishinev Treaty is effective in Belarus, Azerbaijan, Kazakhstan, Kyrgyzstan, Armenia and Tajikistan only.

They strictly apply to relationships between the Russian parties and parties from a another State Party. The rules of jurisdiction reflected in these bilateral agreements override the national Russian rules of jurisdiction.

Judicial practice or case law does not represent a source of law in Russia, except for resolutions issued by the Constitutional Court, resolutions of the Plenum (general assembly of all justices) of the Supreme Court in Russia and, until August 2014, resolutions of the Plenum of the Supreme *Arbitrazh* Court.[57] Also, periodically, collegial groups of the Russian Supreme Court review lower courts' practice and explain the most controversial issues that arise in practice (in addition to a limited number of original jurisdictional matters). The Supreme Court provides normative resolutions on those issues by publishing decrees (*postanovleniia*) and guiding explanations (*raz'iasneniia*). These decrees by the supreme judicial body are accordingly applied by judges. These decrees 'are designed to ensure uniform court practice'.[58] Also, historically, Russian courts have accepted application of law by analogy of legislation (*analogiia zakona*, *analogia legis*) and analogy of law (*analogiia prava*, *analogia juris*), which can be viewed as a type of precedent.[59] Where relations are not regulated by the legislation or by the parties' agreement, and no standard business practice norms apply, judges are directed to proceed by analogy of law, which 'comes to a form of systematic interpretation',[60] looking at the general principles and intent of civil legislation. In addition, the courts are to proceed 'from the demands of good faith, reasonableness, and fairness (*dobrosovestnost, razumnost i spravedlivost*)'.[61]

Finally, the Constitution of the Russian Federation features, inter alia, a number of provisions relevant to private international law and international jurisdiction rules: (i) the rule of law; (ii) the supremacy of international law provisions over the national legal rules (except for the Constitution itself); (iii) the rights and freedoms of individuals (both national and foreign); and (iv) the equality of all before the law and the courts, etc. The Constitution also provides the foundation for the judicial (courts) system, recognises and protects private, state and other forms of property, and mentions the basic rules of prosecution.

Substantively, the jurisdiction of Russian courts is twofold. First, courts are divided by the subject matter of the cases they can handle: criminal, civil,

[57] Formerly, the Supreme Court and Supreme *Arbitrazh* Court constituted two entities, and since August 2014, in light of the ongoing judicial reform in Russia, the Supreme Court has been empowered with the Supreme *Arbitrazh* authorities, while the latter ceased to exist. See text to n 65 below.

[58] V Zhuikov, 'The Supreme Court and the New Civil Code of the Russian Federation' in W Simons (ed), *Private and Civil Law in the Russian Federation. Essays in Honor of FJM Feldbrugge* (Martinus Nijhoff Publishers, 2009) 112.

[59] T Neshataeva, 'International Civil Procedure in the Russian Federation: Sources and Issues' (2003) 28(2) *Review of Central and East European Law* 161.

[60] W Snijders, 'The Civil Codes of the Russian Federation and The Netherlands: Similarities and Contrasts' in W Simons (ed), *Private and Civil Law in the Russian Federation. Essays in Honor of FJM Feldbrugge* (Martinus Nijhoff Publishers, 2009) 20.

[61] V Iakovlev, 'The *Arbitrazh* Courts and the New Civil Code' in W Simons (ed), *Private and Civil Law in the Russian Federation. Essays in Honor of FJM Feldbrugge* (Martinus Nijhoff Publishers, 2009) 102.

commercial, etc. The doctrine of competence (subject matter jurisdiction, *kompetentsiia* or *podvedomstvennost*) sets out the mandate for particular courts to hear and adjudicate disputes. Secondly, in order to determine exactly which court shall be authorised to hear a case, the rules of jurisdiction (*podsudnost*) apply. There are two steps of jurisdiction: vertical jurisdiction (*rodovaia podsudnost*) and horizontal, territorial jurisdiction (*territorialnaia podsudnost*).

Thus, first, according to the rules of the subject matter of jurisdiction, all non-commercial civil matters (family, employment, tenancy, land, ecological and non-economic or commercial matters arising out of administrative offences) in Russia are subject to jurisdiction of the courts of general jurisdiction. Claims of a commercial nature (cases on economic disputes and other cases connected with carrying out business and other economic activity) are heard in *arbitrazh* (commercial) courts. *Arbitrazh* courts handle disputes with the participation of foreign and domestic companies and are the sole proprietors concerning commercial and economic matters. *Arbitrazh* courts also consider economic disputes arising out of administrative and other public legal relationships. The Russian Federation, the subjects of the Russian Federation,[62] state authorities, state officials and foreign sovereigns could also be parties to proceedings in *arbitrazh* courts. Russian *arbitrazh* courts are empowered to consider claims involving foreign parties.[63] In certain cases, *arbitrazh* courts have the exclusive competence to hear a case with a foreign element that cannot be changed by a choice-of-court agreement.[64] These cases include those relating to property owned by the state of the Russian Federation or immovable property or rights to such property located in Russia, registration or issuance of patents registered in Russia, etc.[65]

After a case is characterised as civil or commercial, it is assigned to the jurisdiction of courts of general jurisdiction or *arbitrazh* courts. Then, the rules of vertical jurisdiction determine the order in which a case can progress: from the lowest court to the highest court with the same subject matter jurisdiction category (vertically). A case shall be first brought to a court of first instance. Then, before its entry into force, parties to a case (and in some instances, third parties) have the right to appeal the decision in a court of (first) appeal. Furthermore, the decisions by courts of first appeal that have already entered into force and (or) judgments by the court of first appeal, may be further appealed in courts of *cassation* according

[62] The 'subject of the Russian Federation' is understood as a territorial unit of the Federation: an autonomous area, autonomous republic, city, etc.

[63] CAP art 247. Specific types of case where a foreign defendant or his property is located in Russia, when a managing body, branch, or representative office of a foreign entity is located in Russia, in torts cases for the infliction of damages to property when the act that gave rise to the complaint or the consequences of such occurred in Russia; where a dispute arose from unjust enrichment that happened in Russia, and other instances with a close connection to the disputed legal relationship to Russia.

[64] CAP art 248. M Boguslavskiĭ, *Mezhdunarodnoe Chastnoe Pravo* (*Private International Law*), 5th edn (Iurist, 2005) 250. Also, P Krasheninnikov, *Postateinyĭ Kommentariĭ k Arbitrazhnomu Protsessual'nomu Kodeksu* (*Article-by-Article Commentary on Code of Arbitrazh Procedure*) (Statut, 2007) 434.

[65] CAP art 248.

to the *cassation* (second appeal) procedure.[66] Finally, judgments by these courts which have already entered into force can be reviewed in actions of supervision (*nazdor*) by the Supreme Court.

The rules of territorial (horizontal) jurisdiction determine which exact court among the many courts of that level should have the right to consider the case. There are four types of territorial jurisdiction in Russia: general, alternative, contractual and exclusive jurisdiction. The general rule is that claims shall be filed with a court of a subject (territorial unit) of the Russian Federation at the location or place of residence of the defendant. This general rule of territorial jurisdiction coincides with the domicile principle established by Article 4 of the Brussels I Recast in the EU. The general rule of territorial jurisdiction is subject to a number of exceptions. The rules of alternative jurisdiction foresee situations where a certain connecting factor ties a case with an *arbitrazh* court other than that at the location of the defendant. In such regard, it may be compared with the rules of special jurisdiction in the EU. Moreover, jurisdiction rules may be overridden by a contractual jurisdiction – mutual agreement of the parties before the beginning of court proceedings in a case, except for cases subject to exclusive jurisdiction. This corresponds to the prorogation of jurisdiction in the EU. Finally, exclusive jurisdiction determines the venue (forum) for a number of cases overriding the application of the rules of general, alternative or prorogation jurisdiction. Cases of mandatory (exclusive) jurisdiction include claims concerning immovable property in Russia, bankruptcy proceedings, counterclaims, etc.

Currently, and for the next few years, the Russian judicial system is undergoing reform.[67] The initiative to combine the existing Supreme *Arbitrazh* Court and the Supreme Court of the Russian Federation was considered by the Russian Parliament in November 2013. Changes in this regard were introduced to the Constitution of the Russian Federation and the law on court system and the status of judges in February 2014. They came into effect in August 2014.[68] Notably, no such unification shall take place in relation to lower courts. Lower *arbitrazh* courts will continue to exist alongside the courts of general jurisdiction. Given the historical background of the Russian judicial system, and peculiarities of commercial litigation stipulated by the nature of commercial relationships, preserving the dual system appears to be the most appropriate. The competence of the courts will still be differentiated based on the subject matter of disputes they are authorised to handle.

[66] CCP ss II–IV; CAP ss II–VI.

[67] See M Karayanidi, 'Adjudicative Jurisdiction in Civil and Commercial Matters in Russia: Analysis and Commentary' (2016) 64 *American Journal of Comparative Law* 981.

[68] Federal'nyĭ Zakon RF o Popravke k Konstitutsii RF, o Verhovnom Sude RF i Prokurature RF (Federal Law of the Russian Federation on Changes to the Constitution of the Russian Federation: On the Supreme Court of the Russian Federation and the Prosecutor's Office of the Russian Federation) of 5 February 2014 no 2-FKZ; Federal'nyĭ Konstitutsionnyĭ Zakon RF o Vnesenii Izmeneniĭ v Federal'nyĭ Konstitutsionnyĭ Zakon o Sudebnoĭ Sisteme RF (Federal Constitutional Law of the Russian Federation Introducing Changes to the Law on the Judicial System) of 5 February 2014 no 4-FKZ.

In connection with the ongoing judicial reform, a working group of experts commenced the monumental work of consolidating the Codes of Civil and *Arbitrazh* Procedure. Six months after the experts started, they published a framework for a new united Code of Civil Procedure.[69] The Code shall be applied by both *arbitrazh* courts and courts of general jurisdiction. The framework for the new Code and its structure were approved by the Committee on Civil, Criminal and *Arbitrazh* Procedural Law of the State Duma (Parliament) in December 2014. The main objective of the Framework constitute

> ensuring accessible and equitable justice, carried out in reasonable time, where competent and independent judges follow the procedure … which represents unconditional requirement for democratic development of the rule of law based on the priority of rights and freedoms of individual.[70]

It also aims to improve the effectiveness of the judicial procedure in Russia, by eliminating contradictions between the provisions of the existing Codes of Civil and *Arbitrazh* Procedure. However, as the Framework announces, the rules on jurisdiction are projected to practically remain the same. I believe the reform represents a great opportunity to reconsider the Russian overall approach to jurisdiction and offer a number of solutions that can be taken into account by Russian legislators.

C. Brief Conclusions

Based on this brief overview, a few points need to be noted about the chosen jurisdiction regimes. First, there is a striking similarity between the Brussels and Russian schemes of jurisdiction. Both systems have a similar foundation: asserting jurisdiction at the location of the defendant. Both regimes foresee specific situations in which the defendant can be sued at an alternative forum. Both systems recognise the parties' choice of forum (party autonomy) and provide for exclusive jurisdiction of some courts in certain cases (some uniform, some different). This likeness between the Brussels regime and Russia is predicated by the influence of Roman law and the French and German jurisprudence during the formation of Russian law. However, although the blueprint of the two systems appears the same, application and interpretation of those rules by courts are different. The two systems are distinct by way of applying the law in the context of their social, economic and political climates. In particular, the pan-European Brussels

[69] Kontseptsia Edinogo Grazhdanskogo Processualnogo Kodeksa RF odobrena resheniem Komiteta po Grazhdanskomu, Ugolovnomu, Arbitrazhnomu i Processualnomu zakonodatelstvu GD FS RF ot 8 dekabria 2014 no 124(1) (Framework for the Consolidated Code of Civil Procedure of the RF, approved by the Decision of the Committee on Civil, Criminal and *Arbitrazh* and Procedural legislation of State Duma of the RF of 8 December 2014 no 124(1).

[70] Pavel Krasheninnikov, Opening Statement to the Framework for the Consolidated Code of Civil Procedure (n 69).

jurisdiction regime emerged in the late twentieth century, designed to support the common market. The Russian regime was formed in the nineteenth century and sustained minor adjustments throughout the Soviet era.

Moreover, the two systems stand further apart when analysing residual jurisdiction rules in the EU Member States. As is the case with England, the English and Russian lawmakers take seemingly opposing views towards the jurisdiction system overall. Establishing personal jurisdiction based on physical presence and submission to jurisdiction is foreign to Russia. In addition, a major contrast between the English common law and the Russian rules of jurisdiction is that English jurisdiction is accepted unless disputed. The diametrically opposing approach is taken by Russian courts, which assumes jurisdiction only if specifically afforded by law.

I will continue discussing the differences and the similarities between these regimes throughout this book. At this point, I have only introduced their main features. Throughout my analysis in the chapters that follow, I arrive at certain recommendations for improvement for Russian and EU lawmakers.

PART I

Party Autonomy in Private International Law on Jurisdiction

3

Autonomy as a Foundational Value for Jurisdiction

I. Introduction

In the following two chapters, I describe an ideal jurisdiction regime with party autonomy at its foundation. In the present chapter, I define autonomy, justify it against other values and show why it is appropriate for matters of private international law and jurisdiction.

To define autonomy, I examine its philosophical value in the context of the intellectual traditions from the regions that I focus on. Since German philosophical thought in many ways defined the formation of EU law, I rely on the German philosophical postulates on autonomy. Furthermore, since the creation of the conception of jurisdictional rules in Russia was in many ways influenced by German thought of the eighteenth century, discussion of the German thought on autonomy seems even more fitting. I start with Kant and his understanding of autonomy. I proceed to discuss how Kantian ideas developed into the Enlightenment as an international phenomenon. I argue that the Kantian understanding of individual autonomy of rational beings provides a solid theoretical foundation for my understanding of autonomy in jurisdiction. I further seek support for private party autonomy in jurisdiction from instrumentalist theory.

Furthermore, I connect consent and party autonomy in private law theory to the law on jurisdiction. I draw an understanding of individual sovereignty and power to make one's own decisions and show how it applies to private international law as well. I further note that the modern concept of autonomy is not unlimited; having learned from the failures of nineteenth-century liberalism, the contemporary phenomenon of autonomy aims to balance both parties' interests. In addition, I reflect on cultural constraints, noting that the concept of autonomy has slightly different understandings in different societies. I set aside the ambition to create a universal claim. Instead, I offer my analysis of the existing rules on jurisdiction in the two particular regimes: the EU and Russia. I examine them through the lens of my proposed approach, emphasising the role of party autonomy in jurisdiction.

I propose several arguments for autonomy to be at the foundation of the law on jurisdiction. First, I demonstrate how it naturally evolved in chosen national regimes. I argue that the rationale for its national development should apply to international jurisdiction agreements in cross-border matters. Secondly, I argue that party autonomy to choose a forum can be supported by the concurrent growing recognition of choice of law, and all the arguments in favour of it. Thirdly, I argue that broader recognition of party autonomy facilitates a better flow of international business transactions.

To further support my argument, I show why sovereignty is no longer the proper foundation for the law on jurisdiction. I argue that the combination of factors such as globalisation, development of the open society and a new world order signal the end of parochialism in private international law. Territoriality and sovereignty may remain appropriate for constructing jurisdiction in public international or criminal law, but these values have outgrown their importance for private international law. Wider recognition of foreign law in domestic proceedings shows that states have moved towards liberalisation of judicial procedure. The increased role of individuals as subjects of international law only further accentuates the shift of power from the state to private individuals. In these conditions, the time has come to reconceptualise how we view private international law and the law on jurisdiction in civil and commercial matters. Sovereignty no longer represents an adequate foundation for private international dispute resolution.

I put these ideas to test in chapter four, where I examine the existing rules of jurisdiction in the EU and Russia for their conformity with my view of an ideal jurisdiction regime. I conclude this Part I by defining the minute details of my proposed view and by recommending some general and specific changes to the jurisdiction regimes that I have examined.

II. Definition of and Justification for Autonomy

My understanding of autonomy is synonymous with the idea of freedom of individual actors to make their choices. For the law on jurisdiction, autonomy means freely choosing a forum to resolve disputes in cross-border dealings. It is drawn upon a philosophical understanding of autonomy as individual independence from others and from the state in making one's own decisions.

A. Kantian Autonomy and Enlightenment

My approach to party autonomy echoes the Kantian idea of autonomy. Discussing Kantian ideas is appropriate since they establish the foundation for private law, and private international law can be conceived of as private law on the international scale. According to the classical Kantian philosophy, autonomy is what leads an individual to enlightenment. It empowers an individual to walk by himself, in contrast to having society, the Church, convention and prejudice determine his (or her) decisions. Individual autonomy liberates an individual from the constraints that had been placed upon him (or her).[1] To achieve this liberation, the individual would have to question the truths presented to him by society, and use *reason* to achieve the enlightened understanding.[2] Kant goes further and asserts that through such reasonable assessment of things around the individual, a moral standard evinces. Thus, individual autonomy becomes a 'fundamental moral standard used to weigh and order all other moral considerations'.[3] Morality, according to Kant, takes the form of a categorical imperative: 'I must do the right thing because it is right, not because it will promote my interests or satisfy my desires'.[4] This moral judgement then determines the constraints on the freely chosen act.[5]

The Kantian idea of individual autonomy and morality presents an ideal, according to which individual rational agents would make a choice, and the choice would be morally sound. This is relevant to my argument, because I aim to discern a balanced view of autonomy, which embraces free choice, constrained by moral considerations. Freedom is a property of the will of all rational beings,[6] and I want to start from the understanding of rational beings who act as Kantian rational beings would: doing the right thing because it is right, and not out of selfish interests. That is why I adopt the Kantian understanding of individual autonomy and morality.

The fundamental role of freedom of individuals in law, established by Kant, was further developed by European liberal thinkers.[7] It grew into the international phenomenon of Enlightenment thought. One of the prominent thinkers of the Enlightenment, Savigny, recognised that freedom was an absolute necessity for a man, and law was necessary to secure that freedom.[8] Enlightenment ideas spread and took hold throughout Western Europe and across the Atlantic Ocean. The Enlightenment became associated with believing in the natural goodness of human beings. It attempted to liberate the people from religious and the monarch's authority and to make government depend on the consent of the governed.[9]

Many Russian thinkers accepted the ideas of the Kantian autonomy of individuals. Some of them continued the Kantian tradition, arguing that law is in

[1] A Pagden, *The Enlightenment: And Why it Still Matters* (Random House, 2013) 21.

[2] ibid, referring to *Practical Philosophy* 17: AK 8: 35–36.

[3] R Robb, 'Moral Theory, Autonomy, and Collective Rights: A Response to Dwight Newman' (2012) 25 *Canadian Journal of Law and Jurisprudence* 483.

[4] MJ Sandel (ed), *Justice: A Reader* (Oxford University Press, 2007) 157.

[5] A Somek, 'German Legal Philosophy and Theory in the Nineteenth and Twentieth Centuries' in D Patterson (ed), *A Companion to Philosophy of Law and Legal Theory* (Blackwell Publishing Ltd, 1996).

[6] I Kant, *Groundwork of the Metaphysics of Morals: A German-English Edition* (M Gregor and J Timmermann eds, trs, Cambridge University Press, 2012) 123.

[7] eg, Hedley Bull, and his *Anarchical Society: A Study of Order in World Politics* (Columbia University Press, 1977); Y Fukiyama, *The End of History and the Last Man* (Free Press, 1992) etc.

[8] J Gordley, *The Philosophical Origins of Modern Contract Doctrine* (Clarendon Press, 1993) 225.

[9] J Charvet and E Kaczynska-Nay, *The Liberal Project and Human Rights* (Cambridge University Press, 2008) 314.

deep unity with morals, and the norms of regulatory acts should embody justice and morality.[10] Kantian individual autonomy was accepted to a point, however, because of other popular philosophical postulates and the predominant authority of the state. Similar to other Western ideological traditions,[11] Russian society absorbed only the parts of them that it deemed necessary. Individual autonomy stretched only as far as allowed by the tsarist society and the proliferating ideas of societal solidarity. Notably, the Western ideas of individual autonomy came to Russia around the time of the emancipation of serfs in Russia (1861), at the beginning of the great judicial reform. The Russian ruler was finally abolishing (what essentially could be equated to) slavery. The effects inevitably 'spilled over' to all areas of law and society, recognising the rights and freedoms of the individual. However, Russian liberal judicial reform came 'from the top down'.[12] People were graciously given a leeway of autonomy by the sovereign. Instead of the need for the change to originate in the minds of people, the reform and progressive ideas were instilled upon the minds of the Russian people. Thus, at the time of the reception of Kantian ideas, autonomy was never fully embraced as the Kantian autonomy. It only planted the seed to blossom later, in the context of the great upcoming societal changes (unfortunately, to be stifled again later).[13] Nevertheless, individual autonomy eventually took hold in Russian society.

B. Autonomy in Private Law

In addition to classical Enlightenment thought, I draw my understanding of autonomy from the concept of autonomy in the theory of private law. By private law theory, I mean the principles underpinning private transactions in the civil law tradition, and theoretical works on philosophy of private law in the English judicial tradition. These ideas are relevant because private law theory helps in understanding transactions involving private parties and concerning private matters. Private international law transactions can be conceived as the same private transactions with an international element.

In Russian scholarship, the private parties' right to choose a forum to settle their disputes reflects one of the main principles of civil law and procedure: the parties' right to freely exercise their material and procedural rights (*printsip dispozitivnosti*).[14] A number of classical Soviet works establish this principle.

[10] D Nokhrin, 'Russian National Report: Goals of Civil Justice' in D Maleshin (ed), *Civil Procedure in Cross-Cultural Dialogue: Eurasia Context* (Statut, 2012) 224, referring to S Alekseev, *Teoriya Prava* (*Theory of Law*) (BEK, 1993) 70–71.

[11] In contrast to, however, Marx and Engels' ideology which was accepted and embraced literally by the Bolsheviks.

[12] ibid 9.

[13] Repressed by the communist regime.

[14] Such understanding is advocated by a number of authors; most vividly by Marina Rozhkova: M Rozhkova, 'Teoriya protsessual'nogo dogovora v sootnoshenii s kontseptsieĭ sdelok, napravlennyh na zashchitu prav' ('Theory of Procedural Agreement in Relation to the Concept of Transactions Aimed at Protection of Rights') (2007) 6 *Rossiĭskiĭ Ezhegodnik Grazhdanskogo i Arbitrazhnogo Protsessa* 184.

Krasavchikov, one of the first Russian scholars to speculate about it,[15] understood it as a 'special category of civil procedural law understood in scholarship as the possibility of free disposition by the subject of his material and procedural rights in civil procedure'.[16] Contemporary Russian civil law scholars go further. For instance, Kurochkin contends that: 'the will of the subjects in judicial process, who are directed [by the judge] but remain independent and autonomous, … represents the foundation for making their decisions … resulting in legal consequences'.[17] Rozhkova relies on the principle of *dispozitivnost* as a starting point for her theory and contends that the right of parties to influence the development of the court procedure, such as through procedural agreements, emanates from this principle.[18] Thus, the principle of free exercise of material and procedural rights by the parties represents one of the fundamental values in civil law and procedure in Russia. The right of the parties to choose jurisdiction is recognised alongside other civil procedural agreements, such as the agreement to transfer the case to an arbitration tribunal, or an amicable settlement agreement that parties may conclude at any stage of the civil procedure (unless otherwise stated by federal law).

The principle of free exercise of material and procedural rights is consistent with my argument for party autonomy in jurisdiction. Parties' choice of jurisdiction expresses their mutually negotiated expectations[19] in relation to their future dispute resolution. Enforcement of jurisdiction agreements gives effect to the parties' rights and expectations. It is justified because it helps maintain predictability and certainty in relation to the forum, and it is morally right to give the parties this opportunity to determine their preferences in terms of adjudicating disputes.

Furthermore, my view on placing autonomy at the foundation of the law on jurisdiction can be supported by (common law) private law theory. In private law, autonomy especially proliferates in contract law, where the contract embodies the notions of liberty and free will. Behind the binding nature of contract, there is a voluntary undertaking of obligations in exchange for something in return. Parties consent to any bargain transaction they wish. Consent is important, as it is 'a manifested intention to be legally bound'.[20] Through their consent, individual actors, empowered by their autonomy, conduct their affairs and make

[15] O Krasavchikov, '*Dispozitivnost' v Grazhdansko-Pravovom Regulirovanii*' ('Principle of Free Exercise of Material and Procedural Rights by the Parties in Civil Law') (1970) 1 *Sovetskoe Gosudarstvo i Pravo* 41.

[16] S Kuznetsov, *Sudebnie Obespechitelnie Sredstva v Rossiĭskom Grazhdanskom Prave* (*Legal Enforcement Remedies in Russian Civil Law*) (Wolters Kluwer, 2008) 51, referring to O Krasavchikov, *Ukazannye Sochineniia* (*Selected Works*) (Statut, 2005) 59.

[17] S Kurochkin, 'Soglasheniia v Tsivilisticheskom Protsesse' ('Agreements in Civil Procedure') (2012) *Vestnik Grazhdanskogo Protsessa* 3.

[18] Rozhkova (n 14) 188.

[19] For a similar justification of parties' choice of law, see, M Lehmann, 'Liberating the Individual from Battles between States: Justifying Party Autonomy in Conflict of Laws' (2008) 41 *Vanderbilt Journal of Transnational Law* 381, 392, referring to R Leflar: 'Choice-Influencing Considerations in Conflicts Law' (1966) 41 *New York University Law Review* 267, 283.

[20] R Barnett, 'Contract is not Promise, Contract is Consent' (2012) 45 *Suffolk University Law Review* 647, 655; also, R Barnett, 'A Consent Theory of Contract' (1986) 86 *Columbia Law Review* 269.

their choices. This individual sovereignty presupposes persons' capacity and responsibility for making their decisions, including those concerning entering into contracts.[21] Thus, the autonomy of actors in private law is an expression of their will.[22] In this light, choice of forum can be conceptualised as a right enjoyed by private actors to set the terms of their interaction in the manner most suited to their economic and practical interests. Notably, a neo-Kantian non-instrumentalist approach regards private law as independent of influence from public law and as non-political. Similarly, I envision private international law as non-political. My understanding of the autonomy of private actors is of a non-threatening and non-political character.

C. Consequentialist Justification of Party Autonomy

Apart from the Kantian concept of autonomous moral agents, party autonomy may be justified by consequentialist argument.

Consistent with John Stuart Mill's claim that autonomy is 'one of the elements of well-being',[23] by bringing the practical benefits to each party, party autonomy may be a means to a greater wellbeing. Party autonomy allows individual actors to make choices most suited to their economic and practical interests: by exercising autonomy in private international law, a person takes a step towards litigating in a forum most suitable and beneficial to that person's interests. Such choice of forum contributes to the person's overall fulfilling life, where decisions are made not because of being dictated by state sovereign rules but based on self-government. Such individual wellbeing aggregates, and the overall increase in the aggregate welfare justifies party autonomy as the ultimate basis for jurisdiction.

Parties' choice of forum may be justified as it is a decision that is most effective and efficient under the circumstances. Expression of the parties' will in jurisdiction is justified because it reflects their economic – among other – interests. This applies particularly to corporate actors – especially 'travelling corporations' who 'alter their structures' to 'cherry-pick'[24] what law applies to them – who may not necessarily act as moral agents but seek choices most efficient for them.

In this regard, the pragmatic argument by Whincop and Keyes,[25] based on the general claim by O'Hara and Ribstein, and Guzman, may be applied here. The

[21] J Kraus, 'Personal Sovereignty and Normative Power Skepticism' (2009) 109 *Columbia Law Review Sidebar* 126.

[22] E Weinrib, *The Idea of Private Law* (Oxford University Press, 2012); S Smith, *Contract Theory* (Oxford University Press, 2004).

[23] JS Mill, *On Liberty* (Longman, Roberts, & Green Co, 1859/1975) ch III.

[24] The concept is described by Darren Rosenblum in D Rosenblum, 'How Firms and Nations Compete Through Intellectual Property Law' in H Muir Watt et al (eds), *Global Private International Law: Adjudication without Frontiers* (Edward Elgar Publishing, 2019).

[25] M Whincop and M Keyes, *Policy and Pragmatism in the Conflict of Laws* (Ashgate, 2001).

claim is that economising on litigation should be a priority in private international law,[26] and the most efficient choice of forum should be the most optimal one. Whincop and Keyes narrow down the issue of determining an appropriate jurisdiction to a common denominator – efficiency, where fora are selected based on the efficiency criterion and welfare maximisation rather than a certain set of rights. Having dissected the variables of costs to plaintiff and defendant of litigating here or there, and having mentioned the interests relevant to jurisdictional principles, they contend that choosing, submitting to and, possibly objecting to, jurisdiction may be made taking into account these costs and interests. Whincop's and Keyes' argument is consistent with my claim to the extent that private actors and their interests should determine jurisdiction in international civil and commercial claims.

It differs from their argument, however, because apart from efficiency, there are further considerations of policy and fairness, that I regard as important.

While the Kantian idea of autonomy – reflecting individual moral agency – transposes well to individual actors in private international law, it is arguably not applicable to corporate actors that are motivated at least primarily by shareholder profit.[27] Consequentialist argument more easily provides justification for party autonomy. Resolving disputes at a forum of their choice increases the corporate actors' benefits, thus contributing to the overall wellbeing of the ultimate shareholder individuals who stand behind the corporate actors.

D. Delimiting the Modern Concept of Autonomy for Jurisdiction

To be clear about my understanding of autonomy for the law on jurisdiction, a few words need to be said about the necessary limitations to the concept of autonomy. In particular, taking into consideration the challenges brought by the twentieth century to nineteenth-century individualism, I concede that party autonomy cannot be unlimited. In fact, I argue that constraints define, rather than, destroy freedom. This idea is similar to the Miltonian paradox: Milton portrays Adam and Eve's freedom as 'lost through freedom'.[28] Because Adam and Eve were, in the beginning of time, so free, that they could even relinquish and negate their freedom, their unlimited freedom was lost. Then, enslavement of their wills did not negate their freedom, but expressed it. The chains set them free. Thus, paradoxically, constraints define, rather than, destroy freedom. In further chapters of this book, I describe exactly how freedom to choose a forum should be limited. For now, I note the necessity to limit it and outline the general reasons for such limitation.

[26] E O'Hara and L Ribstein, 'From Politics to Efficiency in Choice of Law' (2000) 67 *University of Chicago Law Review* 1151; A Guzman, 'Choice of Law: New Foundations' (2002) 90 *Georgetown Law Journal* 883.

[27] A Mills, *Party Autonomy in Private International Law* (Cambridge University Press, 2018) 70–71.

[28] B Myers, *Milton's Theology of Freedom* (De Gruyter, 2006) 140.

A valid argument against unlimited party autonomy originates in the main critique of liberalism. To explain it, it would be easiest to project oneself into nineteenth-century capitalist-driven society in Europe.[29] The reforms regarding minimum conditions and maximum hours for workers in various industries were non-existent. This happened not because of 'inhumanity and greed', but from the conviction that the state had no business to interfere in the relationships of master and workman or landlord and tenant, any more than any other form of private contract.[30] A strong belief in governmental non-interference in the market economy dominated in society. Private actors had the freedom to conduct business in the manner they saw fit, as long as in the end, it promoted economic growth. The hardship it caused to certain groups of individuals was accepted as inevitable and unimportant side effects of the system.

Eventually, the critique of the freedom of contract evolved exposing that 'there was no real freedom in a relationship where the starting positions of the two sides were grossly unequal'.[31] An awareness developed 'of the reality of much that went on in the name of freedom of contract'.[32] Questions began to appear: 'if an employer offers a man work in a very unhealthy workshop, and the man accepts the work and its conditions, are the employer and the workman at perfect liberty to carry out such a contract?'[33] The eventual sunset of pure laissez-faire policy began.

There is a parallel between this argument against economic freedom and my argument for party autonomy in jurisdiction. What is the danger here? What disasters may take place similar to those born of the economic liberalism of the nineteenth century, such as atrocities in relation to minimum working conditions?

In an ideal jurisdiction system, party autonomy cannot be absolute. Unlimited party autonomy to choose a forum might ensue in opportunism and advantage taken by a party better positioned to negotiate jurisdiction. With no governmental interference, unrestricted private power to allocate jurisdiction would inevitably sway in the direction beneficial to the actors with stronger bargaining positions. In view of protecting the equality and rights of all market players, including those with weaker bargaining power, some constraints should be placed on party autonomy to choose a forum. Having learned from the nineteenth century's economic liberalism, I confidently suggest that the underlying value of freedom of individuals to choose how they conduct their affairs (including the right to designate the court to handle their disputes) should be limited in the interests of equality. During the nineteenth century's economic liberalism, private businesses flourished in the pure laissez-faire policy, where working conditions and minimal wages were unregulated. However, eventually, society came to a realisation that without governmental protection, certain parties were put at an intolerable

[29] JM Kelly, *A Short History of Western Legal Thought* (Clarendon Press, 1992).
[30] ibid 305–06.
[31] ibid 306.
[32] PS Atiyah, *The Rise and Fall of the Freedom of Contract* (Clarendon Press, 1979) 614.
[33] ibid 615, referring to WS Jevons, *The State in Relation to Labour* (Macmillan and Co, 1882).

disadvantage. Similar to these reasons for the decline of the nineteenth century's economic liberalism, we should be cautious about unlimited freedom to designate a forum for dispute resolution. Forum selection clauses inserted unilaterally in contracts of adhesion should only be given effect where they do not abrogate the weaker party's access to justice.

This view is consistent with the above-mentioned Kantian view of individual autonomy. Although we may 'commonly think that freedom consists in the ability to pursue our desires unimpeded',[34] it is not the case under Kantian enlightenment thought. Where individuals act based on categorical imperative (doing the right thing because it is right), they will act freely, but within the constraints imposed by the considerations of morality. As Stevens argues, 'we can't be half-hearted Kantians – [in other words,] if we're attracted to a Kantian view of the law it must be that we buy into Kantianism generally, and not just when we feel like it'.[35] I advocate for party autonomy and believe that individuals and entities have the autonomy to make their rational choices. I still wholeheartedly embrace the Kantian view, but the concept of party autonomy in this book is constrained by moral considerations that should be backed by governmental protection in certain cases involving weaker parties.

E. Reflection on Cultural Constraints

Having outlined my views on the concept of autonomy, I need to address sensible limitations of my understanding. In particular, party autonomy definition largely depends on the cultural and societal values of a particular state. Party autonomy may be counterintuitive to social and legal patterns in non-liberal and authoritarian societies. Bearing in mind that 'liberalism is … indigenous to the West and imported to non-Western societies through the West's hegemony in international society',[36] I appreciate that various beliefs in different states may not subscribe to the same truths of liberty and freedom of the individual. Even within liberalised and democratic societies, one value does not necessarily mean the same thing in different states. For instance, an enquiry into the intellectual history, legal theory, and legal philosophy of France and England proves that a French jurist and an English common lawyer are not necessarily talking about the same thing when arguing about 'freedom of contract'.[37] Furthermore, the very idea of legal knowledge and legal culture differs greatly between common and civil law, despite the claims of convergence between these two regimes.[38] Law simply cannot be captured by a set

[34] Sandel (n 4) 157.

[35] R Stevens, 'The Conflict of Rights' in A Robertson and HW Tang (eds), *The Goals of Private Law* (Hart Publishing, 2009) 140.

[36] Charvet and Kaczynska-Nay (n 9) 318.

[37] H-W Micklitz, 'On the Intellectual History of Freedom of Contract and Regulation' (2015) 4 *Penn State Journal of Law & International Affairs* 1.

[38] P Legrand, 'European Legal Systems Are Not Converging' (1996) 45 *International & Comparative Law Quarterly* 52, 56.

of neatly organised rules, and even seeming convergence of legal systems in the EU is misleading.[39] Therefore, any fundamental value that lawyers argue may be ascribed different gradations of meaning, and autonomy is not an exception.

Where does this leave my argument? One alternative would be to attempt to construct a universal claim, with a disclaimer of applicability only in liberal and democratic states.[40] I could argue that the claim on prevalence of party autonomy to choose a forum is universal. However, the universality of the claim is only true as far as the national recognition of party autonomy stretches. This book does not fit every single state's approach to the role of state and individual in law. Proving the universality of the claim would require defending the premises of Western liberalism, which would bring me outside the scope of this book. Instead, I confine my argument to interpreting the existing law in the two systems: the EU and Russia. I argue that if my claims on prevalence of party autonomy are accepted, the discussion presented in this book follows. The reason is that the value of party autonomy has to come from within a nation, before it can be enforced in cross-border transactions. A state must first cease being parochial. The historical exercise performed further in this chapter demonstrates that the EU and Russia have had domestic legal norms recognising parties' choice of forum long before adopting them for international jurisdiction. By natural progression, the party autonomy to choose a forum evolved from the nationally recognised principle of an international standard.[41]

Focusing on the EU and Russian definitions of party autonomy, I realise that they have the same broad meaning but differ in detail. A Russian lawyer may embrace Kantian individual autonomy, however, his perceptions of the power of the state would automatically project on the scope of this autonomy, limiting it to private affairs only, or ending where the state apparatus says so. While an English common lawyer may view freedom to choose a forum as an inherent part of freedom of contract, the civil law approach would view the autonomy to choose a forum as a procedural issue, rather separate from general contractual terms.

I concede that these possible variations in understanding party autonomy exist. I bear them in mind but aim to arrive at a common denominator. With this purpose, I proceed with an understanding of party autonomy as the power of the private parties to choose a forum independently of considerations of

[39] ibid 59–61.

[40] In light of Charvet and Kaczynska-Nay's explanation of cultural relativism, liberal ideas apply universally, equally to Taliban perspective on no education for women, although they only extend to members of the respective (Western or Taliban) society. Thus, 'these universal judgements … are valid only from the relevant cultural standpoint': Charvet and Kaczynska-Nay (n 9) 320.

[41] Although, arguably, party autonomy to choose a forum can also be implemented from the top down. This may be relevant in societies where the development of the law emanates from government and is imposed upon the society, rather than being a result of a democratic and representative process. For instance, a national leader of Ruristan (a fictitious neighbouring country to Dicey's fictitious Ruritania), driven by the considerations of popularity in the international arena, may be pressured to adopt the Hague Convention on Choice-of-Court Agreements. This may trigger the process for implementation and development of party autonomy as a principle in the national law as well.

territoriality of the claim. First, however, I establish why exactly party autonomy should be at the foundation of jurisdiction, why it should take the place of other traditionally accepted values such as sovereignty, and why it should be reasonably limited.

III. Autonomy as a Proper Foundation for Matters of Private International Law and Jurisdiction

As an expression of private parties' will regarding jurisdiction, autonomy is the ultimate principle that should determine the appropriate forum to settle disputes between private parties. In this section, I put forward several arguments to support this idea.

A. Development of Autonomy

In my search to justify party autonomy in international dispute resolution, I trace its origins within certain national legal systems. The rationale for doing so is based on the notion that before the party autonomy to choose a forum was recognised in the international setting, it originated from and was enforced within the state. I argue that the logic behind its development can be applied to international dispute resolution.

The three national systems for my historical enquiry are Germany, Russia and the UK, chosen based on their influential role in their corresponding regions. Germany was one of the founding states of the European Union, and it provides an interesting example of evolution of party autonomy, as the cradle of Enlightenment liberalism in Europe. The English example of party autonomy development is important and helpful, since the English case constitutes the main example of applying the EU jurisdiction regime in this book. Finally, it is also interesting and necessary to outline Russian domestic recognition of parties' choice of jurisdiction, considering the unique coexistence of Russian civil and commercial judicial procedure, and the apparent transposition of Russian national jurisdiction rules onto its regulation of international jurisdiction.

i. German Example

Section 38 of the current German Zivilprozessordnung[42] (Code of Civil Procedure) (the ZPO) foresees jurisdiction of a court of first instance by express

[42] German Code of Civil Procedure as promulgated on 5 December 2005 (ZPO) (*Bundesgesetzblatt* (*BGBl, Federal Law Gazette*) I p 3202; 2006 I p 431; 2007 I p 1781), last amended by Article 1 of the Act dated 10 October 2013 (*Federal Law Gazette* I p 3786) (Germany).

or tacit agreement of the parties, where such parties are merchants, legal entities, or public law special funds (*Sondervermögen*).[43] The provision outlines the admissibility of jurisdiction clauses and presupposes local or international jurisdiction.[44] Fascinatingly, when the Code of Civil Procedure Rules of Germany was enacted in 1877, its section 38 already envisaged permitting agreements concerning jurisdiction of the courts.[45] Therefore, one must look prior to the end of the nineteenth century, before the ZPO was promulgated in order to find the preconditions for party autonomy to choose a forum in Germany.

Before the all-German civil procedural code of 1877 and the seminal Bürgerliches Gesetzbuch (Civil Code) (the BGB) 1900, there was no uniform legislation on civil law and civil procedure in Germany. Over 30 different legal systems in the German state mandated various rules. In some of these territories (especially to the west of the river Rhine), French civil law traditions influenced local codification efforts.[46] In particular, early-nineteenth-century French codifications, the Code civil of 1804, the Code de procédure civile of 1806, and the Code de commerce of 1807 had a substantial influence on German statutes, especially in the western territories.[47] For instance, the Bavarian Codex Bavaricus civilis of 1756 was a substantial codification, but still followed the tradition of *ius commune*.[48] In practice, it meant that Germanic customary law still prevailed throughout the whole of Germany,[49] but French statutory law eventually influenced the development of the German ZPO norms.

In parallel, the French Revolution played an 'awakening' role for European societies at the end of the eighteenth century. In particular, the French revolutionary Declaration of the Rights of Man and of the Citizen 1789, proclaiming men free and equal in their rights and the principles of fair trial and due process of law, had its share of influence on the minds of the contemporary German statesmen and scholars.

In addition, recognition of private autonomy in Germany could be attributed to the development of liberal enlightenment in the seventeenth and the eighteenth centuries. Van Caenegem expresses a similar thought in relation to the codified laws in Europe during the period of enlightenment, while legislation and national

[43] ZPO, § 38.

[44] Toussaint, *Beck'scher Online Kommentar (OK)* ZPO (Beck-online, 15th edn, as of 1 January 2015) § 38.

[45] S Goren (tr), *The Code of Civil Procedure Rules of the Federal Republic of Germany* (F Rothman & Co, 1990) 9–10.

[46] CH van Rhee, 'The Influence of the French Code de Procédure Civile (1806) in 19th Century Europe' in L Cadiet and G Canivet (eds), *De la Commémoration d'un Code à l'Autre: 200 Ans de Procedure Civile en France* (*On Commemoration of the Code of Others: 200 Years Anniversary of Civil Procedure in France*) (LexisNexis/Litec, 2008).

[47] F Kawohl, 'Commentary on the Copyright Provisions in the Baden Statute Book of 1809' in L Bently and M Kretschmer (eds), *Primary Sources on Copyright (1450–1900)*, available at: www.copyrighthistory.org.

[48] RC van Caenegem, *An Historical Introduction to Private Law* (Cambridge University Press, 1988) 123.

[49] D Ibbetson, Book Review: 'Van Caenegem's An Historical Introduction to Private Law' (1992) 41 *International & Comparative Law Quarterly* 958.

codes were a means of putting the conceptions of the law of reason into practice.[50] German classical liberal thought set the foundations of the contemporary democratic state and the rule of law. Individual actors were empowered with independence from the sovereign state in their private affairs. The recognition of the parties' right to choose a forum might have been a natural progression of this development. Thus, the Enlightenment provided a favourable environment for the development of party autonomy. The mentality evolved from closed, limited and subjugated, to liberated, free and independent. During this shift, the recognition of party autonomy occurred within the domestic jurisdictional regime in Germany.

ii. Russian Experience

Current Russian law explicitly allows private parties to surpass general and alternative (special) rules of jurisdiction by agreeing on a forum to handle their civil or commercial disputes. This autonomy has developed as a matter of practicality. In his account on the history of jurisdiction agreements in Russian law, Russian scholar Dergachev traces the evolution of Russian statutory rules on jurisdiction agreements in civil and *arbitrazh* (commercial) procedure.[51] He analyses the current legislation, the Soviet period and pre-revolutionary (tsarist) Russia. He demonstrates that the rules allowing jurisdiction by agreement were formed in Russia in the first half of the nineteenth century.[52] First statutory consolidation of the prorogation of jurisdiction by agreement took place in the Ustav sudoproizvodstva torgovogo (Statute of Commercial Procedure) in 1832.[53] The reason behind this enactment was connected with the particularities of trade. Given that commercial courts existed in only a few Russian cities at the time, and merchants were engaged in business activity all over the vast territory of the Russian state, it made practical sense for the parties in certain cases to prorogue jurisdiction in favour of the local civil court of general jurisdiction.[54] The commercial cases could be heard in courts of general jurisdiction, as opposed to specialised commercial courts, with due regard to the commercial procedural rules.

Eventually, a similar rule was prescribed for civil non-commercial cases. Several decades later, the Ustav grazhdanskogo sudoproizvodstva (Statute of Civil Procedure) of 1864 reflected the possibility of parties choosing a forum in all other civil non-commercial transactions. The enactment of the Statute of Civil Procedure in 1864 triggered subsequent doctrinal analysis of jurisdiction agreements of the

[50] van Caenegem (n 48) 122.

[51] S Dergachev, '"Dogovornaia Podsudnost" v Grazhdanskom i Arbitrazhnom Processe Rossii' ('"Jurisdiction" by Agreement in Civil and Commercial Procedure in Russia') (PhD Book, Russian Academy of Justice affiliated with the Supreme Court of the Russian Federation, 2011) (on file with author).

[52] ibid 17.

[53] Ustav Sudoproizvodstva Torgovogo 1832 (Rules of Legal Commercial Procedure) arts 47, 155.

[54] Interview with Symeon Dergachev, Assistant Professor, Chair of Civil, *Arbitrazh* and Administrative Procedural Law, Russian Academy of Justice (Dublin, Ireland–Moscow, Russia (skype) 20 April 2015).

pre-revolutionary period,[55] which mostly took the form of the commentaries to the Statute.[56] Notably, the earlier Statute of Commercial Procedure of 1832, which first prescribed party autonomy to choose a forum, did not generate any scholarly commentary or discussion at all. One author generalises that 'until the nineteenth century there was virtually no legal scholarship, no theory or philosophy of law'.[57] Nevertheless, the wider intellectual thought in Russia espoused individual autonomy in private affairs. As noted above, this was a hybrid of the Western philosophy and local political, social and cultural realities.

After the Revolution of 1917, the Soviet civil procedural statutes[58] did not foresee jurisdiction agreements up until 1964.[59] Nevertheless, the earlier tsarist-timed rules on civil procedure applied, as long as they did not contradict the interests of the proletariat. As resolved by the Higher judicial authority at the time, the possibility for parties to choose jurisdiction was permissible, where no exclusive jurisdiction rules existed.[60] The reason why the Higher judicial authority resolved that lower courts could allow jurisdiction agreements was because this rule had already been applied by the courts since tsarist times, yet it was missing in the legislation at the time.

This temporary absence of jurisdiction agreements in law has divided Soviet scholars into two groups: those in favour of such party autonomy to choose a forum, and those against it. Those in favour of party autonomy[61] contended that it ensued from the general meaning of the law. The civil procedure rules did not explicitly prohibit it. Moreover, separate bits of legislation contained provisions allowing it. In particular, civil law allowed the place of performance of contract to be determined by the parties' agreement; civil procedure allowed bringing disputes arising out of contracts with specified place of performance at the local court; thus, contract suits could be brought at the place chosen by the parties. Filing a suit not at the location specified in the contract deemed violation of the agreement. One scholar openly called the opinion that parties allegedly could not choose a court to handle their disputes a 'misconception'.[62]

[55] ibid.

[56] Dergachev (n 51) 61–63, referring to Vas'kovskiĭ, Nefed'ev, Engel'man, Annenkov, and others.

[57] Z Zile (ed), *Ideas and Forces in Soviet Legal History: A Reader on the Soviet State and Law* (Oxford University Press, 1992) 3.

[58] Dekrety o Sude no 1 ot 24 noiabria (5 dekabria) 1917 g, no 2 ot 15 febralia 1918 g i no 3 ot 7 marta 1919 g (Decrees on Courts no 1 as of 24 November 1917, no 2 as of 15 February 1918 and no 3 as of 7 March 1919; Grazhdanskiĭ Protsessual'nyĭ Kodeks RSFSR (Code of Civil Procedure of the Russian Soviet Federative Socialist Republic (RSFSR)) 1923.

[59] Grazhdanskiĭ Protsessual'nyĭ Kodeks RSFSR 1964 (Code of Civil Procedure of the RSFSR) art 120.

[60] Plenum of the Supreme Court of the RSFSR, Protocol no 1 as of 3 February 1932.

[61] Dergachev (n 51) 68, referring to B Popov, 'K Voprosu Dogovornoi Dodsudnosti' ('On the Issue of Jurisdiction by Agreement') (1927) *Pravo i Zhizn* 77, M Pergament, 'Opredeleniia Grazhdanskoĭ Kassatsionnoĭ Kollegii za 1924' ('Resolutions of Cassation Committee for the Year 1924') (1926) 2 *Ezhenedelnik Sovetskoĭ Justitsii*, and I Osipov, *Podvedomstvennost i Podsudnost Grazhdanskih Del* (GosIurIzdat, 1962) 100.

[62] V Trapeznikov, 'Dopustima li Dogovornaya Podsudnost' Iskov?' ('Is Jurisdiction by Agreement Permissible?') (1924) 33 *Ezhenedelnik Sovetskoi Iustitsii* 770.

Scholars advocating against party autonomy in civil procedure believed that it was impermissible because the civil procedural statute did not explicitly provide for it. Another reason was viewing the concepts of jurisdiction and territorial jurisdiction as one subject matter.[63] In this regard, if all jurisdiction was subject matter jurisdiction – allocating civil cases to civil courts, and commercial cases to commercial courts – it could not be reasonably changed by private parties but could only be prescribed by state rules.

Later, since the enactment of the Code of Civil Procedure in 1964, the rule on jurisdiction by agreement re-entered and has remained in the Russian rules on civil procedure. Notably, the Code of 1964 separated the subject matters of jurisdiction and territorial jurisdiction into two separate sections. Thus, the rules prescribing claims of a certain nature to certain courts remained rigid, but the rules for filing at the location of the defendant were augmented by other possibilities, including the parties' choice of court.

In addition to the reasons of practicality and rationality, party autonomy in jurisdiction evolved due to certain accompanying historical developments. One cannot avoid noticing the correlation with the emancipation of serfs of 1861 and the great judicial reform in the Russian monarchy. Before the great judicial reform of 1864, some critics characterised the Russian judiciary as 'brutal, disorganised, arbitrary and corrupt'.[64] The judicial procedure was inconvenient, insufficient, complicated, expensive, and the judges were 'wildly incompetent and consistently corrupt'.[65] Without legal representation, a jury, and a presumption of innocence, the poor had little chance of securing justice. The need for reform was recognised by the Russian tsar Nikolaĭ I and implemented by Alexander II. To align Russia with the liberal and modernised nations of Europe, judicial reform in Russia was carried out by borrowing from progressive French legislation. The new Russian law on civil procedure was based on the French Code of Civil Procedure.[66] Some parts were literally taken from the French Code. The French Code, in its turn, had drawn upon the Roman tradition, ideas of which were already part of ancient Russian medieval law through Byzantine Canon law. This general acceptance of the Roman tradition, where deemed necessary by the 'social needs of medieval

[63] Dergachev (n 51) 68, referring to A Bugaevskiĭ, 'Dogovornaya Podsudnost' ('Jurisdiction by Agreement') in V Tadevosyan and F Nabok (eds) *Sbornik Stateĭ i Materialov po Grazhdanskomu Protsessu za 1922–1924 gg.* (*Collection of Essays and Materials on Civil Procedure for 1922–24*) (Iuridicheskoe Izdatelstvo Narodnogo Komissariata Iustitsii RSFSR, 1925) 155–60. Also, A Bugaevskiy, *Grazhdanskiĭ Process v ego Dvizhenii s Prilozheniem Tipichnykh Del* (*Civil Procedure in its Development: Typical Cases Attached*), 2nd edn (BI Leningrad, 1924) 13.

[64] B Conlon, 'Dostoevsky v the Judicial Reforms of 1864: How and Why One of Nineteenth-Century Russia's Greatest Writers Criticised the Nation's Most Successful Reform' (2014) 2(4) *Russian Law Journal* 7, 9, citing W Mosse, *Alexander II and the Modernisation of Russia* 23 (English Universities Press, 1958), referring to liberal writer and critic Alexander Herzen.

[65] Conlon, ibid 11.

[66] van Rhee (n 46) 131.

Russian society',[67] combined with progressive French legal thought, resulted in the adoption of the procedural rule that allowed jurisdiction by the parties' agreement.

In addition, recognition of the parties' choice of jurisdiction in Russian domestic law may be attributed to scholarly influence. Although no doctrinal publications can be traced before 1864 regarding the parties' choice of jurisdiction, the fundamental rule on jurisdiction agreements did not simply present itself. Enacted by Alexander II, the Statute of Civil Procedure 1864 was drawn up by a group of experts familiar with the Russian and Western systems (including Zarudnyĭ, Stasov, Bludov, Cherkasova,[68] and others). Authors were inspired by German, French, Austrian and Italian as well as English and American laws.[69] In particular, one of the main names behind the reform, Zarudnyĭ, contended that 'not accepting improvements from a foreign state only because they are foreign is equivalent to not introducing railways, telegraph, and other inventions, just because the citizens of the given state did not have a chance to come to such inventions'.[70] The Western doctrines had a significant influence upon Russian theoretical jurisprudence at the end of the eighteenth and beginning of the nineteenth century.[71] In fact, many scholars at the time in Russian universities were, literally, German nationals. Tomsinov, for instance, mentions that all the professor posts belonged to Germans, with the only Russian scholar Desnitskiĭ being an exception.[72] Thus, it might be argued that German enlightenment thought found its way to Russian academia and the intellectual elite. Notwithstanding the 'heritage of many centuries of autocracy, dictatorship and enforced orthodoxy and unity',[73] Russian society embraced the ideas of individual autonomy as a progressive feature of best contemporary practice abroad. Notably, this adoption of party autonomy by legislators, judicial practitioners and scholars was accepted through the lens of local particular characteristics of Russian society, as I have explained in the previous section on cultural constraints on party autonomy.

iii. English Precedent

Currently, party autonomy to choose a forum and law is largely upheld by English courts. Judges give effect to the parties' agreement on a forum and 'leave it, more

[67] See, eg, F Feldbrugge, *Law in Medieval Russia* (Martinus Nijhoff Publishers, 2009). Also, O Vinnichenko, S Marochkin and S Racheva, 'Internal and External Law of Medieval Russia: A Look from the Current West' (2014) 2(3) *Russian Law Journal* 141, 143.

[68] D Legkiĭ, *Dmitry Vasil'evich Stasov: Sudebnaia Reforma 1864 g* (*Dmitry Stasov: Judicial Reform of 1864*) (Dmitry Bulanin, 2011) 37.

[69] D Maleshin, 'Vmesto Predisloviya: "Pradedy" i "Pravnuki" Sudebnoĭ Reformy 1864' ('In lieu of Introduction: "Great Grandfathers" and "Great Grandchildren" of the Judicial Reform 1864') in *Sudebnye Ustavy Rossiĭskoi Imperii 1984 goda* (*Judicial Codes of the Russian Empire 1864*) (Statut, 2014) 10.

[70] ibid.

[71] V Tomsinov, 'Russkiĭ Zakonoiskusnik Zakhar Anikeevich Goriushkin (1748–1821)' ('The Russian Jurist Zakhar Anikeevich Goriushkin (1748–1821)') (2009) 6 *Zakon* 287, 294.

[72] ibid 289.

[73] Feldbrugge (n 67) 259.

or less, at that'.[74] This recognition of the parties' right to agree on jurisdiction in the UK happened gradually, with a history of refusal to give force to the parties' choice by the courts. Courts used to view forum selection clauses as unwarranted ousting of the courts' jurisdiction and treated them with hostility.

Development of party autonomy to choose a forum in the traditional rules in England was founded on precedent rather than a theoretical framework. Principles developed on a case-by-case basis. Until the end of the Second World War, private international law case law mainly focused on the question of applicable law, not jurisdiction.[75]

At the same time, freedom of contract governed civil and commercial transactions in the nineteenth and the beginning of the twentieth century. Concurrently, conceptually, agreement on jurisdiction has always been viewed as a contractual term. As Briggs put it: 'courts analyse jurisdiction agreements as being contractual … it is almost as though no-one has ever suggested any other way of looking at things'.[76] Many scholars are still convinced that there exists no difference in principle between 'an agreement to sell' and 'an agreement to sue'.[77] With the development of the principle of autonomy in private law (contracts), and regarding forum selection clauses as a contract, gradually, forum selection clauses began to be recognised in case law.

Recognition of parties' power to derogate from English courts' jurisdiction first developed in regard to arbitration and then 'cross-fertilised' over to 'curial agreements'.[78] A milestone case recognising the power of the parties to derogate from a court's jurisdiction was *Scott v Avery*.[79] It was the first precedent that gave force to the parties' power to choose arbitration and oust state courts' jurisdiction. However, the provision was 'buttressed' by section 11 of the Common Law Procedure Act 1854 which gave courts discretion to stay an action where parties had an arbitration agreement.[80] The next important case was *Law v Garrett*.[81] In that case, three British subjects entered into an agreement, according to which all disputes were referred to the Saint Petersburg commercial court. The plaintiff brought proceedings in England, the defendants moved for a stay in proceedings. The court held that the parties' agreement to refer all disputes to the Saint Petersburg court was within section 11 of the Act 1954, thus upholding party autonomy to refer disputes to a foreign court/tribunal.

[74] A Briggs, *Agreements on Jurisdiction and Choice of Law* (Oxford University Press, 2008) viii.

[75] J O'Brien, *Conflict of Laws* (Cavendish Publishing Limited, 1999) 16.

[76] A Briggs, 'Which Law Governs Forum Selection Clauses' (Paper for ASIL Webinar 'The Nature of Natures of Agreement Relating to Jurisdiction to Governing Law', 2 March 2016) 4. Briggs' paper concerns England; however, the same can be inferred about all common law (Anglo-Saxon) systems.

[77] Briggs, Agreements on Jurisdiction and Choice of Law (n 74) 195.

[78] P Nygh, *Autonomy in International Contracts* (Oxford University Press 1999) 21.

[79] *Scott v Avery* (1856) V House of Lords Cases (Clark's) 811; 10 All ER 1121.

[80] Nygh (n 78) 19.

[81] *Law v Garrett* (1878) LR 8 Ch D 26.

In addition to justifying forum selection clauses based on party autonomy, other reasons included, for instance, the basic principle that a party should be held to his word, as established in *Mackender v Feldia*.[82] In that case, a diamond insurance policy was made in England and contained an exclusive choice-of-court and choice-of-law clause in favour of Belgian courts and Belgian law. Damage occurred in Italy. Plaintiffs came to an English court for leave to be granted to serve a writ outside the English jurisdiction. In view of comity between civilised nations, and the parties' express agreement to follow Belgian law, the English court gave force to the exclusive foreign jurisdiction clause.

In my next chapter, I elaborate that party autonomy to designate a court to decide private international disputes manifests itself through (i) jurisdiction agreements *ex ante* and (ii) submission to jurisdiction after the dispute has been lodged (*ex post*). Notably, in England, the rule recognising submission to jurisdiction has been long accepted. In *Boyle v Sacker*,[83] the defendant appeared by counsel, filed affidavits and argued the case on the merits. Subsequently, he decided to object to the order for service, as he was resident in Odessa (Russia at the time). The case rightfully established that where the defendant takes a chance of success by arguing the case on the merits, thus availing the opportunity to be heard, he cannot later object to jurisdiction. LJ Cotton explained that discharging a court order 'does not go on the ground that there has been an erroneous decision, but on the ground that the opposing party has not had an opportunity of being heard'.[84] Thus, accepting service of a writ (personally or through a solicitor) or defending a case on its merits (personally or by counsel) constitutes submission, and, therefore, non-objection to jurisdiction of the English courts. Thus, this principle has been recognised in English common law for over a century and represents one of the fundamental rules of jurisdiction. Notably, appearance merely to contest jurisdiction is not deemed as submission to jurisdiction.[85]

The decision of the UK to join the EU in 1973 prompted adoption and recognition of many legislative acts regulating allocation of jurisdiction. The Civil Jurisdiction and Judgments Act 1982 enacted the provisions of the Brussels Convention into national law.[86] The right of the parties to prorogue jurisdiction by agreement has been included in the British statutes. Thus, combined with the common law rules applicable outside the Brussels regime, autonomy of the parties in jurisdiction has been recognised and enforced in England. As mentioned above, this book relies on the English courts' interpretation of the pan-European rules of jurisdiction and does not account for complexities brought about by Brexit.

[82] *Mackender v Feldia AG* [1967] 2 QB 590, 604.
[83] *Boyle v Sacker* (1888) 39 Ch D 249 (CA).
[84] ibid 251.
[85] *Re Dulles Settlement (No 2)* [1951] Ch 842 (CA).
[86] Brussels Convention on Jurisdiction and the Enforcement of Judgments in Civil and Commercial Matters [1972] OJ L 299/32 (the Brussels Convention).

B. Growing Recognition of Parties' Choice of Law

To defend my claim that party autonomy represents an appropriate foundation for an ideal judicial system, I argue that its growing recognition in another area of private international law – applicable law in contract – can be used as evidence. In particular, the tendency of increased recognition of party autonomy in relation to applicable law in contract signals a liberalisation of court proceedings. This, in turn, supports the need to reconceptualise how we view the foundation of judicial jurisdiction.

Recognition of party autonomy regarding the choice of law has become one of the factors inherent in the late decades of the twentieth century. It is reflected in the main sources of law in Russia, recognised in English common law and American case law, the Rome I Regulation in Europe and other statutes worldwide. This exemplifies the tendency to recognise party autonomy as a 'bedrock' principle of the international law of contractual obligations.[87] A great summary of the new era inaugurating the end of parochial views in private international law[88] may be found in *Bremen v Zapata*.[89] In that case, German and American parties consented that their disputes should be resolved in an English forum. The court reasoned as follows:

> The expansion of American business and industry will hardly be encouraged if, notwithstanding solemn contracts, we insist on a parochial concept that all disputes must be resolved under our laws and in our courts … We cannot have trade and commerce in world markets and international waters exclusively on our terms, governed by our laws, and resolved in our courts.[90]

A similar rationale applies to any global businesses' decisions on governing law with respect to business transactions. This new era of recognition of private choice of law may be viewed as evidence of courts opening their minds to the possibility of private choice, with no detriment to state power or sovereignty. At the same time, it could mean recognition of soft power by economic players on the market. This tendency supports and, to a certain extent, accelerates the need for a similar shift of private power with respect to forum.

C. Promulgation of Party Autonomy and International Commerce

Enforcing the parties' choice of a dispute resolution forum facilitates better flow of international commerce. This argument is similar to Lehmann's justification

[87] J Basedow, *The Law of Open Societies: Private Ordering and Public Regulation of International Relations* (Recueil des cours 360, Martinus Nijhoff Publishers, 2013) 164.

[88] R Brand, 'Balancing Sovereignty and Party Autonomy in Private International Law' in J Erauw, V Tomljenovic and P Volken, *Liber Memorialis Petar Sarcevic: Universalism, Tradition and the Individual* (Sellier European Law Publishers, 2006) 43.

[89] *The Bremen v Zapata Off-Shore Co* 407 US 1 (1972).

[90] ibid 9.

of party autonomy in choice of law pursuant to which honouring freely negotiated choice-of-law clauses ensures the conditions necessary for the functioning of international commerce.[91]

This claim is especially effective in capitalist societies. Encouraging private transactions is inherent to a capitalist societal framework. In this context, liberal and capitalist values are symbiotic. Arguments supporting capitalist-driven trade and commerce also justify private parties' choice of forum. For instance, privatisation of national industries is justified because it encourages higher production rates, attracts innovation and overall leads to faster development of the industry. The presence of several private players on the market amplifies this effect, because now, competition drives them as well. In addition, deregulation by the state breathes fresh air into the industry, stimulating variable ways of succeeding and reaching new heights. Similarly, these arguments can be applied to the law of jurisdiction. Providing parties with the right to choose a forum as a founding principle in international transactions will liberalise and facilitate further development of international commerce. Private parties will be more eager to explore cross-border opportunities to raise their production/revenue/assets.

Moreover, party autonomy to choose a forum can be regarded as an aid for the global governance of international commercial activity. Private claims in national courts involving a foreign element – transnational litigation cases – can be conceived of as part of global transnational governance. Some conceptualise such litigation as part of a pluralist regime for the governance of transnational economic activity.[92] Many internationalists see the aim of such a system as the 'facilitation of international commerce and transactions'.[93] In light of this theory, the increased recognition of party autonomy to choose a forum will help strengthen the enforcement of cross-border contracts and transactions.

IV. Sovereignty: Not a Starting Point for the Law on Jurisdiction

In the jurisdictions that this book focuses on, state territoriality and sovereignty have been foundational for establishing jurisdiction. My contention is that this approach is wrong. In this section, I argue why sovereignty should not be the starting point for the law on jurisdiction. I draw evidence from the changes in international law and society, examine the inherent flaws for sovereignty to form the foundation in the first place, and conclude that the time has come to reconceptualise the hierarchy of values in the law on jurisdiction.

[91] Lehmann (n 19) 394.

[92] R Wai, 'Transnational Private litigation and Transnational Governance' in M Lederer and P Müller, *Criticizing Global Governance* (Palgrave Macmillan, 2005) 244.

[93] ibid.

A. End of Parochialism: Globalisation, Open Society, New World Order

I oppose parochialism and realism in international law. I argue that the significance of territoriality has faded away in the era of globalisation. A state no longer loses any significance or power when private parties choose a foreign court to handle their disputes. States should yield to the private interests, and if those private interests direct a dispute to a foreign forum, the courts should enforce it. There is no competition or rank in the power of states over foreign domiciliary parties. The primary consideration for the courts in civil cases should be the administration of justice in the name of the interests of the parties.

I urge scholars, lawmakers, policymakers and private actors to reconceptualise how we view jurisdiction and private international law in general. I see evidence of the decline in importance of territoriality and sovereignty in many global political and economic changes. For example, globalisation, development of an 'open society', and liberalisation of state judicial procedure support the idea of the supremacy of private interests over state interests in jurisdiction.

Globalisation is the phenomenon of technology advancement, international trade development, and social and cultural internationalisation in all spheres of life. Globalisation leads to opening of borders and the gradual erasing of the boundaries between everything domestic and foreign. Globalisation facilitates the development of a jurisdiction system catering for the choice and interests of private actors engaged in civil and commercial relations in the international arena. As Michaels and Jansen put it: '[p]erhaps the most important development of globalisation is the shift away from states altogether towards the private sphere'.[94]

One of the effects or a consequence of globalisation is the advent of the 'open society' – the 'absence of barriers to entry and exit'.[95] Technological innovation, trade, foreign direct investment, and the flow of migration result in far-reaching social, political and economic consequences. These factors act as a driving force of societal development from closed nation-states to an open society. In these conditions of increasing permeability of national frontiers, a new private ordering emerged. Among other areas, these effects extend to private international law. In relation to the law on jurisdiction, this phenomenon of open society results in an increased number of cross-border transactions, a more frequent presence of international elements in national judicial proceedings, delegation of some authority to resolve certain cases involving local domiciliaries to foreign courts, etc. In the end, it translates into opening the borders to international transactions and the dilution of a clear divide between states' jurisdiction.

[94] R Michaels and N Jansen, 'Private Law beyond the State? Europeanization, Globalization, Privatization' (2006) 54 *American Journal of Comparative Law* 843, 868.

[95] Basedow (n 87) 59. Basedow bases his understanding on the political philosophical concept of the open society by Bergson and Popper (H Bergson, *The Two Sources of Morality and Religion* (1932); and K Popper, *The Open Society and its Enemies*, 1st and 2nd vols (Routledge, 1945).

Schiff-Berman, who proposes a cosmopolitan pluralist conception of jurisdiction, advocates similar ideas.[96] Schiff-Berman discusses globalisation of jurisdiction in the global era associated with the internet. As a reform of conflict of laws in the United States, he proposes a combination of the Restatement (Third) of Foreign Relations Law and three major choice of law regimes (vested rights by Beale, governmental interests by Currie, and substantive law method by von Mehren). His approach focuses less on literal contacts with territorially based sovereign entities and more on the extent to which the various parties might be deemed to have affiliations with the possible communities.[97] Unlike Schiff Berman, I do not necessarily see globalisation of private international law matters as especially associated with the internet. The internet is just another effect of technological innovation, brought about by globalisation. It amplifies the effects of the readiness to cross borders, cover vast distances in seconds, etc. However, I agree with Schiff-Berman's detailed substantiation of globalisation changing the conceptions of private international law across the global community of states.

Another effect of globalisation is fragmentation of monolithic states. As captured by Slaughter,[98] traditionally, the global network of judges has been envisaged as a mechanism of interstate political relationships with judges with differing agendas. Instead, Slaughter argues, a new global legal system has emerged. The new messy system consists of horizontal and vertical networks of national and international judges. When making their decisions, these judges are not guided by their respect for international law or a desire to build a global system, but by 'a host of more prosaic concerns, such as judicial politics, the demands of a heavy caseload, and the new impact of international rules on national litigants'.[99] In addition, the global network of judges is complicated by influence from the lawmakers: legislators talk to judges and give them rules to apply.[100] Often, the lawmaker–judge dialogue takes place across national borders: English judges may follow the EU legislators' direction; American judges apply laws made by state and federal lawmakers, etc.

In this world-view of inter-judge, interinstitutional and inter-private-party relations across the globe, I argue that the role of states diminishes. It is relegated to facilitating enforcement of the interests and rights of private actors. This view resonates with the prediction by Scelle, the French solidarism advocate, who wrote about a world community, consisting of special or regional communities,

[96] P Schiff-Berman, 'Towards a Cosmopolitan Vision of Conflict of Laws: Redefining Governmental Interests in a Global Era' (2005) 153 *University of Pennsylvania Law Review* 1819.

[97] ibid 1822.

[98] A-M Slaughter, *A New World Order* (Princeton University Press, 2004) 67. Also, A Khrebtukova, 'A Call to Freedom: Towards a Philosophy of International Law in an Era of Fragmentation' (2008) 4 *Journal of International Law and International Relations* 51, 102.

[99] Slaughter, ibid 67–68.

[100] Briggs (n 74) 538–39.

integrated with each other through political elements.[101] The world is becoming a small community, where judges engage with the lawmakers and foreign judges on a more personal, rather than interstate level. Among other areas of law, this applies to private international law. Judges allocate, accept or decline jurisdiction in cross-border civil and commercial disputes having consideration for domestic and, on some levels, foreign rules of jurisdiction.

Some lawyers might argue that the world may be slowing down on the course of globalisation. It is evidenced with the election of anti-EU representatives in Europe,[102] Brexit, the Trump Administration's focus on American national interests, or the Ukrainian unrest and the Russian annexation of Crimea, when the states were once again reminded of the importance of their sovereignty. These events may indicate that nations are drawing back to their national identity, away from globalisation. However, the complexity of the political issues pertain to international interstate relations. This book focuses on private international relations. Although some effect of the anti-globalism sentiments may reflect on private international relations, only time will tell how the events will transpire in the end. There are always going to be some factors slowing down globalisation. But there is no scenario in which the world will revert to Bergson's 'closed society',[103] where every state will see no further than its self-preservation. Even if the rate of globalisation remains as it is now without any further development, my argument still stands.

In addition, the end of parochialism and liberalisation of judicial procedure can be evidenced by the growing openness of courts to apply foreign law in domestic proceedings. In particular, the late decades of the twentieth century witnessed a transformation of conflict of laws throughout Europe, including the UK, Russia and the United States in an unprecedented way. Courts began accepting foreign law in judicial proceedings.[104] This readiness of national courts to apply foreign law, with no detriment to state power or authority serves as evidence of the relaxation of

[101] A Loboda, 'Sovremennye Teorii Mezhdunarodnogo Chastnogo Prava v Svete Podhodov Traditsyĭ Kontinentalnogo i Obshego Prava' ('Contemporary Theories of Private International Law in Light of the Traditions of Continental and Common Law') (Lecture, Private International and Civil Law, MGIMO, referring to G Scelle, *Manuel de droit international public: Cours de droit international public* (*Casebook of Public International Law: The Course in Public International Law*), 3rd edn (Domat-Montchrestien, 1948).

[102] The 2014 EU elections showed that the pro-EU camp lost 50 seats from 2009. As reflected by Le Pen, a leader of the French far-right National Front: 'the people have spoken loud and clear … They no longer want to be led by those outside our borders, by EU commissioners and technocrats who are unelected. They want to be protected from globalisation and take back the reins of their destiny'. Mark John and Leila Abboud, 'Far-right National Front Stuns French Elite with EU "Earthquake"' *Reuters* (Paris, 25 May 2014), available at: www.reuters.com/article/2014/05/25/us-eu-election-france-idUSBREA4O0CP20140525.

[103] See Basedow (n 87) 59. *cf* K Waltz, *Theory of International Politics* (Waveland Press, 2010) arguing that international relations systems make states pursue moderate and reserved policies to maintain their security (defensive realism); and John Mearsheimer's offensive realism – blaming anarchic international relations systems for states' aggressive behaviour.

[104] Although some still argue that applying foreign law by a court is essentially making its own law with reference to the foreign legal norms; See, eg, H Maier and T McCoy, 'A Unifying Theory for Judicial Jurisdiction and Choice of Law' (1991) 39 *American Journal of Comparative Law* 249.

state control over judicial procedure overall. States started to accept the importance of comity, reciprocity and globalisation in civil and commercial proceedings. For example, Article 1191 of the Russian Civil Code of 2001[105] and Article 14 of the Code of *Arbitrazh* Procedure of 2002 clearly allow application of foreign substantive rules (*lex causae*) in Russian court trials. This signals of significant liberalisation of the Russian judicial system. It is consistent with the general tendency of letting go of the parochial view of 'only our law, only our courts'.[106]

B. Growing Role of Individual Actors in International Law

Another contemporary development illustrating the shift of power from the state to private parties is the growing role of individuals and corporations in international law. Individuals, international governmental organisations, and international non-governmental organisations are changing the landscape previously dominated by states.[107] The modern trend is that international law no longer deals only with interstate relationships, but also includes private actors.[108] Rosenblum demonstrates an evolving paradigm of state sovereignty being undermined, when large international firms (the so-called 'travelling corporations') undertake activity that competes not with other firms elsewhere, but with states.[109] An example of such a framework would be Apple competing with the state of South Korea and Samsung in the high-profile phone dispute that was heard in the US Supreme Court.[110]

In this new emerging international legal order, states are becoming an instrument to protect the interests (and human rights) of their citizens. States are accountable to individuals to help ensure that all persons have access to institutions that protect basic human rights.[111] In these conditions, jurisdiction is no longer a prerogative of states; it is 'at least to some extent a matter of individual right', an obligation owed by states to individuals.[112] Closely connected with this

[105] Grazhdanskiĭ Kodeks Rossiĭskoĭ Federatsii (Civil Code of the RF) (the Russian Civil Code) pt 3 (2001).

[106] Brand (n 88) 43, citing Chief Justice Burger in *Bremen v Zapata*, 9, encouraging a move away from such parochial views.

[107] C Harding, 'Statist Assumptions, Normative Individualism and New Forms of Personality: Evolving a Philosophy of International Law for the Twenty First Century' (2001) 1 *Non-State Actors and International Law* 107. Also, E Ip, 'Globalization and the Future of the Law of the Sovereign State' (2010) 8 *International Journal of Constitutional Law* 636, 642.

[108] Lehmann (n 19), referring to I Brownlie, *Principles of International Law*, 6th edn (Oxford University Press, 2003) 65; P-M Dupuy, *Droit International Public*, 2nd edn (Broché, 1993) 147–49; K Ipsen, *Völkerrecht*, 5th edn (CH Beck, 2004) 95–96; H Lauterpacht, *International Law and Human Rights* (Garland Publishing, 1973) 27–47; and to *Sosa v Alvarez-Machain* 542 US 692, 732, n 20 (2004).

[109] Rosenblum (n 24) 220.

[110] *USSC Samsung Electronics Co, Ltd, et al v Apple Inc No 15-777* (6 December 2016).

[111] More on the moral foundation for the international legal order can be found in A Buchanan, *Justice, Legitimacy and Self-Determination* (Oxford University Press, 2007) 4–5.

[112] A Mills, 'Rethinking Jurisdiction in International Law' (2014) 84 *British Yearbook of International Law* 187, 229. This echoes the ideas of 'normative individualism', the theory that the primary normative unit is the individual, not the state, encapsulated by Harding (n 107) and Fernando Tesón, 'The Kantian Theory of International Law' (1992) 92 *Columbia Law Review* 1, 53, 54.

reasoning is the principle that law is made for the benefit of people, and not the other way around.[113] The state, the law and the judicial system is there for people and companies. The whole apparatus of the justice system operates for the benefit of those who need to appeal to it.

Thus, power has shifted from the state to the individual players on the international arena. For private international law, I see it translating into the recognition and enforcement of parties' autonomy to choose jurisdiction and governing law. No longer should the rules be dictated based on the sovereign interests of states, but, rather, the rights and interests of individual actors in private international transactions should prevail. A jurisdictional system based on private – rather than state (sovereign) – interests is an ideal jurisdictional system.

C. Overall Tendency of Shift of Power to Private Parties

Several authoritative voices in international law support the idea of a shift of power from the state to private parties. Mills analyses and concludes the wide recognition of party autonomy as a 'unifying' principle of modern private international law.[114] Mills argues for the prevalence of party autonomy in the context of his proposal for a private international law conception, 'that is systemic, international, public and constitutional in nature'.[115] Basedow speaks of the power of individual interests transcending the concepts of state power in private law.[116] He contends that private relations constitute a private realm, thus, it should be up to private actors to decide the regulation of their relations. Schiff-Berman also argues that territorially-based conceptions of legal jurisdiction may no longer be adequate in an era when ideas of bounded nation-state communities operating within fixed territorial borders are under challenge.[117] Lehmann criticises the state-centred conflict of laws and private international law theory.[118] Watt summarises the shift from public to private power.[119] Brand also speaks of the reallocation of authority from the

[113] T Hartley, *International Commercial Litigation: Texts, Cases and Materials on Private International Law* (Cambridge University Press, 2009).

[114] See, generally, Mills, *Party Autonomy in Private International Law* (n 27) 2; A Mills, *The Confluence of Private and Public International Law: Justice, Pluralism and Subsidiarity in the International Constitutional Ordering of Private Law* (Cambridge University Press, 2009). Also Mills, 'Rethinking Jurisdiction in International Law' (n 112) 189.

[115] J Bomhoff, 'The Confluence of Private and Public International Law: Justice, Pluralism and Subsidiarity in the International Constitutional Ordering of Private Law by Alex Mills' (2011) 60 *International & Comparative Law Quarterly* 822.

[116] Basedow (n 87).

[117] P Schiff-Berman, 'The Globalization of Jurisdiction' (2002) 151 *University of Pennsylvania Law Review* 311.

[118] Lehmann (n 19).

[119] H Muir Watt, 'Private International Law Beyond the Schism' (2011) 2 *Transnational Legal Theory* 347, 392.

state to both non-state institutions and private parties in legislative jurisdiction.[120] He examines the history of sovereignty – first, as relationships within a state between a governor and the governed, and, later, as a concept used to describe relationships between nations. He demonstrates how during the latter half of the twentieth century, multilateral organisations and private parties have gained an increased role in choosing a forum for the resolution of their disputes.[121]

All these arguments support my argument for the prevalence of party autonomy in jurisdiction. Now, the question remains: how exactly should this shift to private power be reflected in the rules on jurisdiction?

[120] Brand (n 88) 37.
[121] ibid 40.

4

Autonomy in the Law on Jurisdiction: Harmony and Controversy

I. Linking Theory to Practice

The main argument of this book is that party autonomy should be placed at the foundation of an ideal jurisdiction regime. In this chapter, I analyse the existing rules on jurisdiction agreements pursuant to EU and Russian law. Throughout my analysis, I delineate how existing jurisdiction rules can be improved to better reflect the will of the parties. I point out the inconsistencies (if any) between the existing rules and my normative view.

Both systems recognise and enforce party autonomy in jurisdiction. However, my first criticism is regarding where these regimes place party autonomy. Both see it as an exception to the general rule of suing at the location of the defendant. My main idea is diametrically opposite. Rather than the current predisposition, party autonomy should be given the role of an all-encompassing main rule, with all other rules representing exceptions to it.

In practice, the will of private parties designating a forum is not enforced as an abstract concept. It takes the form of a valid jurisdiction agreement in accordance with the applicable law. The minimum criteria of validity of jurisdiction agreements should include the unequivocal consent of the parties and written (or equivalent) form. First, where included in a contract, a jurisdiction clause should be treated as an agreement severable and not dependent on the validity of the main contract. Secondly, a jurisdiction agreement can take a written or equivalent-to-written form. In addition, courts should enforce jurisdiction agreements in favour of foreign courts. Against these criteria, I test the existing jurisdictional regimes in the EU and Russia to see whether they correspond with my view.

I further discuss complications that may arise in cross-border contractual disputes, where no clear choice of forum is present. I outline the effect of the parties' choice of law on the court's discretion to retain jurisdiction. In addition, I delineate the correlation between the *lis pendens* rule – jurisdiction of the court that first seized jurisdiction – and party autonomy. I recognise that a better view is to prioritise a forum chosen by the parties over the forum that first seized the dispute (as is now reflected in the Brussels I Recast).[1] Finally, I discuss the scenarios of concurrent choices of arbitration and litigation. To find a proper forum, I propose to use the parties' intent and circumstances of the case as guidance.

Finally, in the last section in this chapter, I discuss the rule of voluntary submission. I stress the importance of the rule, representing another part of party autonomy. I define the circumstances when the rule should trigger a court's jurisdiction. I address situations where a party refuses to accept service, fails to appear, and later must fight the enforcement of a default judgment against it. I conclude by summarising my findings for chapters three and four.

II. Party Autonomy *ex ante*

A. Validity and Effectiveness of Jurisdiction Agreements in the EU and Russia

Both the EU and Russia recognise the importance of the autonomy of private parties to designate a forum to settle their disputes. They both explicitly grant prorogation of other jurisdiction rules by the parties' agreement in favour of a competent court. Prorogation of jurisdiction is usually contrasted with derogation of jurisdiction – excluding court(s) which otherwise has(-ve) jurisdiction pursuant to general (territorial) jurisdiction rules. Arguably, an international jurisdiction agreement has prorogation and derogation effects at the same time.[2] Indeed, an exclusive choice-of-court agreement simultaneously confers jurisdiction of a chosen court (prorogation effect) and ousts jurisdiction of otherwise competent courts (derogation effect). A non-exclusive choice-of-court agreement, however, is intended to have prorogation but not derogation effects. Both the EU and Russian legislatures allow prorogation of jurisdiction by agreement, which – in cases of exclusive choice-of-court agreements – means also recognition of the derogation of jurisdiction.

In the EU, by virtue of Article 25 of the Brussels I Recast, except in consumer contracts, if parties have agreed that a court or the courts of a Member State are to have jurisdiction to settle any disputes which have arisen or which may arise in connection with a particular legal relationship, the court(s) shall have jurisdiction. For instance, when parties delegate exclusive jurisdiction to English courts, other Member State courts shall give effect to the agreement by the parties. Likewise, when parties agree that another Member State court should handle their disputes,

[1] Regulation (EU) 1215/2012 of 12 December 2012 on Jurisdiction and the Recognition and Enforcement of Judgments in Civil and Commercial Matters (Recast) [2012] OJ L351/1 (the Brussels I Recast).

[2] U Magnus and P Mankowski (eds), *European Commentaries on Private International Law: Brussels I Regulation*, 2nd edn (Sellier European Law Publishers, 2012) 455.

and then an action is filed with an English court, the English court must stay its proceedings. Jurisdiction agreements supersede the domicile principle (suing at the location of the defendant) but can be overridden by the rules of exclusive jurisdiction.[3] Furthermore, parties may later agree on a different choice of jurisdiction. This latter agreement shall prevail, and the court before which a defendant enters an appearance shall have the jurisdiction.[4] This voluntary submission to a court supersedes the jurisdiction agreements, 'provided [the submission] amounts to a consensual variation of the contract'.[5] Notably, simply by making observations in relation to a proposed claim, a defendant thereby does not enter an appearance in that claim.[6] Therefore, later agreement or submission to jurisdiction overrides an earlier jurisdiction agreement (more details about the rules of submission are in the next section of this chapter).

The revision of the Brussels I Regulation,[7] which resulted in the adoption of the Brussels I Recast in 2012, enhanced the effectiveness of jurisdiction agreements. In particular, jurisdiction agreements were given priority over the *lis pendens rule*.[8] In addition, the Brussels I Regulation used to require at least one party to be domiciled in a Member State for the provision to apply. The Brussels I Recast no longer requires that. It expanded the application of this principle to non-EU domiciled parties. Now, where the non-EU domiciled parties choose a court or courts of the EU Member State in a prorogation of a jurisdiction agreement, it shall be enforced as well. Thus, a step forward was made in an attempt to harmonise the application of the rule beyond EU domiciliaries. These amendments manifested a positive change by increasing legal certainty when determining jurisdiction in the EU.

Similarly, Russian law allows parties to agree on jurisdiction of a court or courts in domestic and international civil and commercial dealings,[9] provided the chosen court(s) has (have) competence over the subject matter of the dispute, and the rules of exclusive (mandatory) jurisdiction are not violated. A choice-of-court agreement signed at the outset of commercial relationships is not a fixed commitment. It is possible to transfer a case in Russia to another court after lodging a claim in a first court, if both parties agree and provide evidence that the majority of evidence is located in the territory within the competence of another court.

[3] Brussels I Recast art 25(4).

[4] Brussels I Recast art 26.

[5] A Briggs and P Rees (eds), *Civil Jurisdiction and Judgments*, 5th edn (Proforma, 2009) 165, para 2.110, referring to Case 150/80 *Elefanten Schuh GmbH v Jacqmain* [1981] ECR 1671 (*Elefanten Schuh*).

[6] *Emerson Electric Co and others v Morgan Crucible Company Plc and others* [2008] CAT 8, para 43.

[7] Regulation (EC) 44/2001 of 22 December 2000 on Jurisdiction and the Recognition and Enforcement of Judgments in Civil and Commercial Matters [2001] OJ L 12/1 (the Brussels I Regulation).

[8] Now, Art 29 (the *lis pendens rule*) of the Brussels I Recast is subject to Art 25 (jurisdiction agreements).

[9] Grazhdanskiĭ Protsessual'nyĭ Kodeks Rossiĭskoĭ Federatsii (Code of Civil Procedure of the RF) of 14 November 2002 no 138-ФЗ (Russia) (the CCP) arts 32 and 404; Arbitrazhno-Protsessual'nyĭ Kodeks Rossiĭskoĭ Federatsii (Code of *Arbitrazh* (Commercial) Procedure of the RF) of 24 July 2002 no 95-ФЗ (Russia) (the CAP) arts 37 and 249.

The right of Russian parties to choose a forum has long applied in domestic economic relationships. However, in cases with foreign parties, the lack of statutory rules before the adoption of the Code on *Arbitrazh* Procedure 2002 led to divergence of opinions on whether the Russian law enabled parties to sign jurisdiction agreements.[10] Although the Code on *Arbitrazh* Procedure 1995 (in force at the time) contained a major improvement by widening the scope of competence of *arbitrazh* courts to consider disputes with participation of foreign parties, it did not contain a clause giving effect to international jurisdiction agreements. In particular, it was arguable whether parties could oust the case from the otherwise proper jurisdiction of the courts of one country and submit it for resolution by the courts of a foreign country.[11] In practice, however, the *arbitrazh* courts in Russia often dealt with claims involving foreign entities and had to establish their jurisdiction based on jurisdiction agreements. In most cases, the courts applied the 'national regime' towards foreign entities, treating cross-border suits the same as domestic.[12]

Since the adoption of the Code of *Arbitrazh* Procedure 2002, the right of parties to choose a forum has explicitly extended to foreign parties. Now, in transactions with a foreign element, a Russian *arbitrazh* court shall have jurisdiction if agreed by the parties, as long as it does not violate the exclusive jurisdiction of a foreign court established by foreign national law or an international treaty. In addition, a Russian *arbitrazh* court shall have jurisdiction in cases prescribed by international treaties when parties from foreign states sign a prorogation jurisdiction agreement in favour of the Russian court.[13]

Globally, choice-of-court agreements are recognised by the states-signatories to the Hague Convention on Choice of Court Agreements.[14] The Hague Convention provides uniform rules on international jurisdiction agreements, and the recognition and enforcement of judgments given in such cases. It was ratified by Mexico, signed and ratified by the EU,[15] Singapore, Montenegro, ratified by the UK, Denmark, and signed by the United States, the People's Republic of China, and Ukraine. The ratification by the EU in 2015 triggered the Convention's entry into force. The effect of this is tremendous – the scope of application of the

[10] O Vorobieva, *Private International Law in Russia* (Kluwer Law International BV, 2012) 169.

[11] ibid.

[12] V Yarkov (ed), *Arbitrazhnyĭ Protsess: Uchebnik* (*Arbitrazh Procedure: Textbook*), 4th edn (Infotropic Media, 2010).

[13] Postanovlenie Plenuma Verkhovnogo Arbitrazhnogo Suda RF ot 11 iiunia 1999 g no 8 o Deĭstvii Mezhdunarodnyh Dogovorov RF Primenitelno k Voprosam Arbitrazhnogo Protsessa (Resolution of the Plenum of the Supreme Arbitrazh Court of the RF of 11 June 1999 no 8 on the Application of International Treaties of the RF Connected with *Arbitrazh* Procedural Issues) art 7, referring to the 1992 Kiev Treaty and the 1993 Minsk Treaty.

[14] Hague Convention on Choice of Court Agreements of 30 June 2005.

[15] Council Decision 2009/397/EC of 26 February 2009 on the signing on behalf of the European Community of the Convention on Choice of Court Agreements [2009] OJ L133/1; Council Decision of 4 December 2014 on the approval, on behalf of the European Union, of the Hague Convention of 30 June 2005 on Choice of Court Agreements [2014] OJ L353/5–8.

Convention is international. It will apply to disputes involving parties from the EU Member States, Mexico, Singapore and Montenegro. Other countries considering ratification of the Convention include Argentina, Australia, Canada, Costa Rica, New Zealand, Russia,[16] Turkey and the United States.[17] Thus, the effectiveness and enforceability of jurisdiction agreements on the global scale should largely improve in the near future.

i. Severability

The minimum criteria that should determine the validity of choice-of-court agreements – severability, written (or equivalent) form, and unequivocal consent of the parties – represent the elements of validity of choice-of-court agreements as reflected in academic scholarship. For instance, Beaumont and Yüksel accentuate the formal and substantive validity of jurisdiction agreements;[18] Ratković and Zgrabljićrotar consider validity as a three-part test: formal validity, formal consent and substantive validity;[19] Tang mentions formal and substantive validity,[20] Camilleri also emphasises formal and material validity,[21] etc.

The severability requirement is harmonious with my approach to jurisdiction. Both in EU and Russia, jurisdiction agreements are treated as separate agreements and do not depend on the validity of the main contracts. The validity of a choice-of-court agreement cannot be contested solely on the ground that the contract is void. In EU, this rule was reaffirmed in *Francesco Benincasa v Dentalkit*[22] and reflected in the new text of the Brussels I Recast.[23] On the national level European jurisdictions also recognise the doctrine of severability. For instance, as a matter of English law, Longmore LJ in *Deutsche Bank v Asia Pacific Broadband Wireless* established that: 'a jurisdiction clause, like an arbitration clause, is a separate agreement from the agreement as a whole. This is uncontroversial both as a matter of domestic law and as a matter of European law'.[24]

[16] Russian officials confirmed their interest regarding the Convention during The Hague Conference Council meeting in 2012, Email from Marta Pertegás to author (11 March 2014).

[17] M Pertegás and M Dogauchi, 'Introducing the 2005 Hague Convention on Choice of Court Agreements' (Conference on International Litigation in the Asia Pacific Region, Wuhan, People's Republic of China, 23 September 2013).

[18] P Beaumont and B Yüksel, 'The Validity of Choice of Court Agreements under the Brussels I Regulation and the Hague Choice of Court Agreements Convention' in K Boele-Woelki, T Einhorn, D Girsberger and S Symeonides (eds), *Convergence and Divergence in Private International Law: Liber Amicorum Kurt Siehr* (Eleven International Publishing, 2010).

[19] T Ratković and D Zgrabljić Rotar, 'Choice-of-Court Agreements under the Brussels I Regulation (Recast)' (2013) 9 *Journal of Private International Law* 245, 260.

[20] ZS Tang, 'Exclusive Choice of Forum Clauses and Consumer Contracts in E-Commerce' (2005) 1 *Journal of Private International Law* 237.

[21] SP Camilleri, 'Article 23: Formal Validity, Material Validity or Both?' (2011) 7 *Journal of Private International Law* 297.

[22] Case C-269/95 *Francesco Benincasa v Dentalkit* Srl [1997] ETMR 447.

[23] Brussels I Recast art 25(5).

[24] *Deutsche Bank v Asia Pacific Broadband Wireless* [2008] EWCA 1091 [24] (Longmore LJ).

Likewise, Russian scholarship distinguishes jurisdiction agreements as severable from the main contract. Invalidity of the main contract does not cancel out the jurisdiction clause contained therein.[25] The choice-of-court clause remains valid regardless of termination or expiration of the main contract, if the dispute in question concerns relationships of the parties arising out of the contract during the time of its operation. Such a position, for instance, was taken by the court in a dispute over the validity of a jurisdiction agreement in Chelyabinsk city.[26] A hire company and an individual entrepreneur had a leasing contract with a choice-of-court clause in favour of the *arbitrazh* court of the Republic of Bashkortostan, one of the autonomous units of the Russian Federation. Later, the plaintiff tried to recover a debt in the *arbitrazh* court of Chelyabinsk *oblast* (region). The court transferred the case to the court chosen by the parties pursuant to the jurisdiction agreement. The plaintiff asked to annul the court order, arguing that termination of the leasing contract a year before invalidated the choice-of-court clause. On appeal, the original order of the first *arbitrazh* court to transfer the case was affirmed. The unilateral termination of the leasing contracts by the plaintiff did not terminate the jurisdiction clause, because the disputed relationship arose during the period of the contracts' validity. This example is not necessarily an authority or a precedent when it comes to enforcing jurisdiction agreements in Russia. However, it demonstrates that Russian law has the same view of severability of a forum selection clause as the EU.

ii. Form

With respect to the requirements to the form of jurisdiction agreements, the EU approach is more accurately aligned with the view of jurisdiction I advocate than the Russian. In the EU, an agreement conferring jurisdiction is required to be made in writing or evidenced in writing, or in a form set by practices between the parties or customary trade observed by the parties.[27] Electronic communications are equated to 'writing',[28] prompted by the tendency at the time to recognise the validity of e-contracts and the clauses and terms contained therein.[29] Thus, jurisdiction agreements are acceptable in a variety of forms.

[25] eg, R Khodykin, 'Prorogatsionnye Usloviia Vneshneekonomicheskikh Sdelok' ('Prorogation Conditions of Foreign Economic Transactions') (2002) 6 *Vestnik Vysshego Arbitrazhnogo Suda RF* 133, 137, referring to A Minakov, *Arbitrazhnye Soglasheniia i Praktika Rassmotreniia Vneshneekonomicheskikh Sporov* (*Jurisdiction Agreements and Practice on Considering Foreign Economic Disputes*) (Iurid Lit, 1985) 68–74; G Dmitrieva, *Mezhdunarodnoe Chastnoe Pravo* (*Private International Law*) (Prospekt, 2001) 609–10; V Zvekov, *Mezhdunarodnoe Chastnoe Pravo* (*Private International Law*) (NORMA, 2000); L Lunts and N Marysheva, *Kurs Mezhdunarodnogo Chastnogo Prava* (*Course on Private International Law*) (Iurid Lit, 1976) and others.

[26] Postanovlenie Vosemnadtsatogo Arbitrazhnogo Apellliatsionnogo Suda ot 8 iiulia 2011 g no 18АП-6934/2011, delo no A76-7966/2011 (Decision of the Eighteenth *Arbitrazh* Court of Appeal of Chelyabinsk) of 8 July 2011 no 18АП-6934/2011 case no A76-7966/2011.

[27] Brussels I Recast art 25.

[28] ibid.

[29] Tang (n 20).

In Russia, an international jurisdiction agreement must be made in writing.[30] There is no differentiation between 'made in writing' and 'evidenced in writing'. On the other hand, a few changes in the Russian legislation give hope for liberalisation of the strict written requirement. Recent changes to the Russian Civil Code eliminated the prerequisite that any international trade transaction must be completed in written form (since September 2013).[31] Moreover, changes introduced to Russian civil legislation in November 2013 deleted the requirement to carry out any cross-border transaction, at least one party to which is a Russian legal entity or a Russian individual entrepreneur, in a form consistent with Russian law.[32] Some practitioners interpret this as liberalisation of Russian civil law.[33] Although the 'written' requirement in relation to jurisdiction agreements still remains, these changes indicate the intent of the Russian legislators to embrace certain changes associated with the increasing number of cross-border transactions.

Some scholars consider it a problem that formal requirements for jurisdiction agreements are absent from Russian legislation. As Rozhkova puts it: 'the main problem of legal regulation of jurisdiction agreements [in Russia] is that in essence such agreements are not regulated by the legislation at all' in contrast with vast regulation of arbitration agreements.[34] She explains this by the lack of interest by Russian jurists regarding this topic.

If seeking formal validity requirements for jurisdiction agreements in Russian law, I contend that the requirements for validity of a civil transaction may apply to the jurisdiction clauses. These overall requirements of formal validity of transactions (including those with a foreign element) are reflected in Articles 160 and 162 of the Russian Civil Code. Article 160 stipulates that a written transaction shall be done by making a document expressing its content and it being signed by a party or parties carrying out the transaction (or their duly authorised representatives). Use of facsimile reproduction of the signature, made with the assistance of the means of mechanical or other kinds of copying, of the electronic signature or of another analogue shall be admitted in the cases and in the order, stipulated by the law and by the other legal acts, or by the agreement of the parties. Article 162 states that non-observance of the simple written form of a transaction shall, in case of a dispute, deprive the parties of the right to refer to the testimony for the confirmation of the deal and of its terms, while not depriving them of the right

[30] CAP art 249(2).

[31] Russian Civil Code art 162.3 (no longer in force) 'Failure to observe written form of a foreign trade agreement shall result in invalidity of the agreement'.

[32] Russian Civil Code art 1209.

[33] A Kucher, A Yadykin and A Asoskov, 'Entry into Law of Bundle of Amendments to Russian Civil Code – Section on Private International Law' (Debevoise & Plimpton Client Update, 18 October 2013).

[34] M Rozhkova et al, *Dogovornoe Pravo Soglasheniya o Podsudnosti, Mezhdunarodnoĭ Podsudnosti, Primiritel'noĭ Protsedure, Arbitrazhnoe (Treteĭskoe) i Mirovie Soglasheniia* (*Contract Law: Agreements on Jurisdiction, International Jurisdiction Agreements, Conciliation Agreements, Arbitration Agreements, Settlement Agreements*) (Statut, 2008) 10.

to cite the written and the other kinds of proof. In practice, the non-observance of the simple written form of the deal shall entail its invalidity. Russia accepts the notion that a jurisdiction agreement is a civil transaction. Then, these requirements can apply to jurisdiction agreements. A similar view has been expressed by Professor Yarkov.[35] However, this view does not prevail in Russian scholarship. Many scholars understand the jurisdiction agreement as procedural in nature, and thus the requirements of substantive civil agreements not applying to jurisdiction agreements.[36]

On the other hand, it may be argued that the absence of special validity criteria for jurisdiction agreements simplifies the matter. For instance, the English Civil Jurisdiction and Judgments Act 1982 incorporates the provisions of the Brussels I Regulation into domestic law and omits the requirement of a jurisdiction agreement to be in writing. It simply states that, 'if the parties have agreed that a court or the courts of a part of the UK are to have jurisdiction to settle any disputes', then certain jurisdiction rules apply. No requirement of writing features there. Such an approach seems more flexible, which, arguably, may be 'the source of the problem with it', according to Briggs.[37] For an English court to retain jurisdiction over a dispute as specified by a jurisdiction agreement, all the court needs is demonstration that the existence of the agreement satisfies the standard of a 'good arguable case'. There are no formal guidelines, and the burden of proof rests with the interested party to show the validity of the agreement.

Is the similar approach, with no explicit requirements to the form of jurisdiction agreements in Russia preferable? Perhaps, the absence of direct regulation of the form of jurisdiction agreements has certain benefits. However, in light of the formalism of Russian legal culture, I would recommend a detailed regulation rather than the absence of such. Judges pay special attention to every little formal detail of legal documents. Absence of exact guidance regarding the form of international jurisdiction agreements may lead to unequal treatment and divergent interpretation of different jurisdiction agreements. To see how formalistic Russian judges can be, one can refer to a series of adoption cases rejected by the Russian courts.[38] Notwithstanding the Hague Apostille Convention specifically stating that the Apostille certificate shall be in a shape of a square with sides at least (and not necessarily) nine centimetres long,[39] and the Hague Conference actively promoting the view that variations in the form and size of Apostilles among Competent Authorities should not be a basis for rejection, as long as the Apostilles are clearly

[35] Yarkov (n 12).

[36] S Dergachev, 'Dogovornaia Podsudnost' v Grazhdanskom i Arbitrazhnom Processe Rossii' ('Jurisdiction by Agreement in Civil and Commercial Procedure in Russia') (PhD Book, Russian Academy of Justice affiliated with the Supreme Court of the Russian Federation, 2011) (on file with author).

[37] Briggs and Rees (n 5) 167, fn 1.

[38] Hague Conference on Private International Law, 'Letter to Mr Lobach, Deputy Director, Ministry of Foreign Affairs' (The Hague, 7 July 2011, on file with author).

[39] The Hague Convention Abolishing the Requirements of Legalisation for Foreign Public Documents of 5 October 1961 art 4 and annex.

identifiable as Apostilles issued under the Convention,[40] Russian judges still treated the Apostilles sceptically. Just because the shape of the Apostille on foreign documents was not exactly a square with sides nine centimetres long, the apostilled documents were repeatedly rejected by various courts.

This type of behaviour is intrinsic to Russian legal culture. Judges are formalistic in relation to all official documents presented in court. This implies a similar pedantic attention to the form of choice-of-forum clauses. To ensure uniform enforcement of valid jurisdiction agreements across the country, better validity criteria need to be set out in law. A simple legislative change explicitly establishing the requirements for the form of jurisdiction agreements would prevent the problem of divergent readings. It would enhance the effectiveness of jurisdiction agreements.

Therefore, EU jurisdiction rules already foresee adequate requirements for the form of jurisdiction agreements. To bring the Russian rules into harmony with my world-view on formal requirements for jurisdiction agreements, the Russian legislators should relax the strict formal requirement of the 'written form'. They might add a qualifier of 'equal to writing' or apply the internal civil code provisions (Articles 160 and 162 of the Civil Code) to the jurisdiction clauses.

iii. Substantive Validity

One of the most important elements of the validity of jurisdiction agreements is consent. Consent can be generally defined as the voluntary undertaking of an obligation in exchange for something in return. In jurisdiction agreements, the will of the parties manifests itself through consent – a meeting of minds regarding the place to resolve potential (or actual) disputes. Without this mutual agreement, the choice-of-court clause shall be invalid. To be capable of expressing mutual consent in jurisdiction, parties must have legal capacity to enter into a jurisdiction agreement. Further material validity requirements include, similar to contract law in general, the absence of fraud, mistake, misinterpretation, duress, grossly inadequate consideration, etc.

In the EU, the Brussels I Recast requires that parties 'agree' on a court(s) to settle their disputes. Therefore, it reflects the basic consent requirement.

Furthermore, following the revision of the Brussels I Regulation, a harmonised conflict of law rule on the substantive validity of choice-of-court agreements has been added to the provision on jurisdiction agreements. In particular, if the parties have agreed that a Member State court(s) shall have jurisdiction, such court(s) shall have jurisdiction 'unless the agreement is null and void as to its substantive

[40] Hague Conference on Private International Law, 'Conclusions and Recommendations of the Special Commission on the Practical Operation of the Hague Apostille, Service, Taking the Evidence and Access to Justice Conventions' (Permanent Bureau, 2–9 February 2009) para 92, available at: www.hcch.net/upload/wop/jac_concl_e.pdf.

validity under the law of that Member State'.[41] This qualification provides a unified conflict of law rule on the validity of choice-of-court agreements. It ensures a similar outcome on the matter of substantive validity 'whatever the court seized' and reflects 'the solutions established in the 2005 Hague Convention on the Choice of Court Agreements'.[42]

Thus, the elements of material validity (capacity, fraud, mistake, etc) are regulated by the applicable national law of the Member State where the chosen court is located. In my normative view on jurisdiction, the fact that the elements of material validity are subject to the domestic law of different jurisdictions does not create a major problem. It is true that it may lead to divergent criteria applicable to jurisdiction agreements throughout the EU. However, European national regimes apply divergent rules in many other areas of law (eg, family law), and it does not ruin the overall integrity of the EU legal regime. As long as they correspond to the minimum widely accepted requirements (such as legal capacity of the parties, absence of fraud or mistake), diverging regulation of the exact material validity of jurisdiction agreements is consonant with my world-view; but harmonisation of its understanding will help enhance the EU regime.

For instance, the common law approach towards formal essential and material validity of jurisdiction agreements leads to the application of norms from one or two different bodies of law.[43] First, validity of a contract containing the jurisdiction clause will be determined under the Rome I Regulation. If the entire contract is void, the jurisdiction clause stands as if the contract was voidable. Validity of the jurisdiction clause is then determined under common law, which stipulates that the governing law shall determine it.[44] The proper law of the contract would be the one chosen by the parties or the legal system with which the contract had the closest and most real connection.[45] If English law applies, validity of jurisdiction agreements may be separated into four categories: enforceability issues (consideration,[46] misrepresentation, duress, etc); construction (interpretation of the scope of the jurisdiction agreement); formality (notice, language, etc); and procedure (standard of proof required). Enforceability issues are governed by the governing law of the contract. Issues of construction are also decided in accordance with the governing law. Matters of formality shall be decided as governed by the law of the country where the agreement was entered into. Finally, questions of procedure are decided according to law of the court. Therefore, the answer to

[41] Brussels I Recast art 25.

[42] Proposal for a Regulation of the European Parliament and the Council on Jurisdiction and the Recognition of Judgments in Civil and Commercial Matters (Recast), 30 January 2014, Brussels, COM (2010) 748 Final, 2010/0383 (COD), art 23(1); Explanatory Memorandum, 9.

[43] L Merrett, 'Article 23 of the Brussels I Regulation: A Comprehensive Code for Jurisdiction Agreements?' (2009) 58 *International & Comparative Law Quarterly* 545, 547.

[44] *Dubai Electricity Co v Islamic Republic of Iran Shipping Lines (The Iran Vodjan)* [1984] 2 Lloyd's Rep 380.

[45] J O'Brien, *Conflict of Laws* (Cavendish Publishing Limited, 1999) 308.

[46] *Dunlop v Selfridge* [1915] AC 847. Also, eg, PS Atiyah, 'Consideration: A Restatement' in PS Atiyah, *Essays on Contract* (Clarendon Press, 1990).

the question of which law determines the validity of a jurisdiction agreement is not straightforward. English law approaches the issues of material and substantive validity of contracts through examining several doctrines.

Notably, under English common law, a foreign jurisdiction clause will be found invalid if it violates an English statutory law, as happened in *The Hollandia*.[47] There, the bill of lading specified that all disputes should be brought in Holland, and the law of the Netherlands applied. Under the Netherlands law, the Hague–Visby Rules were incorporated. According to these Rules, they could not be contracted out, otherwise, it would make any agreement relieving the carrier of liability in case of shipwreck invalid. The Rules were also enacted in England by the Carriage of Goods by Sea Act 1971. The Netherlands law limited liability of the carrier to (what equalled) £250. In an admiralty action in England, the shippers claimed £22,000, after the ship was arrested in an English port. The English court rendered the exclusive jurisdiction clause and the choice of law provision invalid as they violated the Hague–Visby Rules.

Therefore, the rule on jurisdiction agreements in the Brussels I Recast requires the consent of the parties, a certain form of the agreement, and refers to national applicable law to determine material validity requirements.

The question of the validity of jurisdiction agreements in Russian scholarship and case law can be compared with the English common law approach. Issues of material validity are determined in accordance with the proper law of the contract, and the issues of its procedural validity are decided according to the court's law. Conditions of material validity are reflected in the Russian Civil Code. They are met when there is general consent between parties,[48] and the three main conditions are satisfied: (i) the content (*soderzhanie*) and legal effect (*pravovoĭ rezultat*) does not contradict the law; (ii) the parties possess the capacity to make the transaction;[49] and (iii) the parties' intention (*volia*) coincides with their declaration of intent (*voleiz'iavlenie*).[50] Agreements do not meet the material validity requirements when one of these elements fails. Given the fact that Russian civil law drew some of its origin from French legal doctrine, it is easy to see the compatibility of these material requirements with Article 1108 of the French Civil Code encompassing the questions of fraud, duress, mistake and frustration relating to concluding a jurisdiction agreement with a 'general requirement of good faith'.[51]

In practice, the question of determining the procedural validity of a jurisdiction agreement may appear at the stage of recognition and enforcement of a

[47] *Owners of Cargo on Board the Morviken v Owners of the Hollandia (The Hollandia)* [1983] 1 AC 565.

[48] Russian Civil Code art 154(3).

[49] Further information on 'legal capacity' of natural and legal persons can be found in Vorobieva (n 10) 77, 96.

[50] E Vershinina and I Stakheeva, 'Usloviia Deĭstvitelnosti Sdelki v Rossii i Frantsii: Sravnitelno-Pravovoi Analiz' ('Conditions for Validity of Transaction in Russia and France: Comparative Analysis') (2013) 32(5) *Vestnik* 197, 198.

[51] Merrett (n 43) 559, referring to § 242 of the BGB and R Zimmerman and S Whittaker, *Good Faith in European Contract Law* (Cambridge University Press, 2000) 557.

foreign court decision that heard the case based on a foreign jurisdiction agreement.[52] For instance, in a private dispute between companies Uzulgurzhisavdo (Uzbekistan) and El-Delta (Russia),[53] a delivery agreement contained a jurisdiction clause in favour of Uzbekistan state courts. The plaintiff brought a claim in an Uzbekistan court and won the case. He later applied to the Moscow *arbitrazh* court to enforce the decision, since the defendant's assets were in Moscow. The Moscow court had to consider the validity of the jurisdiction clause and whether the competence of the Uzbekistani commercial court was appropriate in accordance with the procedural law of Uzbekistan. After several appeals, the decision was finally enforced in Russia. This case demonstrated that sometimes the question of the procedural validity of a jurisdiction agreement has to involve foreign procedural law. Some view it as improper, because Russian courts end up acting as a supervisory authority over foreign courts' proceedings. Nevertheless, such examination of validity of jurisdiction agreements is necessary in order to avoid situations where parties resolve a dispute in a foreign court in violation of a jurisdiction agreement in favour of a Russian court, and then try to enforce such a decision in Russia. Such a scenario occurred in a case where BTA Bank obtained a decision in Kazakhstan's Almaty commercial court against several defendants based on an assignment agreement. The agreement contained a jurisdiction clause in favour of a Russian court. The court in Kazakhstan found the jurisdiction agreement invalid, considered the case on its merits and produced a decision.[54] Later, when the Bank applied for recognition and enforcement of the decision in Russia, the Russian courts rightfully refused such enforcement[55] because 'invalidity of … a jurisdiction agreement was established by a foreign court which was not competent to consider such invalidity, and recognition and enforcement of such judgment could not be done'.

In addition, the validity of jurisdiction agreements in Russia will also depend on specifying the right type of court (by subject matter) in the agreement. Since commercial and civil disputes are considered by different courts in Russia, when designating a court to handle commercial disputes in Russia, parties should make sure they refer to a proper court that has the authority to hear commercial cases. Jurisdiction agreements will be invalid if they choose courts of general jurisdiction to hear commercial disputes. The claim will be automatically rejected by the

[52] A Kostin, 'Voprosy Deĭstvitelnosti Soglasheniia o Mezhdunarodnoĭ Podsudnosti na Etape Priznaniya i Privedeniya v Ispolnenie Inostrannogo Sudebnogo Resheniia' ('Issues of Validity of International Jurisdiction Agreements at the Stage of Recognition and Enforcement of a Foreign Judgment') (2014) 5 *Arbitrazhnyĭ I Grazhdanskiĭ Protsess* 49.

[53] Postanovlenie Federal'nogo Arbitrazhnogo Suda Moskovskogo Okruga ot 17 maiia 2004 g no KG-A40/3102-04-P (Decision of the Federal *Arbitrazh* Court of Moscow Circuit) of 17 May 2004 no KG-A40/3102-04-P.

[54] Reshenie Spetsializirovannogo Mezhraionnogo Ekonomicheskogo Suda Goroda Almaty ot 4 fevraliia 2010 g (Decision of the Specialised Inter-regional Commercial Court of Almaty City) of 4 February 2010 case no 2-748/10.

[55] Opredelenie Vysshego Arbitrazhnogo Suda RF ot 27 iiunia 2011 g no VAS-6415/11 (Resolution of the Supreme *Arbitrazh* Court of the RF) of 27 June 2011 no VAS-6415/11 no A40-111626/10-63-980.

'chosen' court of general jurisdiction. This makes sense; and the only solution here is for parties to know the subject matter jurisdiction of the Russian courts.

B. Derogation of Jurisdiction: Foreign Jurisdiction Agreements

A few words need to be said regarding party autonomy and jurisdiction agreements in favour of a foreign court. In principle, such agreements should be enforced by courts because they exert the parties' intention.

In the EU, the Brussels I Recast does not directly deal with agreements conferring jurisdiction to a court outside the territory of the EU, as the EU has no competence to regulate the prorogation of courts outside its boundaries.[56] Further questions regarding derogation of jurisdiction in the EU are left for the European Court of Justice (ECJ) to consider.

National laws of the EU Member States already provide solutions in connection with derogation agreements. For instance, where a case falls entirely outside the Brussels I regime, an English court would stay the proceedings and give effect to the jurisdiction agreement in favour of a foreign court, or order restraint on foreign proceedings.[57] The court has an inherent discretion to disregard an express foreign jurisdiction clause.[58] The English court would apply the doctrine of *forum non conveniens* to determine the most appropriate forum. Foreign jurisdiction clauses are recognised unless a good case is shown against it. This can be traced back to *Eleftheria*.[59] In that case, a dispute arose from a bill of lading according to which all disputes were to be referred to a foreign (Greek) court. Plaintiffs initiated proceedings in England, and the defendant applied for a stay of proceedings because of the foreign jurisdiction clause. Brandon J established that: (i) the court has a discretion to decide whether or not to grant a stay when proceedings in England are brought in breach of a foreign jurisdiction clause; (ii) the discretion should be exercised by granting a stay, unless strong cause is shown for not doing so; (iii) the burden of proof to show strong cause is on the plaintiffs. In addition, regard may be had to the circumstances, the location and availability of evidence of facts, the material differences between the English and the applicable foreign law, the connection of the parties to relevant countries, the possibility of prejudice

[56] Magnus and Mankowski (n 2) 458.

[57] A Briggs, 'The Impact of Recent Judgments of the European Court on English Procedural Law and Practice' (2006) University of Oxford, Faculty of Law Legal Studies Research Paper Series, Working Paper No 11/2006, 5.

[58] C Woodruff and K Reed, 'Comparative Study of "Residual Jurisdiction" in Civil and Commercial Disputes in the EU: National Report for England' (National Report on Residual Jurisdiction, England, for the General Report: Study on Residual Jurisdiction edited by Arnaud Nuyts, 3 September 2007) 15, available at: ec.europa.eu/civiljustice/news/docs/study_resid_jurisd_england_en.pdf.

[59] *Owners of Cargo Lately Laden on Board the Eleftheria v Owners of the Eleftheria (The Eleftheria)* [1970] P 94; [1969] 2 WLR 1073.

of plaintiffs if deprived of their claim in England, etc. In that case, the corresponding party failed to show a strong case against staying the English proceedings and the court decided not to stay English proceedings in breach of such an agreement. From my point of view, Brandon J gave the court too much discretion in that case. Had the parties not had an exclusive jurisdiction clause, all those factors and considerations of a strong arguable case, proximity and availability of evidence, possibility of obtaining a fair trial, etc would be helpful to determine the parties' interests. However, where an express choice of jurisdiction by the parties existed, it must have been honoured, and considering other reasons was unnecessary. An exclusively chosen English court must exercise jurisdiction when the Hague Choice of Court Convention 2005 applies (see Article 5(2)).

In another case, *Banco de Honduras*,[60] the English court upheld choice of court by the parties in favour of Lahore (capital of Punjabi province in Pakistan), even though the claimant tried to establish English jurisdiction based on the choice of English law by the parties. The court gave effect to the jurisdiction clause since there was no problem of the Lahore courts applying the English law, and, inter alia, the claimant failed to show why it should not keep to its promise to settle disputes in Lahore.

A similar solution regarding agreements in favour of foreign courts exists in Russia. Where a jurisdiction agreement refers to a competent foreign court, Russian *arbitrazh* courts shall stop the proceedings, at the request of the interested party. This has been recommended by the Supreme *Arbitrazh* Court reviewing lower Russian courts' practice: 'an *arbitrazh* court shall consider itself lacking the jurisdiction if it establishes that parties concluded an enforceable and legally valid agreement on settlement of dispute exclusively in a court of a foreign state'.[61] In such a case, the Russian court is to dismiss any claims without hearing the case on its merits, provided the interested party submits its objection to jurisdiction in time. Vorobieva further elaborates that it is improbable that Russian courts would have the interest or spare time to hear proceedings targeting companies which conclude derogation agreements excluding Russian courts.[62] Russian courts are overloaded with cases as it is, and 'chasing' commercial actors trying to avoid Russian jurisdiction would require additional resources and time that the Russian courts might not have.

In addition, Russian law stipulates that if several courts of different states seize of a case between the same parties on the same subject matter and on the same grounds, a Russian *arbitrazh* court shall terminate the proceedings if it was not the first to seize the proceedings.[63] It might be possible, however, that the case

[60] *Banco de Honduras SA v East West Insurance Co Ltd* [1996] LRLR 74 (QB).

[61] Informatsionnoe Pismo Presidiuma Vysshego Arbitrazhnogo Suda RF ot 9 iiulia 2013 g no 158 'Obzor Praktiki Rassmotreniia Arbitrazhnymi Sudami Del s Uchastiem Inostrannykh Lits' (Information Letter of the Presidium of the Supreme *Arbitrazh* Court of the RF 'Review of Judicial Practice on Certain Issues Connected with Deciding Cases by Russian *Arbitrazh* Courts with Participation of Foreign Entities') of 9 July 2013 no 158, para 6.

[62] Vorobieva (n 10) 170.

[63] Postanovlenie Plenuma Verkhovnogo Suda RF no 6, Plenuma Vysshego Arbitrazhnogo Suda RF no 8 ot 1 iiulia 1996 g o Nekotorykh Voprosah, Sviazannykh s Primeneniem Chasti Pervoĭ Grazhdanskogo Kodeksa RF (Resolution of the Plenum of the Supreme Court of the RF no 6 and the Plenum of the Supreme *Arbitrazh* Court of the RF no 8 on the Effect of International Agreements in the Russian Federation Relating to Questions of International Civil Procedure) of 6 June 1996, art 7.

falls under exclusive jurisdiction provisions prescribing mandatory jurisdiction of a Russian court. Such exclusive jurisdiction of Russian *arbitrazh* courts cannot be changed by a private jurisdiction agreement. Even if the Russian court does not seize the case first, and a foreign court starts proceedings as directed by a jurisdiction agreement, the Russian court would not terminate the proceedings started in accordance with the rules of exclusive jurisdiction.

Therefore, Russian law neither objects to nor prohibits derogation agreements unless Russian jurisdiction is mandatory. The fundamental principle of permissiveness (*obshedozvolitelnyĭ tip pravovogo regulirovaniia*) applies. According to this principle embedded in political and legal theory in Russia, that – which is not expressly prohibited by law – is permitted.[64] However, when such an agreement contradicts the Russian mandatory (exclusive) jurisdiction provisions, it shall not be enforced. For instance, when it concerns relationships of Russian parties with parties from the EU or elsewhere choosing a court in the EU to handle their disputes, Article 25 of the Brussels I Recast applies. The Brussels I Recast elaborates on the prorogation effect of jurisdiction agreements choosing courts of Member States; and it is for third-countries' courts, if seized, 'to decide themselves according to their law whether and when they give effect to such derogation'.[65] In such a case, a Russian court checks if any exclusive (mandatory) jurisdiction provisions of the Russian Federation are breached; and if not, it returns the claim with no action or rejects the proceedings. Thus, the Russian court will uphold the jurisdiction agreement in favour of the EU court, unless it is contrary to Russian mandatory jurisdiction provisions.

An interesting case featuring an exclusive jurisdiction clause in favour of a European court was considered by Russian courts involving sole proprietors from Russia and Belgium, Bagadova and Munro.[66] They signed a contract for delivery of giraffes with an exclusive jurisdiction clause in favour of a Belgian commercial court. The initial claim by the Russian entrepreneur in Russia was returned due to lack of jurisdiction because of the jurisdiction agreement.[67] On appeal, the Russian entrepreneur argued that the jurisdiction clause was not based on full consent, and the dispute should be considered at the place of performance of the contract, in Krasnodar. The Belgian defendant was duly notified of the Russian proceedings but did not appear. The appellate court did not satisfy the claim for the following reasons: the parties expressly chose a Belgian court; jurisdiction of a Russian court based on alternative jurisdiction (at the place of performance of the contract) could not be allowed because of the express jurisdiction agreement. Moreover, no

[64] V Chervoniuk (ed), *Elementarnie Nachala Obshcheĭ Teorii Prava* (*Elementary Foundations of Jurisprudence*) (KolosS, 2003) 264.

[65] Magnus and Mankowski (n 2) 456.

[66] Postanovlenie Piatnadtsatogo Arbitrazhnogo Appelliatsionnogo Suda ot 16 marta 2010 g no 15АП-8482/2009 (Resolution of the Fifteenth *Arbitrazh* Appellate Court) of 16 March 2010 no 15АП-8482/2009 case no A32-15102/2009.

[67] Opredelenie Arbitrazhnogo Suda Krasnodarskogo Kraiia ot 9 iiunia 2009 g (Decision of *Arbitrazh* Court of Krasnodarskii Territory) of 9 June 2009 case no A32-15102/2009.

proof of violation of Russian exclusive jurisdiction rules was provided. Therefore, the decision of the lower Russian court was upheld.

III. Party Autonomy Bordering Other Issues

In addition to the straightforward scenarios where private parties choose jurisdiction by an explicit agreement, there may be nuances and complications associated with choice of forum. In some instances, parties may designate governing law to the contract, but refrain from specifying the forum. In other cases, they may mention both arbitration and litigation as options for dispute resolution. In other instances, litigation started in accordance with a valid jurisdiction agreement may be contested based on earlier proceedings commenced elsewhere. This section will encompass some of these issues and analyse them in light of the profound role of party autonomy that is allotted in my envisioned ideal jurisdiction regime.

A. Applicable Law and Appropriate Forum

The cornerstone of an ideal jurisdiction system should be the will and interests of private parties. How does this approach translate into practice, when parties sign a choice-of-law but not a choice-of-court agreement? Should such choice of law of a state lead to the automatic application of that state's jurisdiction?

The point of the parties choosing a law implies that parties consciously believe that the provisions of that law are likely to be favourable to their contract.[68] However, where parties *ex ante* believe provisions of some law are beneficial to their relationship, it does not necessarily mean the courts of that same place is the most appropriate forum in which to settle their disputes. It does not automatically mean that there is an implicit agreement on jurisdiction. It is merely one of the factors that needs to be taken into account when courts decide whether to stay or dismiss a claim. Courts should explore the parties' intent and reasoning behind the evident choice of law. Was that choice a compromise motivated by commercial reasons? Was it done because of market practice applicable to a certain transaction? Was it based on a substantive connection between a transaction and the forum? Only in combination with other factors, may it be determined that adjudicating the claim is in both parties' interests.

Now, does the practice in the EU and Russia correspond to the attitude outlined above? In the EU, while choice of court may be one of the factors considered while determining whether 'a choice of law has been clearly demonstrated',[69] the same

[68] O'Brien (n 45) 27.

[69] For instance, Recital 12 Regulation (EC) 593/2008 of the European Parliament and the Council of 17 June 2008 on the law applicable to contractual obligations [2008] OJ L177/6 (the Rome I Regulation).

does not apply the other way around. Magnus clearly states that contractual choice of law does not entail even a 'tacit' choice of court; the reason for this being that it is no longer presumed that a chosen law is solely applied by the courts of the country of that law.[70] Such an approach reflects my overall approach set forth above.

In Russian scholarship, the predominant view is that it is impossible not to note the existing connection between choice-of-court agreements and choice-of-law agreements.[71] In particular, these agreements pursue similar objectives: increasing predictability and legal certainty. These agreements are 'mutually interdependent'.[72] Choice of law may indicate the parties' interests and inclination towards a certain jurisdiction. However, an individual approach to each case may be necessary to see whether simple mention of a country's body of law indicates the parties' intention to litigate in that country. Although practically difficult, no unified standard should apply to all situations with choice of law but no choice of forum. Sometimes, parties' choice of law is predicated by their preference of contract law in that country. Sometimes, it may be a simple compromise to choose a third state's law to govern their relationships, in order to avoid favouring the parties' 'home' laws. In those cases, agreements on law should not immediately signal the parties' choice of the corresponding forum, because they are merely a shot in the dark: any other foreign law may be equally successfully chosen. In such cases, proper jurisdiction shall be determined in accordance with other applicable rules.

This approach may be compared with the common law understanding of the connection between the chosen body of law and the chosen forum. For example, an American study of a number of commercial contracts revealed that 'a contract may bear a reasonable relationship to [a forum] merely because of the parties' decision to select the law [of the forum]'.[73] The same study concluded that the majority of commercial contracts failed to designate a forum. The reasons vary when parties fail to specify a forum in their contracts but designate a certain body of law to govern their relationship. 'Bargaining obstacles or agency problems'[74] may be further investigated as the main possible reasons preventing parties choosing a forum for resolution of their disputes. At any rate, when parties did specify a forum of choice, it overwhelmingly corresponded to the contract's choice of law.[75] Thus, a 'heavy weight' in the American case law is given to the parties' intention

[70] Magnus and Mankowski (n 2) 460. The view is also supported by the one expressed in P Schlosser (ed), 'Report on the Convention on the Association of the Kingdom of Denmark, Ireland and the United Kingdom of Great Britain and Northern Ireland to the Convention on jurisdiction and the enforcement of judgments in civil and commercial matters and to the Protocol on its interpretation by the Court of Justice' (1979) OJ C 59/71 (Schlosser Report) para 175; and A Layton and H Mercer, *European Civil Practice*, 2nd edn (Sweet & Maxwell, 2004) para 20.018.

[71] I Timohov, *Inostrannoe Pravo v Sudebnoi Praktike* (*Foreign Law in Judicial Practice*) (Wolters Kluwer, 2004) 32.

[72] ibid.

[73] T Eisenberg and G Miller, 'The Flight to New York: An Empirical Study of Choice of Law and Choice of Forum Clauses in Publicly-Held Companies' Contracts' (2009) 30 *Cardozo Law Review* 1475, 1484.

[74] ibid 1512.

[75] ibid 1503.

and the place of making the contract in determining which jurisdiction has the most significant contacts.[76]

Similarly, in England, a proper forum may heavily depend on the governing law of the contract, in case of absence of a choice of forum clause. An example of choice of law conferring jurisdiction may be found in *Ocean Steamship Co v Queensland State Wheat Board.*[77] In that case, wheat from Australia was delivered to England and Scotland according to a bill of lading. The bill of lading incorporated the Australia Sea Carriage of Goods Act 1924. The Act provided that the parties to a contract of a goods delivery from Australia to any place outside Australia deemed to have intended the law of the place of shipment to apply to their contract. When the shipowners applied in England for leave to serve a writ outside the jurisdiction, the court held that the stipulation of the Australian Act, duly incorporated in the parties' bill of lading, applied and Australian law governed the contract. On appeal, the court reasoned that jurisdiction by both English and Australian courts would be possible. The fact that the Australian and English laws were the same, was found irrelevant. It was further noted that where English law was to be applied, an English court was the proper court to apply it.

Moreover, the Rules of Civil Procedure in England specify that an English court may accept jurisdiction and permit serving a claim outside English jurisdiction in contract cases, when the contract is governed by English law.[78] For instance, in *Navig8 Pte Ltd v Al-Riyadh Co,*[79] in a dispute between a Jordanian and a Singaporean company concerning a shipment ('the Lucky Lady') from Malaysia to Jordan, an English court allowed an application for a negative declaration to be served out of the jurisdiction in Jordan, because the foreign court would not give effect to the parties' English choice of law agreement. The dispute had no other connection to England other than the choice of English law. This case embodies an approach by some English courts that courts should exercise jurisdiction where choice of law would otherwise be defeated in a foreign forum.[80]

In another significant case, *Erste Group Bank v JSC VMZ Red October,*[81] a dispute arose in connection with a loan repayment which was not honoured by a Russian borrower (a steel plant) or the guarantor (its parent company). The loan agreement and the guarantee referred all disputes to arbitration and the exclusive jurisdiction of English courts by request of the lenders (a syndicate of investors including an Austrian bank). The English court allowed service outside the jurisdiction, since the claimant demonstrated that England was the

[76] *Mechanic v Princeton Ski Shop Inc* 1992 US Dist (SDNY) (1992); also, *Haag v Barnes*, 9 NY 2nd 554 (NY 1961).

[77] *Ocean Steamship Co v Queensland State Wheat Board* [1941] 1 KB 402; [1941] All ER 158.

[78] Courts Procedure Rules, Practice Direction 6B – Service Out of the Jurisdiction, para 3.1(6)c (UK).

[79] *Navig8 Pte Ltd v Al-Riyadh Co ('The Lucky Lady')* [2013] EWHC 328, [2013] 2 Lloyd's Rep 104 (Com Ct).

[80] M Hook, 'The Choice of Law Agreement as a Reason for Exercising Jurisdiction' (2014) 63 *International & Comparative Law Quarterly* 963.

[81] *Erste Group Bank AG (London) v JSC (VMZ Red October)* [2013] EWHC 2926 (Comm).

appropriate and proper forum for the dispute resolution. The claimant sustained damages in England. The tort claim was only pleaded as a matter of English law. The defendants could allege that Russian law was applicable, but they failed to plead this in due course. This case demonstrated how the governing law of contractual relationships can play an important role in asserting jurisdiction of the English courts. Above all, this case had a fall-back option of the exclusive jurisdiction of English courts. Given all this, it was appropriate for lender(s) to sue in England.

A more complicated situation arose in another case where a company – incorporated in England and controlled by two Arab individuals – initiated proceedings against a Saudi Arabian company in England, *Global Multimedia v ARA Media Services et al.*[82] The parties had an agency agreement for work in Europe which contained an English choice of law and English non-exclusive jurisdiction clause. Potentially, England and perhaps other fora would be appropriate to adjudicate disputes between the parties. Moreover, the parties had another agreement for agency in Japan, governed by Saudi law and containing a non-exclusive Saudi Arabian jurisdiction clause. In this case, the court had to ascertain whether proceeding with the suit in England or in Saudi Arabia would be more appropriate. There was no claim in Saudi Arabia between the same parties on the same grounds and relating to the agreement for agency services in Europe. Almost all the defendants were domiciled in England, and no evidence was provided that the litigation in England would cause problems or injustice to the parties. For these reasons, England was found a *forum conveniens* for the case.

The reasoning of the courts in these English cases is consistent with my theory of an ideal jurisdiction regime. Where parties specify a non-exclusive choice of forum to settle their disputes, a court should analyse the parties' intent and the circumstances of the case. Why did they choose a certain law? Would considering the case in this jurisdiction cause manifest injustice to the parties, such as depriving them of resources to defend themselves? Were most parties domiciled in this jurisdiction? Have (any) defendants submitted to the jurisdiction already? A combination of answers to all these questions may lead a court to believe that the jurisdiction is appropriate.

B. Jurisdiction Agreements and *lis pendens*

A few words need to be said about the interrelation of prorogation of jurisdiction by agreement and the *lis pendens* rule. The *lis pendens* rule asserts that any court other than the court first seized shall stay its proceedings until the jurisdiction of the court first seized is established. It is enforced in order to avoid parallel proceedings and potentially conflicting judgments. The principle is embedded

[82] *Global Multimedia International Limited v ARA Media Services et al* [2006] EWHC 3612 (Ch).

in the EU Brussels jurisdiction regime and in the Russian Codes on Civil and *Arbitrazh* procedure.[83]

Controversial cases occur where parties sign a jurisdiction agreement, and then one party sues the other in another jurisdiction despite it. Which court shall then have priority? The history of correlation between jurisdiction agreements and the *lis pendens* rule in Europe shows that the court chosen by the parties should have priority in such cases. Otherwise, the effectiveness of jurisdiction agreements is undermined, and parties become entrapped by the procedure.

In particular, where it came to interplay between the party autonomy to choose a forum and the *lis pendens* rule in the EU, the ECJ issued a controversial decision in *Gasser v MISAT*.[84] *Gasser v MISAT* established, and *Turner v Grovit*[85] reaffirmed that courts, allegedly chosen by the parties in the jurisdiction clause, could not assume jurisdiction unless and until the court, first seized, had declined it. The ECJ reasoning was to maintain the legal certainty that Brussels I was trying to achieve. Also, avoidance of risk of irreconcilable judgments was behind the ECJ's grounds to grant the jurisdiction to the court first seized.

However, the decisions undermined the effectiveness of exclusive jurisdiction clauses within the EU. The main problem of the *Gasser* decision was that the ECJ failed to recognise the difficulties of applying *Gasser* to future cases with a similar sets of facts.[86] The cases exhibited failure to enforce jurisdiction agreements, and, 'in London, have left a sense of real disappointment and more than a little indignation'.[87] The question arose why, at all, designate a particular court or courts to resolve disputes, if that decision may be overridden by the *lis pendens* rule, and would not protect the parties from possible delay, uncertainty and inconvenience? Also, since the usefulness of the jurisdiction agreement is 'conditional upon the availability of efficient remedies in case of breach',[88] what use can be derived from the jurisdiction agreement if it cannot be appropriately enforced?

The need to set priorities between party autonomy to choose a forum and the *lis pendens* rule and related actions was noted by the Irish Supreme Court in the *Websense* case.[89] The dispute took place between two companies – one Irish and one Italian. Two law suits were filed, with Italian proceedings lodged a month earlier than the suit in Ireland. The case related to a distribution agreement featuring an exclusive jurisdiction agreement in favour of the Irish courts. The dispute

[83] Brussels I Recast art 29; Russian CCP art 406; CAP art 252.

[84] Case C-116/02 *Erich Gasser GmbH v MISAT Srl* [2005] QB 1; [2004] 1 Lloyd's Rep 22.

[85] Case C-159/02 *Turner v Grovit* [2005] 1 AC 101; [2004] 1 Lloyd's Rep 216.

[86] J Steinle and E Vasiliades, 'The Enforcement of Jurisdiction Agreements under the Brussels I Regulation: Reconsidering the Principle of Party Autonomy' (2010) 6 *Journal of Private International Law* 565, 571.

[87] Briggs, 'The Impact of Recent Judgments of the European Court on English Procedural Law and Practice' (n 57) 232.

[88] G Cuniberti and M Requejo, 'Damages for Breach of a Choice-of-Court Agreement' (2010) *ERA Forum* 7.

[89] *Websense International Technology Ltd v ITWAY SpA* [2014] IESC 5 (2014).

was whether a later agreement subsequently changed the distribution agreement. The Irish court had to decide whether, essentially, the Irish and Italian proceedings were connected, and if so, whether to stay the local proceedings until the Italian court decided on its jurisdiction. Notably, the Italian court would decide on its jurisdiction not in a preliminary hearing on jurisdiction (right away), but at the time of a substantive hearing (in the far future). Although the parties had a jurisdiction agreement, the Irish Supreme Court decided to stay the proceedings, given the significant overlap between the proceedings.

The Court's reasoning included unwillingness to create a situation of conflicting judgments. The Court acted in view of the harmonious application of European law, which, at the time, gave priority to the *lis pendens* rule over jurisdiction agreements. Thus, the *Websense* decision preserved the ECJ logic in *Gasser*. The decision was legally accurate, but it further showed that prioritising jurisdiction agreements over related actions was needed in Europe: 'the more nuanced approach to the rules contained within the Regulation is necessary if the commitment to certainty is not to lead to an impractical situation being mandated'.[90] The Irish court predicted that the case would come back to it in the future: the connection between the two cases was too strong, the facts were too similar, and the possible outcomes closely related to each other. Therefore, only if and until the Italian court decided on its jurisdiction over the case, the Irish court had to stay the proceedings.

Through the lens of my view on ideal jurisdiction, the case once again exposed the problem of not putting party autonomy as the primary value in law on jurisdiction. All facts and circumstances of the case screamed that Irish jurisdiction was appropriate. Nevertheless, the Irish court had to abide by the ECJ precedents and hold back from asserting jurisdiction in the case.

In 2012, during the reform of the Brussels I Regulation, the Commission urged the European Parliament and the Council to enhance the effectiveness of choice-of-court agreements in connection with the *lis pendens* rule in order to address this 'torpedo problem'.[91] The torpedo tactic represents an evasive technique: a party launches proceedings in a jurisdiction other than that chosen by the parties which takes several months or years to decide and decline its jurisdiction. Thus, the party deliberately avoids judicial proceedings. In the meantime, it can hide its assets or evidence in bad faith. The torpedo tactics are not welcome in international practice and should be tackled by the states. The European Commission proposed, and the Parliament and Council approved the proposal and gave the priority to courts specified in choice-of-court agreements over the courts first seized. According to the Brussels I Recast, the *lis pendens* rule now applies subject to prorogation of jurisdiction by agreement.[92] The adoption of the Commission's proposal can be easily supported,

[90] ibid 52.

[91] C Heinze, 'Choice of Court Agreements, Coordination of Proceedings and Provisional Measures in the Reform of the Brussels I Regulation' (2011) Max Planck Private Law Research Paper no 11/5, 3, citing M Franzosi, 'Worldwide Patent Litigation and the Italian Torpedo' (1997) 19 *European Intellectual Property Review* 382.

[92] Brussels I Recast recital 22 and art 29.

as it gives the priority to the forum chosen by the parties, strengthens jurisdiction agreements and underlines the importance of party autonomy in international civil litigation.[93] These changes took effect in early 2015.

By learning from the EU experience, Russia should prioritise the jurisdiction of a court chosen by the parties over the court that first seizes the dispute. At present, no such solution exists; and the *lis pendens* rule is generally enforced. Indeed, the Russian legislators should avoid the pains of *Gasser v MISAT*-like situations and quickly make changes similar to the Brussels I Recast provision prioritising choice-of-court agreements over the *lis pendens* rule. Such legislative change may not appear very crucial to a Russian lawyer, who may be used to expeditious court proceedings in Russia. Russian lawyers may be unfamiliar with some jurisdictions (like Italy) where a single case may last over a decade. Nevertheless, the Russian legislator should be prepared for such situations. Moreover, bringing the Russian procedural law in line with the recently carefully reviewed Brussels I Recast would benefit Russian parties in the long run, in view of the potential convergence of legal regimes or accession of Russia to international instruments on jurisdiction (Lugano Convention on Jurisdiction or the Hague Convention on Choice of Court Agreements).

Therefore, the EU Brussels I Recast now recognises the precedence of jurisdiction agreements over the *lis pendens* rule. Russia needs to head in the same direction. Then, both jurisdictional regimes will be properly aligned with my proposed view emphasising the centrality of party autonomy in jurisdiction.

C. Arbitration and Litigation

Although alternative dispute resolution methods such as arbitration and mediation are outside the scope of this book, a few words need to be said about the instances when litigation and arbitration intersect. For instance, there are mixed jurisdiction and arbitration agreements; there are situations where parties designate arbitration as a method of settling disputes and then end up in state courts; there are court cases invalidating or giving effect to jurisdiction and arbitration agreements, etc. Insofar as the matter of jurisdiction agreements touches arbitration, it warrants consideration. In light of my proposed approach, both jurisdiction and arbitration manifest the expression of the parties' will. Both types of agreement equally deserve effective enforcement. However, how should an ideal jurisdictional system prioritise between the two?

i. Mixed Arbitration and Litigation Agreements

What if parties sign a mixed dispute resolution clause containing conflicting alternatives of arbitration and litigation? An interesting account has been given

[93] ibid 8.

by Garnett on common law courts' response to situations where jurisdiction and arbitration clauses are both included in a single contract.[94] He summarises that the current academic and judicial authority seems to support the idea that in such cases, arbitration must be given preference over litigation.[95] I agree with Garnett who criticises such a view, suggesting that it is 'unjustified' to favour arbitration simply because of an 'abstract superiority' of arbitral process over litigation. In fact, litigation should have the priority because it bears mandatory character backed by state authority.

How would Russia deal with such situations? Arbitration has been found especially attractive by parties conducting business in Russia. This is a widely accepted view in Russian legal scholarship, where arbitration is the 'irrefutably dominating form of dispute resolution of international commercial cases'.[96] First, the reason for that may relate to easier enforcement of arbitral awards in comparison with recognition and enforcement of foreign judgments. Enforcement of foreign judgments in Russia is subject to the existence of a mutual agreement between Russia and the corresponding state(s). In order to avoid the risk of having an unenforceable foreign judgment, many parties choose to resolve their disputes by arbitration. Then, arbitral awards are more easily enforced in Russia in accordance with the New York Convention on Arbitration[97] and the Russian legal provisions envisaging enforcement of foreign arbitral awards.

Popularity of arbitration for commercial relations involving Russian parties may also be explained by historical reasons. Arbitration was practically the only alternative for resolving international commercial disputes in the USSR.[98] Moreover, courts of general jurisdiction in the USSR lacked experience in the application of private law in the field of commercial relations. State *arbitrazh* courts which combined judicial and administrative functions were 'also unfamiliar with the practice of applying private law'.[99] Thus, international commercial arbitration has become a well-developed and preferable means of commercial dispute resolution in Russia. With the evolution of international private law since the collapse of the Soviet Union, state litigation in commercial (*arbitrazh*) courts has improved: the rules of civil procedure have become more comprehensive, the courts have more experience applying these rules, and society took a big leap from the state controlled to a market economy.

[94] R Garnett, 'Coexisting and Conflicting Jurisdiction and Arbitration Clauses' (2013) 9 *Journal of Private International Law* 361.

[95] ibid 361, fn 1.

[96] See, eg, Timohov (n 71) 30.

[97] The New York Convention on the Recognition and Enforcement of Foreign Arbitral Awards of 10 June 1958.

[98] A Komarov, 'The Role and Significance of international Arbitration in the Formation of a Modern Legal System in Russia' in W Simons (ed), *Private and Civil Law in the Russian Federation. Essays in Honor of FJM Feldbrugge* (Martinus Nijhoff Publishers, 2009).

[99] ibid.

Still, arbitration plays an indispensable role in commercial dispute resolution in Russia. The question of the alleged superiority and popularity of arbitration over litigation remains open. The most difficult situations may be found in cases of optional and non-exclusive jurisdiction and arbitration clauses ('any disputes between the parties may be referred to arbitration or litigation in a state court'). What carries weight in such situations?

Perhaps, litigation in state courts would supersede arbitration in Russia. The power of the state in this post-totalitarian and authoritarian society remains strong. Clear hierarchy of power in law and other areas in Russia suggests the undeniable and outweighing power of court decisions, notwithstanding the admitted conclusiveness and incontestability of arbitral awards. The state power would arguably prevail in Russia, based on this notion of superiority of the state over its affairs and principals. Then, litigation would be given effect before arbitration. Is this approach correct? Although it appears logical, this should not be the uniform prescription for every situation of mixed arbitration and litigation clauses. Regard must be had to the parties' will expressed via both wording of their contracts and their actions (such as voluntary submission to the jurisdiction of a state court, for instance). The same view is expressed by Garnett who believes that courts should, most importantly, consider the parties' intention and only give priority to arbitration when parties expressly desire so in clear words.[100] Another approach to prioritise between arbitration and litigation would be to give power to the court (or arbitral tribunal) first seized of the case. In a case where the parties' intention can be equally interpreted preferring either arbitration or litigation, the tribunal first seized should handle the case. In all accounts, the debate regarding mixed arbitration and litigation agreements continues; and further commentary and judicial authority is required regarding the matter.

ii. Regulation of Arbitration and Litigation: Problems Remain

A milestone case highlighting the problems at the borderline between arbitration and litigation in Europe was the *West Tankers* case.[101] In that case, a vessel owned by the West Tankers Company collided with a jetty (pier) owned by Erg in Syracuse, Italy. The charter party was governed by English law and contained a clause providing for arbitration in London. Erg, the owner, claimed compensation from its insurers Allianz and Generali. Arbitration proceedings were commenced in London against West Tankers, and West Tankers denied liability for the damage caused by the collision. Allianz and Generali paid Erg compensation under the insurance policies. Then, Allianz and Generali brought proceedings against West Tankers before the Tribunale di Siracusa (Italy) in order to recover the moneys

[100] Garnett (n 94).

[101] Case C-185/07 *Allianz SpA, Generali Assicurazioni Generali SpA v West Tankers Inc* [2009] ECR I-663 (*West Tankers*).

they had paid to Erg. West Tankers raised an objection of lack of jurisdiction because of the existence of the arbitration agreement.

In parallel, West Tankers brought proceedings before an English court, seeking enforcement of the arbitration agreement, and asking for an anti-suit injunction against proceedings by Allianz and Generali in Italy. The problem with an Italian court seizing the jurisdiction was the allegation that Italian court procedure may take 10 years, thus causing inconvenience and delay. The English court granted the anti-suit injunction. Allianz and Generali appealed to the House of Lords, arguing that granting such an injunction was contrary to the Brussels I Regulation. The House of Lords stayed its proceedings and referred a question to the ECJ. It asked whether it was incompatible with the Brussels I Regulation for a court of a Member State to make an order to restrain a person from commencing or continuing proceedings before the courts of another Member State, on the ground that such proceedings would be contrary to an arbitration agreement, even though Article 1(2)(d) of Brussels I excludes arbitration from its scope.

Essentially, the ECJ ruled that granting the anti-suit injunction in such circumstances would be incompatible with the Brussels I Regulation.[102] Proceedings on anti-suit injunctions in relation to arbitration, although outside the scope of Brussels I, might have had consequences undermining the effectiveness of the common Brussels I jurisdiction regime. They might have prevented the 'attainment of the objectives of unification of the rules of conflict of jurisdiction'.[103] The decision raised much debate with respect to the principle of mutual trust and the scope of civil procedure in Europe. The case exhibited intolerance of the EU jurisdiction regime to the common law procedural devices, such as anti-suit injunctions. Moreover, giving power to the Italian court that first seized the dispute, considering that parties had an arbitration agreement, undermined the effectiveness of enforcement of the principle of autonomy of the parties. The case was severely criticised for providing a loophole in the law allowing for forum shopping. In particular, parties may ignore an arbitration agreement in favour of arbitration in one Member State and bring actions to a forum with particularly long procedural periods, thus avoiding being brought to justice.

During the most recent reform of the Brussels I Regulation, the Commission aimed to enhance the correlation between litigation and arbitration 'in order to give full effect to the will of the parties'.[104] The Commission's Proposal contained

[102] Although incompatible with the Brussels jurisdiction regime, anti-suit injunctions against breach of a dispute resolution agreement remain a valid alternative for the English court where the case involves defendants from outside the EU. See, eg, A Briggs, 'Which Law Governs Forum Selection Clauses' (Paper for ASIL Webinar 'The Nature of Natures of Agreement Relating to Jurisdiction to Governing Law', 2 March 2016) or *AES Ust-Kamenogorsk Hydropower Plant LLP v Ust-Kamenogorsk Hydropower Plant JSC* [2013] 1 WLR 1889, where the English court decided it had jurisdiction while arbitration clause directed so, by issuing an injunction preventing instituting litigation proceedings in Kazakhstan.

[103] *West Tankers* [24].

[104] Proposal for a Regulation of the European Parliament and the Council on Jurisdiction and the Recognition of Judgments in Civil and Commercial Matters (Recast), COM (2010) 748 Final, 2010/0383 (COD), Brussels, 14 December 2010, recital 20.

the introduction of special rules aimed at avoiding parallel proceedings and abusive litigation tactics in cases where the designated seat of arbitration was in a Member State. The rule would fix the problems occurring in cases like *West Tankers*.

However, the idea of coordinating arbitration and litigation within the EU jurisdiction regime stirred a wave of criticism from the arbitration community, viewing 'any intervention of state authorities in the realm of arbitration' as an 'intrusion'.[105] For instance, the Heidelberg Report studying the application of Brussels I, drawn up by Hess, Pfeiffer and Schlosser,[106] analysed national reports from EU Member States considering extension of the Brussels I regime into arbitration. The majority of the national reporters adopted a critical view on such an extension.[107]

The European Parliament's revision of the Commission's proposal reversed all the changes proposed by the Commission. It justified this by referring to the Parliament's Resolution of 7 September 2010 on the implementation and review of the Brussels I Regulation, which set out that the reasons for all aspects of arbitration should be clearly and unambiguously excluded from the scope of the Brussels I Regulation.[108]

The final text of the Brussels I Recast contains a new recital 12 and Article 73(2) which regulate its relationship with arbitration. Article 73(2) states that the Brussels I Recast shall not affect the application of the New York Convention on Arbitration. Recital 12 elaborates that the Brussels I Recast should not apply to arbitration. It clearly states that it should not apply to any proceedings relating to the establishment of an arbitral tribunal, the powers of arbitrators, the conduct of an arbitration procedure or any other aspects of such a procedure, nor to any action or judgment concerning the annulment, review, appeal, recognition or enforcement of an arbitral award. Recognition of arbitral awards shall be done according to the New York Convention on Arbitration which takes precedence over the Brussels I Recast. However, recital 12 distinguishes that in 'mixed' situations, the Brussels I Recast shall apply to the parts of judgments on substance, even if ruled together with respect to the validity of arbitration agreements. In particular, courts of the Member States shall be free to consider matters conferred

[105] Guest Editorial, B Hess, 'Should Arbitration and European Procedural Law be Separated or Coordinated?' (Conflict of Laws.net, Guest Editorial, 14 February 2010), available at: conflictoflaws.net/2010/guest-editorial-hess-should-arbitration-and-european-procedural-law-be-separated-or-coordinated, referring to L Radicati di Brozolo, 'Interference of National Courts with Arbitration' in C Müller and A Rigozzi (eds), *New Developments in International Commercial Arbitration* (Schulthess, 2009).

[106] B Hess, T Pfeiffer and P Schlosser, 'Report on the Application of Regulation Brussels I in the Member States' (Institute for International and Private International Law, Ruprecht-Karls-University Heidelberg, Study JLS/C4/2005/03, Final Version, September 2007).

[107] ibid 51.

[108] Draft Report on the Proposal for Regulation of the European Parliament and of the Council on Jurisdiction and the Enforcement of Judgments in Civil and Commercial Matters (recast) (COM(2010)0748 – C7-0433/2010 – 2010/0383(COD)), 28 June 2011 (Draft Parliament Resolution) recital 11: Justification, available at: www.europarl.europa.eu/meetdocs/2009_2014/documents/juri/pr/869/869709/869709en.pdf.

to arbitration by parties, to stay or dismiss the proceedings, to refer the parties to arbitration or to establish the validity of arbitration agreements. Furthermore, the Brussels I Recast shall not apply in cases of recognition and enforcement of court orders rendered with respect to the validity of arbitration agreements. However, where a court seized of a matter pursuant to the Brussels I Recast decides on invalidity of an arbitration agreement, the court's judgment on the substance of the matter may proceed to recognition and enforcement under the Brussels I Recast.

This partially settles the non-application of the Brussels I Recast to arbitration. However, it is virtually impossible to separate the EU conflict of laws regime from arbitration.[109] Strict separation of the two will lead to continuous issues arising on the border between arbitration and litigation (issues other than those addressed in recital 12 and Article 73(2)). It would be better to address the isolated controversial issues pertaining to litigation where it borders with arbitration in the existing Brussels I Regulation, rather than leave it to the New York Convention on Arbitration, the ECJ case law or a possible future instrument dedicated to arbitration in the EU.

The problem raised in the *West Tankers* case will remain in Europe. Proof of this may be found in *Gazprom v Lithuania*, a case that is similar to *West Tankers*, on which the ECJ ruled in 2015.[110] The case involved Lietuvos Dujos, the Lithuanian natural gas company. Its shareholders (including Gazprom, a Russian oil and gas giant, the Lithuanian Ministry of Energy and others) had a shareholder's agreement (SHA) with an exclusive jurisdiction clause conferring all disputes to arbitration governed by the rules of the Stockholm Chamber of Commerce. Notwithstanding the exclusive jurisdiction agreement, the Lithuanian ministry initiated the proceedings against Gazprom in a Lithuanian court. Gazprom started arbitration proceedings which resulted in the award granting an anti-suit injunction against the Lithuanian litigation. The Lithuanian Supreme Court referred a question to the ECJ as to whether such an anti-suit injunction would be contrary to the Brussels I Regulation. The ECJ ruled that the Brussels I Regulation does not preclude the courts of an EU Member State from recognising and enforcing an arbitral award prohibiting a party from bringing certain claims (characterised as an anti-suit injunction) before a court of that Member State. AG Wathelet further stated that *West Tankers* had been wrongly decided, and had the case been brought under the Brussels I Recast, an analogous anti-suit injunction would not have been held incompatible with the Brussels I Recast regime.[111]

Notably, a recent English High Court case – *Nori Holdings v Bank Otkritie* – covered the issue relating to anti-suit injunctions in protection of arbitration agreements under the Brussels I Recast.[112] That case analysed the question

[109] S Camilleri, 'Recital 12 of the Recast Regulation: A New Hope?' (2013) 62 *International & Comparative Law Quarterly* 899, 915.
[110] Case C-536/13 *'Gazprom' OAO v Lietuvos Respublika*, Judgment of 13 May 2015.
[111] ibid, Opinion, para 133.
[112] *Nori Holdings v Bank Otkritie* [2018] EWHC 1343 (Comm).

of availability of an anti-suit injunction (by an English court) against court proceedings in another EU Member State (Cyprus). Males J criticised the AG's opinion on *Gazprom* and confirmed that anti-suit injunctions continue to not be available where they would restrain proceedings in another EU Member State. *Nori Holdings* thus confirmed *West Tankers* as rightfully decided.

Overall, open questions remain regarding the interrelation between arbitration and litigation in the EU under the Brussels I Recast. In this, I join scholars who advocate revision in this area, as long as the parties' intent and mutual interests are the driving force behind a to-be-adopted solution.

IV. Party Autonomy *ex post*

Party autonomy in jurisdiction can also manifest itself after the proceedings have been commenced. In that case, parties may agree on a competent forum de facto. The claimant files an action in a particular forum, and the defendant does not protest against the choice and takes part in the proceedings. This type of parties' tacit agreement on jurisdiction also fits within my approach to party autonomy in jurisdiction. It is a form of consent and another expression of party autonomy. The rule of jurisdiction recognising parties' voluntary submission should be enforced in an ideal jurisdiction regime. Notably, the parties' agreement on jurisdiction *ex post* should override the parties' jurisdiction agreement *ex ante* (either signed at the outset or signed after the contract has been executed but before the commencement of proceedings).

A. Summary and Justification

The importance of the rule of submission to jurisdiction is significant, because it gives effect to the parties' intention. It enforces the idea that private parties may agree on a competent jurisdiction to hear their dispute even after the initiation of court proceedings.

Submission to jurisdiction should supersede other rules of jurisdiction that are otherwise applicable. The policy behind the recognition of the parties' consent on jurisdiction after the beginning of the dispute is simple: it is predicated by the risks and problems that may arise if parties have a case heard and then complain about jurisdiction. By fighting a case on its merits, a party shows its acceptance of the possibility of winning the case. A case may be decided in favour of either party. After such participation in the court proceedings, no party to judicial proceedings should contest the ruling made on the merits after the ruling, based on lack of jurisdiction. Conditional appearances represent an exception to the rule. However, where there is no objection to the competence of the court before hearing a case on its merits, such jurisdiction of the court should be considered valid. In addition, when the defendant enters an appearance, contests jurisdiction, and makes a point on the merits of the case, it would be undesirable for the court to make a stand on that substantive point, and then declare that it has no jurisdiction over the case.[113]

Thus, voluntary submission represents an easily administered test of the parties' will regarding jurisdiction, because the parties' appearance indicates consent and approval of a particular forum. It cannot be contested later, due to mere inconvenience or some other disadvantages experienced by the complaining party. Motivation (such as turning up at court out of fear), or lack of knowledge of another competent forum do not matter. The defendant can hardly complain about being unfairly disadvantaged by the choice of forum, if he consents to the choice by voluntary submission.[114] Even where the defendant may learn about another competent court, after the court proceedings have taken place, submission to jurisdiction should not be contested. In such cases, one cannot allege one's ignorance of the rules as a basis for challenging a valid court decision.

The EU and Russian international jurisdiction rules and case law show differing levels of recognition of the rule on submission to jurisdiction. In the EU, it is explicitly recognised in the Brussels I Recast: appearance by the defendant in a Member State court gives the court jurisdiction over the case. The rule does not apply, however, where appearance was entered to contest the jurisdiction, or where another court has exclusive jurisdiction.[115] Notably, in contractual matters in the EU where a 'weaker' party (a policyholder, an insured, a beneficiary of the insurance contract, a consumer or an employee) is the defendant, a court seized of proceedings must inform the defendant of his right to contest the jurisdiction of the court and of the consequences of entering or not entering an appearance.[116] Thus, the EU jurisdiction regime safeguards and protects the interests of the 'weaker' parties. This reflects the social and economic attitude of the EU legislators to consumers and other 'weaker' parties in the EU.[117] My approach to jurisdiction, presented in this book, is consistent with this: it is quite beneficial for any defendant, be it a weaker or a stronger party, to know about their rights and the consequences of non-appearance.

A precise and excellent justification for voluntary submission has been given by the ECJ in *Elefanten Schuh*. The dispute arose between a Belgian national and a German company involved in a shoe business. An agreement of agency existed between the parties, featuring a jurisdiction clause in favour of German courts at the location of the German company. The Belgian individual subsequently brought a suit at a labour tribunal in Belgium. The German company entered an appearance before that tribunal and argued on the substance of the case. Consequently, the

[113] A similar point has been made by AG Slynn in *Elefanten Schuh* (n 5) 1694.

[114] A von Mehren and D Trautman, 'Jurisdiction to Adjudicate' (1966) 79 *Harvard Law Review* 1121, 1138.

[115] Brussels I Recast art 26.

[116] Brussels I Recast art 26(2).

[117] For more on my position regarding the 'weaker' parties, see further chs 5 and 6.

German company tried to contest the jurisdiction of the Belgian labour tribunal that was in violation of the original exclusive jurisdiction clause. Finally, the Belgian Hof van Cassatie (court of cassation) referred some questions to the ECJ regarding Articles 17 and 18 of the Brussels Convention (jurisdiction by agreement and by submission, equivalent to Articles 25 and 26 of the Brussels I Recast). The Court explained that jurisdiction agreements and submission to jurisdiction represent two ways in which a party may consent to jurisdiction: by contract or by the act of entering an appearance.[118] The difference between these two ways is in the nature of the agreement: in writing or by consensual understanding.[119] Both simply represent two sides of the same coin.

Contrary to the EU, no provision on the submission rule exists in the primary sources of law on jurisdiction in Russia (the Codes of Civil and *Arbitrazh* Procedure). Parties fully take part in the proceedings and later argue about jurisdiction. This clutters the courts of appeal. A reform of the current regulation is necessary providing that voluntary appearance of parties to argue the case on its merits should be interpreted as final submission to jurisdiction.[120] Even where parties had a preliminary jurisdiction agreement *ex ante*, their later act of appearance in a different court clearly demonstrates a willingness to change their original jurisdiction agreement. It should be treated as their voluntary submission. If the defendant does not object to jurisdiction at the beginning of the proceedings, it makes him equally responsible for submitting to jurisdiction and thus deprived of the right to contest the jurisdiction later. A common argument against the submission to jurisdiction in Russia is that a jurisdiction agreement made in writing must be later changed in a written form as well.[121] This focuses more on the strict formal requirement for a valid jurisdiction agreement than on the parties' intent. It only promotes formalism and bureaucracy instead of focusing on an effective solution respecting the parties' choice.

Notably, a quasi-recognition of the parties' choice of jurisdiction after the commencement of judicial proceedings may be found in Article 39 of the Code of *Arbitrazh* Procedure and the almost identical Article 33 of the Code of Civil Procedure. These Articles establish that 'an (*arbitrazh*) court shall transfer a case for consideration by another (*arbitrazh*) court (of the same level) if: … both parties file a request to transfer the case to a court at the location of the majority of evidence'.[122] Some Russian legal scholars consider this rule as a form of enforcement of a jurisdiction agreement concluded during an ongoing judicial proceeding

[118] *Elefanten Schuh*, Opinion of AG Slynn, 1693.

[119] ibid 1678.

[120] A quasi-rule on submission to jurisdiction entitled 'estoppel' is being considered by the Russian Parliament at the moment, as a part of the greater ongoing judicial reform. See, M Karayanidi, 'Adjudicative Jurisdiction in Civil and Commercial Matters in Russia: Analysis and Commentary' (2016) 64 *American Journal of Comparative Law* 981.

[121] S Komaritsky, 'Dogovornaya Podsudnost – Est N'iuansi' ('Contractual Jurisdiction – There are Nuances') (2003) 11 *Arbitrazh and Civil Procedure Journal* 18.

[122] CAP art 39(2)(2); CCP art 33(2)(2).

(eg, Rozhkova, Kurochkin).[123] Dergachev classifies such agreements as 'posterior' (subsequent) jurisdiction agreements (as opposed to 'preliminary' jurisdiction agreements, ie, signed before the initiation of judicial procedure).[124] Therefore, Russian legal culture intuitively recognises the importance of the jurisdiction rule of submission. However, the absence of a clear codification of the submission rule represents a serious gap in the Russian jurisdiction mechanism. It creates room for dishonest business practice. It potentially allows parties to abuse the loopholes in the law to their own advantage. Unfortunately, the chance remains that some judges may still decide that 'silent' acceptance does not necessarily entail actual submission to jurisdiction. This may lead to the unattractiveness of Russian fora in which to settle disputes. It may result in an understanding that no court decision is final in Russia. It creates an impression that ways exist to contest a court's jurisdiction after the fact, and anyone can do it if they do not like a court decision. That is not the message that Russia wants to convey in on the international arena; therefore, this gap should be eliminated.

B. Nuances in Submission to Jurisdiction

In this section, I define some details of the submission to jurisdiction rule considering my overall approach to law on jurisdiction. First, I argue that the proper procedural moment to determine when the defendant voluntarily submitted is before the first substantive defence is raised. Secondly, I contend that understanding of 'discussing a case on its merits' should include raising the defence arguments with a hope to win on the substantive matter of the claim. EU law provides a vague definition of 'discussing a case on its merits' and Russian law, as noted above, lacks the rule on submission altogether. I conclude that both regimes can be improved in this regard. Finally, I consider a possibility of default judgments being issued in cases where defendants fail to appear altogether. I conclude that where the defendant refuses to accept service, does not appear but nevertheless is deemed to be notified, his non-appearance should not be equated to submission.

i. *Suitable Time to Contest Jurisdiction:* in limine litis

To ensure that voluntary submission is distinguished from appearance in court to contest jurisdiction, a precise moment for raising the objection regarding jurisdiction should be defined. An acceptable resolution of this issue can be found in the *Elefanten Schuh* case mentioned above. In that case, the ECJ clarified that jurisdiction must be contested before the first substantive defence. What constitutes a first defence should be determined in accordance with applicable national

[123] Rozhkova et al (n 34).
[124] Dergachev (n 36) 100.

procedural law. A similar approach is recommended for Russia. When introducing the rule on voluntary submission, the Russian legislators should provide that the defendant who wishes to contest jurisdiction of a court must raise his objection *in limine litis*, at the start of the procedure, and before the substantive argument in his defence. Otherwise, his appearance and participation in the case should be understood as voluntary submission.

ii. Discussing a Case on its Merits

Remarkably, the ECJ allows a defendant to raise a 'subsidiary defence on the substance or a subsidiary counterclaim against the plaintiff'[125] without it being understood as 'discussing a case on its merits'. Magnus and Mankowski refer to *Elefanten Schuh* and confirm that the ECJ supports this statement.[126] Such an approach may appear contrary to, and counterintuitive to the legal certainty, clarity and finality that the rule of submission to jurisdiction strives to achieve. Why did the ECJ adopt a view that sometimes the rule on submission does not apply, and the defendant is allowed to simultaneously contest jurisdiction and argue his defence? A closer look on the statement submitted by the UK government in the case partially clarifies the reasoning behind such a 'flexible' interpretation of the rule on submission. The case represented a complicated scenario where proceedings were accompanied by provisional or protective measures, 'which the defendant can only prevent by addressing arguments to the substance of the case'.[127] There may be a time limit for the lodging of a defence that may run out before the issue on jurisdiction is settled. Thus, the UK government advised the ECJ to interpret Article 18 of the Brussels Convention (predecessor of Article 26 of the Brussels I Recast) in a flexible manner, especially where the arguments to the substance are clearly subsidiary to the main objective of contesting the jurisdiction. In addition, the ECJ cited a number of cases from Germany, Italy and the Netherlands, where a defendant who denies jurisdiction may plead on the substance of the case in the alternative.[128] Then, the ECJ reserved the solution whether the defendant may put forward submissions in his defence, and contest the jurisdiction, to the procedural laws of the EU Contracting States. At the same time, it advised that the interpretation where the defendant may contest jurisdiction as well as argue on the substance of the claim, is 'more in keeping with the objectives and spirit of the Convention', where under the law of some Contracting States, the defendant may be barred from making his submissions as to the substance later if, at

[125] Magnus and Mankowski (n 2) 441.

[126] *Elefanten Schuh*, 1700.

[127] ibid 1679.

[128] ibid referring to Bundersgerichtshod, 3 March 1976, Recht der international Wirtschaft 1976, 447; Italian Court of Cassation, 23 June and 10 November 1977, Giustizia Civile 1978, No 1, 44–47; Arrondissementsrechtbank, Oermond, 31 October 1974, Nederlandse Jurisprudentie 1975, No 405; Tribunale di Bassano del Grappe, 13 February 1976, EEG – Dcoumentatie No 36; Tribunale de Pinerolo, 31 March 1976, Rivista di Diritto Internazionale Privato e Processuale 1977, No 1, 78).

the beginning, he only confines himself to contesting jurisdiction and the court happens to reject his plea and assumes jurisdiction.[129] Thus, the ECJ offered a controversial solution. Depending on the national law of civil procedure, it allows the defendant to submit certain arguments regarding the substance of the case, as long as the defendant clearly indicates that he intends to contest the jurisdiction of the court before he makes that subsidiary submission.

As remarked by Lord Denning in *Re Dulles Settlement*,[130] by fighting the case on its merits, a party hopes to win that case. In that case, an American father, resident abroad, appeared before an English court by counsel to oppose application, and to seek protection of the (French) court order for custody. The current law in England was (and still is) that if a party fights a case, not only on the jurisdiction, but also on the merits of the case, such actions would be understood as submission to jurisdiction. The party should not be allowed to have a choice of accepting the court's decision if it is favourable to them or rejecting submitting to it if the decision is made against them. In that case, Lord Denning continued, however, that in addition to vigorous protest to English jurisdiction by an American person, seeking to protect an already issued court order for custody from the French courts, would not amount to 'fighting the case on its merits'. Therefore, it was found insufficient to qualify as a submission to the English jurisdiction. The case seems to provide an example of an EU national procedural case where appearing in court, protesting against the jurisdiction, and then fighting on an additional issue is not necessarily interpreted as equivalent to submission.

It is recommended that Russian legislators should adopt a similar approach to 'conditional appearance'. Contesting the jurisdiction of a court but having it available to argue some subsidiary matters as to substance, may be motivated by the desire to avoid penalties, or not to miss the statute of limitations for certain claims. For instance, sometimes a defendant might urgently need to lodge a counter claim against the protective measures, before the issue of jurisdiction is resolved. In such cases, disputing jurisdiction at a later stage is permissible, as the defendant's appearance cannot be seen as full, but only conditional.

In harmony with existing concepts in Russian civil procedure, 'discussing a case on its merits' should mean submission of relevant evidence in one's defence before the court session on the substance of the case, or when the defendant decides to file a counter claim (*vstrechnyĭ isk*) to offset the claim by the claimant. Even though this involves submission of documents and not physical participation in the court proceedings per se, these actions should be interpreted as if the defendant is taking them in the hope of winning the case. Thus, in the context of Russian civil procedure, 'discussing a case on its merits' should be understood as any action by the defendant where he expresses his acquiescence to the court's jurisdiction.

[129] *Elefanten Schuh*, 1685.

[130] *In Re Dulles Settlement (No 2) Dulles v Vidler* [1948 D 231]; [1951] Ch 842.

iii. Non-Appearance

A peculiar situation may arise on the borderline of what could be viewed as submission to jurisdiction and failure to appear to defend. Where the defendant fails to appear, a court may issue a default judgment. Normally, countries will be entitled to reject the default judgment if it contradicts their own requirements of fair procedure. Depending on their public policy, recognition of such a judgment may or may not happen. Even among the EU Member States, a default judgment might fall under unfair procedures and may not be recognised and enforced. However, this is a question of enforcement jurisdiction, and answering it will bring this discussion outside the scope of this book. In this subsection, I am only interested in the question of whether and why a court can issue a default judgment in absence of the defendant's appearance.

Article 28 of the Brussels I Recast provides that where a defendant domiciled in another Member State is served and does not enter an appearance, the court shall declare it has no jurisdiction unless it is derived from the provisions of this Regulation. 'Unless it is derived from the provisions of this Regulation' underscores the imperative nature of the Brussels I regime, by which parties domiciled in the EU submit (assent) to EU jurisdiction simply by being there. A court shall stay the proceedings if not shown that the defendant has been served with process in sufficient time to enable him to arrange for his defence, or that all necessary steps have been taken to this end.[131] The necessary steps on notification within Europe shall be carried out in accordance with Article 19 of the EU Regulation on service of documents,[132] or, outside its application, Article 15 of the Hague Service Convention.[133]

In Russia, a default judgment may be issued against a no-show defendant who has been properly notified about the judicial proceedings as required by Russian law. *Arbitrazh* courts will consider cases even in the absence of a statement of defence or necessary evidence or in the absence of the defendant himself, provided that the defendant has been properly notified of the time and place of the proceedings.[134] In international cases heard by Russian courts, if the foreign party is from a state-signatory to The Hague Service Convention[135] or another Convention with relevant provisions on service of process, notification is carried out through the channels established by the Convention. Where no international

[131] Brussels I Recast art 28(1–2).

[132] Regulation (EC) 1393/2007 of the European Parliament and of the Council of 13 November 2007 on the service in the Member States of judicial and extrajudicial documents in civil or commercial matters (service of documents), and repealing Council Regulation (EC) 1348/2000 [2007] OJ L324/79.

[133] The Hague Convention on the Service Abroad of Judicial and Extrajudicial Documents in Civil or Commercial Matters of 15 November 1965 (the Hague Service Convention).

[134] CAP art 156.

[135] The Hague Service Convention.

agreement regulates this issue, the Russian court sends the notification to a judicial authority or other competent authority of the foreign state (including consular and diplomatic channels) to perform the service of process. Notably, in such cases, the time for case consideration shall be extended for the period specified in the international agreement, or in the absence of such, for a period not exceeding six months.[136]

Complications may arise when a foreign addressee refuses to accept the writ of summons or another court notice from Russia. In such situations, the person delivering or serving the writ makes a note on the writ of summons. The writ or notice is then returned to the Russian court. For the purposes of Russian law, the addressee who refuses to accept the writ of summons or another court notice is nevertheless deemed to have been notified of the place, date, and time of the relevant court proceeding or another particular proceeding. The Russian court will draw up a certificate confirming that the documents have been served or setting out the reasons that have prevented execution of the request.[137] Unfortunately, in such a case, a default judgment against the foreign party may be issued if the Russian court assumes the foreign defendant has been properly notified. This represents an undesirable side of the Russian law. It can be countered by fighting against the enforcement of such a decision based on the lack of opportunity to be heard.

Therefore, non-appearance by the defendant should not be interpreted as submission. Further protection of the interests of non-appearing defendants is required in cross-border matters in Russian law.

V. Conclusion

In these two chapters, I have focused on the power of private actors to shape the rules of judicial jurisdiction.

In chapter three, I have defined party autonomy as I view it for the law on jurisdiction. I have argued for its prevalence in the hierarchy of values behind jurisdiction rules. I have suggested a number of arguments to support my claim that party autonomy, and not sovereignty, should form the foundation of an ideal jurisdiction regime. I traced the development of recognition of party autonomy in certain national jurisdictional systems. I demonstrated the 'snowball' effect (recognition of party autonomy in other areas of law such as applicable law), growing recognition of individuals and companies as actors in international law, globalisation, advent of the open society, and others. The combination of these factors support and confirm my conclusion that the time has come to re-evaluate the

[136] CAP art 253(3).
[137] See The Hague Conference on Private International Law, Russian Federation-Central Authority & Practical Information, available at: www.hcch.net/index_en.php?act=authorities.details&aid=699.

values we see in jurisdiction in civil and commercial matters, and to prioritise party autonomy as a foundational value and a general rule of jurisdiction.

In chapter four, I have analysed the existing law on jurisdiction in the EU and Russia through the prism of my ideal view on law on jurisdiction. I have focused on the EU and Russian rules regarding private parties' choice of forum. At first sight, it appeared that the EU and Russia have adequate statutory provisions for enforcement of jurisdiction agreements. On a closer look, I noticed unnecessary rigidity and, at the same time, ambiguity regarding the (written) form of jurisdiction agreements in Russia.

Furthermore, I have shown that neither directly prohibited nor advised by the law, derogation agreements excluding domestic courts are accepted according to the EU Brussels jurisdiction regime and Russian private international law. I have further analysed the connection between choice-of-law and choice-of-forum in both jurisdictions. My analysis has shown that, to a lesser extent in the EU and to a larger extent in Russia, parties' choice of law may be associated with their intent and may lead to their litigation in the corresponding forum. I have asserted that selection of a certain body of law should not immediately mean parties' choice of that forum. Instead, courts should explore the parties' intent and reasoning behind their choice of law.

In addition, I have recognised as exemplary the EU approach that prioritises party autonomy to choose a forum over the *lis pendens* rule. During the reform of the Brussels I Regulation, the question was addressed and the Recast of Brussels I prioritised the court exclusively chosen by the parties over any courts that have seized jurisdiction. I have recommended the same solution for Russia to this presently unregulated question.

In the last part of chapter four, I argued that strong backing of the rule of submission to jurisdiction constitutes a cornerstone in an ideal jurisdiction regime. The rule of voluntary submission upholds the parties' de facto choice of jurisdiction. Both in contractual and non-contractual cases, actual participation of parties in the proceedings and arguing the case on its merits shall be understood as their consent to jurisdiction. Strong enforcement of this rule not only supports the party autonomy to choose a forum, but also reflects a sense of order and logic, and complements the finality of court proceedings.

Analysis of the Russian and EU jurisdiction regimes has shown contrasting levels of recognition of the submission rule. While in Europe, the Brussels I Recast explicitly recognises the expression of the parties' will by way of submission to jurisdiction, the situation in Russia is less clear. There is no manifest legislative declaration of jurisdiction by silent acceptance. It may be partially revealed from the meaning of the rule allowing the parties to transfer a case to another competent court after the proceedings have been started. It also features in commercial arbitration regulation (as opposed to adjudication by state courts), where a party's appearance and discussing a case on its merits at an arbitration tribunal is recognised as the party's submission to the tribunal's jurisdiction. I have criticised the absence of a clear rule on submission in

Russian civil procedure and have recommended its enactment as a part of the ongoing judicial reform.

Therefore, I have demonstrated that a choice of forum by private parties should take the principal place in an ideal jurisdictional system. Interests and the will of private parties should be the driving force behind determination of an appropriate forum in private international law. The parties' will is most effectively recognised through enforcement of the parties' choice of forum. It reflects the principle of free exercise of material and procedural rights by the parties to legal proceedings. In addition, establishing jurisdiction based on the parties' agreement brings legal certainty to civil and commercial relationships. By directing to a specific forum, jurisdiction agreements (both *ex ante* and *ex post*) provide security in terms of how disputes should be resolved, saving time and expense for the parties and the judiciary.

From the analysis of the EU and Russian approaches to sovereignty and private autonomy, my proposal to reverse their positions in the hierarchy of values is easier to realise in the EU than in Russia. In Russia, although there are advocates for the growing role of individuals in private and public international law,[138] the view that an individual represents a subject in international law has not yet become an accepted reality.[139] A derogative phrase originating from Soviet times '*Pishite hot' v OON*' (feel free to write to the UN as a higher power) still rings true in some respects. It suggests that it is futile for individuals to appeal against the actions of the governmental apparatus or state decisions. This means that the ideas of this book are going to take longer to be accepted in Russian society.

With this analysis complete, I will proceed to discuss limitations on the scope of recognition of party autonomy in light of considerations of party inequality and some limited state sovereignty interests.

[138] A Sultanov, 'Chelovek protiv Gosudarstva, Mezhdunarodnye Organy, Rossiia' ('Individual against the State, International Authorities, Russia') [2008] 1 *Gosudarstvennaya Vlast I Samoupravlenie* 1, fn 8, referring to Sergey Kargopolov, Ilya Iushkarev, Natalia Zakharova, etc.

[139] ibid 26–30.

PART II

Party Equality

5

Categorical Equality in the Law on Jurisdiction

I. Introduction

In this part I continue describing an ideal jurisdiction regime. I reflect on what autonomy means in the world where people do not deal as equals. I emphasise that equality should act as a balancing factor, providing certain exceptions to party autonomy as the foundation of jurisdiction. Equality is needed to ensure that full effect is given equally to the will of both parties. To that end, I explain that it is necessary to limit the power of some private parties to choose a forum in order to protect the interests of all the parties in the case.

In the first section of chapter five, I explore the quality of consent in transactions between parties of unequal bargaining power. Bargaining power can be understood as a party's level of sophistication in conducting business, informational awareness, and access to resources. I argue that an unequal arrangement is fair if the parties truly consent to it. This is most evident from my analysis of asymmetric jurisdiction clauses – agreements on jurisdiction providing parties with differing options to sue. I first argue that private parties, being rational subjects, possess the power to negotiate and agree on the admissibility of various clauses, including the right to sue in several places or restriction to sue in one place only.

At the same time, I call attention to the difference between voluntary and coerced asymmetric jurisdiction clauses. This brings the discussion to the need to protect certain categories of private parties. In the second part of this chapter, I discuss protective jurisdiction, sometimes referred to as privileged jurisdiction (Briggs) or exclusionary jurisdiction (Kaye).[1] These rules apply to disputes involving parties with the weaker bargaining power: consumers, employees or insurance holders. A party to a contract may be characterised as a consumer when acting outside their trade or profession. This EU definition is derived from *Société Bertrand v Paul Ott KG*[2] and *Benincasa v Dentalkit*[3] as well as being adopted in the

[1] Notably, the term of protective jurisdiction is not to be confused with the protective jurisdiction in the United States, referring to situations where federal courts, extended by the power of Congress, may have jurisdiction over state claims, although the claims may not involve a question subject to regulation by the federal law.

[2] Case 150/77 *Société Bertrand v Paul Ott KG* [1978] ECR I-139, I-188, para 19.

[3] Case C-269/95 *Benincasa v Dentalkit Srl* [1997] ECR I-3767.

European conflict of laws.[4] A similar definition can be found in Russian civil law as well: an individual who intends to or acquires products or services solely for personal, family, home and other needs, unconnected with carrying out commercial activity.[5]

Some may argue that the practical importance of private international law in transactions with weaker parties may be 'exaggerated',[6] as the value of consumer, employment and insurance disputes may be insignificant for the purposes of litigation.[7] Only a small percentage of consumer contracts made on the internet result in a dissatisfactory outcome.[8] In addition, controversies involving weaker parties are often resolved through discussion, negotiation or alternative dispute resolution. Potentially, a very small number of the disputes would result in actual court proceedings since, as Judge Posner once noted, 'only a lunatic or a fanatic sues for $30'.[9] Given the low value of the suits and the low chance of the transactions being disputed in state courts, the practical significance of protective jurisdiction within private international law may seem very limited.

Nevertheless, conceptually, the issue of jurisdiction in cases involving weaker parties is of utmost importance. Without it, my view on an ideal jurisdiction regime would be incomplete. Inequality of parties in transactions involving these weaker parties may lead to situations where large corporate entities take advantage or, worse, potentially abuse their power, by coercing their choice of jurisdiction. The weaker parties are especially vulnerable when agreeing to contracts of adhesion, which often contain non-negotiable jurisdiction clauses referring all disputes to the location convenient to the dominating party. In such cases, my suggestion is to safeguard a 'categorical' equality – equality of certain categories of parties, in order to give effect to their autonomy. Protecting this sort of equality therefore provides better protection for autonomy overall. To demonstrate my point,

[4] Regulation (EU) 1215/2012 of 12 December 2012 on Jurisdiction and the Recognition and Enforcement of Judgments in Civil and Commercial Matters (Recast) [2012] OJ L351/1 (the Brussels I Recast) art 17(1); Convention on the Law Applicable to Contractual Obligations [1980] OJ L266/1 (the Rome Convention) art 5; M Giuliano and P Lagarde, 'Report on the Convention on the Law Applicable to Contractual Obligations' (1980) OJ C 282/1, 23.

[5] Zakon RF o Zashchite Prav Potrebitelеĭ ot 7 fevralia 1992 g (Law of the RF on Protection of the Rights of Consumers) of 7 February 1992 no 2300-1, preamble.

[6] ZS Tang, 'Private International Law in Consumer Contracts: A European Perspective' (2010) 6 *Journal of Private International Law* 225, 227, referring to J Hill, *Cross-Border Consumer Contracts* (Oxford University Press, 2008).

[7] eg, statistical data proves that fewer than one in five consumers (18%) in the EU made an online purchase with a retailer based in another EU country in 2014. The figure contrasts with the number of consumers who made an online purchase from a business in the same country (55%). See, EU Commission, 'Common European Sales Law Proposals to be Replaced as New Consultation is Opened on Online Sales Barriers', June 2015, available at: www.out-law.com/en/articles/2015/june/common-european-sales-law-proposals-to-be-replaced-as-new-consultation-is-opened-on-online-sales-barriers.

[8] Hill (n 6) 18.

[9] B Wardhaugh, 'Bogeymen, Lunatics and Fanatics: Collective Actions and the Private Enforcement of European Competition Law' (2014) 34 *Legal Studies* 1, citing *Carnegie v Household International Inc* 376 F 3d 656, 661 (CA7 2004) (Posner J).

I engage with the provisions of positive law involving weaker parties and suggest certain corrections in line with my normative approach.

Therefore, in this chapter, I elaborate on the notions of differing bargaining power, fairness, access to justice, and the balancing of private interests. I aim to construct an approach reconciling these values with party autonomy in the law on jurisdiction.

II. Equality Limiting Party Autonomy: Normative View

A. Quality of Consent

In contractual relations between parties with unequal bargaining power, provided there is meaningful consent by the parties, party autonomy should play the leading role in determining proper jurisdiction. In such cases, what matters is quality of consent. In the commercial sphere, bargaining inequality is a frequent occurrence. The compromises of commercial negotiations lead to different terms benefiting different parties. A compromise regarding choice of jurisdiction may be offset by a better price for the contract, or other intangible benefits, such as a right to use the franchise name, or even the very possibility of signing a deal with the stronger party. It is normal that the pendulum may sway in favour of the party with stronger bargaining power, preferring to litigate in a certain forum. Similar to the adequacy (or inadequacy) of consideration, it is not up to the court's discretion to determine the adequacy of the parties' choice of forum, as long as that choice was made based on informed and full consent.

An unequal arrangement is fair if the parties truly consent to it. I understand the concept of fairness as the balance of interests among private actors in civil procedure. It transpires through equal treatment of the parties. Actors in civil and commercial relationships may in fact be unequal, and there is no solution to their general contextual inequality. However, they are regarded as equal before the court and law. The will of one party cannot entirely dominate the transaction to the point that it crushes the autonomy of the other party. Parties should have an equal chance to express their autonomy. A jurisdiction agreement reflects both parties' will regarding jurisdiction; and in commercial transactions a compromise regarding jurisdiction comes along with compromises in other aspects of the deal. Where a jurisdiction agreement is signed with the full consent of both parties, it should be considered fair even if on the surface it seems to benefit only one party. A jurisdiction agreement should normally be enforced if properly negotiated, incorporated into a contract and signed without any undue influence or duress.

In the global community of states, democratic states cherish equality and fairness as part of their constitutional regimes. Fairness closely relates to justice. The importance of fairness is reflected in the cosmopolitan view on global justice: 'justice is an obligation owed to individuals because of their moral status as human beings, independent of whatever social relations and institutions they find themselves in'.[10] Fairness forms a part of an organisation of a just society. This view is harmonious with Rawls' account on justice.[11] Rawls envisions a society of people 'untainted by differences of bargaining power and knowledge'.[12] He then asks which principles of justice would be chosen by these free and rational persons concerned to further their own interests. This hypothetical social contract constitutes the Rawlsian theory of justice – justice as fairness.[13] In line with this theory, I accept equality in the original position of private parties. I recognise the equal importance of the interests of all free rational actors in private international law.

However, for certain categories of private parties, a choice to sue at their domicile should be available, where an existing jurisdiction agreement abrogates the weaker party's right to access to justice. These categorically weaker parties are understood as the parties whose economic status, bargaining power and savvy in the business world are weaker (by default) than that of their counterparts. I concede to the possibility of limiting party autonomy in transactions involving these weaker parties in the interests of access to justice. Considerations of equal access to court by the parties can justify curbing unlimited party autonomy to choose a forum.

Why have special rules favourable to weaker parties? One of the reasons is connected with less-than-meaningful consent in such cases. In transactions involving weaker parties, choice of jurisdiction is often incorporated in non-negotiated standard-form contracts (contracts of adhesion). These standard-form contracts are usually drafted unilaterally and presented to the party with the weaker bargaining power in a 'take-it-or-leave-it' form. Particular examples of such transactions include consumer contracts. Very often, these contracts are made online, in click-wrap or browse-wrap forms. In such transactions, it cannot be maintained that the weaker party fully consents to the jurisdiction clause when forming a contract (clicking 'I agree'). Its assent, at best, can be described as blanket assent, less-than-fully-voluntary assent to the terms of contracts of adhesion, conceived as acceptance of all 'not unreasonable and indecent terms … which do not alter or eviscerate the reasonable meaning of the dickered terms'.[14] Traditionally, such assent has been found satisfactory, and a party's signature has been understood

[10] C Carmody, F Garsia and J Linarelli (eds), *Global Justice and International Economic Law* (Cambridge University Press, 2012) 6–7.

[11] J Rawls, *A Theory of Justice* (Clarendon Press, 1972 and rev edn, Oxford University Press, 1999).

[12] M Sandel (ed), *Justice: A Reader* (Oxford University Press, 2007) 203.

[13] Rawls imagines that 'in a just society the liberties of equal citizenship are taken as settled; the rights secured by justice not subject to political bargaining or to the calculus of social interests'. He formulates two principles of justice: first, 'each person is to have an equal right to the most extensive basic liberty compatible with a similar liberty for others'; second, 'social and economic inequalities are to be arranged so that they are both (a) reasonably expected to be to everyone's advantage, and (b) attached to positions and offices open to all'; see J Rawls, 'A Theory of Justice' in M Sandel (ed), *Justice: A Reader* (Oxford University Press, 2007) 214.

[14] K Llewellyn, *The Common Law Tradition: Deciding Appeals* (Quid Pro Books, 1960) 370.

as sufficient legal assent to contract terms (including in cases of contracts of adhesion).

To what extent does a contract between parties, based on the 'blanket assent' truly promote party autonomy? The worry associated with such contracts constitutes potential abuse of the rights of a large group of people and companies. In view of what we learned during the decline of freedom of contract, we came to believe that absolute freedom leads to unfair outcomes.[15] An understanding evolved that no real freedom can exist where the parties are in grossly unequal positions. That is why equality ought to curb party autonomy. Otherwise, unlimited party autonomy in jurisdiction will inevitably lead to opportunism by the stronger party who will take advantage of the weaker party. Certain protections from the government of certain categories of private parties actually enforces the autonomy of weaker parties, which is otherwise lost in comparison to the autonomy of stronger parties dictating their contract conditions.

Party expectations as regards convenient forum can and should be met, as the forum most convenient to the parties reflects their interests that an ideal jurisdiction regime should respect. However, in light of categorical equality, a balance needs to be found between the parties' expectations regarding efficiency and independence from the state, and the state's interests to protect weaker parties and account for the wellbeing of their domiciliaries.

B. Asymmetric Jurisdiction Clauses in the Commercial Context Versus in Contracts of Adhesion with Weaker Parties

As outlined above, asymmetric jurisdiction agreements, when signed, express the will of the parties. Parties should be at liberty to choose to sign a contract or not, to negotiate certain unfavourable terms. Implicit agreements favouring one party can be enforced where 'there is no ambiguity as to the parties' intentions'.[16] Where parties have unequal access to information, resources, negotiation skills, etc, but are originally equal market participants, free to consent to any agreement they choose, their asymmetric jurisdiction clauses should be given force. However, a certain degree of limitation towards party autonomy may be appropriate. Unilateral jurisdiction agreements in contracts of adhesion should only be given effect where they do not abrogate the weaker party's access to justice.

This analysis is best explained when illustrated by enforcement of asymmetric jurisdiction clauses in practice. These clauses represent a type of jurisdiction

[15] See earlier discussion on 'Delimiting the Modern Concept of Autonomy for Jurisdiction' in ch 3 of this book.

[16] U Magnus and P Mankowski (eds), *European Commentaries on Private International Law: Brussels I Regulation*, 2nd edn (Sellier European Law Publishers, 2012) 504. However, the rule is limited in cases involving the categorically 'weaker' parties.

agreement, granting one choice for one party and a different (or several) choice(s) to the other.

Unilateral jurisdiction clauses constitute the subject of debate both in Russia and the EU. In a couple of Russian cases, asymmetric jurisdiction clauses were found invalid. In its review of lower courts' practice in 2018, the Supreme Court in Russia describes a case where disputes were to be resolved by commercial arbitration, but one party – the seller – had an option to sue at state courts.[17] The Supreme Court commented on the imbalance of rights of such asymmetric agreements and declared such agreements invalid in part by not providing the same choice to sue at state courts to the other party.[18] Relying on general principles of fair trial, the Court summarised that a dispute resolution agreement may not provide one party only with the right to sue at a competent court and deprive the other party of the same right.[19]

In a case involving Sony Ericsson,[20] the Supreme *Arbitrazh* Court in Russia examined the validity of jurisdiction clauses where one party was provided with an option to initiate court litigation and the other was to resolve disputes by arbitration. The Court noted that such unilateral prorogation agreements put one party at an advantage and violated the balance of interests of the parties. The agreement was determined void because it violated the parties' rights of equal access to justice.

This outcome is surprising given a number of previous Russian court decisions validating asymmetric jurisdiction clauses.[21] In those cases, parties agreed on two or more options of dispute resolution different for each party, and Russian courts enforced such agreements. Some practitioners in Russia maintain that such situations occur often, especially where one party bears higher financial risks and prefers to have several alternatives for dispute resolution.

This coincides with Fentiman's commentary on unilateral jurisdiction clauses in England. Where there is one financially dominant party, it is common to have a non-exclusive jurisdiction agreement, conferring jurisdiction to one forum but allowing each party to sue another in any other competent court.[22] Fentiman asserts

[17] Obzor Praktiki Rassmotreniia Sudami Del, Sviazannykh s Ispolneniem Funktsiĭ Sodeĭstviia I Kontrolia v Otnoshenii Treteĭskikh Sudov I Arbitrazheĭ (Review of Practice by Courts of Cases Connected to Fulfilling the Function of Assistance and Control of Arbitral Tribunals and Arbitration), approved by the Presidium of the Supreme Court 26 December 2018.

[18] ibid.

[19] ibid.

[20] Postanovlenie Presidiuma Vysshego Arbitrazhnogo Suda ot 19 iiunia 2012 (Resolution of the Supreme *Arbitrazh* Court) no 1831/12 of 19 June 2012.

[21] See, for instance, A Kucher, A Yadykin and A Asoskov, 'Are Asymmetric Jurisdiction Clauses Valid According to the Russian Law Following the Supreme *Arbitrazh* Court Decree in Sony Ericsson Case?' (Debevoise & Plimpton Client Update, 28 November, 2012), available at: documents.lexology.com/ba1a3296-1ef5-489a-8c48-a7b06dac2125.pdf, referring to Postanovlenie Federal'nogo Arbitrazhnogo Suda Moskovskogo Okruga ot 21 dekabria 2009 g (Decision of the Federal *Arbitrazh* Court of Moscow Circuit) of 21 December 2009 case no КГ-A40/11967; Postanovlenie Federal'nogo Arbitrazhnogo Suda Severo-Zapadnogo Okruga ot 23 sentiabria 2004 g (Decision of the Federal *Arbitrazh* Court of Northern-Western Circuit) of 23 September 2004 case no A21-2499/03-C1.

[22] R Fentiman, 'Unilateral Jurisdiction Agreements in Europe' (2013) 72 *Cambridge Law Journal* 24.

that such agreements contribute to the readiness of banks to provide finance. They minimise the risks that a debtor's obligations would be unenforceable. He finds it difficult to conceive that such agreements may be invalidated in English law.

The validity of such asymmetric agreements has been affirmed in common law, for instance, in *Continental Bank v Aeakos*.[23] There, a jurisdiction agreement stated that each defendant 'irrevocably submits to the jurisdiction of the English courts … but the bank reserves the right to proceed under this agreement in the court of any other country claiming or having jurisdiction in respect thereof'. In that case, Greek loan borrowers filed a suit in Greece against an American bank, in spite of the jurisdiction clause obliging them to submit all claims to England. The bank sought an injunction in England against the defendants to restrain them from taking any further steps in the Greek proceedings. The injunction was granted and subsequently upheld on appeal. The English court enforced the jurisdiction agreement between the parties and viewed the commencement of the Greek proceedings as a clear breach of the jurisdiction agreement. That alone was enough to grant the injunction. Additionally, the American bank incurred losses as a result of the default of the borrowers. The bank had the right to recover damages, and the English court was the most appropriate forum in which to do so, because the borrowers preliminarily agreed on resorting to English jurisdiction. As Gatehouse J emphasised, the option reserved in favour of the bank to sue in England and elsewhere was 'deliberately omitted' in relation to the borrowers.[24] Those were the terms of the agreement, under which the bank took the risk of facilitating the loan. The jurisdiction clause was upheld because on its true construction it obliged the defendants to submit irrevocably to the jurisdiction of English courts. The injunction was the only effective remedy for the defendants' breach of contract. The party who breached the jurisdiction agreement 'set at naught [the jurisdiction agreement] which was the product of the free will of the parties'.[25] Another policy factor that transpired in the decision was the notion that the best court to decide questions of exclusive jurisdiction is the court chosen by the parties in the jurisdiction agreement.

A different view has been taken by a French court in the *Rothschild* case (involving a weaker party).[26] There, a French citizen, Ms X, had a contract with a Luxembourg bank. The contract stipulated that Luxembourg courts had exclusive jurisdiction, but the bank reserved the right to also sue at the defendant's domicile or in any other competent court. Thus, the asymmetric jurisdiction clause resembled the same form as the Sony Ericsson case in Russia. The *Cour de cassation* regarded the forum selection clause invalid. It decided that Ms X was free to sue in France. It found that uncertainty about the unilateral jurisdiction clause was

[23] *Continental Bank NA v Aeakos SA* [1994] 1 WLR 588.
[24] ibid 593.
[25] ibid 597.
[26] Cour de cassation, Arrêt 983 du 26 septembre 2012 (Decision of the Court of Cassation) of 26 September 2012 no 983 (11-26.022), available at: www.courdecassation.fr/jurisprudence_2/premiere_chambre_civile_568/983_26_24187.html.

incompatible with the Brussels jurisdiction regime. The clause was drafted to the sole benefit of the bank, and the court invalidated it in its entirety. The French court interpreted the forum clause 'potestative' or merely granting an option for the bank to sue in Luxembourg. The decision was based on the French concept of *potestativité* from Article 1174 of the French Civil Code. It reflected the cultural attitude of France towards jurisdiction over French nationals. (France is renowned for the 'exorbitant' French jurisdiction over its nationals, notwithstanding whether the suit is connected with France, based on well-known Article 14 of the French Civil Code.) It also illustrated the French commitment to protect weaker parties.[27]

This also echoes another Russian domestic case involving an individual (Mr Ponedelnikov) and a bank (Tusarbank).[28] The parties had a bank deposit contract. The contract was offered to Mr Ponedelnikov by the bank as its standard agreement for bank deposit; it contained a dispute resolution clause directing all claims to the courts at the location of the bank. The clause was subsequently disputed as violating Mr Ponedelnikov's rights. Since he was a weaker party (consumer), he claimed his right to sue either at his location, or at the place of signing or performance of the contract, or at the location of the defendant. The Supreme Court of the Russian Federation, when considering the case at the last instance, decided that the dispute resolution clause in favour of the bank in the contract of adhesion violated the statutory rights of the consumer. Under statutory rights, the Court meant, inter alia, the right of access to court. Therefore, the case was resolved with an outcome similar to the *Rothschild* case in France but based on a slightly different rationale.

C. Protective Jurisdiction: Counterarguments

The approach to afford jurisdictional protection to certain categories of parties corresponds to the existing regimes in the EU and Russia. Kaye notes that the 'perceived need to protect certain economically weak parties to international transactions' urged drafters of the original Brussels Convention[29] and subsequent Accession Convention 1978 to provide a more favourable jurisdictional environment to these weak parties.[30] Similarly, Briggs contends that, presumably, it was inequality of power that 'triggered' the application of these privileged jurisdiction rules in the first place.[31] Dickinson calls the European concern for protection of

[27] MJA société v Apple Sales International [2016] ILPr 13 where the Cour de Cassation gave effect to an asymmetric agreement under Brussels I. See the follow up in C-595/17 CJEU judgment of 24 October 2018 and the AG's Opinion para 37 of 5 July 2018.

[28] Opredelenie Verkhovnogo Suda RF ot 10 maia 2011 g (Decision of the Supreme Court of the RF) of 10 May 2011 no 5-B11-46.

[29] Brussels Convention on Jurisdiction and the Enforcement of Judgments in Civil and Commercial Matters [1972] OJ L299/32 (the Brussels Convention).

[30] P Kaye, *Civil Jurisdiction and Enforcement of Foreign Judgments* (Professional Books Ltd, 1987) 824.

[31] A Briggs, *Civil Jurisdiction and Judgments* (Oxford University Press, 2008) 134.

those vulnerable to exploitation, especially consumers, a 'legitimate' one.[32] The Brussels jurisdiction regime sets out protective jurisdiction rules to balance out the disadvantages of weaker parties in negotiations and contracting. Employees, insurance bearers and consumers are allowed to sue defendants at their own domicile. This also corresponds with the protective jurisdiction rules in Russia, as I detail in my analysis of positive law in the next section of this chapter.

Nevertheless, several counterarguments to having protective jurisdiction need to be addressed. First, it could be argued that weaker parties are not really subject to exploitation in the context of purchasing goods or services, concluding employment contracts or signing up for insurance plans. In the modern interconnected, fast-developing, and technology-driven society, the practical understanding of the average consumer these days can be demonstrated by their behaviour. A survey coordinated by the European Commission, Directorate General for Communication and conducted by TNS Political & Social[33] shows that the proportion of consumers who made at least one purchase across the border in 2012 has nearly tripled since 2006, to reach an average of 15 per cent.

Where consumers search and actively pursue obtaining a certain product beyond their domicile, it seems reasonable to assume that they should be ready to bear the cost and inconvenience that may be associated with dealing with a foreign supplier. They exercise their autonomy in reaching beyond the borders of their state. In exchange for the possibility of obtaining a certain product (not available at their location), they enter into the contracts of adhesion with a foreign supplier.

Moreover, enforcement of jurisdiction clauses in consumer contracts actually benefits consumers. Suppliers of certain products, when deprived of the possibility of a standard dispute resolution clause, would be compelled to litigate in the fora of their potential consumers. Subjecting companies to jurisdiction at the domicile of all their consumers means increased (potential and actual) expenses for businesses. This will inevitably increase the cost of the product. In this regard, are the interests of the majority of weaker parties, those who may never dispute anything in relation to the transaction, really taken care of? This point may be further demonstrated in light of a theory of price as liquidated damages illustrated by Markovits.[34] In his argument, he mentions that consumers paying a comparatively high price for a toaster, in essence, pay for the possibility of a lifetime warranty, unlimited returns and other benefits. Therefore, companies offering products of

[32] A Dickinson, 'Surveying the Proposed Brussels I *bis* Regulation: Solid Foundations but Renovation Needed' in A Bonomi and GP Romano (eds) *Yearbook of Private International Law Vol XII* (De Gruyter, 2010).

[33] European Commission, 'Consumer Attitude towards Cross-Border Trade and Consumer Protection' (Flash Eurobarometer 358 Report 2013), available at: ec.europa.eu/public_opinion/flash/fl_358_en.pdf.

[34] D Markovits, 'Sharing Ex Ante and Sharing Ex Post: The Non-Contractual Basis of Fiduciary Relations' (Max Planck Institute for Comparative and International Private law, Aktuelle Stunde (weekly discussions on comparative law), Hamburg, Germany, July 2014). Also, D Markovits and A Schwartz, 'The Myth of Efficient Breach: New Defenses of the Expectation Interest' (2011) 97 *Virginia Law Review* 1939.

ordinary daily needs for an astronomical price do so to account for future expenses in association with the product. The same principle may be applied to the present discussion on jurisdiction. To account for the cost and inconvenience of being sued at the various locations of their consumers, suppliers will simply raise the price. In a bad case scenario, consumers will get the product for a raised price. In the worst case scenario, producers will be discouraged from offering the product in a particular area altogether, and consumers will suffer from the lack of a possibility of acquiring the product.

Of course, in addition to protective jurisdiction, protection of weaker parties is done through other areas of law. Consumer law is central in EU private law; the interests of consumers are given great protection in the EU.[35] Russia protects the rights of consumers and employees though the Law on Protecting the Rights of the Consumers. Likewise, the Consumer Protection Act 1987 in the UK ensures protection of consumers against potential defects in acquired products and liability of the supplier. The point is that protecting the interests of weaker parties is also done in the realm of contract law, labour law and other areas at the national and supranational level.

What would a jurisdiction regime look like without these special protective jurisdiction rules for weaker parties? English residual jurisdiction rules provide one example. Common law determines jurisdiction in disputes with UK weaker parties against foreign employers, insurance agents and sellers,[36] and in disputes relating to non-EU domiciled weaker parties and English 'stronger' parties. Unlike the EU jurisdiction regime, traditional English common law treats insurance, consumer and employment contracts no differently from any other contracts. Jurisdiction agreements are given effect if properly incorporated into a contract. Voluntary appearance in court is interpreted as submission to jurisdiction, unless expressly declared that the appearance was made only to dispute the matter of jurisdiction. UK-domiciled weaker parties do not have any special jurisdictional provision under UK law to bring a claim against a non-EU domiciled 'stronger' party in England. Rather, general rules of jurisdiction apply. Foreign suppliers, insurers and employers may be sued in England, and permission may be sought to serve them outside English jurisdiction. Having considered the circumstances, an English court will accept the claim (and permit serving out the jurisdiction, if applicable) only if it finds sufficient connection of the claim with English jurisdiction. Notably, claims by British employees against non-EU businesses can rarely hold in an English court, unless there is some close connection with the UK or EU.[37]

[35] See, eg, C Twigg-Flesner (ed), *The Cambridge Companion to European Union Private Law* (Cambridge University Press, 2010) 7.

[36] Not treated as having domicile or a 'deemed' domicile in the EU by having a branch, agency or other establishment in the EU.

[37] C Woodruff and K Reed, 'Comparative Study of "Residual Jurisdiction" in Civil and Commercial Disputes in the EU: National Report for England' (National Report on Residual Jurisdiction, England, for the General Report: Study on Residual Jurisdiction edited by Arnaud Nuyts, 3 September 2007) 10, available at: ec.europa.eu/civiljustice/news/docs/study_resid_jurisd_england_en.pdf.

Absence of special exclusionary treatment of weaker parties when it comes to jurisdiction does not mean disregarding the interests of the weaker parties. They are protected, while the suits involving their interests are filed under the usual procedure. One additional important feature of the English common law is the doctrine of *forum conveniens* which helps determine the most appropriate forum in which to conduct proceedings. Existence of the doctrine distinguishes the English common law from most EU European jurisdictions. At the EU level, the doctrine does not apply. This may explain the rigidity of the structure of Brussels I, and its attempt to encompass all the specific cases where special jurisdictional rules may be necessary. In addition, in contrast to England, the EU lawmakers aim to protect the common market, about which English lawmakers did not have to worry at the time of setting up the jurisdictional mechanism. The considerations of the common market and consumer protection across the EU might have been another reason behind the design of EU protective jurisdiction.

D. Access to Justice and Categorical Equality

Notwithstanding the counterarguments to protective jurisdiction above, an approach based on party autonomy and categorical equality would account for the possibility of providing weaker parties with the right to surpass jurisdiction agreements in adhesion contracts. The justification for this emanates from consideration of access to justice. The idea of equal access to justice is closely connected with the theory of corrective and distributive justice. In essence, it declares that people are entitled to their right for a fair trial, defence, representation, protection of their interests, judicial solution delivered in a timely fashion, etc. The right of access to justice means that there should be no gaps in law where a person cannot get effective justice. The fair allocation of claims to appropriate courts constitutes an integral part of the overall access to justice (although not the totality of it).

The understanding of access to justice differs from one geographical region to another. For instance, in Europe, access to justice developed as an entitlement granted by the state in the aftermath of distribution of power within the state. The power belonged to the European sovereigns. The power eventually transformed (and transferred) to governmental power. The government then conferred the rights on individuals. Eventually, all members of society were granted the benefit of enjoying equal rights, as is now reflected in the European Convention on Human Rights (ECHR)[38] and implemented in the laws of the EU Member States. Some credit could be attributed to enlightenment thought and the ideas of individual rights in the Western intellectual tradition that transpired into all areas of

[38] The European Convention on Human Rights of 4 November 1950.

European law. Furthermore, distributive justice aspirations promoted by Marx and Engels have left an impact in political and legal thinking in European states, emphasising equality in economic, social and legal spheres.

A recent tendency regarding access to justice in Europe constitutes a shift from equality to efficiency. For instance, a study evaluating various criteria of justice in 47 countries in Europe[39] revealed that access to justice is not solely implemented through a wider forum selection or having an attorney. It is not simply about flexibility for a claimant to bring suits at a certain location. Many other aspects of efficiency of judicial systems[40] need to be at work. Having a day in court is paramount; however, it also matters whether that day in court is spent meaningfully (making the aggrieved party 'whole'). This would depend on availability of legal aid, time required to meet with a judge, etc. Thus, many factors need to work in order to provide the parties to a civil suit with the right to protect their interests, resolve disputes and recover damages.

The European approach towards equality and access to justice concentrates on the equality of position. In this regard, it contrasts with the American equality of opportunity. Whereas Europe views the need to provide reasonable access to court for all, the US approach focuses on equal opportunity to have a day in court. In the US, the meaning of 'access to justice' is predicated upon the historic turmoil that occurred during the fight for independence and the civil war. The utmost necessity of access to the court was forged during the making of the state (hence, the judicial discretion granted by the Constitution). At the outset of the American state, the function of the court constituted proper allocation of governmental authority: 'imposing restraints on governments'.[41] Further commitment to equality and individual rights in the US was established through the struggle for equal rights, recognised in the constitutional amendments.

In a comparative perspective, English legal tradition views access to justice as a right to a remedy. The right to open access to the courts to obtain a remedy for injury is 'rooted in Magna Carta' and 'nourished in the English struggle for individual liberty and conscience rights'.[42] These elements of access to justice are

[39] European Commission for the Efficiency of Justice (CEPEJ), *European Judicial Systems – Edition 2014* (2012 *data*): *Efficiency and Quality of Justice*, available at: www.coe.int/t/dghl/cooperation/cepej/evaluation/2014/Rapport_2014_en.pdf, a comprehensive study of access to justice in 47 European countries beyond the territorial boundaries of the European Union, including the EU Member States, the EEA, Switzerland, Russia and other former Soviet states, Turkey and the former Yugoslav states.

[40] eg, public expenditure allocated to courts, the prosecution system and legal aid, variation of the absolute number of all courts, level of computerisation of courts, number of professional judges in courts per 100,000 inhabitants, the clearance rate (the number of resolved cases within the year divided by the number of incoming cases within the same period and multiplied by 100), average length of proceedings, salaries of judges and prosecutors, etc.

[41] A von Mehren and P Murray, *Law in the United States* (Cambridge University Press, 2007) 146.

[42] T Phillips, 'The Constitutional Right to a Remedy' (2003) 78 *New York University Law Review* 1309, 1310, referring to ch 29 of the 1225 version of Magna Carta, and to D Howard, *The Road from Runnymede: Magna Carta and Constitutionalism in America* (University of Virginia Press, 1968) 6–8.

consistent with the general European protection of human rights (Article 6 of the ECHR, guaranteeing the right to a fair trial).[43]

At the same time, in Russia, access to justice is a constitutionally protected right.[44] More particularly, the Code of Civil Procedure reflects the goals of judicial procedure which include the 'correct and timely examination and settlement of civil cases in order to protect the infringed or challenged rights, freedoms and legitimate interests of people, institutions, rights and interests of the Russian Federation'.[45] The Code of *Arbitrazh* Procedure envisions similar goals for commercial and economic dispute resolution including 'the protection of violated or challenged rights and legal interests of persons … provision of accessibility of justice … fair, public judicial examination … etc'.[46] Naturally, such a right of access to justice implies the capacity of the party, admissibility of the claim, competence of the corresponding court, and other formal requirements for submitting a claim. As best summarised by Nokhrin:

> [W]here it comes to access to justice, [Russian] scholars traditionally draw analytical schematics … accentuating its territorial component (territorial accessibility of courts [etc]), its managerial aspect (sufficient number of courts, judges [etc]), and its institutional (integration of courts into the overall system of social protection, such as public defenders' office, etc) and procedural aspects (accessibility, simplicity, swiftness, low-cost and effectiveness of the procedure), etc'.[47]

The scholarly understanding of the right to access to justice in Russia may be traced back to German jurisprudence (Savigny, Windscheid) in the mid-nineteenth century.[48] Following these traditions, Nefed'ev,[49] Degenkolb and Vach formulated understanding of the public and procedural nature of access to justice in Russia in the end of the nineteenth century. Contemporary Russian scholars connect the right of access to justice to a number of different aspects.[50] One contemporary scholar views access to justice (*obespechenie dostupnosti*

[43] The right to a fair trial (the right to an effective remedy and to a fair trial guaranteed) is further foreseen in Art 47 of the Charter of Fundamental Rights of the EU [2000] OJ C 364/1.

[44] Konstitutsiia Rossiĭskoĭ Federatsii (Constitution of the RF) art 2 (Russia).

[45] Grazhdanskiĭ Protsessual'nyĭ Kodeks Rossiĭskoĭ Federatsii (Code of Civil Procedure of the RF) of 14 November 2002 no 138-ФЗ (the CCP) art 2.

[46] Arbitrazhno-Protsessual'nyĭ Kodeks Rossiĭskoĭ Federatsii (Code of *Arbitrazh* (Commercial) Procedure of the RF) of 24 July 2002 no 95-ФЗ (Russia) (the CAP) art 2.

[47] Email from Dmitry Nokhrin to author (8 May 2015). Also, D Nokhrin, 'Russian National Report: Goals of Civil Justice' in D Maleshin (ed), *Civil Procedure in Cross-Cultural Dialogue: Eurasia Context* (Statut, 2012).

[48] T Sakhnova, *Tsivilisticheskiĭ Protsess* (*Civil Procedure*) (Prospect, 2014) ch 9.

[49] E Nefed'ev, *Osnovnye Nachala Grazhdanskogo Sudoproizvodstva* (*Fundamental Principles of Civil Procedure*) (Kazan, 1895).

[50] V Yarkov, 'Access to Justice: Foreign Persons and Russia's New Arbitration Procedure Code (Part I)' (2007) 32 *Review of Central and East European Law* 121, 123. Also, V Yarkov, *Juridicheskie Fakty v Mekhanizme Realisatsii Norm Grazhdanskogo Protsessualnogo Prava* (*Legal Facts in the Mechanism of Application of Rules of Civil Procedure*) (SYuI, 1992) 110, 122.

pravosudiia) as the general task at the stage of initiation of judicial procedure, which is attained by bringing the matter before the court and of providing its acceptance by the court.[51] Others set forth essential basics of access to justice,[52] viewing it as a manifestation of the right to submit a claim to the court and the duty of the court to accept the duly submitted claim, the right to appeal, the right to extend certain time frames, and the right to have the court fees waived. The principle is implemented in practice 'in actual organisational management of court work'.[53] The right of access to justice is directly linked to the effectiveness of civil procedure. The effectiveness depends on court workload, reasonableness of court fees,[54] and exemption of fees for certain categories of claimants (in alimony cases, in claims for damages by the injured party, etc), the guarantee of access to competent legal counsel (which should be free in certain cases) and other factors.

Consistent with the above understandings of access to justice, my normative view on jurisdiction provides for protection of some categories of private parties. I see an allocation of jurisdiction in direct relation to the access to justice. Exclusive enforcement of jurisdiction agreements in adhesion contracts may limit some parties' access to justice. To prevent that, jurisdiction of additional courts may be allocated by special rules of protective jurisdiction (as is done already in the EU and Russia).

E. State as a Fiduciary of Weaker Parties

Suppose the claim is accepted that weaker parties should have equal access to justice, which sometimes translates into overriding a jurisdiction agreement drawn by a stronger party in a contract of adhesion. Does that mean that the state ought to provide access to a *convenient* jurisdiction to weaker parties?

[51] G Zhilin, 'Tseli Grazhdanskogo Sudoproizvodstva i Ikh Realizatsiia v Sude Pervoi Instantsii' ('Goals of Civil Procedure and their Realisation in a Court of First Instance') (LLD Book, Institute of Law and Comparative Law adjunct to the Government of Russia 2000) s II, para 6.

[52] I Prihodko, 'Dostupnost' Pravosudiia v Arbitrazhnom i Grazhdanskom Protsesse: Osnovnye Problemy ('Access to Justice in Arbitrazh and Civil Procedure: Main Issues') (Izdatelsvo of Law Faculty of Saint-Petersburg State University, 2005); V Zhuikov, *Sudebnaia Reforma: Problemy Dostupa k Pravosudiiu* (*Judicial Reform: Problems of Access to Justice*) (Statut, 2006).

[53] I Prihod'ko, 'Dostupnost' Pravosudiia v Arbitrazhnom i Grazhdanskom Protsesse: Osnovnye Problemy' ('Access to Justice in Arbitrazh and Civil Procedure: Main Issues') (speech at the All-Russian Research and Practice Conference on Access to Justice, Moscow, January–February 2001), available at: www.legist.ru/conf.html.

[54] A famous reference by Prihod'ko goes as follows: 'Even amidst the poverty of the majority of the population, a court fee for civil claim should hardly be equated to the cost of a bottle of beer, a pack of cigarettes or two trips in the subway. Access to justice should have its reasonable limits, which includes, inter alia, respect for the judge and his work': Prihod'ko, ibid.

In this regard, protection of categorical equality in jurisdiction may be conceived through the theory of the state as a fiduciary. The concept of fiduciary stipulates acting in the best interests and on behalf of another. Fiduciary relationships appear where one person grants another a mandate and conferred associated powers to advance the specific interests of another person or an abstract purpose.[55] Fiduciary relationships usually refer to relationships between a doctor and a patient, a parent and a child, or a legal counsel and a client. Similar to these relationships, a state can be viewed as a fiduciary of its domiciliary parties. The fiduciary theory of the state exists as an alternative to the social contract tradition. As Finn suggested decades ago, the 'authority of the state is inherently fiduciary'.[56] The idea of using the state apparatus to protect the people and legal entities is not new. As John Stuart Mill contended: 'in a liberal society, the machinery of the state can be legitimately used to prevent harm to others'.[57] Furthermore, Marx warned against the laissez-faire style of contracting, with contracts negotiated without any governmental interference, and stronger market players taking advantage of the weaker.

In light of these theories, it can be further argued that individuals entrust control to public bodies which have the moral authority to protect the weakest.[58] This echoes the morality of unequal autonomy as illustrated by the insight by Castro: 'though we cherish freedom and equality, we nevertheless generally accept the asymmetry of autonomy involved in some kinds of relations, protesting only in specific cases that something has gone morally wrong'.[59] To prevent the tipping of the balance in favour of large corporate enterprises, state interference to protect weaker parties is required. This delegation of authority to the state makes sense if regarding the state as a fiduciary of its citizens.

How does inequality of consent, access to justice and fiduciary role of the government to protect weaker parties manifest itself in practice? In the following section, I analyse the existing rules on jurisdiction involving weaker parties in the EU and Russia, to determine their adequacy in light of my normative view.

[55] P Miller, 'Dimensions of Fiduciary Loyalty' (Private Law Workshop at Harvard Law School Working Paper, Fall 2015, on file with author).

[56] P Miller, 'Principles of Public Fiduciary Administration' in A Scolnicov and T Kahana (eds), *Boundaries of State, Boundaries of Rights* (Cambridge University Press, 2016), available at: ssrn.com/abstract=2613948, referring to P Finn, 'The Forgotten "Trust": The People and the State' in M Cope (ed), *Equity: Issues and Trends* (Federation Press, 1995).

[57] N Oman, 'Unity and Pluralism in Contract Law' (2005) 103 *Michigan Law Review*, 1483, 1487, referring to JS Mill, *On Liberty* (Longman, Roberts, & Green Co, 1859).

[58] Questions of who constructs such moral authority and whether it varies are outside the scope of this book. For the purpose of jurisdiction, it is assumed we are talking about a generally accepted duty of the state to protect its domiciliaries.

[59] S Castro, 'The Morality of Unequal Autonomy: Revising Kant's Concept of Status for Shareholders' (2014) 121 *Journal of Business Ethics* 593. Based on the Kantian theory of status as a nexus, duties of virtue and duties of right, Castro takes the premise beyond domestic interpersonal relationship, and applies it to relationships between individuals and organisations. More particularly, she justifies the position of stakeholders in corporations, and the morality of responsibility entrusted in them.

III. Critical Analysis of Positive Law on Protective Jurisdiction

A. Protective Jurisdiction in the EU

The Brussels jurisdiction regime provides a comprehensive system of rules protecting EU weaker parties (consumers, insured individuals and employees). Existence of protective jurisdictional rules in Europe has overall been accepted and approved. In fact, EU developments in consumers' access to justice have been called 'the first comprehensive and sophisticated' and 'the most influential' conflicts of law system in the world.[60]

In particular, by virtue of sections 3, 4 and 5 of the Brussels I Recast, weaker parties are guaranteed predictability and the convenience of being sued at the place of their domicile, and suing at their domicile or at the location of the other party. This jurisdictional protection applies, no matter whether the dispute involves an EU or a foreign entrepreneur represented in the EU through a branch or agency, or by directing its activity towards the particular Member State (thus, 'deemed' to have a domicile in the EU). These principles carry an exclusionary nature: they surpass the general rule of jurisdiction (suing at the location of the defendant), special jurisdictional rules and, in certain cases, jurisdiction based on the parties' agreement. In addition, foreign judicial decisions violating these protective jurisdictional provisions cannot be enforced in the EU. This protective rule in the Brussels jurisdiction regime can be aligned with the protection of 'weaker parties' via the choice of law Rome I Regulation. In particular, the Rome I Regulation limits choice of law in a contract where it unreasonably or unfairly affects consumers, employees and insured persons.[61]

As a result of the recast of the Brussels I Regulation[62] (by the Brussels I Recast), jurisdictional protection now extends beyond the EU. EU consumers can also bring suits against non-EU defendants at the place of their domicile in the EU.[63] This amendment appears significant for non-EU companies that provide goods and services to EU consumers. However, the magnitude of the rule may be overestimated. Brand refers to this change as, perhaps, 'another of those rules that creates theoretical problems with little practical impact'.[64] It may potentially open EU courts to a large number of consumer suits. At the same time, most of

[60] Tang, 'Private International Law in Consumer Contracts' (n 6) 226.

[61] Regulation (EC) 593/2008 of the European Parliament and of the Council of 17 June 2008 on the law applicable to contractual obligations [2008] L177/6, arts 6–8 (the Rome I Regulation).

[62] Regulation (EC) 44/2001 of 22 December 2000 on Jurisdiction and the Recognition and Enforcement of Judgments in Civil and Commercial Matters [2001] OJ L12/1 (the Brussels I Regulation).

[63] Brussels I Recast art 18(1).

[64] R Brand, 'Jurisdictional Developments and The New Hague Judgments Project' in *A Commitment to Private International Law: Essays in Honour of Hans van Loon* (Intersentia 2013) 98.

the consumer claims are too small to take to court, and we have yet to see how this change impacts business-to-consumer activity in the EU.

During the revision of the Brussels I Regulation, the European Commission also proposed to extend protective jurisdiction for EU-domiciled employees and insured persons beyond the EU territory, by deleting the wording 'domiciled in a Member State' in the corresponding articles stating that insurers and employers can be sued at the state of their domicile, or at the place where the corresponding weaker party is domiciled.[65] Such a change would result in any actions by EU-domiciled employees and insurance holders against foreign insurers and employers to be brought to EU courts, rather than pursuant to relevant national law. Upon its review, the European Parliament rejected this proposal justifying doing so by suggesting that it does nothing to improve the position of non-EU defendants, plus the Commission had no mandate to make such changes.[66]

In the final text of the Brussels I Recast, however, the protective jurisdiction of EU employees was nevertheless extended to claims against non-EU domiciled defendants in certain cases. Non-EU employers may be sued in a Member State court if their employees habitually carry out work in the EU, or where the business was situated in the EU.[67] This reflects the debate raised in *Mahamdia v Algeria*,[68] regarding whether the protective jurisdiction rules in relation to EU-domiciled employees could also apply to a dispute relating to employment between a foreign state embassy in Germany and its former employee. The European Court of Justice (ECJ) interpreted that the embassy in a Member State should be considered an 'establishment', therefore, the Brussels regime applied to the dispute in question.

Nonetheless, some scholars have discussed the notion of jurisdiction over employers domiciled abroad. For instance, Gulotta calls the extension of the jurisdiction of EU Member States' courts towards non-EU employers the 'most innovative feature of the Brussels I Recast'.[69] She does not see the new rule labelled as giving rise to exorbitant grounds of jurisdiction. She elaborates that the extension of jurisdiction is justified by a very strong connection of a case with the

[65] Proposal for a Regulation of the European Parliament and the Council on Jurisdiction and the Recognition of Judgments in Civil and Commercial Matters (Recast), 30 January 2014, Brussels, COM (2010) 748 final, 2010/0383 (COD) Brussels, 14 December 2010 (the Commission's Proposal) arts 9, 19.

[66] Draft Report on the Proposal for Regulation of the European Parliament and of the Council on Jurisdiction and the Enforcement of Judgments in Civil and Commercial Matters (recast) (COM(2010)0748 – C7-0433/2010 – 2010/0383(COD)), 28 June 2011 (the Draft Parliament Resolution) recitals 16 and 17: justification.

[67] Brussels I Recast art 21(2).

[68] Case C-154/11 *Mahamdia v Algeria* [2012] ILPr 41; [2014] All ER (EC) 96.

[69] C Gulotta, 'L'Estensione Della Giurisdizione Nei Confronti Dei Datori di Lavoro Domiciliati All'estero: il Caso Mahamdia e il Nuovo Regime del Regolamento Bruxelles I-bis' ('The Extension of Jurisdiction over Employers Domiciled Abroad: The Mahamdia Case and the New Regime under the Brussels I-bis Regulation') (2013) 49 *Rivista di diritto internazionale privato e processuale* 619, summary by Francesca Villata in Conflict of Laws.net, available at: conflictoflaws.net/2014/third-issue-of-2013s-rivista-di-diritto-internazionale-privato-e-processuale.

European system.[70] If employers choose to base themselves in the EU, they should expect to be bound by EU imperative norms protecting EU employees.

Extension of EU protective jurisdiction beyond EU borders inadvertently implies exorbitance, excessiveness and disrespect towards non-EU domiciliary parties. Unreasonable extension of EU power beyond its territory is not desirable. Perhaps, this extension would be more acceptable where the third states' legislatures deliberately agreed to it. The extension of EU provisions that provide protective jurisdiction for EU-domiciled employees beyond the EU territory inadvertently implies exorbitance and excessiveness towards non-EU domiciliary parties. At the same time, plaintiffs with weaker bargaining power, in some cases, need to be afforded a wider choice of jurisdiction than that prescribed in a form contract provided by a stronger party. To reconcile this contradiction, a balance needs to be found. There is still the necessity to account for the stronger parties' interests, which seem abridged by the EU rules unilaterally extending onto non-EU domiciled parties. Perhaps protecting individuals (but not small companies acting as consumers) should be the line where protection of EU weaker parties is acceptable beyond the EU.

In practice, EU consumers are afforded jurisdictional protection – to sue at their domicile – if they act as passive consumers.[71] This means that a consumer is deprived of protection when actively pursuing the transaction with a foreign supplier carrying out his business activity outside the consumer's domicile. According to this interpretation, weaker parties will not have the privilege of being sued at the convenience of their location if they sought the transaction with the stronger party outside their state of abode. With these limitations, the rule is properly interpreted in a way that a party must not enjoy the privilege of protective jurisdiction if it purposefully avails itself to foreign litigation by crossing the borders of its country, including the 'virtual' borders.

At the same time, it must be considered whether the supplier actively pursues conducting business at the location of potential consumers. As outlined by Oren and Vasiljeva and derived from ECJ case law, for protective jurisdiction to apply, the supplier has to specifically aim at the country of a consumer's domicile; and the consumer has to take all the steps necessary on his part for the conclusion of the contract.[72] Therefore, a business must *pursue* commercial or professional activities in the Member State of the consumers' domicile or *direct* such activities to that Member State. Oren expresses that 'the exact meaning of "pursue" in cross-border commerce contexts seems somewhat uncertain and difficult to state … [T]he expression might be given a wide interpretation ranging from continuous

[70] Email from Carla Gulotta to author (22 March 2014).

[71] P Nielsen, 'Jurisdiction over Consumer Contracts' in U Magnus and P Mankowski (eds), *European Commentaries on Private International Law: Brussels I Regulation*, 2nd edn (Sellier European Law Publishers, 2012).

[72] K Vasiljeva, '1968 Brussels Convention and EU Council Regulation No 44/2001: Jurisdiction in Consumer Contract Concluded Online' (2004) 10 *European Law Journal* 123, 126.

business management, to more sporadic occurrences of commercial activities'.[73] As for 'directing' business activity towards the consumers' state of domicile, case law provides some further guidance. In *Gabriel v Schlank & Schick GmbH*,[74] the court decided that the action of a professional vendor having contacted a consumer at his home by one or more letters, which led the consumer to buy goods to obtain a prize, could be interpreted as a specific invitation addressed to the consumer or advertising within the meaning of the Brussels jurisdiction regime.

Same further requirements apply to electronic consumer contracts. A question was previously raised, whether the mere accessibility of a website in a Member State would be sufficient to trigger the application of the protective rules of jurisdiction. First, *Rayner v Davies*[75] set certain restrictions for the Brussels I Regulation provisions to apply in consumer contracts. It specified that the provisions only apply to 'private, final consumers contracting for their own private use or consumption', with sufficient connection between the contract and the consumer's domicile.[76] Furthermore, the *Ilsinger*[77] case confirmed that the seller's activity must enable consumers to conclude contracts in the place of their domicile. In other words, for protective jurisdiction to apply, a business' website should be construed as directing commercial activity towards consumers domiciled in a Member State. Finally, *Peter v Reeder* and *Hotel Alpenhof v Oliver Heller* confirmed the requirement of intention of the business to target doing business in a corresponding Member State, 'rather than simply falling foul [of protective jurisdiction rule] by virtue of "mere accessibility" of their website'.[78]

Therefore, certain categories of parties may require additional state protection, given their inequality of status, access to information and vulnerability. In the EU, consumers, employees and insurance holders enjoy protective jurisdiction, which transcends the parties' agreement on jurisdiction (which is usually in such cases done in contracts of adhesion). However, the EU protective approach borders closely with excessiveness. It stretches way beyond the EU Member States, affecting businesses outside the EU, which may be sued by EU consumers and employees in EU courts. The extent of protective jurisdiction before the Brussels I Regulation revision (before extending to non-EU defendants) would be more optimal.

A further suggestion for improving the EU jurisdiction regime in cases involving weaker parties concerns consistency. For instance, Rühl[79] demonstrates

[73] J Oren, 'International Jurisdiction over Consumer Contracts in e-Europe' (2003) 52 *International & Comparative Law Quarterly* 676.

[74] Case C-96/00 *Gabriel v Schlank & Schick GmbH* [2002] ECR I-6367.

[75] *Rayner v Davies* [2003] 1 All ER (Comm) 394 (CA).

[76] L Gillies, 'Clarifying the "Philosophy of Article 15" in the Brussels I Regulation: C-585/08 *Peter v Reeder Karl Schluter GmbH and Co* and C-144/09 *Hotel Alpenhof Gesmbh v Oliver Heller*' (2011) 60 *International & Comparative Law Quarterly* 557, 559.

[77] Case C-180/06 *Renate Ilsinger v Martin Dreschers*, Judgment of 14 May 2009.

[78] Gillies (n 76) 562.

[79] G Rühl, 'The Protection of Weaker Parties in the Private International Law of the European Union: A Portrait of Inconsistency and Conceptual Truancy' (2014) 10 *Journal of Private International Law* 335.

how the EU lawmakers employ the 'sectoral' approach by enacting 'specific legal instruments geared for individual legal areas and specific legal issues', without a clear unified vision. This is reflected in the fact that some EU weaker parties (consumers) are protected from choice of law and choice of court in contracts, where the requirements of 'targeted' commercial activities are met, while other weaker parties (employees, (mass) insurance policyholders, passengers and maintenance creditors) enjoy such privileges without any requirements.[80] As Rühl points out, there is a lack of coherence and conceptual vision in the EU protection of weaker parties. Therefore, upon closer analysis of state protection of vulnerable parties, it seems that EU regulation protecting weaker parties could improve further in terms of consistency.

B. Protective Jurisdiction in Russia

During the Soviet era (1917–90), consumers did not receive adequate attention or protection under civil legislation, but the reforms and transition to a market economy in Russia have changed the picture.[81] For instance, Article 179 of the Civil Code[82] declares any transactions void if 'concluded under the influence of fraud, coercion, threat, or unfavourable circumstances'. Furthermore, the interests of consumers are protected by Article 16 of the Law on Consumer Protection, which renders a transaction or an agreement, infringing upon the rights of consumers, invalid.[83] In particular, it is unlawful for suppliers of goods and services to limit consumer rights in contracts, or to offer to give up their rights guaranteed by the law (alluding to freedom of contract). For instance, compounding of interest in bank loans given to individuals (consumers) has been previously held as breaching consumer rights.[84]

In addition, Russia enforces protective jurisdiction rules in relation to consumers in Russia. Similar to the EU, in addition to suing at the location of the defendant, claims on protecting the rights of consumers in Russia can be brought at the plaintiff's place of residence, or at the place of entering into or execution of a corresponding contract, or at the defendant's location. The choice between these places belongs to the consumer.[85] Moreover, a consumer can dispute burdensome provisions of contracts of adhesion,[86] including claiming invalidity of a forum

[80] ibid 356.

[81] J Henderson, 'Entrepreneurs and Consumers as Subjects of Civil Law' in W Simons (ed), *Private and Civil Law in the Russian Federation. Essays in Honor of FJM Feldbrugge* (Martinus Nijhoff Publishers, 2009).

[82] Grazhdanskiĭ Kodeks Rossiĭskoĭ Federatsii (Civil Code of the RF) of 30 November 1994 no 51-ФЗ (pt 1) (the Russian Civil Code).

[83] Law of the RF on Protection of the Rights of Consumers.

[84] Informatsionnoe Pismo Presidiuma Vysshego Arbitrazhnogo Suda RF ot 13 sentiabria 2011 g no 146 (Information Letter of the Presidium of the Supreme *Arbitrazh* Court of the RF) of 13 September 2011 no 146.

[85] CCP art 29(7); Law of the RF on Protection of the Rights of Consumers art 17.

[86] Russian Civil Code art 428(2).

selection clause in an adhesion contract, which directs all disputes to the location of a bank.[87] Special jurisdictional rules also apply to the contracts on insurance (both personal and property) when concluded for personal, family and other use unconnected with commercial activity. The claimant has a choice whether to sue at an earlier agreed forum, or at his own location, or at the place of performance of the contract.[88]

The Russian rules on protective jurisdiction differ somewhat from the EU. First, the Brussels I Recast states that, in consumer contracts, protective jurisdiction prevails over jurisdiction agreements, unless the latter were entered into *ex post* or where they create an additional choice for the weaker party. The Russian rule appears to foresee the possibility where the consumer chooses to abide by an earlier jurisdiction agreement. Another slight difference is that while the Brussels I Recast refers to disputes connected with consumer contracts, the Russian rule refers to 'claims on protection of rights of consumers' and foresees both presence and absence of contracts. The EU rule presupposes that a consumer has the right to sue the other party (business, seller, provider, etc) at the place of their residence. In Russia, pursuant to this jurisdictional provision, claims may also be brought by third persons, state authorities and organisations protecting the interests of consumers, at the location of those entities. In this regard, the Russian approach provides an even wider protection of consumer interests than Europe.

This difference is illustrated in practice. A frequently cited example is that of Mr Solomonis, a lawyer in Saint Petersburg, who filed 11 suits seeking to protect the rights of consumers in 2008.[89] His suits urged to declare unlawful: the liability to pay for utilities by citizens before the issuance of their titles to housing; the prohibition of sale of imported goods with no information about them in Russian; the restriction of the right of passengers for free use of toilets, etc. Some of the claims were satisfied, and some were not. Notably, the claims were brought by a third person, and some of those suits did not relate to a business-to-consumer contract. Mr Solomonis brought the suits at his location, using the jurisdiction rule allowing suing at the location of the plaintiff in matters relating to the protection of consumer rights.

[87] N Eliseev, 'Dogovornaia Podsudnost' – Kakoĭ eĭ byt v Edinom Protsessual'nom Kodekse RF?' ('Jurisdiction by Agreement – What it Should be Like in the Single Civil Procedural Code of the RF') (2015) 12 *Zakon* 191, fn 8, referring to Obzor Sudebnoĭ Praktiki po Grazhdanskim Delam, Sviazannym s Razreshenie Sporov ob Ispolnenii Kreditnykh Obiazatelstv, utv Presidiumom Verkhovnogo Suda RF 22 maiia 2013 g (Review of Court Practice in Civil Cases, Connected to Resolution of Disputes on Fulfilment of Loan Obligations adopted by the Presidium of the Supreme Court of the RF) of 22 May 2013.

[88] Postanovlenie Plenuma Verkhovnogo Suda RF ot 28 iiunia 2012 g no 17 o Rassmotrenii Sudami Grazhdanskikh Del po Sporam o Zashchite Prav Potrebiteleĭ (Resolution of the Supreme Court of the RF on Court Practice in Cases Protecting the Rights of Consumers) of 28 June 2012 no 17, paras 22–26.

[89] The cases were filed in 2008 in courts in Saint-Petersburg; and recent examples of Mr Solomonis' activity may be found in Case no 2-550/2012 (2-7430/2011)~M-7545/2011 in Vyborgskiĭ Circuit Court in Saint-Petersburg, or Case no 2-1453/2012~M-443/2012 in Kirovskiĭ Circuit Court in Saint-Petersburg; both cases concern protecting consumers' rights associated with the sale of products.

Lately, however, the Russian Supreme Court slightly limited this rule. Now, the suits on consumer protection can be brought at the location of the claimant only where the claim is made by the consumer or a representative of a particular consumer (or a specific group of consumers). A claim in relation to an indefinite range of consumers shall be filed in accordance with the general jurisdiction rule, ie, at the location of the defendant.[90] This indicates partial adoption of the EU understanding, where a claim brought by a representative on behalf of the consumer will not fall under protective jurisdiction. For instance, in *VKI v Henkel*,[91] the ECJ specifically noted that a consumer protection organisation cannot be regarded as a consumer, even if the case in its substance deals with consumer contracts. In that case, application of the corresponding provisions of the Brussels jurisdiction regime over consumer contracts could not be invoked. As Tang properly remarked, a direct contractual link between the real litigating parties was missing.[92]

In this regard, a recent proposal by the EU Commission warrants consideration: a directive on representative actions for protection of the collective interests of consumers.[93] Article 16 of this directive specified that any qualified – placed on a publicly available list in a Member State – entity may apply to courts of another Member State that shall accept the claim on infringement of rights of consumers. This paves the way to class actions in Europe that are conceptually equivalent to consumer claims in Russia that may be brought by a representative of their interests.

In relation to employment contracts, Russian law does not provide any special jurisdictional protection. Employment disputes are filed ordinarily in courts of general jurisdiction. However, there is a quasi-protective jurisdiction rule mentioning employment: in cases directly provided by the law, claims connected with rights of employees may be filed at the location of the claimant.[94] Such cases include restoration of employment, pension and housing rights and return of property or the monetary equivalent in case of restitution of damages incurred by a person because of unlawful criminal sentence, placement under custody, or imposition of administrative penalty. With the exception of these cases of unlawful sentence or the other above-mentioned circumstances, normally, employment-related issues are filed in accordance with the general jurisdiction rule, at the location of the defendant.

Where insurance policyholders (individuals) sign insurance contracts for personal, family, household and other purposes unrelated to business activity,

[90] Resolution of the Supreme Court of the RF no 17 (n 88) para 25.

[91] Case C-167/00 *Verein fur Konsumenteninformation v Karl Heinz Henkel* [2002] ECR I-8111.

[92] ZS Tang, 'Consumer Collective Redress in European Private International Law' (2011) 7 *Journal of Private International Law* 101, 110.

[93] Proposal for a Directive of the European Parliament and of the Council on representative actions for the protection of the collective interests of consumers, and repealing Directive 2009/22/EC (COM (2018) 184 final, Brussels, 11 April 2018.

[94] CCP art 29(6).

they are treated as consumers.[95] The rule of protective jurisdiction in consumer relationships allows them to sue at their place of residence. Any other insurance-related claims are to be filed according to the general rules. In comparison, the EU regulation of jurisdiction in insurance contracts goes to a greater degree of elaboration, covering actions against co-insurers, insurance of immovable property, actions of injured persons against liable insured persons, jurisdictional rules in cases relating to legal actions of an insurer against another person, and counterclaims, contractual derogation from the statutory jurisdiction rules, etc. This incredibly detailed regulation of jurisdiction in insurance contracts seems yet too foreign for Russia. In fact, the Russian regulation exemplifies what constitutes normal around the world, while the Brussels I approach on protecting the insured appears to be rather 'out of the ordinary'.[96]

Special protective jurisdiction rules in Russia are designed to protect the uninformed or economically subordinate (*ekonomichski zavisimyĭ*) party in civil procedure, in order to avoid cases of 'imposition' of jurisdiction clauses.[97] The law limits party autonomy where necessary for safeguarding public interests, moral considerations and the interests of third parties. Any imbalance in the interests of the parties is the main reason for these rules.

Court practice appears inconsistent in applying the legal provisions on protective jurisdiction. For instance, in a case at a court of appeal in the Trans-Baikal territory in Russia,[98] a claimant signed an agreement with the defendant, whereby the latter took an obligation to assist the claimant with purchasing a car. The agreement contained a dispute resolution clause designating a court at the location of the defendant to handle any disputes. The claimant performed his part of the agreement (he made the payment), and the defendant failed to fulfil his obligations. Then, the claimant sent a notice to the defendant requesting termination of the agreement and return of the money. The defendant refused. The claimant

[95] Postanovlenie Plenuma Verkhovnogo Suda RF ot 27 iiunia 2013 g no 20 o Primenenii Sudami Zakonodatel'stva o Dobrovol'nom Strakhovanii Imushchestva Grazhdan (Resolution of the Supreme Court of the RF on Application of the Law by Courts on Voluntary Insurance of Property of Citizens) of 27 June 2013 no 20.

[96] Out of 27 (at that time) European countries, only four featured the rights of the insured to bring proceedings at home (France, Italy, Luxembourg and Slovakia), according to a comparative study officially commissioned by the European Commission in 2007. See, A Nuyts, 'General Report on Study on Residual Jurisdiction (Review of the Member States' Rules concerning the "Residual Jurisdiction" of their courts in Civil and Commercial Matters pursuant to the Brussels I and II Regulations)' (3 September 2007, 3rd version) 47–48 available at: ec.europa.eu/civiljustice/news/docs/study_residual_jurisdiction_en.pdf (the Nuyts Study).

[97] S Dergachev, '"Dogovornaia Podsudnost" v Grazhdanskom i Arbitrazhnom Processe Rossii' ('"Jurisdiction" by Agreement in Civil and Commercial Procedure in Russia') (PhD Book, Russian Academy of Justice affiliated with the Supreme Court of the Russian Federation, 2011) (on file with author) 96, referring to M Rozhkova et al, *Dogovornoe Pravo: Soglasheniya o Podsudnosti, Mezhdunarodnoĭ Podsudnosti, Primiritel'noĭ Protsedure, Arbitrazhnoe (Treteĭskoe) i Mirovie Soglasheniia* (*Contract Law: Agreements on Jurisdiction, International Jurisdiction Agreements, Conciliation Agreements, Arbitration Agreements, Settlement Agreements*) (Statut, 2008) 37–38.

[98] Apelliatsionnoe Opredelenie Zabaĭkal'nogo Kraevogo Suda ot 21 maiia 2014 (Appellate Decision of the Trans-Baikal Territory Court) of 21 May 2004 case no 33-2070-2014.

sued the defendant in a court at the location of the claimant, seeking nullification of the agreement and compensation. The court of first instance decided that the relationships did not constitute the business-to-consumer type and refused to accept the claim due to the lack of jurisdiction. On appeal, the court of appeal corrected the lower court, having classified the relationships as consumer-related, since the claimant signed the contract with the sole purpose of acquiring the car for his personal use.

Nevertheless, the court of appeal still decided that courts at the location of the claimant lacked jurisdiction. Citing Resolution No 17 by the Supreme Court,[99] the court decided that the claimant had to specifically dispute the jurisdiction agreement. Thus, it interpreted the Resolution by the Supreme Court literally; the claimant had to officially contest the jurisdiction clause (as if the act of filing the suit at his location did not make that choice clear). Such a paradoxical interpretation appears to deviate from the above-mentioned Supreme Court's guidance. The rule states that the claimant (a consumer) has to right to choose whether to abide by the jurisdiction agreement or whether to bring a claim at his location. Yet, the court refused the consumer his access to justice by turning the statement by the Supreme Court upside down.

On the other hand, Russian courts are at times too zealous in protecting the economically weaker parties. For instance, the Supreme *Arbitrazh* Court, while summarising principles of court practice in disputes relating to loan obligations for lower courts, stated that an asymmetric jurisdiction agreement between a bank and a consumer violates consumer rights. The agreement in question specified that (i) all claims against the borrower would be brought at the location of the bank, and (ii) claims by the borrower against the bank could be brought, at the discretion of the consumer, at the location of the borrower, at the location of the bank, or at the place of performance of the loan agreement. Earlier, the RosPotrebNadzor (Russian Federal Service on Protection of Consumers)[100] argued, on behalf of the consumer, for invalidity of such an asymmetric agreement, as violating the rights of the consumer. The court deemed such provision unlawful, since it was incorporated into a contract of adhesion with the bank, and the bank was subject to administrative liability.[101] In my view, such judicial interpretation was erroneous. The said jurisdiction agreement aimed to enforce the rights of the economically weaker party, by providing several alternatives as to where to bring claims. In fact, the jurisdiction clause offered in that case is what would be recommended for all

[99] Resolution of the Supreme Court of the RF no 17 (n 88).

[100] RosPotrebNadzor, 'O Postanovlenii Plenuma Verkhovnogo Suda RF ot 28 iiunia 2012 g no 17 o Rassmotrnii Sudami Grazhdanskikh Del po Sporam o Zashchite Prav Potrebitelei' (Federal Service for Supervision in the Area of Consumer Protection and Human Well-Being, On Resolution by the Supreme Court of the Russian Federation of 28 June 2012 no 17 'On Court Practice in Cases Protecting the Rights of Consumers') of 23 July 2012 no 01/8179-12-32, para 7. The official letter from RosPotrebNadzor is considered as guidance for consumer protection in Russia, both outside court and in relation to judicial proceedings.

[101] The Supreme *Arbitrazh* Court, Letter no 146 (n 84) s 7.

consumer-related jurisdiction rules in Russia. Such claims need to be filed according to a jurisdiction agreement, with an alternative for the weaker party to bring actions at his location.

IV. Conclusion

In this chapter, I outlined the value of equality in an ideal jurisdiction regime. I discussed what equality is, why it is important for private relations, and how it is connected to the central claim made in this book on re-evaluating the values behind a jurisdiction regime. I have aimed to reconcile the considerations of party autonomy and equality, arguing that party autonomy to choose a forum must be enforced in a way mindful of equality.

I presented my normative view which supports enforcement of the parties' full consent on jurisdiction, except for certain categories of parties whose equality needs to be protected. I unpacked the reasons for consumer protection and traced their justification to a number of philosophical axioms. I laid out the theoretical underpinnings for individual equality, reflected in the ideas of many Western and Russian scholars. I analysed state policy towards protection of weaker parties. Considerations of access to justice and the role of the state as a fiduciary helped justify the need for categorical equality in jurisdiction.

Thus, normally, all parties should be treated as rational and independent subjects capable of expressing their intent to adjudicate in a specific forum. Parties entering in private international transactions should be aware of risks associated therewith. However, choice-of-court agreements with participation of a weaker party may be limited, where exclusiveness of the choice-of-court agreement limits the weaker party's access to justice. Moreover, where the jurisdiction clause was not properly and fairly incorporated into a contract, the weaker party should have an alternative to bring a suit at their domicile, in addition to the earlier-agreed-upon forum.

By analysing unilateral jurisdiction agreements and relationships involving the weaker parties, I demonstrated the significance of quality of consent. I have argued that where parties' equal rights to allocate jurisdiction are respected, and all parties can enjoy proper access to justice (with or without an agreement on jurisdiction), such a system may be considered fair (meaning fair to the parties, not to other countries and their competing claims to jurisdiction).[102]

I advocated this position and compared it with the existing protective jurisdiction rules in the EU and Russia. Both in Europe and Russia, protective jurisdiction

[102] Similar to the understanding of fairness in the American jurisdictional model; see R Michaels, 'Two Paradigms of Jurisdiction' (2006) 27 *Michigan Journal of International Law* 1003, 1022, portraying the American and the EU jurisdictional systems as two diverging paradigms (ie, thought patterns, an epistemic background for analysis, the way participants in a legal system discuss matters of jurisdiction).

rules override party autonomy to designate a forum. In particular, Articles 15, 19 and 23 of the Brussels I Recast only give effect to jurisdiction agreements with the weaker parties *ex post* where such agreement expands the choice of available fora for the weaker party. In addition, parties can agree to confer jurisdiction to courts of a Member State where they are both domiciled, if the law of that Member State permits it.[103] The reasoning behind the prevalence of protective jurisdiction over party autonomy in the EU is based on a clear inequality in the position of the parties, and the desire to prevent imposition of solutions (including regarding forum selection) by the stronger party.[104] As regards submission to jurisdiction (which is another side of party autonomy to choose jurisdiction), the EU jurisdiction regime reasonably recognises its superiority over protective jurisdiction. The above-mentioned Articles 15, 19 and 23 give effect to jurisdiction agreements made after the dispute has arisen. Thus, for example, where an employee and an employer expressly submit to a court in a Member State after the proceedings start, such submission overrides protective jurisdiction. Submission to jurisdiction similarly applies to disputes involving consumer and insurance contracts.[105]

However, the EU goes too far in its protection of weaker parties. After the most recent reform of the Brussels jurisdiction regime, the right of European weaker parties (consumers and employees) to sue at their domicile extends to certain non-EU defendants as well. This undermines the autonomy of non-EU parties. Particularly, if EU weaker parties preliminarily agree to a third-country forum when entering into relationships with non-EU vendors, and later sue the vendors at their domicile in the EU under EU jurisdiction rules, this contradicts the non-EU parties' autonomy. Whereas EU-domiciled businesses and employers consent to the EU jurisdiction regime by virtue of their domicile there, non-EU parties do not. It is inappropriate to bring them to EU courts for the sake of protection of EU weaker parties.

In Russia, the regulation of the issue is similar. The Russian jurisdiction regime provides for protective jurisdiction in cases involving consumers and insured individuals. As for employment contracts, they are filed in accordance with the general rule, except for a few limited cases. Where a claim is brought to a court by a consumer in accordance with a jurisdiction agreement by both parties, the judge shall not refuse accepting it due to the lack of jurisdiction. The judge shall not return the claim of a consumer disputing an agreement on forum, because the choice among several competent courts belongs to the claimant.[106] Therefore, the Russian official judicial position prioritises the interests of weaker parties (consumers) over jurisdiction agreements made prior to the start of judicial proceedings.

[103] ibid 345.

[104] Magnus and Mankowski (n 16) 411, citing G Palao Moreno, *Derecho Internacional y de la integración 2* (*International Law and Integration 2*) (2003) 7, 27.

[105] eg, in relation to consumer contracts, Kaye (n 30) 841.

[106] Resolution of the Supreme Court of the RF no 17 (n 88) para 26.

However, the court practice lacks uniformity in this regard. Furthermore, the correlation between the submission rule (party autonomy to choose a forum *ex post*) and protective jurisdiction is quite moot in Russia. As mentioned in chapter four on Submission to Jurisdiction, current Russian procedural rules do not recognise silent acceptance of jurisdiction by parties. Therefore, although intuitive to common sense, it is unclear whether the actual submission prevails over protective jurisdiction in accordance with statutory Russian law. This situation needs to be corrected, and submission to jurisdiction should evidently supersede protective jurisdiction rules.

6

Jurisdiction in Tort and Contract in the Absence of Choice of Forum: Balance Exercise

I. Introduction

My overall approach to law on jurisdiction advocates having party autonomy at the basis of an ideal jurisdiction regime. I believe in giving force to party autonomy since it is the ultimate expression of the parties' will in relation to jurisdiction. However, in unplanned tort actions or contracts with no jurisdiction clause, such a clear choice is absent. Such cases are best resolved based on balancing the interests of private parties in light of considerations of equality. My main claim in relation to tort is that equality of private parties and fairness should condition the claimant's right of choosing an appropriate jurisdiction (again, fairness in the sense of fairness to the parties to the transaction, not to other countries and their competing claims to jurisdiction).

The necessity to balance fair treatment of both defendants' and claimants' interests may be found in Mills' account on the international ordering of state power and the objectives of 'classical' private international law.[1] In particular, he lists criteria for localising disputes in classical tradition, which include 'reliance on both personal and territorial connections … as well as considerations of balancing fairness to claimants and respondents, and balancing predictability [etc]'.[2] Mills proceeds to support this statement by the findings of the Report from the International Law Association (ILA).[3] A group of experts prepared this report as a guideline for national courts facing international civil litigation against corporations, individuals and other non-state actors to redress human rights violations. The Report proposes a framework for ascertaining international jurisdiction, applicable law and recognition and enforcement of civil claims relating to the

[1] A Mills, 'The Identities of Private International Law: Lessons from the US and EU Revolutions' (2013) 23 *Duke Journal of Comparative & International Law* 445, 449.

[2] ibid.

[3] International Law Association (ILA), 'International Civil Litigation for Human Rights Violations' (C Kessedjian, E Ho and J van de Velden (eds), *ILA Sofia Conference Final Report*, 2012) (the ILA Report).

protection of human rights based on the survey of national reports in a range of countries in Europe, Asia and America.[4] Among other grounds for jurisdiction, the report mentions exceptional circumstances where courts may assume jurisdiction on the sole basis of necessity, to avoid a denial of justice.[5] The Report defines the 'denial of justice' as situations in which no other court is available, or the claimant cannot be reasonably expected to seize another court, such as, for example, during civil unrest or war.[6] It also mentions situations where a local judgment cannot be recognised and enforced within the forum. Where there is some obstacle preventing the claimant from obtaining justice in a foreign state, where justice so demands,[7] it may be permissible for a court to retain jurisdiction in that particular case.[8]

Philosophical justification of the idea to balance the rights of the private parties stems from the essence of corrective justice, the Aristotelian view that disturbance of the balance of equality of parties is a violation of justice.[9] The Aristotelian normative equilibrium proclaims that a party wronged in some respect possesses the right to restorative justice. For tortious relationships, where party autonomy in choice of forum provides little guidance, corrective justice may assist in understanding not only *why* the aggrieved party has the right to restorative justice, but also whether it should be done at the venue convenient to the aggrieved party. For contracts, it explains why both parties' intentions and interests must be equally taken into account.

Further support for this position can be found in works of many scholars who rekindle the ideas on corrective justice. For instance, in accordance with the Rawlsian theory of justice: 'each person is to have an equal right to the most extensive scheme of equal basic liberties compatible with a similar scheme of liberties for others'.[10] In addition, the very fundamental theses of private law, as envisaged by Weinrib, put corrective justice as an ideal, while the Kantian rights supply the moral standpoint for the structure. Corrective justice represents 'the form of the private law relationship',[11] which helps maintain the indispensable equilibrium of equality.

[4] Australia, England and Wales, Japan, The Netherlands, South Africa, Switzerland, and the United States of America.

[5] ILA Report, 6.

[6] ILA Report, 33.

[7] R Michaels, 'Two Paradigms of Jurisdiction' (2006) 27 *Michigan Journal of International Law* 1003, 1047.

[8] This, in turn, is consistent with Principle 2.2 of the American Law Institute (ALI)/UNIDROIT 'Principles of Transnational Civil Procedure' (2004) 9 *Uniform Law Review* 758.

[9] Although applicability by the Ancient Greek judiciaries of the principle is questionable, the coherence of the principle itself remains.

[10] J Rawls, *A Theory of Justice* (Clarendon Press, 1972 and rev edn, Oxford University Press, 1999) 53.

[11] E Weinrib, *The Idea of Private Law* (Oxford University Press, 2012) 75. Further rationale for the right of action in tort may be found, eg, in J Goldberg and B Zipursky, 'Unrealised Torts' (2002) 88 *Virginia Law Review* 1625, 1643.

These ideas of corrective justice manifest the rationality of relationship of plaintiff and defendant. They help explain the nature of tortious relationships and the underlying reasoning for equality in jurisdiction. For the purpose of my research, they help me justify upholding the balance of the parties in situations where a clear choice of forum is absent.

To further support my argument, I discuss the merits and values of the existing EU and Russian jurisdictional solutions in torts and contracts without a clear choice of forum. The chapter consists of two main parts. The first is devoted to tort actions, with no pre-meditated choice of forum. The second discusses disputes arising out of contracts without any jurisdiction clauses. I analyse the rules through the prism of my world-view to determine similarities and differences in the EU and Russia, to find gaps in application of the rules and to give recommendations for their improvement.

II. Jurisdiction in Torts: Interpretation and Justification

The existing rules on jurisdiction in tort in the EU and Russia allow actions to be brought at the location of the defendant, or at the place where the torts occurred or the damage was sustained. In addition, Russia specifically allows plaintiffs to bring certain tort claims at the place of their residence. In particular, in EU disputes, a person domiciled in a Member State may be sued in matters relating to torts, delict or quasi-delict in the court of the Member State where the harmful event occurred or may occur, in addition to the possibility to sue at the domicile of the defendant.[12] In cases involving non-EU defendants, the national laws of EU Member States regulate the proper allocation of jurisdiction in tort actions.

Russian courts have the competence to handle international cases with foreign persons if the physical injury and harm to property occurred in Russia, or the plaintiff resides in Russia.[13] Further domestic jurisdiction rules determine which local court shall have jurisdiction. Four types of tort cases can be distinguished in accordance with the Russian Codes on Civil and *Arbitrazh* procedure. First, claims for damages based on physical injury[14] may be brought by a plaintiff to the court at the place of his (her) residence or at the place where the damage was inflicted.[15] Disputes arising from the infliction of damage to property with a foreign element shall be heard in Russian *arbitrazh* courts, where the act that gave rise to the

[12] Regulation (EU) 1215/2012 of 12 December 2012 on Jurisdiction and the Recognition and Enforcement of Judgments in Civil and Commercial Matters (Recast) [2012] OJ L351/1, art 7(2) (the Brussels I Recast).

[13] Grazhdanskiĭ Protsessual'nyĭ Kodeks Rossiĭskoĭ Federatsii (Code of Civil Procedure) of 14 November 2002 no 138-ФЗ (Russia) art 402(3)(4–5) (the CCP).

[14] Severe injury or any other type of injury, or a wrongful death of the family breadwinner.

[15] CCP art 29(5).

complaint occurred or the damage was sustained in Russia.[16] Moreover, where individuals suffered damage as a result of unlawful conviction, unlawful attachment (*arest na imushchestvo*), or violation of employment rights, etc, a claim for restitution to restore the labour, pension, and/or property rights may be filed at the residence of the plaintiff.[17] In addition, Russian law foresees special jurisdiction in claims for damages caused by the collision of ships. Such claims and claims seeking to collect fees for rendering rescue and salvage at sea may be submitted to the *arbitrazh* court at the location of the defendant's ship or home port of the ship or the place where the damage was inflicted.[18] Finally, actions for damages arising out of a ship collision, actions by ship personnel to recover salary and social benefits for work at sea, concerning salary and social payment actions for compensation for providing assistance and rescue at sea, may be brought in a court of general jurisdiction at the location of the defendant's ship or the home port of the ship.[19]

Does this existing tradition of connecting a suit to jurisdiction by a certain subject matter fit a hierarchy of values in jurisdiction proposed in this book? It does, as long as the rationale behind it is balancing the interests between the parties. In the following sections, I discuss nuances of the jurisdiction rules in light of my normative approach, in different types of tort cases (personal injury, damage to property, and defamation).

A. Place Where the Harmful Event Occurred: Economic Loss and Damage to Property

A commonly accepted place for bringing actions in torts is the place where the harmful event occurred. A harmful event is an event attributed to the defendant which is alleged to have caused damage to another party.[20] The place where the harmful event occurred is understood both as the place where the harmful act was committed (*locus delicti commissi*) and the place where the injury arose (*locus damni*). A few significant EU cases define the 'place of tort'.[21] The first case to clarify the concept was *Bier v Mines de Potasse d'Alsace*[22] in 1976, which explained that 'a plaintiff has an option to commence proceedings either at the place where the damage occurred or the place of the event giving rise to it'. In that case, a Netherlands undertaking, Bier, had large nurseries near Rotterdam, irrigated by

[16] Arbitrazhno-Protsessual'nyĭ Kodeks Rossiĭskoĭ Federatsii (Code of *Arbitrazh* (Commercial) Procedure) of 24 July 2002 no 95-ФЗ (Russia) art 247(1)(4) (the CAP).

[17] CCP art 29(6).

[18] CAP art 36(6).

[19] CCP art 29(8).

[20] Case C-572/14 *Austro Mechana*, Opinion of AG Saugmandsgaard Oe of 17 February 2016, para 67.

[21] Case C-21/76 *Bier v Mines de potasse* [1976] ECR 1735 (*Bier v Mines de potasse*); Case C-167/00 *Konsumenteninformation v Henkel* [2002] ECR I-8111; Case C-168/02 *Kronhofer v Maier et al* [2004] ECR I-6009; Case C-189/08 *Zuid-Chemie v Philippo's* [2009] ECR I-6917 (*Zuid-Chemie v Philippo's*).

[22] *Bier v Mines de potasse*.

water from the river Rhine. The defendant, a French mining company, allegedly committed a wrongful act by pouring pollutants into the Rhine in France. The Dutch nurseryman had to use the water from the river to water his plants and use a purification process, which cost him a pretty penny. The alleged wrongful act was committed in France, but the damage was sustained in the Netherlands. The claim was brought in the Netherlands; and the defendant objected to jurisdiction of the Dutch courts, since the unlawful act allegedly occurred in France. Having considered varying national interpretations of the 'place where the harmful event occurred', the court issued an independent definition, for the purpose of the Brussels Convention. Guided by the purpose of sound administration of justice and effective conduct of proceedings, the European Court of Justice (ECJ) emphasised that there must be a particularly close connecting factor between the dispute and the courts of the place where the harmful event occurred. The existence of the close connecting factor would justify the attribution of jurisdiction to those courts.

Later, *Marinari v Lloyds Bank*[23] clarified that the 'place where the harmful event occurred' could not be interpreted as referring to the place where the victim claims to have suffered financial loss consequential upon initial damage arising and suffered by him in another Member State.

Furthermore, *Zuid-Chemie* elaborated that the 'place where the harmful event occurred' refers to the place 'where the initial damage occurred as a result of the normal use of the product for the purpose for which it was intended'.[24] In that case, a Dutch undertaking, Zuid-Chemie, manufactured fertiliser. Its Belgian deliverer of a product, Philippo's, had a dispute regarding an alleged unlawful act by Phillippo's (delivering a contaminated product used for production of the fertiliser). The product was manufactured by Phillippo's in Belgium. Zuid-Chemie took delivery of the product in Belgium. Then, Zuid-Chemie processed the product in the Netherlands, where the fertiliser was produced. Subsequently, some consignments of the fertiliser were sold to customers of Zuid-Chemie. When the fertiliser was found unusable or of substandard quality, Zuid-Chemie claimed to have suffered economic loss. Seeking compensation, Zuid-Chemie instituted proceedings against Phillipo's in the Netherlands.

Further interpretation was needed of the 'place where the harmful event occurred', since opinions in the Dutch court became divided. The ECJ was asked to interpret Article 5(3) of the Brussels Regulation (now, Article 7(2) of the Brussels I Recast) and determine whether the 'place where the harmful event occurred' designated the place where the defective product was delivered, or where the damage occurred following normal use of the product. Furthermore, the ECJ was asked whether Article 5(3) should apply to physical damage only or financial loss as well. With an objective to further describe the 'place where harmful event occurred', the ECJ correctly used the wording the 'place where the event which gave rise to the

[23] Case C-364/93 *Marinari v Lloyds Bank* [1995] ECR I-2719.

[24] *Zuid-Chemie v Philippo's*, para 33.

damage produces its harmful effects' or the 'place where the damage caused by the defective product actually manifests itself'.[25] Having regard to this, the place where the damage occurred was rightfully determined as being in the Netherlands, ie, where the defective product was processed into fertiliser, which subsequently led to the damages suffered by Zuid-Chemie.[26] Thus, the 'place where the harmful event occurred' was understood as the 'place where the damage occurred as a result of the normal use of the product'.

An ECJ case clarifying the meaning of the place of a tort was *Concurrence Sarl v Samsung and Amazon*.[27] In that case, the French Cour de cassation submitted a request to the ECJ relating to interpretation of the Brussels jurisdictional rule in tort. The question was whether, in the event of an alleged infringement of prohibitions on resale outside a selective distribution network and on a marketplace by means of online offers on several websites operating in various Member States, an affected party has the right to bring an action seeking an injunction in the courts of the territory where the online content is or was accessible, or whether there must be some other clear connecting factor. The ECJ referred to the established case law, stating that the Brussels jurisdictional rule in tort is based on the existence of a particularly close connecting factor between the dispute and the courts of the place where the harmful event occurred or may occur, 'which justifies the attribution of jurisdiction to those courts for reasons relating to the sound administration of justice and the efficacious conduct of proceedings'.[28] In *Concurrence Sarl v Samsung and Amazon*, not only did the appellant suffer a reduction of sales in France because of Samsung's breach of distribution agreement, but the law of France gave effect to prohibition of infringement of resale outside the distribution network, which established a natural link between the forum and the dispute.[29] The fact that the Samsung and Amazon websites where online offers were posted were accessible in other Member States was found irrelevant.

In Russia, a 'place of tort' can be interpreted as: a place where event causing damage occurred, or where the harm was sustained. Understanding of the 'place where the harmful event occurred' was derived from Soviet judicial tradition. During Soviet times, courts understood it in the light of the circumstances of the case. It could be a place where the harmful action or inaction happened, or a place where the result of the harmful event was sustained. This choice was for the court to make in the interests of the party that suffered the damage.[30] Now, Russian legal scholarship takes the view that the interpretation of the corresponding Russian provision includes both the place where the harmful event occurred, and where

[25] ibid para 27.

[26] ibid para 29.

[27] Case C-618/15 *Concurrence Sarl v Samsung Electronics France SAS, Amazon Services Europe Sarl*, Judgment of 21 December 2016 (*Concurrence v Samsung*).

[28] Case C-47/14 *Holterman Ferho Exploitatie and Others*, Judgment of 10 September 2015, para 73.

[29] *Concurrence v Samsung*, para 32.

[30] L Lunts, *Mezhdunarodnoe Chastnoe Pravo* (*International Private Law*), 3rd edn (Iuridicheskaia Literatura, 1973) 258–59.

the damage was sustained.[31] The authority to interpret the place where harmful events occurred (*mesto sovers heniia pravonarusheniia*) still belongs to the courts.

What is the reasoning behind the jurisdiction of courts at the place where the damage was inflicted? A classical view is that jurisdiction in torts manifests extension of state authority over events happening within its realm of power. The state enforces certain laws on its territory, and where a civil wrong is committed at the territory of the state, the majority view is that the state possesses the (moral) power to bring the tortfeasor to its courts.[32] For instance, in relation to state public policy on protection of intellectual property rights, violation of that policy should empower the state's courts to adjudicate.

Such justification does not concur with my general theory on civil jurisdiction. I contend that the interests of private parties should be the driving force behind the jurisdiction rules, and not state public policy. State power over civil wrongs committed within the state territory should be the last reason why tort actions should be adjudicated at the place where the tort was committed.

A better explanation of the rule – filing at the place where the tort was committed – stems from the inherent connection between jurisdiction and choice of law. Since the law of the place where the wrong was committed appears to be the most appropriate, it is natural to also confer jurisdiction on the courts at the place where the tort occurred. In this interpretation, the justification of the rule is sensible and beneficial to the parties. They enjoy predictability in terms of appropriate courts in tort. In some cases (depending on the unpredictable nature of torts), the place may be more convenient to one party than to the other.

In addition, the local courts have better access to evidence, witnesses, etc; they are familiar with local customs and public policy. As noted in *Henkel*: 'the courts for the place where the harmful event occurred are usually the most appropriate for deciding the case, in particular on the grounds of proximity and ease of taking evidence'.[33] Such considerations of practicality and common sense provide better rationale for this rule, because they accentuate the parties' interests to resolve the case in a speedy and effective manner rather than the interests of the state as sovereign.

Therefore, the 'place where the harmful event occurred' should be interpreted as meaning the place where the tort occurred, where the damage was sustained by the alleged victim, or where the event that caused damage took place. Such a broad interpretation may be criticised for providing too much choice for the plaintiff and undermining predictability for defendants where they may be potentially sued. However, such interpretation facilitates better access to justice to potential victims. It contains a lot of value, 'particularly … in product liability actions, since it would

[31] D Karapetyan, 'Jurisdiction, Recognition, and Enforcement of Court Judgments and Arbitral Awards: Analyses and Recommendations to Improve Armenian and Russian Legislation' (2002–03) 28 *Review of Central and East European Law* 211, 227.

[32] R Cappalli, 'Locke as the Key: A Unifying and Coherent Theory of *in Personam* Jurisdiction' (1992) 43 *Case Western Reserve Law Review* 97.

[33] Case-167/00 *Verein für Konsumenteninformation v Karl Heinz Henkel* [2002] ECR I-8111, para 46.

make clear that a person injured by a defective product could bring his action where the injury took place'.[34]

B. Location of Victim: Personal Injury

The main narrative of this book suggests that the interests of private parties should be placed first and foremost when determining jurisdiction in civil matters. In the absence of a clear choice-of-forum, what matters is what best reflects the parties' interests in a way that is fair to each party. At any rate, I contend the question should be resolved by reference to private interests, and not state interests (of power over the events happening in its territory). For instance, if an accident occurs outside a person's usual state of abode and leads to a personal injury, where should the victim have the opportunity to file a tort action? Should the claimant sue at his domicile? How should the justice system allocate jurisdiction, taking into consideration the interests of the defendant as well?

As I envision an ideal jurisdiction, directing personal injury cases to the place of the victim is appropriate. Generally, a claimant has to come to the defendant and prove his case. It is fair, considering that the interests of the parties should be the most important consideration when allocating jurisdiction. The defendant does not start the judicial proceedings; the claimant does. It seems reasonable that the claimant has to come to the defendant to satisfy a claim (more detail on this reasoning in chapter eight). However, the special nature of tort actions, and physical injury cases in particular, presents an example where the interests of the injured party may outweigh the normal conjuncture of bringing suits at the location of the defendant. Claimants in physical injury actions should be given the benefit of local jurisdiction. Considering the necessity to balance both parties' interests, and the reasoning of corrective justice, personal injury victims should have the option to bring suits at their location.

In personal injury cases, pursuant to Article 29(5) of the Code of Civil Procedure, claimants in Russia can sue at the location of the defendant, or at the place where a tortious act took place or damage was sustained, or at the place of residence of the claimant.[35] In addition, the law waives the filing fee for persons bringing personal injury actions.[36] Therefore, in this regard, the Russian approach

[34] T Hartley, *International Commercial Litigation: Texts, Cases and Materials on Private International Law* (Cambridge University Press, 2009) 55.

[35] Postanovlenie Plenuma Verkhovnogo Suda ot 26 ianvaria 2010 no 1 o Primenenii Sudami Grazhdanskogo Zakonodatel'stva, Reguliruiushchego Otnosheniia po Obiazatel'stvam vsledstvie Prichinenii Vreda Zhizni ili Zdorov'iu Grazhdanina (Resolution of the Supreme Court of the RF on Application by Courts of Civil Law regulating Relations on Liability Resulting from Death or Personal Injury of a Citizen) of 26 January 2010 no 1. The Resolution guides Russian courts in adjudicating claims arising out of personal injury or death (damage to life or health of a citizen).

[36] Postanovlenie Plenuma Verkhovnogo Suda RF ot 10 marta 2011 no 2 o Primenenii Sudami Zakonodatel'stva ob Obiazatel'nom Strakhovanii ot Neschastnykh Sluchaev na Proizvodstve i

is very plaintiff-friendly and appears to provide great protection for the aggrieved persons. The rule aims to ensure proper access to justice for wronged individuals who need the protection of the state. It directly relates to the fundamental constitutional right to life and health. Even where the tort was committed abroad, and even where the tortfeasor was domiciled in a third state (neither in Russia, nor at the place where the tort was committed), Russia provides very protective conditions to the victims resident in Russia.

This rule may be explained by several historical reasons. During the post-Soviet economic collapse, many people were wronged by the negligent behaviour of employers and force majeure circumstances. The rule attained great importance because of numerous disadvantaged groups of the population in Russia who suddenly lost protection of the socialist state. Previously, the state, as the major provider of jobs and social welfare, was expected to support all social groups. Furthermore, prior to the communist regime, the relationship between the state and its people carried paternalistic undertones: Father-Tsar (*tsar-batyushka*, affectionate name for the tsar in Russia) was expected to take care of his dominion and his people. This cultural attitude of the need to protect certain classes carried through centuries and generations. One of the manifestations of this phenomenon is the present-day rule, allowing people who were wronged to bring suits at their convenience, at the place of their residence.

In this regard, a parallel may be drawn with the French justice system. In torts, an action in France may be filed where the event causing the damage occurred or damage was suffered, ie, where a French citizen suffers damage. In addition, in France, victims of certain criminal offences resulting in personal injury (even if committed abroad) may claim compensation from a French public fund. The fund subrogates the rights of the victim and takes an action to recover the money from the tortfeasor. This scheme was established after the Cour de cassation ruling relating to a French national who was injured while jet-skiing in the US.[37] The French national was first denied compensation by the Versailles court of appeal, because the conduct that caused him harm (jet-skiing) could not be classified as a tort under American law. The Cour de cassation reversed the judgment, totally excluding the relevance of the foreign law. It satisfied the action for damages and set the precedent for compensation for an act committed abroad, notwithstanding whether the act constituted a tort there. The claimant who suffered the injury only had to prove the offence according to French law. Moreover, the public fund in France provided immediate compensation to the victim. Finally, the French

Professiona'nykh Zabolevaniĭ (Resolution of the Supreme Court of the RF On Application by the Courts of Law on Accident Insurance Occurring at the Place of Work and Sickness resulting from Work) of 10 March 2011 no 2, para 2.

[37] Cour de cassation, Chambre civile 2, 25 janvier 2007, 06-10.514, *Publié au bulletin* (Court of Cassation, Civil Chamber, published in the Bulletin 25 January 2007, 06-10.514), available at: www.legifrance.gouv.fr/affichJuriJudi.do?oldAction=rechJuriJudi&idTexte=JURITEXT000017626232&fastReqId=1259025937&fastPos=2.

judgment would not need to be enforced by the victim himself outside France. Notably, if the same happened in relation to a Russian victim of a jet-skiing accident in the US, a Russian court would accept jurisdiction and follow Russian law when classifying the alleged wrong committed. The difference, however, would be in the enforcement of the judgment. No public fund in Russia would compensate the victim. The claimant would have to enforce the Russian court order in America, and its enforceability would depend on a whole list of factors. Thus, allowing the claimant to bring a suit at his place of residence is protective and may seem plaintiff-friendly. However, sometimes, enforcement considerations might preclude the victim from appealing to the justice system to recover damages altogether.

In comparison, in the EU regulation of jurisdiction, the Brussels I Recast only refers to the place where the harmful event or damage occurred (although the place of damage may often be the domicile of the injured party). Thus, the EU approach recognises the right to file at the location of the injured party, but only where it coincides with the jurisdiction where the act giving rise to a claim took place or where the damage was sustained. The right to bring suit at the place of residence of a victim was not included in the EU jurisdiction regime, starting from the very conception of the Brussels Convention.[38] The original contracting parties to the Brussels Convention on jurisdiction regarded the possibility of a plaintiff bringing a tort case at his domicile to be excessive and undesirable and the rule did not find its way into the EU jurisdiction regime. Instead, a more widely accepted and practised rule of allocating jurisdiction in tort actions was adopted – connecting the case with the place where damage was sustained.

Except for a few EU Member States that have no specific jurisdictional basis for tort (Finland, Greece, Poland), most European countries recognise the place of the causal event and where the damage was sustained as the basis for jurisdiction in tort.[39] Notably, two EU countries – Latvia and Lithuania – foresee the possibility for tort victims to sue at the place of their residence. In particular, claims for personal injury and actions for the recovery of property (in Latvia), and any claims for damage to property (in Lithuania) may be brought at the domicile of the plaintiff. Such a protective attitude towards victims of torts in Latvia and Lithuania obviously emanates from their common past with Soviet Russia, and the influence of Russian law in the Baltic states. Apart from these two republics, bringing claims at the place of residence of the alleged victim is not explicitly envisaged in the EU.

[38] This may be inferred from the absence of its mention in the Jenard Report, usually referred to as an explanatory report in conjunction with the adoption of the Brussels Convention 1968: P Jenard (ed), 'Report on the Convention on Jurisdiction and Enforcement of Judgments in Civil and Commercial Matters' (1979) OJ C 59/1 (Jenard Report).

[39] A Nuyts, 'General Report on Study on Residual Jurisdiction (Review of the Member States' Rules concerning the "Residual Jurisdiction" of their courts in Civil and Commercial Matters pursuant to the Brussels I and II Regulations)' (3 September 2007, 3rd version) 34, available at: ec.europa.eu/civiljustice/news/docs/study_residual_jurisdiction_en.pdf (the Nuyts Study).

Similarly, English residual rules of jurisdiction do not permit tort actions based on the domicile of the claimant. Claims made in tort involving non-EU defendants may be brought in England pursuant to ground 9 of rule 3.1 of the Practice Direction. English courts may accept jurisdiction and permit servicing out of the jurisdiction where the damage was sustained or resulted from an act committed in England.[40] Additionally, there may be other ways to keep the jurisdiction of an English court in tort cases. For instance, an injured individual has a choice to base his claim on tort or contract when suing his employer for negligence, as in *Matthews v Kuwait Bechtel*,[41] where the English court permitted serving a claim against a foreign employer with no office in England, out of the jurisdiction. The jurisdiction was based on a contract governed by English law and made in England, even though the injury occurred in Kuwait. The contract had enough connection to England, and the claimant successfully recovered damages in the English court.

C. Place of Damage to Reputation: Defamation

A special mention needs to be given to defamation cases. Reputational damage is hard to quantify or attach to a certain place. In addition, specificity of damage to reputation exemplifies an interesting interrelation between the interests of the involved parties as well as certain territorial interests of the states.

Both the EU and Russian legal systems appropriately allocate jurisdiction at the place where the damage to reputation was sustained. In addition, a victim whose reputation has been damaged has the option of bringing the suit at the location of the defendant. This broadens the number of places where the suit could be brought. This properly provides access to justice for the plaintiff both at his own residence and at the location of the defendant. It also appears practical to separate the scope of damage to the reputation to a few jurisdictions, each exercising its share in damage at the corresponding territory, except in some cases involving publication on the internet.

In particular, defamation in Russia is viewed as dissemination of false and defamatory information discrediting honour, dignity or business reputation (Article 152 of the Civil Code). The provision on protection of business reputation equally applies to individuals and legal entities.[42] In addition to tangible

[40] Courts Procedure Rules, Practice Direction 6B – Service Out of the Jurisdiction, para 3.1(9) (UK). (The rule used to be known previously as Order 11 r 1(1)(f)).

[41] *Matthews v Kuwait Bechtel Corp* [1959] 2 QB 57.

[42] Grazhdanskiĭ Kodeks Rossiĭskoĭ Federatsii (Civil Code of the RF) of 30 November 1994 no 51-ФЗ (pt 1) of 2001 art 152(7) (Russian Civil Code). Also, Opredelenie Konstitutsionnogo Suda RF ot 4 dekabria 2003 g no 508-O ob Otkaze v Priniatii k Rassmotreniiu Zhaloby Grazhdanina Shlafmana Vladimira Arkad'evicha na Narushenie ego Konstitutsionnykh Prav punktom 7 stat'i 152

(economic, financial) damage, legal entities have the right to claim non-pecuniary harm.[43] Victims of defamation can file for damages in a court of general jurisdiction in Russia (since individuals normally cannot bring actions to *arbitrazh* courts) relying on the provisions of the Civil Code[44] and other statutory law.[45] They would have to prove the falsity of the opinion expressed in a publication; the actual injury to reputation; the causal effect of the publication and the injury to reputation, etc – ie, all the attributes of a defamation claim. If they could show that the damage occurred in Russia, the local court would accept jurisdiction and hear the case. In addition to the tort-related jurisdiction rule, Article 402(9) of the Code of Civil Procedure contains the rule on the protection of business reputation of Russian residents in Russian courts.

In the EU, defamation actions fall under the claims concerning liability in tort and delict, pursuant to Article 7(2) of Brussels Ia. In *Shevill*,[46] the ECJ has resolved that courts of each Member State where the injury was suffered shall have jurisdiction relating to the harm caused in that state and the courts of the state of the domicile of the defendant shall have jurisdiction relating to all harm caused.[47] In that case, Ms Shevill, a UK resident, temporarily employed in Paris, and other claimants argued against Presse Alliance SA, a company registered under French law with no activity in England. After a defamatory article was published, claimants sued Presse Alliance SA in England asking for damages for libel in relation to the copies of the publication in France and in England. Jurisdiction of the English High Court was disputed, since, according to Presse Alliance SA, no harmful event had occurred in England. The English court asked for guidance from the ECJ. AG Darmon and AG Léger deliberated on the appropriateness of bringing an action in England (at the place where the damage to the claimant's reputation occurred) and in France (at the location of the defendant, and at the place where the article was published). They decided that the Member State's courts should

Grazhdanskogo Kodeksa RF (Decision of the Constitutional Court of the RF of 4 December 2003 no 508-O on Rejecting Consideration of a Claim by Mr Shlafman V A on Violation of His Constitutional Rights by Article 152(7) of the Civil Code of the Russian Federation' (2004) *Vestnik Konstitutsionnogo Suda* RF, no 3. Also, Postanovlenie Plenuma Verkhovnogo Suda RF ot 20 dekabria 1994 g no 10 'Nekotorye Voprosy Primeneniia Zakonodatel'stva o Kompensatsii Moral'nogo Vreda' (Resolution of the Plenum of Supreme Court of the Russian Federation 'Certain Issues on Application of Legislation on Compensation for Moral Harm') of 20 December 1994 no 10.

[43] See, Resolution of the Constitutional Court no 10 (n 42).

[44] CCP art 402(9).

[45] Postanovlenie Plenuma Verkhovnogo Suda RF ot 24 fevralia 2005 no 3 o Sudebnoĭ Praktike po Delam o Zashchite Chesti i Dostoinstva Grazhdan, a takzhe Delovoĭ Reputatsii Grazhdan i Iuridicheskikh Lits (Resolution of the Supreme Court of the RF on Court Practice in Cases of Protection of Honour and Dignity of Individuals as Well as Business Reputation of Individuals and Legal Entities) of 24 February 2005 no 3.

[46] Case-68/93 *Shevill v Presse Alliance SA* [1995] ECR I-415, para 33.

[47] This is also consistent with the interpretation of the Lugano Convention on jurisdiction 2007 applicable among the EU Member States and Iceland, Switzerland, Norway and Denmark: F Pocar, 'Explanatory Report on the Convention on Jurisdiction and the Recognition and Enforcement of Judgments in Civil and Commercial Matters, signed in Lugano on 30 October 2007' OJ C 319/1.

have jurisdiction for damage sustained within that jurisdiction, and the courts at the location of the defendant should have full jurisdiction in relation to all the damage in several Member States. Although such an approach, admittedly, appeared disadvantageous because of the different courts' competence and potential of diverging decisions, such a solution was the most appropriate. The victim was not deprived of access to justice at her domicile, where she enjoys a certain reputation. At the same time, the plaintiff always had the option to bring a suit in relation to all the damages at the location of the publishing company. This decision allowed 'a plaintiff freedom to forum shop to a very great degree' reasonably limiting it 'in terms of recovering damages'.[48] The interests of the aggrieved party were properly taken care of. I find the decision appropriate, since its rationale had little to do with state sovereignty: it did not interfere with it or concern it. Jurisdiction of courts at the location where the aggrieved party suffered reputational damage was justified in consideration of that party's interests, not state sovereignty.

The ECJ's position towards jurisdiction in defamation cases further developed in the *eDate* case and in *Martinez v MGN*.[49] The two joint cases raised questions of jurisdiction in civil liability suits for information and photographs published on the internet. In *eDate*, a German national brought an action before a German court seeking an injunction against eDate, a company operating an advertising internet portal, ordering eDate to refrain from publishing any information about the German individual. The injunction would apply throughout the German territory. EDate argued against the jurisdiction of the German court in this matter. In *Martinez v MGN*, a British newspaper published (online) some photographs and commentary regarding a certain celebrity's relationship with Mr Martinez. The plaintiff then, with his father (both of French nationality), brought an action in France and argued infringement of their right to privacy and the right of Mr Martinez to his own image. The defendant disputed jurisdiction of the French courts.

The ECJ considered both cases together. Taking into consideration the profound changes brought by the internet regarding dissemination of information, the Court had to consider adapting the *Shevill* ruling to the internet publications. In the most crucial part of his opinion, AG Cruz Villalón speculated on assessing the damage inflicted by the internet publication. He explains that the particularity of the internet is such that no reliable criteria could precisely indicate the impact of a certain publication on a certain territory. Even the number of 'hits'

[48] D Kenny and L Heffernan, 'Defamation and Privacy and the Rome II Regulation' in P Stone and Y Farah (eds), *Research Handbook on EU Private International Law* (Edward Elgar Publishing, 2015).

[49] Cases C-509/09 *eDate Advertising Gmbh v X* and C-161/10 *Martinez v MGN* [2011] ECR I-10269 (*eDate*). Also see the ECJ's diverging decision tying the reputational damage only to the place where the tort was committed in Case C-441/13 *Pez Hejduk v EnergieAgentur NRW GmbH* [2015] Judgment of 22 January 2015; Marta Requejo, 'Is the Shevill Doctrine Still Up to Date? Some Further Thoughts on CJEU's Judgment in Hejduk (Case C-441/13)' (*ConflictofLaws*.net, 24 January 2015), available at: conflictoflaws.net/2015/is-the-shevill-doctrine-still-up-to-date-some-further-thoughts-on-cjeus-judgment-in-hejduk-c-44113.

on a website 'do not provide sufficient guarantees for the purposes of establishing conclusively and definitively that unlawful damage has occurred'.[50] Therefore, he recommended allowing the plaintiff to bring an action for all the damage caused in the place which could be characterised as the 'centre of gravity of the dispute'. In accordance with this recommendation, the ECJ relaxed its earlier *Shevill* approach. It concluded that an action for all the damage caused may be brought either where the publisher is established or before the courts of the Member State where the centre of the plaintiff's interests is based. This updated approach fits my world-view on jurisdiction. Relaxing the requirement to bring the action in full only at the location of the publisher (the defendant) fits well with the general liberalisation of jurisdiction rules. It takes into consideration current developments in the media where damaging content can be published/accessed anywhere. Perhaps, it does not fairly account for the interests of media publishers who have to expect to be sued virtually anywhere their content affected someone. However, in the end, on the scales of justice, the interests of the aggrieved party outweigh the interests of the media publishers. Moreover, it adds an additional incentive for the media to be cautious in publishing damaging information.

One of the most famous and most compelling examples of a defamation case involving a Russian national is, undoubtedly, *Berezovsky v Michaels*.[51] In that case, Russian businessmen Berezovsky and Glouchkov filed a claim in England against an American publisher, Forbes, for defamation in a magazine with a circulation of 748,123 copies in the United States, 566 in England and Wales and 13 in Russia. The allegedly defamatory article was also published via the internet; however the specific issues arising out of the defamation over the internet were not given special attention in this case due to an insufficient number of 'published' online copies. Why did Berezovsky and Glouchkov bring an action in England? The main reason must have been the strict approach to defamation (libel) in England. English libel law has been characterised as 'pro-claimant oriented',[52] giving reputation an overwhelming status vis-a-vis free speech,[53] and perhaps one of the strictest in the world,[54] especially identified through the *McLibel* saga.[55] It may be argued, that the

[50] *eDate*, Opinion of AG Cruz Villalon, para 50, referring to DJB Svantesson, *Private International Law and the Internet* (Kluwer Law International, 2007) 324; and I Roth, *Die internationale Zuständigkeit Deutscher Gerichte bei Persönlichkeitsrechtverletzungen im Internet* (*The International Jurisdiction of German Courts in the Case of Violations of Personality Rights on the Internet*) (Peter Lang, 2006) 283.

[51] *Berezovsky v Michaels*) [2000] 1 WLR 1004 (*Berezovsky*).

[52] See T Hartley, 'Libel Tourism" and Conflict of Laws' (2010) 59 *International & Comparative Law Quarterly* 25.

[53] R Garnett and M Richardson, 'Libel Tourism or Just Redress?' (2009) 5 *Journal of Private International Law* 471, 487.

[54] Recently, an opinion has been proposed that Australia is becoming the strictest forum in the world when it comes to libel, attracting many international claims. See, eg, D Rolph, 'Splendid Isolation? Australia as a Destination for "Libel Tourism"' (2012) 19 *Australian International Law Journal* 79.

[55] *McDonald's Corporation v Steel & Morris* [1997] EWHC QB 366. US based McDonald's Corporation and its British subsidiary McDonald's Restaurants Ltd sued five protesters from the London Greenpeace group (independent from the International Greenpeace movement) for distributing

Russian businessmen searched for a court which in their opinion was most likely to provide a favourable judgment (libel tourism). It may be speculated further, that their motivation to sue in England was supported by their ability to afford the expenses associated with suing in England.

The main question in *Berezovsky* concerned whether the English forum was the most appropriate forum. The claimants sought compensation for damage to their reputations in England, for which, they argued, the English court represented the most appropriate forum. To determine whether England was the most appropriate forum, the *Cordoba Shipping*[56] and *Spiliada*[57] cases were considered. *Cordoba Shipping* provides that the most appropriate court to try the claim is where it is manifestly just and reasonable that the defendant should answer for his wrongdoing.[58] The *Spiliada* case establishes the classic test to see if England was the 'most appropriate forum'. It required that the case be tried in a forum more suitable to the interests of all the parties and the ends of justice. The burden of proof rests on the defendant to show that a more appropriate forum for the trial exists. Regard must be had to other factors, including the availability of witnesses, the governing law of the transaction, etc. Finally, the court has the discretion to stay or refuse to stay the proceedings, as justice so requires.[59]

These criteria were discussed in *Berezovsky*. At first instance, Popplewell LJ found that the plaintiffs' connection with England was tenuous, and that they failed to show that England was an appropriate forum for trial of action. On appeal by the plaintiffs, however, the Court of Appeal admitted new evidence and held that the plaintiffs' connections with England were in fact significant which gave them a strong prima facie case for a trial in England. Forbes believed that Russia or the United States would be more appropriate jurisdictions for the trial. However, both the US and Russia were found unsuitable. Because the plaintiffs' connection with the US was slight, the US was not an appropriate forum. Although Russia was the centre of the claimants' sphere of operations, the circulation of the magazine there was minimal. By a majority, the House of Lords believed that 'it is clear that a judgment in favour of the plaintiffs in Russia will not be seen to redress the damage to the reputations of the plaintiffs in England', and Russia, therefore, could not realistically be treated as an appropriate forum where the ends of justice could be achieved.[60] The most appropriate (the natural) forum for the dispute was the one where the tort was committed. The claim purported to recover compensation

leaflets attacking McDonald's corporate practices. Two of the protesters refused to capitulate and fought the lawsuit for several years: D Vick and K Campbell, 'Public Protests, Private Lawsuits, and the Market: The Investor Response to the McLibel Case' (2001) 28 *Journal of Law and Society* 204; and Douglas Vick and Kevin Campbell, 'McLibel: Longest Case in English History' (*BBC News*, 15 February 2005), available at: news.bbc.co.uk/2/hi/uk_news/4266741.stm.

[56] *Cordoba Shipping Co Ltd v National State Bank* [1984] 2 Lloyd's Rep 91 (CA) (*Cordoba Shipping*).

[57] *Spiliada Maritime Corporation v Cansulex Ltd* [1987] AC 460 (*Spiliada*).

[58] *Cordoba Shipping*, 96.

[59] *Spiliada*, 476–78.

[60] *Berezovsky*, 1015.

for damage to reputation suffered in England. It did not deal with the entirety of the claim worldwide; the dispute concerned whether the English courts had jurisdiction over the claim for damage to reputation in England. The claimants could still sue independently for damage suffered in the US, Russia, etc (although they believed those jurisdictions were inappropriate).

The case demonstrated a good example of the deliberation of factors involved while considering the fairness of adjudicating a defamation claim in different courts. It described nuances and considerations that need to be accounted for when determining an appropriate forum to hear and decide a reputational damage claim. It provided an appropriate solution – adjudicating a claim in a forum where reputational damage was sustained.

D. Place of Potential Tort

Regardless of some changes recommended below, my analysis shows that the interests of private parties to civil transactions are accounted for in the law on jurisdiction in cases of potential torts in the EU and Russia. In the EU, in addition to actual torts, the jurisdictional rule embraces harmful events that 'may occur'. In Russia, at least in relation to proprietary rights, claimants are provided with jurisdictional provisions allowing them to bring suits at their location or at the place of the prospective harmful event.

In particular, the EU rule on jurisdiction in torts also applies in actions for negative declaration, ie, seeking to declare that no tort has been committed. This approach by the ECJ has been embodied in *Folien v Ritrama*.[61] In that case, two Swiss companies sued an Italian company. Folien sought to declare that no tort had been committed, and no compensation should have been paid. After the initial rejection by German courts to accept the claim based on Article 5(3) of the Brussels I Regulation, the ECJ later concluded that an action for a negative declaration seeking to establish the absence of liability in tort can fall within Article 5(3) of Brussels I as well. If an action shows a connection with the state in which the damage occurred (or may occur), and a connection with the state in which the causal event giving rise to that damage took place, the court in one of those two places has to hear such an action.[62] This decision aimed to provide better certainty and predictability within the Brussels jurisdiction regime. Classifying cases relating to tort, even if the tort is absent, in the same category with torts improves legal certainty and predictability. This approach benefits the interests of potential tort victims: they can rely on the existing jurisdictional rules in torts, which helps them to reasonably predict an appropriate forum in which to bring their suits.

[61] Case C-133/11 *Folien Fischer AG and another v Ritrama SpA* [2012] Judgment of 25 October 2012.
[62] ibid para 52.

In comparison, the Russian Codes of Civil and *Arbitrazh* Procedure fail to envisage jurisdiction rules for torts that 'may occur'. The jurisdictional rules relating to torts only refer to harmful events that have already taken place, without mentioning potential or non-existent torts. Thus, to bring a tort-related suit, a person must actually suffer damage in Russia before seeking compensation. However, Russian law envisages preventive actions that may be interpreted as claims for compensation resulting from potential violations (comparable in character to preventive measures against imminent torts in English law, where damages may be claimed 'in respect of a failure to do or the doing of a certain thing').[63] In fact, Russia foresees preventive sanctions in many types of cases, such as intellectual property rights protection, legal implications of invalidity of a transaction, and others.[64] In those cases, claims may be brought in several locations, including the place of residence of the plaintiff or the place of violation of the plaintiff's rights. In particular, injunction applications concerning property interests can be filed at the location of the plaintiff, or at the location of monetary funds or other property in relation to which the applicant petitions for the preventive measures to be taken, or at the place of violation of the rights of the applicant.[65] In addition, Russian law provides for special regulation of injunction applications connected with corporate disputes. The 'corporate disputes' are understood as disputes connected with the establishment, management and ownership of legal entities. They may include claims relating to the attribution of shares of a corporation, management of a company, complaints regarding decisions of the organs of the corporation, the issuing of securities, and other disputes.[66] The Code provides that the injunction application protecting proprietary interests relating to these disputes shall be brought at the location of the legal entity concerned, or, where the dispute arises from the activity of a registrar of securities holders – at the location of the securities issuer.

In practice, bringing an application for injunction at the claimant's location may not always be advisable, in the interest of the claimant himself. As elaborated by the Russian Supreme *Arbitrazh* Court, for the purpose of effective enforcement of the preventive measures, it is more advisable to bring the injunction application at the location of the infringement of rights of the applicant.[67] The Court stressed that when bringing the application at the claimant's own location, the applicant, inter alia, must present evidence that his appearance at the location of the defendant or the defendant's property is 'problematic', such as causing financial hardship,

[63] JHC Morris et al, *Dicey and Morris on the Conflict of Laws*, 9th edn (Stevens & Sons Ltd, 1973) 189.
[64] Russian Civil Code art 1065(1).
[65] CAP art 99(3).
[66] CAP art 225.1.
[67] Informatsionnoe Pismo Presidiuma Vysshego Arbitrazhnogo Suda RF ot 7 iiulia 2004 g no 78 'Obzor Praktiki Primeneniia Arbitrazhnymi Predvaritel'nykh Obespechitelnykh Mer' (Information Letter of the Presidium of the Supreme *Arbitrazh* Court of the RF 'Review of *Arbitrazh* Court Practice on Preventive Measures') of 9 July 2004 no 78, para 31.

long travel distance, etc. Also, courts at the location of the alleged civil wrong, for example, the distribution of counterfeit goods in relation to which an injunction is sought for attachment, may have greater access to the evidence of such counterfeit goods on the local market. The Court accentuated the point made in its earlier Resolution,[68] specifying that injunctions can only be accepted where failure to take the measures may result in significant irreversible harmful consequences for the applicant.

Therefore, the Russian rules of jurisdiction in torts and in actions relating to potential torts are segmented into separate provisions. For the purpose of clarity and certainty, the Russian legislators should consider bringing these provisions together. It can be done by incorporating potential tort (delict) activity into the range of claims embraced by the provision of special jurisdiction in torts. Simply adding the wording 'harmful events that may occur' will suffice. Alternatively, the rule on jurisdiction in preventive measures could be put together with the relevant articles elaborating on special (alternative) jurisdiction.

III. No Choice of Forum in Contract: Jurisdiction at the Place of Performance

In addition to jurisdiction in torts, a proper mechanism of jurisdiction needs to be considered for contractual cases with no choice of forum. The absence of choice of forum in contract may result from different reasons. In some situations, the very absence of the forum selection clause reflects the autonomy of the parties not to include it on purpose. In such cases, the interests of party autonomy will be well accounted for by application of the default rules.

Besides the default rule of bringing claims to the courts at the domicile of the defendant, an alternative place of jurisdiction in contract-related claims may be the place of performance of a contract. Both EU and Russian jurisdiction systems envisage this rule. The Brussels I Recast asserts that a person domiciled in a Member State may be sued in the courts for the place of performance of the obligation in question in matters relating to a contract.[69] The rule has been polished by decades of practice within the EU states (Benelux, for instance). The Brussels Convention[70] incorporated this rule, and now it continues to be applied by courts in the EU.

[68] Postanovlenie Plenuma Vysshego Arbitrazhnogo Suda RF ot 9 dekabriia 2002 g no 11 o Nekotorykh Voprosakh, Sviazannykh s Vvedeniem v Deĭstvie Arbitrazhnogo Protsessual'nogo Kodeksa RF (Resolution of the Plenum of the Supreme *Arbitrazh* Court of the RF on Certain Issues Connected to the Code on *Arbitrazh* Procedure of the Russian Federation Coming into Effect) of 9 December 2002 no 11, para 13.

[69] Brussels I Recast art 7(1).

[70] Jenard Report, 23.

Similarly, in Russia, in disputes involving Russian parties or Russian and foreign parties, Russian courts shall have jurisdiction in cases with participation of foreign persons in claims arising out of a contract, according to which full or partial performance should take place or took place in Russia.[71] A suit arising out of a contract in which the place of its execution is specified, may be brought to a court at the place of execution or performance of the contract in Russia, at the discretion of the plaintiff.[72]

Why empower the court with jurisdiction at the place of performance of a contract? Most importantly, the rule accounts to the parties' will. Parties choose to enter into contractual relationships voluntarily. They negotiate various terms of the contract, including where it ought to be performed. They consent to a particular place (or places) of performance when signing the contract. It could be further argued that where parties conclude a contract to be performed at a certain location, they open their minds to the possibility of a potential dispute at that location. Empowering the courts at the place of performance of the contract with jurisdiction, although indirectly, enforces party autonomy. Further rationale for the rule is practicality. Similar to the above-mentioned situations in torts, a court at the place of performance of the obligation in question is best placed to collect the necessary evidence. Also, a plaintiff may be inclined to sue at the place of performance of the obligation in anticipation of recovery of damages at the place where the contract was performed. Additionally, a court at the place of performance may be better situated to apply the local customs or public policy relating to the contractual obligations. Therefore, the objectives of the rule include effectiveness of judicial process, proper access to justice, and legal certainty. All these objectives benefit the parties to the contract.

A lot depends on understanding of the 'place of performance'. In my view, courts should interpret the place of performance as the place of carrying out the (main) obligation in question. To see whether the rule satisfies the test of placing the interests of the parties at the forefront, I analyse the EU and Russian definitions of 'place of performance'.

A. Understanding of 'Place of Performance'

Normally, the place of performance of a contract can be deduced from the content of the contract. In some cases, however, there may be a disagreement. The Brussels I Recast provides a uniform definition of place of performance in contracts for sale of goods or provision of services for the purpose of jurisdiction in cross-border disputes involving EU parties. It specifies that 'unless otherwise agreed, the place of performance of the obligation in question shall be … the place

[71] CCP art 402(5).
[72] CCP art 29(9); and CAP arts 36(4) and 247(1)(3).

where the goods were or should have been delivered' or 'where the services were or should have been provided'.[73]

In contrast to the EU, Russia takes a stricter stance towards the understanding of 'place of performance' of a contract for the purpose of jurisdiction. In particular, the Russian rules specifically require the place of performance to be identified within the text of a contract: 'suits arising out of contracts, in which a place of performance is specified, may be brought to a(n) (*arbitrazh*) court at the place of performance of such a contract'.[74] An appropriate venue to bring claims is easy to determine if the contract mentions its sole place of performance. What about other cases? Should it be inferred from the content of the contract, or from the nature of the obligation in question?

In its explanatory resolutions, the Russian Supreme Court has shed some light on the issue. In particular, in transactions with promissory notes, the Court established that where the place of payment of obligations on a promissory note does not coincide with the location or place of residence of the person under the obligation in question, a claim may be filed either at the place of payment or at the location of the defendant.[75] In claims arising out of copyright agreements, the Supreme Court clarified that they may be brought at the place of performance, ie, at the place of submission of the manuscript to the editor, place of payment of remuneration, or a presentation of author's copies.[76] However, what about the vast variety of all other types of civil and commercial contracts?

Two contrasting views coexist in practice. One approach is to interpret the jurisdiction rule literally. Supporters of this strict approach, including a number of judges, deem that the rule applies only where the specific place of performance is directly stated in the contract.[77] They draw their support from the opinion of Vaskovskiĭ, a prominent classical Russian jurist and scholar.[78] Vaskovskiĭ believed that the alternative to bringing a suit at the place of performance of a contract may

[73] Brussels I Recast art 7(1). As explained in *Falco*, the concept of service 'implies, at least, that the party who provides the service carries out a particular activity in return for remuneration' (Case C-533/07 *Falco Privatstiftung and Rabitsch* [2009] ECR I-3327, para 29).

[74] CCP art 29(9); and CAP art 36(4).

[75] Postanovlenie Plenuma Verkhovnogo Suda RF no 33, Plenuma Vysshego Arbitrazhnogo Suda no 14 ot 4 dekabria 2000 g o Nekotorykh Voprosakh Praktiki Rassmotreniia Sporov, Sviazannykh s Obrashcheniem Vekseleĭ (Resolution of the Plenum of the Supreme Court of the RF no 33 and the Plenum of the Supreme *Arbitrazh* Court of the RF no 14 of 4 December 2000 on Certain Questions in Court Practice of Dispute Resolution Regarding Promissory Notes).

[76] Postanovlenie Plenuma Verkhovnogo Suda RF ot 19 iiunia 2006 g no 15 o Voprosakh, Voznikshikh u Sudov pri Rassmotrenii Grazhdanskikh Del, Sviazannykh s Primeneniem Zakonodatel'stva ob Avtorskom Prave i Smezhnykh Pravah (Resolution of the Plenum of the Supreme Court of the RF on Questions Arising in Courts Consideration Civil Cases Connected with Application of the Law on Copyright and Connected Rights) of 19 June 2006 no 15, art 9.

[77] eg, P Krasheninnikov, Postateinyĭ Kommentariĭ k Arbitrazhnomu Protsessual'nomu Kodeksu (Article-by-Article Commentary on Code of Arbitrazh Procedure) (Statut, 2007) 212.

[78] R Opalev and E Rebrova, 'Rassmotrenie Spora po Mestu Ispolneniia Dogovora' ('Adjudication at the Place of Performance of Contract') (2011) 10 *EZh-Jurist* 3, referring to E Vas'kovskiĭ, *Uchebnik*

only be permitted where the contract is due to be performed at a particular place, and such types of contract usually specify that place. He also foresaw a possibility to deduce the place of performance from the nature of a contract. However, since 1917, the statutory embodiment of Vaskovskiĭ's ideas have eventually developed into a shorter version, allocating all claims in relation to a contract with a specific place of performance to courts at that location. Russian judges have inherited from the times of the former Soviet Union 'a rather legalistic tradition' in interpreting the law, where literal meaning and systematic arguments prevail, in the interests of certainty.[79] This style of literal interpretation explains why some courts strictly require the place of performance to be stated in a contract for the claim to be brought at that location.

A better approach is to understand the place of performance from the content of the contract, even if it does not specify it. Divergence in application of the rule persists in court practice. The first variation manifests itself in applying the jurisdiction rule where performance of obligations by both parties is done at the same place. The second group of cases dictate that the place of performance of obligations in question should be understood as the place where the party bringing a suit performs its liabilities. The third option gives preference to the principal obligation as inferred from the nature of the contract, and then basing jurisdiction on the place of performance of that obligation. Rightfully so, uncertainty existing in relation to this rule objectively requires clarification by the Russian Supreme Court.[80]

I argue that by analogy of legislation (*analogia legis*), deemed to fill in the gaps in law, place of performance of a contract could be determined pursuant to Article 316 of the Russian Civil Code explaining 'the place of performance of an obligation in question'. Article 316 reads:

> If not otherwise defined by the law, or provided in the contract, or clear from business practice or the nature of the obligation, the place of performance of an obligation is understood as:
>
> - In obligations to transfer immovable property – the location of the property.
> - In obligations of delivery of goods or other property – the place of delivery to the first carrier to deliver it to the creditor.
> - In other commercial obligations on transfer of goods or other property – the place of manufacture or storage of the property, if the place was known to the creditor at the time of the obligation.

Grazhdanskogo Protsessa (*Textbook on Civil Procedure*) (Statut, 1917). Also, A Anisimov, 'Podsudnost' Dela: Pravila Chasti 4 stat'I 36 APK RF dlia Podachi Iska' ('Jurisdiction of a Case: Rules of Article 36(4) of CAP RF for Filing a Claim') (2011) *EZh-Jurist* 22; and D Bulgakov, 'Spornaia Podsudnost' ('Disputable Jurisdiction') (2010) 10 *EZh-Jurist* 6.

[79] W Snijders, 'The Civil Codes of the Russian Federation and The Netherlands: Similarities and Contrasts' in W Simons (ed), *Private and Civil Law in the Russian Federation. Essays in Honor of FJM Feldbrugge* (Martinus Nijhoff Publishers, 2009) 19, 25.

[80] Opalev and Rebrova (n 78) 4.

- In monetary obligations – the place of residence or location of the lender at the time of commitment.
- In all other obligations – the place of residence or location of the debtor.[81]

Although the statutory law does not explicitly state that the 'place of performance of an obligation' could mean the 'place of performance of a contract' for the purpose of jurisdiction, it should flow from the meaning of the law. If the Russian legislators implement these changes, it will decrease ambiguity and improve foreseeability regarding jurisdiction in claims arising out of contractual relationships. That, in turn, will benefit the private parties to a transaction.

Many courts already adhere to this position. For instance, in a dispute regarding failure to pay for construction services carried out at a facility in Krasnodar district, jurisdiction of the local court was reaffirmed at the appellate instance.[82] Although the contract did not identify the 'place of performance of the contract', the obligation (construction services) was clearly performed in Krasnodar area. Thus, the court in Krasnodar rightfully assumed jurisdiction based on the place of performance of the defendant's obligations, overriding the general rule of jurisdiction – filing at the location of the state registration of the defendant, which was not in Krasnodar but in the Samara oblast (area). In another case with similar circumstances, an *arbitrazh* court decided that the place of performance can be established through construction of a contract. In that case, a contract for production and installation of metal parts of a tower on a construction site included the address of the construction site. The court interpreted the place of the construction site as the place of performance of the contract, and thus, the place of proper jurisdiction.[83]

B. Several Places of Performance

Some difficulties may arise where contracts, without any clear choice of forum, are performed in several places. In which of those places shall the courts have jurisdiction? Alternatively, rather, should all the competent courts in all those places be available for the plaintiff to bring a suit?

It may seem that narrowing down the choice between a few eligible courts guarantees certainty regarding allocation of jurisdiction among several courts. In addition, practicality may dictate bringing all suits in one place, at the place of performance of the main obligation in question. However, I argue that multiple

[81] Russian Civil Code art 316.

[82] Postanovlenie Federal'nogo Arbitrazhnogo Suda Severo-Kavkazskogo Okruga ot 16 dekabria 2009 (Decision of the Federal *Arbitrazh* Court of North Caucasian Circuit) of 16 December 2009 case no A32-349/2009.

[83] Postenovlenie Arbitrazhnogo Suda Tsentral'nogo Okruga ot 6 oktiabria 2016 g no Ф10-4129/16 (Decision of *Arbitrazh* Court of the Central Circuit) of 6 October 2016 no Ф10-4129/16 case no A14-9741/2016.

places of performance should not raise concerns, but, rather, provide the parties with multiple options. This plurality of options, although diluting legal certainty and predictability, allows for more options, and thus, more freedom of choice for the parties. Having a few fora to choose from increases the parties' access to justice. Why is this approach preferable? To find out, I will evaluate the existing solutions in the EU and Russia.

In the EU, a few ECJ judgments considered contractual obligations performed in several places. In *Color Drack*,[84] goods were delivered in several places within one Member State. The ECJ ruled that the court of the principal place of delivery had jurisdiction. The principal place of delivery had to be determined based on economic criteria. Thus, the ECJ reserved the authority to adjudicate to the court at the main or principal place of performance of the contract. In a later case, *Rehder*,[85] the ECJ decided that the same principle was valid with regard to contracts for the provision of services, including cases where such provision is not effected in one single Member State. In that case, a passenger sought compensation against an airline company for a cancelled flight. The air transport was carried out from one Member State to another, and the airline was established in a third Member State. The places of departure and arrival were equal in terms of provision of services, and it was hard to distinguish them on the basis of a single economic criterion, therefore both places could exercise contract jurisdiction.

This solution is appropriate in light of my overall approach to jurisdiction. Allocation of jurisdiction without any clear parties' choice becomes a balancing exercise. In this case, the airline company carried out activity in both places of departure and arrival, and these places were equally important in terms of performance of the main obligation in question.

In *Wood Floor Solutions*,[86] a question came up again regarding several places of performance. The applicant in the main proceedings, an Austrian company, provided services in several countries, including Austria, Italy, the Baltic states, Poland and Switzerland. When it brought an action in Austria, the court decided it lacked jurisdiction since only a quarter of the company's turnover was generated through its activity in Austria. The applicant took the view that the forum should be determined based on the defendant's centre of business. The defendant argued that *Color Drack* could not have applied in this case, since *Color Drack* only concerned delivery of goods within one single Member State. AG Trstenjak indicated that from the text of Article 5(1)(b) of Brussels I (now Article 7(1)(b) of Brussels Ia), it was unclear whether it applied to contracts performed in one or several Member States. Nevertheless, the question should have been answered in the affirmative as to whether it applied

[84] Case C-386/05 *Color Drack GmbH v Lexx International Vertriebs GmbH* [2007] ECR I-3699.
[85] Case C-204/08 *Peter Rehder v Air Baltic Corporation* [2009] ECR I-6073.
[86] Case C-19/09 *Wood Floor Solutions Andreas Domberger GmbH v Silva Trade SA* [2010] ECR I-2121.

to cases with several Member States involved.[87] Thus, the ECJ, basing its assessment on *Color Drack* and *Rehder*, extended the scope of application of the special jurisdiction rule in contractual obligations with several places of performance. The *Wood Floor Solutions* decision reinforced the principles of proximity and predictability. A different interpretation would contradict these principles of Brussels I, which was adopted to unify the rules governing conflicts of jurisdiction in the EU. Notably, the view that Article 5(1)(b) should apply to contracts for the provision of services in several Member States, was long before expressed by European legal scholars.[88]

In Russia, the jurisdiction rule in contracts with no choice of forum requires the place of performance of a contract to be specified in the contract. Then, that place becomes an alternative venue to bring suits, in addition to the location of the defendant. However, complex civil and commercial transactions may present situations of several places of performance. Some courts in Russia deduce the principal obligation from the nature of the contract, and then base jurisdiction on the place of performance of that obligation.[89] Therefore, the Russian method draws near the EU solution.

Therefore, as already provided for in the EU jurisdiction regime, cases with several places of performance should be heard at the place of the main obligation or main provision of services. In the event, if that is not possible to determine, for example, in regard to commercial agency contracts, the place of establishment of the commercial agent may be viewed as the place of the provision of services. This solution is satisfactory in light of putting the parties' interests at the basis of the law on jurisdiction.

IV. Conclusion

In chapters five and six, I aimed to demonstrate how balancing the private interests of the parties involved in a transaction may help organise jurisdictional rules. I sought to find the balance between access to justice and the interests of persons held liable.

I first analysed the EU and Russian rules on unilateral jurisdiction agreements – agreements providing the parties with differing options to sue.

[87] ibid paras 61–62.

[88] ibid para 66, referring to S Leible, 'Zuständiges Gericht für Entschädigungsansprüche von Flugpassagieren' ('Competent Court for Compensation of Air Passengers') (2009) 16 *Europäische Zeitschrift für Wirtschaftsrecht* 572; H Gaudemet-Tallon, *Compétence et Exécution des Jugements en Europe. Règlement no 44/2001, Conventions de Bruxelles et de Lugano* (*Jurisdiction and Enforcement of Judgments in Europe. Regulation no 44/2001, the Brussels and the Lugano Conventions*), 3rd edn (Librairie Générale de Droit et de Jurisprudence, 2002) 159; and U Magnus and P Mankowski (eds), *European Commentaries on Private International Law: Brussels I Regulation*, 2nd edn (Sellier European Law Publishers, 2012) 147.

[89] Opalev and Rebrova (n 78) 1.

Such agreements may seem to violate the equal treatment of the parties in terms of giving them varying degrees of opportunity to sue. As noted by Keyes and Marshall, unilateral jurisdiction clauses are problematic as they frustrate the very benefits that a jurisdiction agreement is aimed to achieve: clarity, predictability, reducing the risk of multiple proceedings, etc.[90] Further complications are associated with divergent treatment of these clauses in different jurisdictions (such as England and France, as described above). However, provided there is full consent, the asymmetric jurisdiction clauses reflect the will of the parties through their voluntary signing of a contract. I have argued that optional jurisdiction agreements should be enforced unless signed in violation of due procedure or when breaching one party's right to access to justice.

I continued my analysis of jurisdiction clauses included in contracts of adhesion with vulnerable categories of parties. My analysis revealed that the EU approach to jurisdiction strongly protects the interests of weaker parties (consumers, employees and insured persons). In the EU, the weaker parties are provided with access to justice by having the right to sue and being sued at their domicile. In comparison, Russia prescribes special jurisdictional provisions protecting the interests of consumers and, in certain cases, employees as well. It allows the weaker parties to file a suit at the place of their residence or at the place of entering into or performing the contract, in addition to the possibility of bringing the action at the location of the defendant.

I have argued that parties' choice of jurisdiction should be recognised. However, given the nature of contracts of adhesion and less-than-full consent on the part of weaker parties, I conceded to the idea that for certain categories of parties, the right to sue at their domicile may override party autonomy, in cases where this is needed to ensure the weaker party's access to justice. Where there is a risk or evidence of undue influence or duress in imposing a jurisdiction clause of one party on another, there should be an alternative to sue at another forum depending on the nature of the claim. In such situations, protective jurisdiction rules in the EU and Russia appear appropriate.

In chapter six, I evaluated the existing Russian and EU official positions towards jurisdiction in torts for their compatibility with my view on ideal jurisdiction. I selected several categories of torts including personal injury, economic loss, defamation and potential torts, as these areas represent the most interesting issues from the private international law perspective. I have determined that both jurisdictions provide solutions that are acceptable in light of the paramount significance of the interests of the parties. The existing rules allow filing at the location of the defendant, supplemented by the alternative to bring suits at the place where the harmful event was committed, or the place where injury arose, at the discretion of the plaintiff. In addition, Russia permits bringing suits at the location of

[90] M Keyes and BA Marshall, 'Optional Jurisdiction Agreements' (2015) 11 *Journal of Private International Law* 345, 377.

the claimant in personal injury cases, and the EU treats imminent 'torts that may occur' alongside actual torts.

I concluded that it is important for an ideal jurisdiction system to provide several alternatives for the injured party as to where to bring tort actions. In personal injury cases especially, it is crucial to ensure the victim's access to justice at their own location (be it by direct permission, as Russia does, or in the EU way, by interpreting the place where the harm was sustained as a viable place to bring action). At the same time, obtaining a local court's decision may bear potential limitations and delay considerations associated with subsequent enforcement of the decision at the location of the property of the defendant. It may be advisable, in such cases, to bring tort claims at the defendant's location. Either way, the choice should belong to the aggrieved party. The function of a jurisdiction system should be to avail the potential victims of a possibility to seek justice at their closest convenience.

The EU and Russian approaches to jurisdiction in contractual relations with no choice of forum both allocate jurisdiction to courts at the place of performance of a contract. The rule is acceptable, if justified by serving the interests of the parties. Furthermore, the parties' choice of place of performance reflects their will. Thus, empowering courts at the place of performance of contracts implicitly gives effect to the parties' will. My further recommendation for the Russian legislators would be to ease the strict requirement of specifying the place of performance in the contract, and to allow determining it from the meaning of the contract, depending on the main obligation in question.

PART III

Sovereignty and Party Autonomy

7

Sovereignty and Party Autonomy in Civil and Commercial Jurisdiction

I. Introduction

In part III of this book, I finalise the description of a jurisdiction system based on party autonomy, equality and state sovereignty that could fit existing values in the EU and Russia. This part addresses the notion of sovereignty, currently regarded as foundational for jurisdiction in the EU and Russia. I challenge the viability of this traditional approach. I argue that it is time to abandon sovereignty as the starting point of determining an appropriate forum. Instead, it should be allotted a limited place in the hierarchy of values underlying jurisdiction, where party autonomy should be given the priority. I discuss the tension between sovereignty and party autonomy in private cross-border disputes and aim to construct a reasoned reconciliation of these values for the law on jurisdiction.

I envision sovereignty having three dimensions: international sovereignty, home sovereignty, and national public interest represented by the state. Each of these categories embodies different kinds of state interests. The international or public international law sovereignty reflects the state's position in relation to other states and includes its interests of territorial integrity, non-interference in its affairs, equal representation in international affairs, etc. Home sovereignty unites the state's interests within its own borders: its desire for political and economic advancement, control over its own affairs, power over its territory, etc. Finally, the national public interest represents the collective will of state residents/private parties, as opposed to the machinery of the state. In this chapter, I address these types of state sovereignty. Classification between these categories is important because the boundaries of each type of sovereignty in relation to party autonomy are going to be different. In the chapter that follows, I demonstrate how the proposed reconceptualisation could reflect in the existing rules of jurisdiction in the EU and Russia.

II. Extent of International Sovereignty in Private International Law

International sovereignty represents states' positions in relation to other states. International sovereignty (sovereign equality) provides the foundation for the law of nations. It is not the Westphalian constitutional conception of sovereignty, not the Hobbesian 'absolute' sovereignty,[1] not the Austinian sovereignty[2] but a much more limited understanding consistent with neoliberal interpretation in international relations. It is that without which the global system of states would collapse. It is the core of the states' integrity – respect of their territorial borders. It is independence of states from the authority of other states.

Based on this concept of international sovereignty, adjudication is understood as 'an exercise of sovereign power'.[3] The reason why territoriality is seen as foundational for state jurisdiction (legislative, judicial and enforcement jurisdiction) is that it embodies the principles of inviolability of territorial borders and non-interference in the affairs of foreign states. Thus, state international sovereignty (and state immunity) limits the jurisdiction of other states on its territory. More vividly, it is evident in state penal, revenue, antitrust or other public laws. States aim not to encroach into each other's regulation and prosecution of crime or regulation of economy and owe no duty to aid each other unless specifically agreed otherwise. Such non-interference in each other's affairs on criminal or antitrust matters appears universal and holds true both for legislative and judicial jurisdiction. The idea is that where each state's jurisdiction is limited by its territory, it helps maintain the integrity of international relations. Thus, in the broad sense, jurisdiction of state courts is limited at the outset by considerations of international sovereignty.

However, when it comes to states' jurisdiction in civil and commercial matters, it could be argued that adjudication of civil and commercial matters is out of the reach of public international law (the 'local theory' in private international law). The 'local theory' asserts that public international law imposes no significant restrictions on private international law; private international law is a branch of domestic law, and decisions of private international law are non-political.[4]

Nevertheless, I cannot agree with the local theory of private international law in its entirety. Rather, I contend that public and private international law are so intertwined, that in some cases it is rather difficult to discern where 'public' ends and 'private' begins in international law. In this light, I argue that the law of nations draws the initial lines and restricts extraterritoriality of state courts' jurisdiction. States are obliged to avoid undue encroachment on a jurisdiction, more properly

[1] An absolute power of sovereign – that has now become 'impotent': see, E Ip, 'Globalization and the Future of the Law of the Sovereign State' (2010) 8 *International Journal of Constitutional Law* 636, 638.

[2] State sovereignty that is above the law, where the principles of customary international law are enforceable where voluntarily accepted by the sovereign. For further discussion of Austin's view, see A Mills, 'Rethinking Jurisdiction in International Law' (2014) 84 *British Yearbook of International Law* 187, 191.

[3] A Briggs, 'Recognition of Foreign Judgments: A Matter of Obligation' (2013) 129 *Law Quarterly Review* 87.

[4] For more about 'local theory', see A Mills, 'Dimensions of Public Policy in Private International Law' (2008) 4 *Journal of Private International Law* 201, 204.

appertaining to or more appropriately exercisable by, another state.[5] No matter whether private international law is construed as a completely different branch of law, or confluent with public international law,[6] some public international law considerations place constraints on private international law.

One such constraint is international sovereignty. There are always going to be limitations on party autonomy in civil jurisdiction predicated by international sovereignty. These limitations are unavoidable in view of states' conduct of foreign affairs and the functioning of the mechanism of international relations. International sovereignty comes up only rarely, but nevertheless matters. Its limitations constitute the bare minimum 'outer' limits placed on private party autonomy in determining jurisdiction in civil and commercial matters. For this purpose, state interests need to be ascertained to determine to what extent it is acceptable for state sovereign interests to limit private parties' power to select a forum.

My understanding of state sovereign interests comprises a combination of concepts from international relations, the conduct of diplomacy and the study of international politics. I see the evolution of state interests from the will of the sovereign, to economic and strategic self-interest of the states, to facilitation of respect for global human interests. In particular, in classical (conventional) international relations theory,[7] an older (1930s) concept of 'national interest' by Beard[8] traced it back to the Italian and English 'reasons of state' (*raison d'état*), 'dynastic interests' and the 'will of the sovereign'.[9] With the rise of the nation-state in its modern form, and the protection of state commercial and territorial expansion, a new understanding emerged. It was connected to the economic self-interest of the state that started to account for state 'national interests' on the international arena. Since globalisation, trade liberalisation and privatisation of government-owned enterprises (which could be united under the term neoliberalism), the understanding of state interests evolved further. A state can now be viewed as a fiduciary to its people, which is obliged to 'respect legal principles constitutive of the rule of law'.[10]

In formulating state interests in adjudication of claims, some relevance should be given to a state's foreign policy. International relations theory determines what concepts, 'substantially defined in a democracy by public consensus under

[5] A Dutta, 'Jurisdiction of Domestic Courts (Public International Law)' in J Basedow, K Hopt and R Zimmermann (eds), *The Max Planck Encyclopaedia of European Private Law* (Oxford University Press, 2012) 1028, referring to the *Barcelona Traction Case* (ICJ 5 February 1970, ICJ Rep 1970, 3, 105).

[6] eg, A Mills, *The Confluence of Public and Private International Law: Justice, Pluralism and Subsidiarity in the International Constitutional Ordering of Private Law* (Cambridge University Press, 2009).

[7] Realist theoretical tradition remains the most influential in international relations theory. There are also critical (Marxist and anarchist) approaches to the conventional examination of national interests, which are not very useful for the present analysis. They can be found in S Burchill, *The National Interest in International Relations Theory* (Palgrave MacMillan, 2005) ch 2.

[8] C Beard, *The Idea of National Interest* (Macmillan, 1934 and 1966).

[9] Burchill (n 7) 1.

[10] E Fox-Decent, *Sovereignty's Promise: The State as Fiduciary* (Oxford University Press, 2011). Further elaboration on the state as a fiduciary of its people is outlined in ch 3 of this book.

government leadership',[11] are relevant in formulating a state's foreign policy. For instance, Frankel viewed it as a combination of geopolitical, cultural and psychological dimensions of a state's foreign policy.[12] He distinguished between 'objective national interests' (permanent interests relating to a nation-state's ultimate foreign policy goals, taking into account the nation's history, resources and other factors),[13] and 'subjective national interests' (the changing preferences of a state's decision-makers, or governments). This distinction was subsequently adopted by George and Keohane.[14] Liberals also followed this conception seeing the objective goals of foreign policy (minimal state, free trade, unfettered commerce) and the 'subjective claims of sectional interests' that they were highly suspicious of.[15] These concepts of state foreign policy matter when states administer justice (through their courts) in juxtaposition to the courts of other sovereigns.

A. Accepted International Standard: *Lotus* Case

One often-cited case that exemplifies the effect of public international law on private international law is the *Lotus* case.[16] The case arose in the aftermath of a collision between the French 'Lotus' and the Turkish 'Boz-Kourt' steamships at sea. As a result of the collision, eight Turkish nationals died. Turkey started criminal proceedings under Turkish law against the captain of the Turkish ship and Mr Demons, an officer of the watch on board the 'Lotus' at the time of the collision. The Permanent Court of Justice (PCIJ) was asked to determine whether Turkey acted in violation of principles of international law by instituting the proceedings. France argued that jurisdiction for criminal proceedings against the French officer belonged exclusively to the French courts. Turkey insisted it had jurisdiction to prosecute the individuals.

The Court upheld Turkish jurisdiction in this case. It had to ascertain which principles of international law (meaning international law as it is applied between all nations belonging to the community of states) might have been breached by the prosecution of the French national. It narrowed the discussion down to the one utmost important principle:

> International law governs relations between independent States … Restrictions upon the independence of States cannot therefore be presumed. Now the first and foremost restriction imposed by international law upon a State is that – failing the existence of a

[11] Burchill (n 7) 47, citing T Millar, *Australia in Peace and War* (Palgrave Macmillan, 1978) 40.
[12] J Frankel, *National Interest* (Macmillan, 1970).
[13] Burchill (n 7) 3.
[14] A George and R Keohane, 'The Concept of National Interests: Uses and Limitations' in A George, *Presidential Decision-making in Foreign Policy: The Effective Use of Information and Advice* (Westview-press, 1980).
[15] Burchill (n 7) 150.
[16] *SS 'Lotus' (France v Turkey)* (1927) PCIJ Ser A, no 10.

> permissive rule to the contrary – it may not exercise its power in any form in the territory of another State.

The Court also determined the limits that public international law places on a state's exercise of jurisdiction in criminal and civil cases:

> Far from laying down a general prohibition to the effect that States may not extend the application of their laws and the jurisdiction of their courts to persons, property and acts outside their territory, it leaves them in this respect a wide measure of discretion which is only limited in certain cases by prohibitive rules; as regards other cases, every State remains free to adopt the principles which it regards as best and most suitable.[17]

The *Lotus* case helps perceive the limits of state jurisdiction over nationals and crimes beyond state frontiers. It shows the precedence of public international law over national rules on jurisdiction. Although *Lotus* concerned Turkish criminal jurisdiction, it provides a general standard for all types of case with a foreign element adjudicated by state courts. The difference between criminal and civil jurisdiction in this regard only consists of the degree to which considerations of state public policy on its territory are paramount. In criminal cases, adjudication of crimes guarantees public safety. Prosecution of crimes in accordance with state laws constitutes one of the state's top priorities. Similarly, antitrust cases pertain to important state economic interests. Regulation of business activity via enforcement of state antitrust laws exemplify another area where public policy considerations are of the utmost importance. Civil cases raise issues of lesser significance to the state than war-and-peace questions. Nevertheless, a range of important state interests may be affected by another state's adjudication of, for example, rights and obligations relating to an individual's assets in a state.

The principles of *Lotus* sketch the outer limits of domestic jurisdiction to restrain states from exorbitant jurisdiction. In the end, there remains some significance given to public international law and its general requirement for state jurisdiction not to overreach over another sovereign's domain. In the following section of this chapter, I elaborate further which exact (domestic) sovereign values need or don't need protection from such 'foreign' encroachment.

B. Sovereign Immunity and Acts of State

Another illustration of state jurisdiction limited by public international law transpires through the concept of sovereign immunity and the act of state doctrine. Certain matters simply cannot be brought to a court chosen by private parties because states themselves and their property are immune from other states' courts. Also, states do not have jurisdiction over claims which may require making decisions in relation to foreign acts of state. This serves as a different kind of limitation

[17] ibid 19.

on a state's jurisdiction: a limitation in the context of conducting foreign affairs. A normative approach to jurisdiction ought to recognise these boundaries set by the state's desire not to interfere with the political decisions of another state.

For example, the conjoined UK Supreme Court case of *Belhaj* and *Rahmatullah*[18] outlines the Court's position regarding the existence and exercise of jurisdiction by the English courts in claims by foreign nationals against the UK government for torts allegedly committed by various other states in various overseas jurisdictions.

In *Belhaj*, two Libyan citizens alleged suffering mistreatment amounting to torture from US agents in Thailand and Libyan officials in Libya, while the UK conspired in, assisted and acquiesced in torture, inhumane and degrading treatment, batteries and assaults inflicted upon them.

In *Rahmatullah*, two Pakistani citizens were detained by British forces in Iraq, and transferred to US forces in Afghanistan. Subsequently, they filed a claim against the British authorities for damages in tort concerning their detention and ill treatment by the British and American forces by their acting in concert and being complicit. At first instance in that case,[19] Leggatt J ruled that although the defence based on foreign acts of state was found insufficient to bar the claims, the claims were barred based on the Crown act of state doctrine. The doctrine is similar to the US non-justiciability doctrine, and it explains the courts' abstention from adjudicating acts done while carrying out the state's own foreign policy. That aspect was appealed and considered together with *Mohammed (Serdar) v MOD*,[20] which previously established that the action of the British command in capturing and detaining an Afghani citizen fell within the 'class of protected governmental acts known as acts of state' (hence, no jurisdiction). The conjoined appeals, *Rahmatullah* and *Serdar Mohammed*,[21] resulted in a conclusion that there must be a trial on the facts in relation to the Crown act of state, and the doctrine applies only where 'there are compelling considerations of public policy which require the court to deny a claim founded on an act of the Executive performed abroad'.[22]

On appeal, the UK Supreme Court concluded that the issues before the Court were justiciable, and the British authorities' pleas of (i) state immunity and (ii) the doctrine of foreign act of state doctrine failed.

The state immunity rule establishes that any foreign or Commonwealth state is immune from the jurisdiction of the UK courts.[23] The doctrine of state immunity prevents an independent sovereign from asserting its sovereign authority

[18] *Belhaj and another (Respondents) v Straw and others (Appellants), Rahmatullah (No 1) (Respondent) v Ministry of Defence and another (Appellants)* [2017] UKSC 3 (*Belhaj and Rahmatullah*).

[19] *Yunus Rahmatullah v the Ministry of Defence, the Foreign and Commonwealth Office* [2014] EWHC 3846 (QB) (*Rahmatullah v MOD*).

[20] *Serdar Mohammed v Ministry of Defence* [2014] EWHC 1369 (QB).

[21] *Serdar Mohammed and others v Secretary of State for Defence, Yunus Rahmatullah & Iraqi Civilian Claimants v MOD and Foreign and Commonwealth Office* [2015] EWCA Civ 843.

[22] ibid [359].

[23] State Immunity Act 1978 s 1(1) (UK).

in a way that would encroach on the authority of another.[24] The UK Supreme Court concluded (concurring to the earlier decision by Leggatt J) that an immunity conferred on the US did not render the UK officials immune from the claim, 'because the legal position of the foreign states, the conduct of whose officials is alleged to have been tortious in the places where such conduct occurred, will not be affected in any legal sense by proceedings to which they are not party'.[25] The foreign states would be capable of being pursued in their own courts, and the UK government would enjoy state immunity anywhere but in England, and suits against it would be precluded by state immunity.

The Court further reasoned that the claims were not barred by the doctrine of foreign act of state. Described by Mann as 'one of the most difficult and most perplexing topics which, in the field of foreign affairs, may face the municipal judge in England',[26] the foreign act of state doctrine applies in suits where giving a judgment would make the judge uncomfortable as it would infringe upon a foreign state's foreign policy territory. The Court provided a nuanced definition of the doctrine, describing the three types of foreign act of state: (i) a private international law rule recognising a foreign state's legislation in so far it affects property (movable and immovable); (ii) a rule whereby the English court will not question a foreign governmental act in respect of property situated within the jurisdiction of the foreign government in question; and (iii) the rule that an English court will treat as non-justiciable certain categories of sovereign act by a foreign state abroad (both within and outside the foreign state's jurisdiction).[27] With regard to the third type, non-justiciability of an issue has to be established on a case-by-case basis, with the English law having regard 'to the extent to which the fundamental rights of liberty, access to justice and freedom from torture are engaged by the issues raised'.[28]

Therefore, the Court's reasoning in *Belhaj* and *Rahmatullah* has demonstrated that certain public international law concepts (state immunity, the doctrines of foreign and domestic act of state) may limit a state court's jurisdiction. This discussion is relevant when seeking to identify the state's interests in jurisdiction over private matters with a foreign element. In such cases, a cautious evaluation of the jurisdictional interests of the state should be made, before it may be concluded what should overweigh the scales of justice. Judicial abstention from adjudicating foreign acts is justified in view of respecting a state's sovereign immunity. This international dimension of sovereignty is inevitable, and I do not challenge the adequacy of these public international law concepts putting certain limits on jurisdiction in civil and commercial matters.

[24] *Rahmatullah v MOD* [155].

[25] *Belhaj and Rahmatullah* [31].

[26] ibid [33], referring to FA Mann, *Foreign Affairs in English Courts* (Oxford University Press, 1986) 164.

[27] *Belhaj* and *Rahmatullah* [35], [38], [40].

[28] ibid [98].

III. Home Sovereignty and its Limited Role in the Law on Jurisdiction

In this section, I make two claims. First, having traced the concepts of sovereignty and territoriality in the conflict of laws, I argue that the traditional outlook on jurisdiction, with sovereignty at its foundation, has outlived its time. Using the rule of suing at the location of the defendant as an example, I demonstrate how the rule can be re-purposed to reflect the interests of the parties, rather than as an assertion of the power of the state over its residents. My second claim in this section deals with the acceptable limits that home sovereignty can place on party autonomy – by rules of mandatory jurisdiction.

A. Concepts of Sovereignty and Territoriality in Conflict of Laws

i. Classical Tradition

The classical tradition in the conflict of laws is associated with the names of renowned scholars like Story, Beale, Dicey, Mann, Akehurst, Kahn-Feund, Steenhoff, Collier and others. These scholars focused on the exclusive territorial sovereignty of states.[29] When Story wrote about jurisdiction in 1834 (influenced by the European traditions aiming for legal certainty and predictability), he put exclusive sovereignty within a state's territory at the foundation of the theory of 'vested rights'. The idea of vested rights purported that persons acquired rights on a particular territory, and those rights stayed with them forever, and the rules from that territory regarding those rights applied universally across the world. Story's teachings dominated in England for some time.[30] They were adopted in Dicey's *Conflict of Laws*, which reads that state authority was accepted as coincident with, and limited by, its power, and the territorial power enabled the state to legislate and give judgments affecting things and persons within its territory.[31] Across the ocean, Story's ideas have inspired American scholars for some time. Beale established a territorial concept of the sovereign power and the theoretical foundation for territoriality in the United States. His understanding of the 'vested rights' theory also derived from a strictly territorial notion of sovereign power.[32] The sovereign

[29] A Mills, 'The Identities of Private International Law: Lessons from the US and EU Revolutions' (2013) 23 *Duke Journal of Comparative & International Law* 445, 452.

[30] In 1972, Pryles still wrote that 'in no other area … Story's territorial precepts better appear to accord with [court] practice than with respect to jurisdiction'. See M Pryles, 'The Basis of Adjudicatory Competence in Private International Law' (1972) 21 *International & Comparative Law Quarterly* 61, 66.

[31] JHC Morris, *Dicey's Conflict of Laws*, 6th edn (Stevens & Son Ltd, 1949) 13.

[32] P Schiff Berman, 'Choice of Law and Jurisdiction on the Internet: Towards a Cosmopolitan Vision on Conflict-of-Laws: Redefining Governmental Interests in a Global Era' (2005) 153 *University of Pennsylvania Law Review* 1819, 1840.

power within its territory was accepted as supreme.[33] The theory of vested rights prevailed in American legal thought and provided the foundation for the American conflict of laws. However, over time, the foundation laid by Story and Beale began to deteriorate. The system of strict territoriality was breaking down. With the development of trade, infrastructure and the increased mobility of people, the need for a better conflict of laws system emerged.

One of the first scholars to criticise the ideas of territoriality was Cook. He challenged the rigid system of rules of Beale and Story. Cook advocated for a set of guiding principles,[34] aiming to establish a scientific method for allocating applicable law and appropriate jurisdiction through categorisation of cases (by contract, tort, property, corporations). His ideas helped the evolution of the conflict of laws. However, even after categorisation of cases, they were still linked to a particular territory where an event happened or a contract was signed, except now this attribution was a little more flexible.

Cavers and Currie continued the debate. Cavers ascertained that when a court was presented with a dilemma of which law to apply, it should look at the conflicting rules and policies behind them, and then ensure justice for the private parties.[35] Later, Currie aimed to revolutionise the existing conflict of laws system and proposed an interest analysis method. He sought to detect a literal conflict of laws, rather than resolve a potential conflict of regulatory authority.[36] The premise of state interests analysis was that the law was understood as an instrument of social control.[37] Currie argued that where a certain state has an interest in application of its law and policy, a court of that state should apply the local law. Courts should apply a body of law when it benefits the state's domiciliaries.[38] His idea was to look at the purpose of the statute and decide how far that statute needed to apply to serve that purpose, ensuring that it did not apply where the interests of other states were at stake.[39] Currie argued that judges should only rely on state-sanctioned law.[40]

Subsequently, Von Mehren, Juenger and McDougal criticised the state interests analysis. They sought a substantive law method that would determine applicable law not based on the provisions of the forum law in view of governmental interests, but as a compromise among the interests of states involved in a multistate case.

[33] J Beale, *A Treatise on the Conflict of Laws* (Baker, Voorhis & Co, 1935) 311.

[34] S Symeonides, *The American Choice-of-Law Revolution in the Courts: Today and Tomorrow* (Martinus Nijhoff Publishers, 2003) 36, referring to W Cook, *The Logical and Legal Bases of the Conflict of Laws* (Harvard University Press, 1942) 97.

[35] D Cavers, 'A Critique of the Choice-of-Law Problem' (1933) 47 *Harvard Law Review* 173.

[36] Mills, 'The Identities of Private International Law' (n 29) 459.

[37] S Peari, 'Savigny's Theory of Choice-of-Law as a Principle of "Voluntary Submission"' (2014) 64 *University of Toronto Law Journal* 106, 139, referring to B Currie, *Selected Essays on the Conflict of Laws* (Duke University Press, 1963) 64.

[38] Symeonides (n 34) 42.

[39] C Nelson, 'State and Federal Models of the Interaction between Statutes and Unwritten Law (2013) 80 *University of Chicago Law Review* 657, 689.

[40] Schiff Berman (n 32) 1845.

ii. Modern Tendencies

In continuation of the discussion on the role of sovereignty and territoriality in jurisdiction in Europe, works by Mann warrant consideration. In 1964, and 1984, Mann laid the foundation for scholars examining judicial jurisdiction. He established that the territorial doctrine of jurisdiction 'allows the sovereign to exercise jurisdiction over any person within his territory, merely by reason of … allegiance'.[41] He saw jurisdiction and sovereignty as two equal and inseparable notions.

In 1975, Akehurst proposed his view on civil jurisdiction, ascertaining jurisdiction based on assets, physical presence, nationality (domicile), and the subject matter of a suit.[42] His approach differed from Mann's as it was more pragmatic. He systemised the bases for exercising jurisdiction by English courts based on the case law. According to his observations, territoriality – expressed through physical presence, assets, and domicile at the state territory – still dominated the rules of staying or declining jurisdiction.

A more recent comprehensive book on legislative jurisdiction by the Dutch scholar Ryngaert featured a noteworthy academic view on the extent of state power beyond its territory, taking jurisdiction in a territorial sense as a given. Ryngaert attempted to embrace all areas of law, including criminal, civil, competition, family, etc. In all these areas, he advocated that the principle of reasonableness (in the American sense) should guide courts in asserting jurisdiction.[43] His approach, although impressive, appears more applicable to criminal and other matters. In civil and commercial cases, 'reasonableness' as such may mean different things to different people and different judges. Moreover, Ryngaert still accepts territoriality as the foundation for jurisdiction, which, I argue below, needs to be reassessed.

iii. Russian Scholarship

In Russian scholarship on private international law, territoriality has been seen and remains seen as foundational for jurisdiction in civil matters. The Russian pre-revolutionary history of private international law is associated with the names of Ivanov, Malyshev, Martens, Kazanskiĭ, Brun, Kapustin and others. Notably, the question of international jurisdiction as part of international civil procedure has been traditionally understood as part of private international law. In any case, the doctrines on judicial and legislative jurisdiction have developed in close connection and with mutual influence on each other. In this regard, Ivanov, inspired by

[41] FA Mann, *The Doctrine of Jurisdiction in International Law* (Martinus Nijhoff Publishers, 1964) 77; and FA Mann, *The Doctrine of International Jurisdiction Revisited After Twenty Years* (Martinus Nijhoff Publishers, 1984).

[42] M Akehurst, 'Jurisdiction in International Law' (1972–73) 46 *British Yearbook of International Law* 151.

[43] C Ryngaert, *Jurisdiction in International Law* (Oxford University Press, 2008).

the works of Savigny,[44] wrote: 'Each state has sovereignty, which means acting at its territory based on issued laws. However, the interests of mutual cooperation between nations demand recognition of legal force of foreign laws within [the state's] territorial borders'.[45]

Malyshev, another pre-revolutionary Russian jurist, regarded private international law as civil (private) relations in international context. He created the dogma of Russian domestic jurisdiction and applicable law, working on Russian inter-*oblast* (formations of the Federation) conflict rules. Professor Kazanskiĭ considered private and public international law as two distinct disciplines. In addition to the study of jurisdiction, he included the rights of foreigners into the system of private international law.[46]

Later, Yablochkov wrote on international jurisdiction in international civil procedure.[47] In his course on international civil procedure in 1909, he laid the fundamental bases for jurisdiction, including the place of performance of an obligation, location of a legal entity, location of the immovable property, the place of committing a civil wrong, etc. No mention of party autonomy to dedicate a forum can be traced in his work. He understood and presented jurisdiction as an imperative set of norms based on state sovereignty and territoriality. Notably, Yablochkov saw the issue of judicial jurisdiction as a primary matter before the question of applicable law; and his works provided the foundation for many contemporary studies on jurisdiction.

Further development of Russian scholarship on private international law still regarded state territoriality and sovereignty as the foundations of jurisdiction. The scholarship of the twentieth century can be conditionally divided into the Soviet studies and works by Russian scholars in exile (emigrated from Russia because of the Bolshevik revolution). During this period, the major works were by Makarov, Pereterskiĭ, Krylov, Lunts', Boguslavkiĭ and, outside Russia, Gilcher, Zimmerman, Pilenko, Zaĭtsev and others. They all made contributions to the field and all viewed jurisdiction based on the state's territoriality.

Contemporary legal scholarship in Russia is still based on territorial and sovereign notions, although it admits the important role of party autonomy in contractual relations. As Dmitrieva notes: 'in the Russian Federation, designation of competence of domestic and foreign courts is mainly built by using the territorial criterion (location of the defendant)'.[48] Mitina also affirms that the principle

[44] For more on Savigny's ideas of universality of private international law see, eg, A Mills, 'The Private History of International Law' (2006) 55 *International & Comparative Law Quarterly* 1.

[45] N Ivanov, *Osnovaniia Chastnoĭ Mezhdunarodnoĭ Iurisdiktsii* (*Foundations of Private International Jurisdiction*) (Scientific Papers of Kazan University, 1865).

[46] P Kazanskiĭ, *Vvedenie v Kurs Mezhdunarodnogo Prava* (*Introduction to the Course on International Law*) (Ekonomicheskaia. 1901).

[47] T Yablochkov, *Kurs Mezhdunarodnogo Protsessualnogo Prava* (*The Course of International Procedural Law*) (Tipografiia Gubernskogo Pravleniia, 1909).

[48] G Dmitrieva, *Mezhdunarodnoe Chastnoe Pravo* (*International Private Law*), 2nd edn (Prospect, 2009) 593–94, 600.

of state sovereignty remains pertinent in the field of international jurisdiction.[49] Russian understanding of sovereignty is similar to the general ideas expressed above – it includes its judicial power that extends on its territory, over its residents and property on its territory.

B. Revised Outlook on Jurisdiction

As illustrated above, home sovereignty (state power over its territory) has been traditionally and systematically viewed as the foundation of jurisdiction in private international law in Europe and Russia. Claims of adjudicatory authority developed under three theories: a relational theory, a power theory and an instrumental theory. The relational theory was pertinent to feudalism, when tenants relied on their lord for rendering protection and justice. Eventually, it was replaced by the power theory. Power became the major justification of governmental authority, as the modern state emerged.[50] The Austinian theory of legal sovereign explained the reasoning for the sovereign limiting people's rights as a matter of right of that sovereign. Hobbesian followers saw the power – or authority – as being indispensable to 'ordered civil society', and the Lockeans regarded voluntary consent among free men as the foundation for governmental authority. In this regard, Rousseau criticised the possibility of private interests seizing governmental decision-making. Furthermore, critical (Marxist and anarchist) approaches to the conventional examination of national interests elaborated on the dangers of private interests overtaking the governmental apparatus.[51] In line with the power theory, later scholars have also portrayed jurisdiction as a matter of right: 'jurisdiction involves a state's right to exercise certain of its powers'.[52] On this foundation, utilitarian instrumentalism evolved, which justified state jurisdiction based on pragmatic or 'hedonic' reasons.[53]

The problem I see is that all these theories approach the issue of jurisdiction as a struggle for power. Notwithstanding their validity and relevance at different points in time, they fail to provide an adequate justification for state jurisdiction at the present time. I argue that this approach needs to be revisited. I see jurisdiction differently. Civil jurisdiction is a question of choice by the parties, which needs to be facilitated by the states, whose home sovereignty should be preserved for the sake of overall peace. The theory of legal sovereignty and the thinking associated

[49] M Mitina, 'O Ponimanii Sushchnosti Regulirovaniia Mezhdunarodnoĭ Podsudnosti: Sovremennye Tendentsii' ('On Understanding the Substance of Regulation of International Jurisdiction: Contemporary Tendencies') (2010) 4 *Izvestiia VUZov Pravovedenie* 229.

[50] A von Mehren, *Adjudicatory Authority in Private International Law* (Martinus Nijhoff Publishers, 2007) 18.

[51] More in Burchill (n 7) ch 2.

[52] Mann, The Doctrine of Jurisdiction in International Law (n 41) 9.

[53] ibid 19, referring to DH Monro, 'Jeremy Bentham' in P Edwards (ed), *The Encyclopaedia of Philosophy* (Macmillan, 1967) 280.

with it has declined. Instead, the interests of private parties have come to the forefront, leaving a small place for state sovereign interests in jurisdiction. Thus, my overall argument is that the significance of state sovereignty for jurisdiction in civil and commercial matters is in decline.

The need to reconceptualise the traditional approach can be supported by a number of scholarly works. For instance, Schiff Berman criticises territoriality-based conceptions of legal jurisdiction, 'in an era when ideas of bounded nation-state communities operating within fixed territorial borders are under challenge'.[54] He proposes a 'cosmopolitan pluralist conception of jurisdiction' in relation to the applicable law, incorporating vested rights, governmental interests and the substantive law method.

Brand also speaks of reallocation of authority from the state to both non-state institutions and private parties in legislative jurisdiction.[55] Brand addresses a very interesting aspect of 'selfishness' of the states. By applying only their own law in their dominions, and accepting only their own jurisdiction, they pose as unattractive sovereigns, since such an attitude is inconsistent with the primary purpose of the state which is taking care of its residents.[56] He sees the inevitable growth of private power and the state's recognition of it, not as a diminution of the sovereignty of the state but rather as the proper exercise of the state's sovereignty in the modern world.[57]

i. Reconceptualisation in Practice

The way jurisdiction based on state sovereign power can be reconceptualised can be demonstrated by analysing the rule of suing at the location of the defendant. Rather than a general rule that a system would start with, I see it as a back-up rule. I propose a revised justification for suing at the location of the defendant: fairness to the defendant and practicality.

As the law stands in the EU and Russia, suing at the location of the defendant represents the general rule of jurisdiction. Pursuant to Article 4 of the Brussels I Recast,[58] natural and legal persons domiciled in a Member State shall, whatever their nationality, be sued in the courts of that Member State. The analogous approach is

[54] Further excellent detailed account on the so-called 'revolution' in the American Conflict of Laws has been given by Symeonides in his general course in the Hague Academy (n 34), and by Schiff Berman in his article on cosmopolitan approach to conflict of laws (n 32).

[55] R Brand, 'Balancing Sovereignty and Party Autonomy in Private International Law' in J Erauw, V Tomljenovic and P Volken, *Liber Memorialis Petar Sarcevic: Universalism, Tradition and the Individual* (Sellier European Law Publishers, 2006) 37.

[56] ibid 45.

[57] ibid.

[58] Regulation (EU) No 1215/2012 of 12 December 2012 on Jurisdiction and the Recognition and Enforcement of Judgments in Civil and Commercial Matters (Recast) [2012] OJ L351/1 (the Brussels I Recast).

enforced in Russia: claims are generally filed with a court at the location of the defendant. In particular, in private disputes involving individuals, Article 22 of the Code of Civil Procedure[59] attributes civil non-commercial claims to courts of general jurisdiction at the place of residence of the defendant.[60] Furthermore, Article 35 of the Code of *Arbitrazh* Procedure[61] establishes that disputes related to commercial or economic activity of legal entities shall be subject to jurisdiction of an *arbitrazh* court at the location of the defendant.[62] Therefore, both EU and Russian jurisdictional rules accept the rule of general jurisdiction at the location of the defendant.

This practice corresponds with most countries in the world: many jurisdictions agree that for an individual, the paradigm forum for the exercise of general jurisdiction is the individual's domicile; for a corporation, it is an equivalent place, where the corporation is fairly regarded as at home.[63] However, does residence (or location) represent an adequate basis for general jurisdiction over individuals and corporations? Why is this rule rendered the fundamental position in jurisdiction systems? Does it provide adequate protection of the parties' rights, including the right to a fair trial? What is the more appropriate place for this rule in the hierarchy of jurisdiction rules?

I contend that reconceptualisation of the rationale behind this rule is needed. A widely accepted rationale regards the rule as a matter of state territoriality and state power over its subjects. As mentioned above, the territorial doctrine of jurisdiction 'allows the sovereign to exercise jurisdiction over any person within his territory, merely by reason of … allegiance'.[64] Having the rule of suing at the location of the defendant at the core of a jurisdictional system respects the territoriality of a state's power and reflects the doctrine of territoriality of jurisdiction. The fact that a person resides in a state appears to be the reason for that state to have jurisdiction over that person. The rule facilitates efficient distribution of cases according to individuals' and companies' allegiance to the place of their domicile or residence. Thus, from the states' perspective, the domicile or residence provides a solid foundation for jurisdiction; it is desirable and appropriate.

Contrary to this majority view, the rule should be justified differently. Suing at the location of the defendant, as a fall-back or default rule (meaning, unless other rules state otherwise), provides an adequate basis for jurisdiction, because it balances the interests of the defendant and the plaintiff. In particular, before the judicial proceedings, the defendant has no power to influence the initiation of the court actions. Establishing jurisdiction at the location of the defendant

[59] Grazhdanskiĭ Protsessual'nyĭ Kodeks Rossiĭskoĭ Federatsii (Code of Civil Procedure) of 14 November 2002 no 138-ФЗ (Russia) (the CCP).

[60] CCP art 22.

[61] Arbitrazhno-Protsessual'nyĭ Kodeks Rossiĭskoĭ Federatsii (Code of *Arbitrazh* (Commercial) Procedure) of 24 July 2002 no 95-ФЗ (Russia) (the CAP).

[62] CAP art 35.

[63] *Goodyear v Brown* 564 US 915, 921 (2011) (US).

[64] Mann, *The Doctrine of International Jurisdiction Revisited After Twenty Years* (n 41) 77.

for his convenience seems appropriate to counterbalance such absence of power. It is appropriate that if a person wants to sue another person, he must bear the associated expense and inconvenience of travelling and appearing in court at the location of the defendant.

This perceived preference given to the defendant by directing to the forum at the defendant's location appears reasonably substantiated. Further support of this may be found in the works of many scholars. As mentioned by von Mehren and Trautman and expressed by Sunderland, allowing suit at the domicile or residence of the defendant is fair: 'since the plaintiff controls the institution of suit, he might behave oppressively towards the defendant unless restricted. Accordingly, many statutes require transitory actions to be brought in the county of a defendant's residence, which, of course, generally serves his convenience'.[65] Borchers also argued that jurisdiction based upon a defendant's 'home' connection, such as domicile or habitual residence, is fair.[66] Brilmayer[67] and Eng[68] also agreed that the domicile rule is fair and not unfair to the defendant.

One might argue that this presents certain challenges for the claimant, especially if the claimant is a victim seeking access to justice. Indeed, in certain cases, the convenience for the defendant may be trumped by exclusive or specific jurisdiction rules allowing bringing the suit at the location of the claimant (for instance, suing by the weaker parties at their domicile in the EU, bringing claims for child support at the location of the claimant in Russia, etc). Then, in the big picture, both parties are given an equal chance and opportunity to obtain justice.

An additional rationale for the rule of suing at the location of the defendant concerns predictability. Basing jurisdiction on the domicile of the defendant benefits the parties, by providing them with the necessary degree of predictability and certainty in international civil disputes. If jurisdiction is based on the location of the defendant, then the task of finding the appropriate forum becomes relatively easy: just find the defendant. This contributes to the overall objective of having a just and fair system, which requires a certain and predictable place where a person can be reached by those having claims against him.[69]

In addition, it is practical to bring a claim at the defendant's location in hope of its future effective enforcement. Subsequent enforcement of a judgment against the defendant would most likely be performed at the location of the defendant. Having a local (rather than a distant) court order facilitates its faster and easier enforcement.

[65] A von Mehren and D Trautman, 'Jurisdiction to Adjudicate: A Suggested Analysis' (1966) 79 *Harvard Law Review* 1121, 1128, referring to E Sunderland, 'The Provisions Relating to Trial Practice in the New Illinois Civil Practice Act' (1933) 1 *University of Chicago Law Review* 192.

[66] P Borchers, 'J McIntyre Machinery, Goodyear, and the Incoherence of the Minimum Contacts Test' (2011) 44 *Creighton Law Review* 1268, 136.

[67] L Brilmayer et al, 'A General Look at General Jurisdiction' (1988) 66 *Texas Law Review* 721.

[68] E Eng, 'A New Paradigm: Domicile as the Exclusive Basis for the Exercise of General Jurisdiction Over Individual Defendants' (2012) 32 *Cardozo Law Review* 849, 861.

[69] Von Mehren and Trautman (n 65) 1137.

This revised rationale fits the normative approach I describe in this book, which establishes that the interests of private parties should guide allocation of jurisdiction in conflict of laws.

ii. Place for Home Sovereignty in Jurisdiction

Some place for state sovereign interests is still appropriate in the hierarchy of values behind an ideal jurisdiction regime. In limited cases, the necessity to protect the basic policies, the institutions and the integrity of the state (in other words, the state home sovereignty) may justify overriding private parties' autonomy to choose a forum. These considerations are important as they constitute the very foundation of the state, securing its internal political and economic stability. Internal stability of the state helps maintain the integrity of the international legal order, and an ideal jurisdictional system would strive for such stability. Therefore, it is conceivable to accept the necessity to limit party autonomy designating a forum for the sake of maintaining the integrity of the state as sovereign. The problem is that as the core interests of the state are so vague, it is difficult to determine when exactly state interests may override party autonomy to choose a forum.

In practice, state mandatory rules of jurisdiction perform the function of maintaining the integrity of the state and its institutions. Mandatory rules are characteristic of every legal regime. They limit the rights and freedoms of the individual to protect the foundations of the state constitutional system, morals, health, rights and legitimate interests of other persons, to maintain the defence and safety of the state. Where the question of legitimate threat to these core legal values is at stake, it is feasible to limit the private party autonomy to choose jurisdiction. It must be emphasised that such public interference into private matters should be limited in scope and should only apply in exceptional cases. In particular, in matters relating to rights *in rem* in immovable property, issues connected with the registration of trademarks and in a few other cases, the state may claim exclusive right to adjudicate claims regarding these issues at their territory. This minimal state interference in jurisdiction may be allowed in exceptional cases.

IV. Ultimate State Sovereignty: Public Interest

An additional angle to understand state sovereignty is to view it as a collective public interest. The collective public interest is a combination of private interests united under the umbrella of a particular state. The idea that ultimate sovereignty resides in the people is not new; it has been recognised in a number of scholarly works.[70] It may be traced back to Rousseau who once claimed that 'sovereignty … [is]

[70] This is consonant with the US model of government, where people possess the ultimate sovereignty and then assign various responsibilities to other actors, including the federal government and

no more than the exercise of the general will'.[71] The notion of collective public interest may also be traced back to reflect the Lockean ideas in political theory. The will of society in general encompasses the common interests of the members of the community, forming the basis for overall decision-making and policy. On a more basic level, it is the common preservation and wellbeing of all. This 'collective' interest of nationals of a sovereign may be regarded as a form of state sovereignty.

Objectively, the interests of many state nationals need protection. An optimal judicial system would account for the interests of third parties or public interest which may be affected by a suit. The ultimate state sovereignty – expressing its citizens' interests – may limit the extent of individual parties' will in jurisdiction. Because the collective public interest represents the combined private interests of persons domiciled in the state, adjusting individual litigants' absolute party autonomy helps balance all private interests in the state. The relationship between party autonomy and mandatory jurisdiction in this case represents a correlation between particular private interests and costs and benefits to a larger state community. On the boundary between protecting the individual and public interests, interests of a broader community may outweigh the convenience of satisfying the particular private needs and intentions (to resolve disputes in a particular place). Where, however, it makes no practical or principle difference to the general community of a state, private parties' choice of jurisdiction should be enforced. Thus, individual litigants' interests (such as the right to choose jurisdiction) in civil and commercial suits needs to be enforced in a way mindful of the general public interest.

This argument has little to do with public power. While international and home sovereignty concerns preservation of state territory and state power, accounting for collective public interest only supports my argument that jurisdiction should be flowing from private interests. It is time to reconsider the beginnings of jurisdiction and review the classical approach where the principles of state power provided the basis for jurisdiction. Instead of territoriality – an expression of a state's sovereignty and power – jurisdiction rules shall be based on private interests. State sovereign interests can only come in as a limitation to party autonomy in jurisdiction. In the case of collective public interest, they are still private interests, and this reflects the changing reality where private interests should guide the mechanisms of jurisdiction in civil and commercial matters.

In an ideal jurisdictional system, the public interest is particularly relevant in cases where no clear choice of forum is present. In such cases, a balance needs to be attained between the individual and general private interests. In certain cases (as I mention throughout this book), the state may step in to protect the general interest and override private decisions regarding an appropriate forum.

state governments. eg, D Wood, 'The Structure of Sovereignty' (2014) 18 *Lewis & Clark Law Review* 215, 217.

[71] J-J Rousseau, 'The Social Contract' in E Barker, *Social Contract: Essays by Locke, Hume, and Rousseau* (Oxford University Press, 1960) 190.

8

Sovereignty and Territoriality in the Law on Jurisdiction

I. Defining Domicile for the Purpose of Jurisdiction

In the previous chapter, I have argued that sovereignty should play only a limited role in the dichotomy of sovereignty and party autonomy. In this chapter, I demonstrate how the proposed reconceptualised view would fit the existing rules in the EU and Russia. In particular, I demonstrate (i) how the rule of suing at the location can be re-purposed to reflect the interests of the parties, rather than the assertion of power of the state over its residents, and (ii) what acceptable limits there should be for sovereignty in the law on jurisdiction. I analyse the existing law in the EU and Russia to show in which cases the current law needs to be adjusted accordingly.

Regarding the rule of suing at the location of the defendant, one downside of this rule is the ambiguity in understanding what the terms 'domicile' or 'residence' entail. Indeed, uncertainty in determining the place of residence or domicile sometimes creates room for forum shopping.[1] Forum shopping is regarded as a negative and undesirable phenomenon in private international law. One of the downsides of forum shopping is the potential that a plaintiff will abuse the system at the expense of the defendants, choosing a forum most convenient for him. This would raise concerns in terms of equality of the parties and would have to be balanced out by the default rule of suing at the location of the defendant (except in some cases where categorical equality dictates otherwise, as discussed in part II of this book). After all, ideally, a jurisdiction system should provide a mechanism where a single court shall have competence to hear and decide a dispute. Having one clearly competent court eliminates lengthy battles over jurisdiction and any potential conflicting judgments. Where a dispute may be brought to several courts, the room for forum shopping naturally appears, and the risk of irreconcilable judgments increases. Nevertheless, having a few alternative fora is preferable, if such a system takes into account the will of the parties and the principles of equality and fairness. The reason for that is connected with the overall idea of this book: in the hierarchy of values behind the rules of jurisdiction, it is the parties' interests that

[1] Forum shopping is referred to when parties are searching for a court which, in their opinion, is most likely to provide a favourable judgment.

should prevail. The balance of their private interests should determine the appropriate forum, not the external considerations of effectiveness of a state regime for the sake of the regime itself.

Therefore, it is preferable that in cases where a clear choice of forum is missing, an additional (special) jurisdiction rule directs to a few fora, and a fall-back rule of suing at the location of the defendant is available. To avoid the discrepancies in application of the rule, a better uniform definition of domicile may be needed. I aim to find such a perfect formula for determining residence and location of the defendant for the purpose of jurisdiction.

What should constitute an individual's residence in a particular country for the purpose of jurisdiction? Is it citizenship? Or is it physical residence? Or is it numerous and substantial contacts with the state? Should understanding of 'domicile' differ when ascertained for the purpose of taxation, or general jurisdiction? What should be the required duration of residence for an individual in a forum state? As for corporations, what constitutes the most appropriate affiliation and determines location of companies for the purpose of jurisdiction? Is it a physical address, location of the managing body, a place of residence of the directors, or the 'brain centre' of a company, from where all the business decisions originate?

The answers to the above listed questions are not uniform and unambiguous across jurisdictions. In this section, I consider a number of alternatives and argue that, for the target regimes, the most optimal tests of domicile for individuals are (a) residence and (b) substantial connection, and for corporations (a) seat or (b) place of central administration.

A. Individuals: Residence

The concept of domicile of an individual for the purpose of jurisdiction in the EU is determined according to the national laws of the EU Member States. From a perspective of states that drafted the original Brussels Convention on jurisdiction,[2] the domicile for the purpose of jurisdiction denotes the place where a person physically resides. For instance, the German law determines the general venue of a person by his place of residence.[3] *Wohnsitz* or residence of natural persons entails a place where the person settles permanently.[4] For a person with no place of residence, his general venue is determined by that person's place of

[2] Brussels Convention on Jurisdiction and the Enforcement of Judgments in Civil and Commercial Matters [1972] OJ L299/32 (the Brussels Convention or the Brussels Convention 1968).

[3] German Code of Civil Procedure as promulgated on 5 December 2005 (ZPO) (*Bundesgesetzblatt* (BGBl, *Federal Law Gazette*) I p 3202; 2006 I p 431; 2007 I p 1781), last amended by Article 1 of the Act dated 10 October 2013 (*Federal Law Gazette* I p 3786) s 13 (Germany) (BGB).

[4] Bürgerliches Gesetzbuch, German Civil Code of 18 August 1896 as promulgated on 2 January 2002 (*Bundesgesetzblatt* (*Federal Law Gazette*) I p 42, 2909; 2003 I p 738), last amended by Article 2 (16) of the statute of 19 February 2007 (*Bundesgesetzblatt* (BGBl, *Federal Law Gazette*) I p 122) s 7, available at: www.gesetze-im-internet.de/bgb/index.html.

abode in Germany; where no such place of abode is known, by his last place of residence.[5] For comparison, French civil law defines domicile as the place where a person has his principal establishment, evidenced by the actual character of such establishment and his intention to remain there.[6] Therefore, the domicile of individuals in continental Europe is understood as their particular place of residence.

Certain peculiarities evolved in the UK, given the existence of the concept of domicile prior to the British accession to the EU jurisdiction regime. The traditional English understanding of 'domicile' does not imply connection of a person to a certain place, but rather encompasses the relation of a person to a particular legal system. To denote the connection of a person to a particular place, English courts have traditionally used the word 'residence'. So, for the purpose of this discussion, we will concentrate on the English understanding of 'residence' when mentioning domicile, keeping this conceptual difference in mind.

English authority on the definition of 'residence' can be found in *Levene*.[7] The case related to residence for the purpose of taxation; nevertheless, observations from the case on the meaning of 'resident' and 'ordinarily resident' have applied to various civil and commercial matters for almost a century.[8] The dispute concerned whether the appellant was a resident or a visitor to the UK, and the clarification was needed to determine whether England was the defendant's permanent home. The facts of the case indicated that the appellant came back to England for five months a year during the years in question, while spending the rest of the time in France and Monaco. The argument by the appellant was based on the notion that a man might have ordinary residences in different places at the same time. However, in the case, the appellant argued that he definitely gave up his London residence, and never returned to England with the intention of 'establishing his residence' there.[9] On appeal, it was established that 'a person with a home or fixed abode … might well satisfy the tests of residence, although he was absent for most of the year'.[10]

[5] ZPO s 16 (Germany).

[6] Code civil (Civil Code) (Version consolidée au 2 mars 2017) (updated version as of 2 March 2017), available at: www.legifrance.gouv.fr/affichCode.do;jsessionid=CC69880F16CDA9131323C2CE533419BE.tpdila13v_2?cidTexte=LEGITEXT000006070721&dateTexte=20170323, art 102 (France). Also, P Raoul-Duval and M Stoyanov, 'Comparative Study of "Residual Jurisdiction" in Civil and Commercial Disputes in the EU: National Report for: France' (National Report on Residual Jurisdiction, France, for The General Report: Study on Residual Jurisdiction edited by Arnaud Nuyts, 3 September 2007), available at: ec.europa.eu/civiljustice/news/docs/study_residual_jurisdiction_en.pdf.

[7] *Levene v Commissioners of Inland Revenue* [1928] AC 217 (*Levene*).

[8] eg, *Varsani v Relfo Ltd (In Liquidation)* [2010] EWCA Civ 560; *Grace v Revenue and Customs Commissioners* [2008] EWHC 2708 (Ch); *Gaines-Cooper v Revenue and Customs Commissioners* [2007] STC (SCD) 23; 9 ITL Rep 274; *Reed (Inspector of Taxes) v Clark* [1986] Ch 1; [1985] 3 WLR 142; *R v Barnet LBC Ex p Shah (Nilish)* [1983] 2 AC 309; *Stransky v Stransky* [1954] 3 WLR 123; [1954] 2 All ER 536; *Re Adoption Application (No 52 of 1951)* [1952] Ch 16; [1951] 2 All ER 931; *Hopkins v Hopkins (Divorce: Domicile)* [1951] P 116; [1950] 2 All ER 1035, etc.

[9] *Latter KC* and *Cyril King* for the appellant in *Levene* [1927] 2 KB 38, 44.

[10] *Levene*, 218.

In this understanding, an individual located outside the UK but connected with England (by spending a few months in England, or intending to return there) could be regarded as domiciled in the UK. At the same time, the individual's physical location in another country could identify him as domiciled there as well. This can lead to divergent interpretations and confusion. As indicated in the Schlosser Report concerning the UK joining the Brussels Convention 1968, the UK and Ireland were free to retain their traditional concept of domicile; however, this could have led to a certain imbalance of application of the Convention.[11] Dual or triple understanding of a person's domicile would contradict the legal certainty, which the Brussels jurisdiction regime was trying to achieve. The UK and Ireland were requested to adopt in their legislation a concept of domicile as understood in the original states of the EU.[12]

Upon the British entrance to the EU jurisdiction regime with the domicile principle at its core, the UK adopted a slightly more restricted definition of domicile for the purpose of jurisdiction. The Select Committee of the House of Lords on the European Communities stated, concerning the accession of the UK to the Brussels Convention:

> [L]egislation will be needed in the UK to modify, for the purposes only of the Convention, the English and Scottish concept of 'domicile' of an individual so as to equate it to residence of a sufficiently established nature in the UK.[13]

This adjusted statutory understanding has been reflected in the Civil Jurisdiction and Judgments Acts 1982 and 1991 and the Civil Jurisdiction and Judgments Order 2001, section 41. It included the requirements of 'residence' and substantial connection with the UK, in order to consider individuals domiciled in the UK.[14] To show evidence of residence in the UK, a person might produce an original passport, travel document or Home Office records. Failing these, a person may show other evidence instead of official registration of residence, such as employers' letters, a Seaman's Record Book, tax and national insurance letters, etc.[15]

Notably, the traditional English notion of domicile still influences judicial interpretation when applying the domicile principle according to the Brussels jurisdiction regime. For example, in *Bank of Dubai Ltd v Abbas*,[16] Saville LJ

[11] P Schlosser (ed), 'Report on the Convention on the Association of the Kingdom of Denmark, Ireland and the United Kingdom of Great Britain and Northern Ireland to the Convention on jurisdiction and the enforcement of judgments in civil and commercial matters and to the Protocol on its interpretation by the Court of Justice' (1979) OJ C 59/71 (Schlosser Report) para 73.

[12] ibid.

[13] P Kaye, *Civil Jurisdiction and Enforcement of Foreign Judgments* (Professional Books Ltd, 1987) 345.

[14] The Civil Jurisdiction and Judgments Act 1982 s 41, sub-s (2), and the Civil Jurisdiction and Judgments Order 2001 s 41, sub-s 2 (UK).

[15] The UK Border Agency, 'Nationality Instructions: Registering British nationals (nationality instructions)' (29 November 2013), available at: www.gov.uk/government/publications/chapter-12-registering-british-nationals-nationality-instructions.

[16] *Bank of Dubai Limited v Fouad Haji Abbas* [1997] ILPr 308.

clarified that on the basis of *Levene* 'a person is resident … in a particular part of the United Kingdom if that part is for him a settled or usual place of abode', which connotes 'some degree of permanence or continuity'.[17] Although the British joining the EU jurisdiction regime has led to redefining British domicile for the purpose of jurisdiction, the common law approach of interpreting 'residence' remained. Now, judges apply both the 'Europeanised' and the common law understanding of 'residence'. As a result of the merged concepts, domicile is understood as a place of usual abode with some degree of permanence and continuity.

In comparison, the Russian approach towards the residence of individuals for the purpose of jurisdiction appears simpler and closer to the European *Wohnsitz* concept. Natural persons' place of residence is recognised as a place where they permanently or predominantly reside.[18] Registration (*registratsiia* or *propiska*) at a particular physical address is mandatory for Russian residents. Citizens and legal residents (including foreign nationals residing in Russia beyond a short-term visit of 90 days) are free to travel across the Federation, choose a place to work and live. However, when moving to a different location permanently or temporarily, they are required to terminate registration at their original address and register at the new location in accordance with the law.[19] The system of *registratsiia* originates from a long time ago, when *krepostnie krest'iane* (serfs) were attached to their *pomeshchik* (landlord) in tsarist Russia. The serfs were accounted for and any runaways were strictly punished. In Soviet Russia, the government established the system of *propiska* maintaining close monitoring and control over everybody in the Soviet Union, mostly due to the fear of spying activity or potential overthrow of the government.

The remnants of the old system, nowadays the official address of *registratsiia*, serves as the sole basis for general personal jurisdiction in Russia. A claimant must provide the address of the defendant when filing a suit.[20] If the address of the Russian defendant is unknown, the information may be obtained from the

[17] ibid [10–11].

[18] Grazhdanskiĭ Kodeks Rossiĭskoĭ Federatsii (Civil Code of the RF) of 30 November 1994 no 51-ФЗ (the Russian Civil Code) pt 1 (1994) art 20.

[19] Zakon RF o Prave Grazhdan RF na Svobodu Peredvizheniia, Vybor Mesta Prebyvaniia i Zhitelstva v Predelakh RF ot 25 iiunia 1993 g (Law on the Right of Citizens of the RF to Freedom of Movement and Choice of Place of Stay and Residence in the RF) of 25 June 1993 no 5242-1; Postanovlenie Pravitel'stva Rossiĭskoĭ Federatsii Ob Utverzhdenii Pravil Registratsii i Sniatiia Grazhdan Rossiĭskoĭ Federatsii s Registratsionnogo Ucheta po Mestu Prebyvaniia i po Mestu Zhitelstva v predelakh Rossiĭskoĭ Federatsii I Perechnia Lits, Otvetsvennykh za Priem i Peredachu v Organy Registratsionnogo Ucheta Dokumentov dlia Registratsii i Sniatiia s Registratsionnogo Ucheta Grazhdan Rossiĭskoĭ Federatsii po Mestu Prebyvaniia i po Mestu Zhitelstva v Predelakh Rossiĭskoĭ Federatsii ot 17 iiunia 1995 g (Regulation of the Government of the RF on Adoption of the Rules of Registration and De-registration of the Citizens of the RF at the Place of Stay and Residence within the RF and the List of Officials Responsible for Acceptance and Transfer of the Documents for Registration and De-registration of the Citizens of the RF at the Place of Stay and Residence within the RF to the State Authorities on State Registration) of 17 June 1995 no 713.

[20] Code of Civil Procedure of the Russian Federation of 14 November 2002 No 138-ФЗ art 131 (the CCP).

state authorities (immigration authorities, an address bureau, or the police) upon request.[21] Foreign citizens or companies also have the right to obtain such information. They would have to go through the same procedure of requesting the information from the government authorities as any Russian interested party. Once the address of the potential defendant is known, the civil claim may be filed at the corresponding court.

Therefore, Russian law views the residence of individuals in a quite straightforward fashion, aiming to embrace any type of housing where a person may live: a house, an apartment, corporate housing and other residential premises.[22] This approach refers to a particular physical location at a certain point in time (when the proceedings are brought to court). In contrast, for example, English 'residence' is understood more in the sense of a geographical location and a country to which a person is tied. In this regard, the Russian notion of residence is very much more literal than in England. Perhaps, it is necessary to maintain the specifics and particularity of the Russian understanding of residence in Russia, rather than simply indicating that 'an individual must be resident in Russia'. While the English domicile of the defendant attributes jurisdiction of English courts in general, versus any other state's jurisdiction, in Russia it is done to distinguish between many national courts of the same level. Given the vastness of the Russian Federation, the system of *registratsiia* (or *propiska*) must remain intact (at least for purpose of jurisdiction in private international law). Determining jurisdiction based on the official address of the defendant should help determine a single district court best suited to handle a dispute. Filing with the proper court would expedite the proceedings and thus contribute to a better administration of justice.

However, the strict and formalistic Russian approach towards the residence of individuals may have a downside. A person may be nominally registered in one location (a remote location in Siberia), but reside elsewhere (renting a place in Moscow). Common sense would dictate suing the defendant in Moscow; and a claimant, who knows the defendant resides in Moscow, might file a suit with a Moscow city court. However, the court may reject the claim because the defendant is officially resident somewhere else. Then, this may result in delay, inconvenience and additional travel expenses for the parties, in order to have a trial at the appropriate court. Therefore, strict formalism in the Russian understanding of

[21] In particular, an application may be filed with the immigration authorities, or address information bureau, or the law enforcement organs. The procedure is straightforward: an interested party files an application with the immigration authorities (by mail or online), indicating the name and the date of birth (if available) of the person of interest. The applicant would have to explain the reason for such a search (for instance: seeking to recover a debt in court), and produce their passport or identification documents. It takes one to four weeks, and is free. In addition, this information may be obtained from an address bureau for a 'quite moderate fee'. (See Relevant Media LLC, 'How to Find an Address of a Person' (*KakProsto* (online magazine) 2012). Based on a compelling reason, where actual current permanent or predominant location of an individual is difficult to determine, a request to find an address of a person may be filed with the police authorities.

[22] Law on the Freedom of Movement (n 19) art 2 and Rules of Registration and De-registration (n 19) art 3.

'residence' may create some hindrance to the overall administration of justice, but the benefits outweigh the disadvantages of the system.

B. Substantial Connection

In addition to residence at a particular address, there might be another component of domicile for the purpose of jurisdiction: substantial connection. How necessary is it for establishing adjudicatory jurisdiction over individuals? For instance, in the UK, for a person to be considered domiciled in the UK, the law requires existence of substantial connection to the forum in addition to residence there. English law attaches importance to the intent of a person to reside at a particular location, rather than simply looking at the address indicated in the address bureau's records. As put by Cheshire et al: 'whether a person is … resident in a particular country is said to be a question of fact, to be decided by reference to all the circumstances of any particular case'.[23] Thus, English law appears more objective in determining an individual's domicile. The requirement of 'substantial connection' is presumed fulfilled, unless proven otherwise if the person is resident in England for the consecutive three months or more.[24] Ownership of a house in England does not mean a person is domiciled in England if the visits to this house by the individual are 'infrequent, intermittent, and generally fleeting'.[25] Notably, an individual is also to be regarded as domiciled in England if he is resident in England but the nature and circumstances of his residence do not indicate that he has a substantial connection with any particular part of the UK.[26] A person's visit to England and his enforced presence in England due to conditions of bail would not constitute substantial connection to England.[27]

In contrast to the English approach, Russian understanding of 'residence' of an individual has no such requirement of substantial connection with Russia. It seems that the Russian concept of 'permanence' of residence rather depends on a subjective decision of an individual. People register at addresses for a period of time that they find necessary; and it is not the period of stay in that place that ties them to that place, but the fact of their official registration there.

It is worth considering introducing this additional qualifying element of 'substantial connection' into Russian law. In particular, the wording, 'the individual must have substantial connection with Russia', can be added to Article 20 of the Russian Civil Code. Then, it will require more than an address to connect a person to Russia when suing him there. This will help define residence more clearly, in this

[23] J Fawcett, J Carruthers and P North, *Cheshire, North and Fawcett: Private International Law*, 14th edn (Oxford University Press, 2008) 185.

[24] The Civil Jurisdiction and Judgments Act 1982 s 41, para 6, and the Civil Jurisdiction and Judgments Order 2001 s 41, para 9(2) (UK).

[25] *Cherney v Deripaska* [2007] 2 All ER (Comm) 785 [45].

[26] Civil Jurisdiction and Judgments Order 2001 s 41, para 9(5) (UK).

[27] *Petrograde Inc v Smith* [1999] 1 WLR 457, 461–62.

rapidly developing and globalised world, where persons move so easily and have several places of abode. In terms of my suggested normative approach to jurisdiction, this would benefit the parties, because it adds more qualification to the determination of residence. Moreover, in view of the convergence of legal regimes worldwide, bringing the Russian understanding of 'residence' closer to that of English law ('personal, physical presence other than that which is casual, fleeting, transient')[28] could benefit Russia in the long run: whether considering acceding to the European jurisdiction regime (Lugano Convention) or whether engaging in relations with common law systems.

On the other hand, incorporating the 'substantial connection' requirement into the Russian notion of residence may complicate things. How should the requirements of 'substantiality' of the connection be determined? What should the courts in Russia understand as close connection of a person to Russia? Should circumstances be examined in each particular case to assess the degree of a person's connection to a place? Should a certain period of time satisfy the requirement of substantial connection? Should a person's intention determine his or her place of abode? Rather than unambiguously stating a period of time (such as three months) to determine a person's substantial connection to the forum, a number of other various factual elements need to be taken into account by Russian judges. They may include habitual residence in the past, the course of a person's life, language, professional activities, etc. Intricacies of each particular case may further assist in determining the substantial connection. Lastly, these criteria should affect jurisdiction because they ensure that jurisdiction rules are not abstract concepts but an actual reflection of the parties' circumstances and interests in particular cases.

C. Corporations: Corporate Seat

In the next three subsections, I discuss location of legal entities for the purpose of the rule of suing at the location of the defendant. According to the normative approach to jurisdiction I construct in this book, the location of corporations for the purpose of jurisdiction should include not only the place of their state registration, but also their management and operations centre. Relaxing the strict territorial approach of viewing a corporate seat at the place of incorporation is attuned to my overall theory of reflecting the interests of parties in jurisdiction. It is in the interests of a claimant aiming to recover damages from a corporate defendant to have several options of where to bring such claims, where the activity of the defendant cannot be strictly connected with one particular place.

In the EU, a common definition of domicile for companies was proposed by the European Commission and adopted when the Brussels I Regulation[29] replaced

[28] Kaye (n 13) 352.

[29] Regulation (EC) 44/2001 of 22 December 2000 on Jurisdiction and the Recognition and Enforcement of Judgments in Civil and Commercial Matters [2001] OJ L12/1 (the Brussels I Regulation).

the Brussels Convention in 2002. The reason was not necessarily that the domestic rules of the Member States varied widely, and problems arose in practice. Rather, theoretically, it might have nevertheless created difficulties in the future; and, therefore, a common definition of domicile for companies was adopted.[30] Since the purpose of Brussels I was to establish jurisdiction at the location with which the potential defendant had a real connection at the relevant time, the Brussels I Regulation established that the legal entities' domicile represents the place where they (i) have their statutory seat, or (ii) central administration, or (iii) principal place of business.[31] Notably, Article 60(2) of the Brussels I Regulation specified that for the purposes of the UK and Ireland (and Cyprus, according to the Brussels I Recast), the 'statutory seat' shall mean registered office or, where there is no such office anywhere, the place of incorporation or, where there is no such place anywhere, the place under the law of which the formation took place.

This unique definition of a corporate seat for the UK, Ireland and Cyprus reflects the theory of incorporation in common law. The essence of the traditional English theory of incorporation is that domicile of legal entities is determined as the country under the laws of which it is incorporated. The legal system where a company is formed 'gives birth' to it and 'endows it with legal personality'.[32] The law of the place where the company is incorporated determines the validity of such incorporation, the requisite corporate documents, the structure of its main bodies and their powers, the order for dissolution of the company, etc.

The Anglo-Saxon theory of incorporation may be contrasted with the *Sitztheorie* (real seat theory), dominant in Germany, Austria, France, Italy and Luxembourg. The real seat theory reflects the European continental view that a company's actual domicile or real seat should be used as the main criterion to determine jurisdictional issues.[33] For instance, the doctrine is reflected in German legislation and case law. Article 17 of the German Code of Civil Procedure (ZPO) prescribes that 'unless anything to the contrary is stipulated elsewhere, a legal person's registered seat shall be deemed to be the place at which it has its administrative centre (*der Ort, wo die Verwaltung geführt wird*)'.[34] As the Bundesgerichtshof (BGH), the highest German court for civil and criminal law, elaborated in one of its decisions: 'the domicile of a legal person would be calculated according to § 17 ZPO, according

[30] F Pocar, 'Explanatory Report on the Convention on Jurisdiction and the Recognition and Enforcement of Judgments in Civil and Commercial Matters, signed in Lugano on 30 October 2007' OJ C 319/1, para 27.

[31] Regulation (EU) 1215/2012 of 12 December 2012 on Jurisdiction and the Recognition and Enforcement of Judgments in Civil and Commercial Matters (Recast) [2012] OJ L351/1, art 63 (the Brussels I Recast).

[32] T Hartley, *International Commercial Litigation: Texts, Cases and Materials on Private International Law* (Cambridge University Press, 2009) 27.

[33] K Baelz and T Baldwin, 'The End of the Real Seat Theory (*Sitztheorie*): The European Court of Justice Decision in *Ueberseering* of 5 November 2002 and its impact on German and European Company Law' (2002) 3 *German Law Journal* 85.

[34] BGB s 17.

to its founding seat and not its effective management seat'.[35] Also, as noted in another BGH decision 'if there is nothing else, the place where the administration is performed applies as the seat'.[36] These clarifications demonstrate that the continental legal approach stresses the place where the main decisions of management are made, as the domicile of companies for the purpose of jurisdiction.

Now, how does all this compare with the Russian understanding of location of legal entities? Such location is understood in Russia strictly as the place of state registration of the legal entity.[37] State registration shall be carried out at the location of the legal entity's managing body or a person empowered to act on its behalf.[38] In claims against state authorities, their location is the one indicated in the founding document regulating their activity. For example, since the federal tax authority is based in Moscow city pursuant to the Regulation on Federal Tax Authority,[39] it would be sued in the *arbitrazh* court in Moscow city. As for the state officials, their location is understood as the location of the state authority that they represent.

Ideally, the actual location of legal entities (*phizicheskiĭ adres*) and their legal addresses (*iuridicheskiĭ adres*) coincide. However, in practice, many companies have their legal address at one location, and carry out their activity in another place. In such cases, the legal address of the company provides the basis of choosing the appropriate court to file a claim against the company. What if the entity has no office or its location is unknown? How is jurisdiction conferred then? A claimant may choose to file with an *arbitrazh* court at the location of the legal person's property or at its last known location in the territory of the Russian Federation.

However, both during the Soviet period and until the present day,[40] location of legal entities still does not seem to take into account the place from where a company is actually controlled. Russian law does not appear to provide guidance in relation to jurisdiction over companies incorporated abroad but controlled from Russia. England provides a more qualified solution in such cases. For instance, in

[35] Decision of the BGH of 15 March 2010, Case no II ZR 27/09.

[36] Decision of the BGH of 10 November 2009, Case no VI ZB 25/09, available at: www.anwalt24.de/rund-ums-recht/BGH_10_11_2009_VI_ZB_25_09_Zustaendigkeit_des_Oberlandesgerichts_bei_bestehe_-d3908339.html.

[37] Russian Civil Code art 54(2).

[38] ibid. Also, Federal'nyĭ Zakon RF ot 8 avgusta no 129-Ф3 o Gosudarstvennoĭ Registratsii Iuridicheskikh Litz i Individual'nykh Predprinimateleĭ (Federal Law of the RF on State Registration of Legal Entities and Sole Proprietors) of 8 August 2001 no 129-Ф3, art 8(2).

[39] Postanovlenie Pravitel'stva RF ot 30 sentiabria 2004 g no 506 ob Utverzhdenii Polozheniia o Federal'noĭ Nalogovoĭ Sluzhbe (Regulation of the Government of the RF on Approving the Decree on the State Tax Authority) of 30 September 2004 no 506.

[40] See A Makarov, *Osnovnye Nachala Mezhdunarodnogo Chastnogo Prava* (*Fundamentals of Private International Law*) (IurIzdat NarkomIusta RSFSR, 1924); I Pereterskiĭ, *Ocherki Mezhdunarodnogo Chastnogo Prava* (*Essays on Private International Law*) (Gosud Izdatelstvo, 1924); S Krylov, *Mezhdunarodnoe Chastnoe Pravo: Posobie k Lektsiiam* (*Private International Law: Textbook for Lectures*) (Priboĭ, 1930); I Pereterskiĭ and S Krylov, *Mezhdunarodnoe Chastnoe Pravo* (*Private International Law*) (IuridIz NKIu SSSR, 1940).

Harada v Turner,[41] it was contended whether the Harada Company was domiciled in England, considering it was incorporated in Ireland, but had an official address in England. As accurately noted by Lindsay J: 'it rather depends on what one means by "a registered office"'.[42] The court held that although Harada's 'registered office' was in Ireland, its sole business was carried out in the UK. On that basis, it had its central management and control in the UK; and the English court had the jurisdiction. Had this situation arisen in a Russian court, a Russian judge would not be able to establish general jurisdiction over a company incorporated elsewhere but operating solely in Russia, unless the company's property tied it to a particular place in Russia. To remedy the situation, an alternative test of location of companies should be adopted in Russia.

i. Corporations: Central Management and/or Principal Place of Business

As mentioned above, the EU jurisdiction regime envisages domicile of a company not only at the place of its statutory seat, but also where it has its 'central administration' or 'principal place of business'. So far, there have been no European Court of Justice (ECJ) cases interpreting these terms, and their exact meaning at the EU level is uncertain. One could nevertheless speculate on the meaning and relationship between these terms within the frames of the EU Member States' national laws.

For instance, in English common law, the 'principal place of business' concept can be traced back to *Daimler v Continental Tyre*.[43] There, Lord Atkinson established that the test of residence was the 'place where the real business centre from which the governing and directing minds of the company operated, regulating and controlling its important affairs'.[44] Furthermore, the leading modern authorities on the term of 'principal place of business' of a company can be found in *The Deichland*[45] and *The Rewia*[46] cases. *The Deichland* vessel was chartered by Deich, a Panamanian corporation, whose central control and management was exercised in West Germany (Federal Republic of Germany). The plaintiffs issued and served a writ on the defendants relating to damage to the cargo, while the vessel was in Kent in the UK. The ownership of the vessel changed; and the new owners responded to the plaintiffs, guaranteeing the damages. The plaintiffs argued that Article 2 of the Brussels Convention 1968 conferred jurisdiction at the location of the defendant; the defendants argued that the court had no jurisdiction. It was common ground

[41] *Harada Ltd T/A Chequepoint UK Ltd v GP Turner* [2000] ILPr 574.
[42] ibid [17].
[43] *Daimler Co Ltd v Continental Tyre & Rubber Co (Great Britain) Ltd* [1916] 2 AC 307.
[44] ibid 319.
[45] *The* Deichland [1990] 1 QB 361 (*The Deichland*).
[46] *Owners of Cargo Lately Laden on Board the Rewia v Caribbean Liners (Caribtainer) Ltd* [1991] 2 Lloyd's Rep 325; [1993] ILPr 507; *Financial Times*, 12 July 1991 (*The Rewia*).

that Deich was incorporated in Panama, but West Germany would regard Deich as having its seat there. The argument was whether a corporation could have more than one seat, and it was decided that a corporation might satisfy the test for the location of its seat in relation to more than one state. Although the charterers were incorporated in Panama, their central control and management was exercised in the Federal Republic of Germany. Accordingly, their seat for the purpose of jurisdiction was in West Germany.[47] In *The Rewia*, the Court of Appeal held that the principal place of business did not necessarily mean the place where most of the business was carried out. Although day-to-day management of the company took place in Hong Kong, the company was controlled from Germany. Its shareholders, directors and mortgagee banks were German; the meetings of directors took place in Hamburg, the charter was in German, etc. Therefore, the 'principal place of business' was understood as the centre from which instructions were given and the ultimate control was exercised. Significantly, the reference to the 'principal place' did not require identification of a particular building. Following *The Rewia*, case law established that 'central administration' was more clearly identifiable for large corporations, rather than small companies, where 'there may be a considerable blurring of functions because the same person often [discharges] a variety of roles'.[48]

In contrast to the EU, where the concept of a company's domicile includes the place of its central management and control, the Russian approach strictly understands it as the place of their state registration (the corporate 'seat'). The current Russian definition of location of corporations should be adjusted. Additional elements – the company's central administration, or its principal place of business – should be added to Article 54(2) of the Russian Civil Code denoting the location of corporations. Introducing these two additional qualifiers will allow Russian courts to adjudicate claims involving companies not necessarily registered in Russia but carrying out most of their business operations from Russia.

Central administration or principal place of business could be understood as a place of residence of a company's directors or the place of a company's day-to-day management. An example of such interpretation may be found in common law. For instance, in *Latchin*,[49] the first defendant, the GMH Company, was incorporated and registered in Luxembourg. The second defendant, the company's director, was domiciled in England. The claimant had to show a good arguable case that GMH was domiciled in the UK in order for the English court to retain jurisdiction. The defendants argued that all the employees, meeting rooms and facilities for clients of GMH were in Luxembourg, and that no board meetings were ever held in London. There was, however, a UK subsidiary of GMH in London, with 'no connection with any of the matters in dispute', according to the defendants. At the same time, it was common ground that the parties had meetings in London regarding some

[47] *The Deichland*, 375, 379 and 388.
[48] *King v Crown Energy Trading AG and Another* [2003] EWHC 163 (Comm); [2003] ILPr 28.
[49] *Latchin v General Mediterranean Holdings SA & Anor* [2002] CLC 330.

architectural services to be performed in Morocco. In the end, the claimant failed to show a good arguable case that GMH was domiciled in the UK. As noted by Andrew Smith J in that case: 'the question of a corporation's seat or domicile is concerned not with its day-to-day operational decisions, but its central control and management'. Although the claimant contended that the second defendant's decisions took place in London, it was not of relevance, since no evidence of a major controlling decision made in London was provided. The Justice used the wording by Lord Loreburn from an old case *De Beers Consolidated*, asserting that London was not the place where GMH 'kept house and did its real business'.[50]

An analogous discussion occurred in *Royal & Sun Alliance v MK Digital FZE*,[51] where an interested party had to make a good arguable case that a company was domiciled in England. English addresses of the directors did not show that the central management and control of a Danish company was exercised in England. There was no evidence of business dealings in the UK, and the company did not represent itself to the world as operating from the UK. Therefore, both *Latchin* and *Royal & Sun* demonstrated that the mere existence of English directors, even if clearly domiciled in the UK, may not constitute a domicile of a corporation in the UK. Also, these cases show that a company may be domiciled in a state when its central administration is carried out in that state, notwithstanding that it might be incorporated elsewhere.

Further guidance may be found in another English case, which interpreted and applied *The Rewia* definition of principal place of business. This case is *MODSAF v Faz Aviation*.[52] There, the claimant, MODSAF, sued Faz Aviation Ltd, a company incorporated in Cyprus. The proceedings were initiated in England based on Article 2 of the Brussels I Regulation. The claimant argued that the defendant was 'domiciled' in England with its central administration or principal place of business there. The defendants opposed this, however, arguing that Cypriot courts had the jurisdiction to deal with the matter. They insisted that Faz became dormant and had ceased to have any administration or place of business before the proceedings were initiated; and that the place of central administration used to be in Cyprus, where the company's registered office, bank, lawyers, accountants, company secretary and directors were resident. In the end, MODSAF failed to prove a good arguable case that the defendant had any business either to administer or to operate after a date more than 12 months before proceedings were issued. The court held that the company had no principal place of business anywhere apart from Cyprus; and it followed that the English court had no jurisdiction over the claim.

[50] *De Beers Consolidated Mines Ltd v Howe* [1906] AC 455, 458.

[51] *Royal & Sun Alliance Insurance plc & Anor v MK Digital FZE (Cyprus) Ltd & Ors* [2006] EWCA Civ 629; [2006] 1 CLC 787.

[52] *Ministry of Defence and Support of the Armed Forces for Iran v Faz Aviation Ltd (Formerly FN Aviation Ltd) and Al-Zayat* [2007] EWHC 1042 (Comm); [2007] ILPr 42.

Significantly, Langley J listed a number of points regarding the domicile of a company:

i. The central administration and principal place of business of a company … frequently will be in the same country.
ii. The focus, in matters of jurisdiction, is on the country rather than any more particular location.
iii. The principal place of business (if there is one) is likely to be the place where the corporate authority is to be found (shareholders and directors), and to be the place from where the company is controlled and managed.
iv. The place where the day-to-day activities of the company are carried out may not be the principal place of business if those activities are subject to the control of senior management located elsewhere.[53]

These observations, although appearing obvious in some regards, are very important. They emphasise that the court should be mainly interested in which country the principal place of business (rather than an exact physical address) is situated. This view is similar to the domicile of individuals, where the law should focus on the country, rather than on a particular building. This may seem obvious for an English lawyer. However, from a point of view of a Russian legislator, determination of an exact city or district where the company is located is indispensable for the internal jurisdiction system. So, the seemingly obvious additional qualifiers of 'central administration' by Langley J, outlined above, may assist the Russian legislators in their understanding of location of a company.

It is of interest what should occur if the place of registration and the place of administration of a company differ. Which should be given priority? Some scholars might argue that perhaps it is not the place of incorporation but the place of daily or central management and control (of a company) that should assume a more prominent role.[54] The Brussels I Recast does not prioritise between the two, nor does it put the 'statutory seat' before 'central management' or 'principal place of business'. Objectively, all these locations equally qualify as companies' domicile.

A test of the closest connection might provide the most appropriate response to the question when principal management should prevail over official company's address. As emphasised in *889457 Alberta Inc v Katanga Mining Ltd*,[55] it is important to base jurisdiction at the location with which the potential defendant had the closest and most real connection. In that case, the first defendant, Katanga, was nominally a Bermuda corporation, resident in Canada for tax purposes. It had some connection to Canada when the proceedings were started, but its connection to England was much more real. England was where the entirety of the administration took place and where all known management resided. Thus, the central

[53] ibid [29].

[54] R Drury, 'The Regulation and Recognition of Foreign Corporations: Responses to the "Delaware Syndrome"' (1998) 57 *Cambridge Law Journal* 165.

[55] *889457 Alberta Inc v Katanga Mining Ltd* [2008] EWHC 2679 (Comm); [2009] ILPr 14.

administration of the first defendant was in England. Professor Briggs' approach appears in line with this thinking: to determine a company's central administration, one may examine where those who have the serious responsibilities in the company have their place of work.[56]

The validity of the test set out in *889457 Alberta* is however now doubtful after *Young v Anglo American South Africa Ltd*.[57] *Young* establishes that the place where those who have serious responsibility in the company work is not necessarily the place where the 'central administration' of the company will be. The court in *Young* continued that the correct interpretation would be 'to find the place where the essential decisions are taken by the company through its organs for that company's operation and where the company takes its entrepreneurial decisions'. The place of work of those who have 'serious responsibility' for decisions and the place where the essential decisions of the company are made could be different. The court further elaborates that the aim behind the definition of corporate domicile was to provide a claimant with a wider choice of where the claimant can sue the company.

This approach may be useful for Russian courts when establishing jurisdiction. When dealing with divergent locations of company registration and its central management, to determine corporate domicile, courts should take into consideration the place which reflects the most real and the closest connection to the company. Thus, if a company is registered outside Russian jurisdiction, but its entire managing body is in Russia or its essential decisions are made in Russia, this approach might reveal the actual location of the company, preventing avoiding jurisdiction and, possibly, avoiding liability.

This may seem to be a pure academic discussion; however it has a very useful practical application. Frequently, Russian companies get registered in tax havens (such as the Seychelles) to avoid taxation, while their principal management is situated in Moscow. Briggs' approach could help determine the realistic domicile of companies. Then, the appropriate local courts would be in a better position to enforce orders of a commercial nature against such companies and their management.

However, asserting jurisdiction by state courts over entities registered in other jurisdictions may result in parallel actions in multiple courts in different states, potentially leading to conflicting judgments. Nevertheless, a multiple fora approach benefits the interests of the parties seeking access to court. Having more (rather than limited) options regarding competent courts improves the chances for parties to attain justice. In the end, states should facilitate access to their courts, and jurisdiction rules should reflect such facilitation appropriately. That is why my view favours a multiple jurisdictions regime. In addition, conflicting judgments can be avoided by enforcing an effective mechanism such as *lis pendens* and related actions.

[56] A Briggs and P Rees (eds), *Civil Jurisdiction and Judgments*, 5th edn (Proforma, 2009) para 2.115.
[57] *Young v Anglo American South Africa Ltd* [2014] EWCA Civ 1130.

ii. Carrying Out Business Activity in a Forum Via Branches and Agents

In this subsection, I review the relevant provisions of the Brussels I Recast and the Russian Codes of Civil and *Arbitrazh* Procedure foreseeing jurisdiction at the location of branches or agents of foreign corporations (deemed to be domiciled or located in the state). Both regimes accept the notion of retaining jurisdiction over the branches or agencies of foreign companies, if the dispute relates to the activity of such branch or agency. The rule appears fair; if foreign principals choose to carry out business activity in an EU Member State or in Russia via permanent establishment or agency, they open themselves up to local jurisdiction. Plus, in some instances there may be additional connection with the forum, such as the agent signing a contract in the forum, etc.

Now, how are these rules formulated and implemented in statutory law? In the EU, Article 7(5) of the Brussels I Recast assigns jurisdiction to courts at the place where the branch (or other establishment) is situated. In cases involving non-EU companies and their branches in a Member State, pursuant to the residual jurisdiction rule, national law applies. For instance, in England, when a foreign principal company maintains an agent within English jurisdiction, English courts can retain jurisdiction when a claim is served on that agent relating to a contractual dispute.[58] For instance, in *National Mortgage v Gosselin*,[59] a London agent of a foreign company 'merely sent the claimant the defendant's price list and forwarded the claimant's order to the defendant'.[60] These actions, however, were enough for an English court to retain jurisdiction. In another significant case, *Union International Insurance v Jubilee Insurance*,[61] a company registered in Bermuda signed a contract with a Kenyan company via its agents in England. The Bermuda company sought damages for breach of contract. The request to serve out of an English jurisdiction was set aside, because the 'agent' rule only applied when the foreigners chose to carry out business in England by using an agent. A claimant's use of an English agent was, rightfully, in that case, of no relevance.

Russian law is similar to English law: it confers jurisdiction on a Russian court where foreign companies have an establishment or an agent in the UK. In Russia, actions arising out of the activity of a branch or representative office of a company may be filed at a court (or an *arbitrazh* court, depending on the nature of the claim) at the location of the main legal entity, or at the location of the branch or the representative office.[62] This rule applies where the parent company is abroad, and

[58] Civil Procedure Rules r 6.12 (UK).

[59] *National Mortgage and Agency Co of New Zealand v Gosselin* (1922) 38 TLR 832.

[60] S Sime, *A Practical Approach to Civil Procedure*, 10th edn (Oxford University Press, 2007) 152.

[61] *Union International Insurance Co v Jubilee Insurance Co* [1991] 1 WLR 415.

[62] CCP arts 29(2) and 402(1); Code of *Arbitrazh* Procedure of the Russian Federation of 24 July 2002 No 95-FZ 2002 arts 36(5) and 247(2) (the CAP).

its subsidiary is in Russia. Alternatively, it applies where the parent and its branch are located in different parts of the Russian Federation. The plaintiff must provide evidence that the legal action arises out of the activity of the branch or representative office. Otherwise, the claim must be brought to the court at the location of the defendant according to the general rule of jurisdiction. Thus, Russia accepts the notion of retaining jurisdiction over foreign entities represented in Russia via branches or agents in a similar way to the EU.

Upon examining available cases, however, it is noticeable that in many cases, claims against local branches of foreign companies get rejected at first instance in Russia. This occurs notwithstanding the explanatory report by the Russian Supreme Court that clearly calls such rejection contrary to due procedure.[63] Perhaps, this may be explained by the unfamiliarity of judges with this comparatively novel rule. It was impossible and unimaginable during Soviet times for foreign companies to carry out commercial activity in Russia, let alone basing Russian jurisdiction over foreign companies represented in Russia via an agent. It may still appear intrusive on foreign sovereignty, in the eyes of some judges, to retain jurisdiction at the location of the branches or representative offices of foreign corporations in Russia.

For instance, the Russian Supreme *Arbitrazh* Court re-examined a case relating to the branch of a foreign company in Russia in order to reaffirm the jurisdiction of a Russian court.[64] A tax office filed a case against a branch of a Turkish company, Yamata, to collect a fine for tax evasion at an *arbitrazh* court of first instance, which rejected the claim.[65] On appeal, the *arbitrazh* court of appeal left the decision unchanged.[66] Among the main reasons for rejection were that the courts believed that the Russian courts did not have jurisdiction, and the claim should have been addressed to the foreign company itself. The Russian courts thought that Turkey was a more appropriate forum in which to hear the case. The Federal *Arbitrazh* Court cancelled the previous courts' decisions and redirected the case back to the court of first instance for a retrial, because the status of the foreign legal entity (its representative office in Russia) was not analysed correctly for the purposes of applying tax rules and jurisdiction rules.[67]

[63] Obzor Sudebnoĭ Praktiki Verkhovnogo Suda RF 'Nekotorye Vorporsy Sudebnoĭ Praktiki po Grazhdanskim Delam' ('Review of Court Practice by the Supreme Court of the RF, 'Certain Issues of Court Practice in Civil Cases' (1998) 10 *Bulletin of the Supreme Court of the RF* 22.

[64] Postanovlenie Prezidiuma Vysshego Arbitrazhnogo Suda RF ot 4 iiulia 2006 g (Decision of the Presidium of the Supreme *Arbitrazh* Court of the RF) of 4 July 2006 no 1782/06.

[65] Reshenie Arbitrazhnogo Suda Yamalo-Nenetskogo Avtonomnogo Okruga ot 16 avgusta 2004 g (Decision of the *Arbitrazh* Court of Yamalo-Nenetskiĭ Autonomous Area) of 16 August 2004 no A81-2346/3177A-04.

[66] Postanovlenie Vos'mogo Arbitrazhnogo Apelliatsionnog Suda ot 24 noiabria 2004 g (Decision of the Eighth *Arbitrazh* Court of Appeal) of 24 November 2004.

[67] Postanovlenie Federal'nogo Arbitrazhnogo Suda Zapadno-Sibirskogo Okruga ot 28 febralia 2005 g (Decision of the Federal *Arbitrazh* Court of the West Siberian Circuit) of 28 February 2005.

Again, the courts of first instance and of appeal rejected satisfying the claim.[68] On the second appeal, the Federal *Arbitrazh* Court stayed the proceedings concluding that Russian *arbitrazh* courts had jurisdiction in relation to foreign entities, but not their representative offices.[69] No further reasoning was provided in this court decision. The tax office appealed again to the Supreme *Arbitrazh* Court for re-examination of the case. The Supreme *Arbitrazh* Court cancelled the judgments by the *cassation* court and ordered a retrial: it proved the previous judgments erroneous in application of the jurisdictional provisions relating to branches of foreign entities. It affirmed that the *arbitrazh* court at the location of the branch of the foreign company in Russia had jurisdiction.[70] The Supreme *Arbitrazh* Court's decision was right in the end, conferring jurisdiction on Russian courts over foreign companies domiciled elsewhere but carrying out business activity in Russia though an agent.

Although this example demonstrates an extreme case of double revision at all instances, it shows that Russian courts may yet take some time before becoming fully comfortable with asserting jurisdiction over foreign entities represented in Russia.

Therefore, based on the analysis of substantive rule of domicile – suing at the location of the defendant – a few recommendations can be made for Russia. First, it could supplement the statutory definition of residence of an individual with an additional requirement of 'substantial connection'. Secondly, the location of legal entities for the purpose of jurisdiction should be also amended, adding a company's place of central management and/or principal place of business. In addition, application of the existing rules of suing at the location of the branches and representative offices can be further streamlined. Further, the analysis has shown that the EU is in need of a harmonised solution regarding the domicile of an individual for the purpose of jurisdiction. A definition 'based on objective criteria such as eg, habitual residence for a certain time would be preferable'.[71]

[68] Reshenie Arbitrahznogo Suda Yamalo-Nenetskogo Avtonomnogo Okruga ot 11 iiulia 2005 (Decision of the *Arbitrazh* Court of the Yamalo-Nenetskiĭ Autonomous Area) of 11 July 2005; and Postanovlenie Arbitrazhnogo Suda Apelliatsionnoĭ Instantsii Yamalo-Nenetskogo Avtonomnogo Okruga ot 21 sentiabria 2005 g (Decision of the *Arbitrazh* Court of Appeal of Yamalo-Nenetskiĭ Autonomous Area) of 21 September 2005 no A81-3177A-04.

[69] Postanovlenie Federal'nogo Arbitrazhnogo Suda Zapadno-Sibirskogo Okruga ot 21 noiabria 2005 g (Decision of the Federal *Arbitrazh* Court of the West Siberian Circuit) of 21 November 2005.

[70] Postanovlenie Presidiuma Vysshego Arbitrazhnogo Suda RF ot 4 iiulia 2006 g (Decision of the Presidium of the Supreme *Arbitrazh* Court of the RF) of 4 July 2006 no 1782/06.

[71] B Hess, T Pfeiffer and P Schlosser, 'Report on the Application of Regulation Brussels I in the Member States' (Institute for International and Private International Law, Ruprecht-Karls-University Heidelberg, Study JLS/C4/2005/03, Final Version September 2007) 88.

II. State Sovereign Interests Overriding Party Autonomy to Protect the Integrity of the State

A. Acceptable Exclusive Jurisdiction: Immovable Property, Patents and Public Registers

In this section, I analyse exclusive jurisdiction rules that may override party autonomy to choose a forum to handle civil and commercial disputes. Both jurisdiction regimes I analyse (the EU and Russia) recognise state mandatory jurisdiction in certain cases. In those cases, jurisdiction becomes extraterritorial, transcending state borders. Both Europe and Russia agree on such mandatory jurisdiction of their courts in a number of instances. In this subsection, I review the rules that are most uniformly recognised and where not much debate exists: those in relation to immovable property, patents and public registers.

The EU exclusive jurisdiction rules are all contained in Article 24 of the Brussels I Recast. These rules prevail over any other conflicting jurisdictional terms of the regulation. When a court seizes a claim concerning a matter over which courts of another Member State have exclusive jurisdiction by virtue of Article 24, it should declare of its own motion that it has no jurisdiction.[72] This helps maintain mutual trust in administration of justice and reinforce judicial cooperation among the EU Member States. The binding nature of the exclusive jurisdiction rule ensures predictability and legal certainty regarding jurisdiction. Furthermore, Article 24 applies 'regardless of domicile', unlike the rest of the Brussels I Recast pertinent to disputes where defendants are domiciled in an EU Member State. The rules on exclusive jurisdiction extend both to infra-EU and international disputes with non-EU defendants. The EU courts have mandatory jurisdiction if a strong connection exists with an EU Member State, even if a claim involves defendants domiciled in third states. This mechanism may appear exorbitant in relation to parties from non-EU countries. However, the extensive character of Article 24 is not unreasonable, considering that similar rules most likely confer exclusive jurisdiction on the third states' courts regardless of the domicile of defendants in their legislatures as well.

In Russia, Russian courts have exclusive jurisdiction in a number of situations. The rules of exclusive jurisdiction override other Russian rules of general, alternative and contractual jurisdiction. A comprehensive list of cases where Russian courts shall have the exclusive jurisdiction appears in the Codes of Civil and *Arbitrazh* Procedure.[73] Some of them coincide with Article 24 of Brussels I and these are the rules to be reviewed in this chapter. The exclusive jurisdiction of

[72] Brussels I Recast art 27.

[73] CCP; and Code of *Arbitrazh* Procedure of the Russian Federation of 24 July 2002 No 95-FZ 2002 (the 'CAP').

Russian courts cannot be overridden by a private agreement between the parties; only an international intergovernmental treaty can override these provisions. Moreover, in the case of an attempt to enforce a foreign court's decision in Russia regarding a subject matter that makes jurisdiction of Russian courts exclusive, a Russian court shall deny such enforcement.[74]

i. Immovable Property

The most vivid example where it is acceptable for state home sovereignty to override party autonomy concerns immovable property. Immovable property is precisely located on a certain territory: it is registered in appropriate state registers. It is only proper, for the sake of maintaining the integrity of state territorial borders, to accept that states shall have exclusive jurisdiction over titles to immovable property or claims changing rights to immovable property. Not all disputes mentioning immovable property should be subject to the mandatory jurisdiction of state courts.

The tradition to confer jurisdiction on courts at the location of immovable property is recognised across the world. Application of this rule corresponds to the international principle of comity: states' mutual cooperation and recognition of each other's power. Immovable property is inseparably connected with territory of a state; and the sovereignty of the state dominates over that state's property. Adjudicating claims concerning foreign property would intrude on foreign sovereignty, which is strictly undesirable in interstate relations.[75]

In addition to comity and sovereignty, the rule of exclusive jurisdiction in actions *in rem* in property is stipulated by the principle of effectiveness. Suppose a foreign court handles a case concerning state property. Enforcing a foreign court's decision regarding the property in the home state will most likely run into difficulties anyway. Thus, yielding to a state's jurisdiction over the state's property appears reasonable in view of effectiveness of judicial process. Otherwise, why conduct judicial proceedings and have a court order that might fail? A similar idea is convened in *The Tolten*, a case relating to damage done by a ship in foreign waters. An English court ends up retaining jurisdiction in the action *in rem* against the owners of the ship. The cases provide support for the efficiency and practicality argument: 'the reason why common law and chancery courts do not exercise their jurisdiction over foreign soil ought to be regarded as applying also to Admiralty Courts, ie, they cannot make their decree effective in a foreign jurisdiction'.[76]

Pursuant to the Brussels jurisdiction regime, in proceedings which have as their object rights *in rem* in immovable property or tenancies of immovable property,

[74] CCP art 412(3); CAP art 244 (1)(3).

[75] As Story noted over a century ago, 'no court in this country has direct original jurisdiction with respect to real estate abroad'. *Attorney-General v Stewart* (1817) 2 Mer 143, 156; Story's *Conflict of Laws* ss 550–55.

[76] *The Tolten* [1946] P 135, 136.

the courts of Member States where the immovable property is located shall have exclusive jurisdiction.[77] Notably, there is an exception in relation to tenancy of property *in rem*. Where the immovable property is contracted out for private use for a maximum period of six months and the tenant is a natural person, and both the tenant and the landlord are domiciled in the same Member State, the courts of the Member State where the defendant is domiciled would have jurisdiction as well.[78] National laws of the EU Member States 'tend to generally coincide' with this exclusive jurisdiction rule pursuant to the Brussels I regime.[79] For instance, in the UK, the *Mocambique* rule states that English courts shall not have jurisdiction over claims regarding titles to foreign property.[80]

Similarly, Russia confers exclusive jurisdiction on courts at the location of the immovable property in Russia (*forum rei sitae*).[81] This applies in domestic as well as international disputes.[82] In addition, *arbitrazh* courts have exclusive jurisdiction relating to property owned by the state of the Russian Federation, including claims connected with the privatisation of state property and expropriation of property for state needs. Notably, the disputes regarding immovable property cannot be attributed to consideration by arbitration tribunals. This can be reasonably explained because issues of public importance cannot be decided by private parties: changes in state registers of immovable property, for instance, can only be made by involving a state authority (court). In relation to tenancy, the Russian jurisdiction regime does not require a minimum tenancy period in comparison with the Brussels I Regulation. In practice, arguments in this regard do not seem to stir much controversy.

Since many jurisdictions in the world recognise the exclusive jurisdiction of courts at the location of the immovable property, no conflict of jurisdiction should arise. Ideally, each state would assume jurisdiction where a claim concerned immovable property on its territory. Likewise, a state would decline jurisdiction when claims concern foreign property. However, practice brings to light scenarios where controversial issues still appear. One point of interest might be a divergent understanding of 'immovable property'. Next, tenancy for private use may be an exception. In addition, there seems to be a different understanding of subject of a claim involving immovable property. Finally, potential conflict may arise between the exclusive jurisdiction rules of two countries in claims relating to property in both of those countries. These points will be discussed now.

[77] Brussels I Recast art 24(1).

[78] ibid.

[79] The Nuyts Study (n 6) 7.

[80] *BSA v Mocambique* [1893] AC 602. Notably, in actions *in personam*, 'Proceedings for a declaration of trust in land and for the legal owner to transfer ownership did not constitute an action in rem', and therefore, do not fall under exclusive jurisdiction of the state where the land is situated; see *Webb v Webb* [1991] 1 WLR 1410 (Ch). Also, J Wass, 'The Court's *In Personam* Jurisdiction in Cases Involving Foreign Land' (2014) 63 *International & Comparative Law Quarterly* 103.

[81] CCP art 30(1); CAP art 38(1–2).

[82] CCP art 403(1); CAP art 247(1–2).

ii. Diverging Classification of Immovable Property

Article 130 of the Russian Civil Code defines immovable property as everything that is closely connected to land and cannot be moved without substantial damage to the purpose of the property.[83] It includes buildings, structures, land plots, sites of subsurface resources, residential and non-residential premises, forests and certain incomplete construction projects.[84] Also, sea vessels and aircraft are regarded as 'immovable property' because of their high value and importance for the economy of the state. Things that cannot be characterised as immovable, including money and securities, shall be understood as movable.[85]

Questions may arise regarding interpretation of the Russian terminology: 'firmly connected with the land' and 'substantial damage to [the property's] purpose'. The need for clarification was pointed out by the Russian Union of Industrialists and Entrepreneurs (Rossiyskiĭ Soiuz Promyshlennikov i Predprinimateleĭ), the lobby group representing the interests of businesses in Russia. The Union submitted its notes during the Russian parliamentary sessions considering certain changes to the Civil Code pointing out that that the wording of Article 130 of the Civil Code was ambiguous.[86] The Union remarked, that the 'firm connection with land' may mistakenly characterise some objects as immovable property. For example, fences or roads cannot be removed or moved without substantial damage. However, they should be understood as additions or improvements to the immovable property, rather than immovable property. The Parliament, however, determined that the practice of the application of Article 130 in its present form shows that this ambiguity is not sufficient to require an immediate change. Therefore, at this time, no further criteria regarding 'firm connection with the land' or 'substantial damage to the purpose' were introduced. The definition of the immovable property remains the same.[87]

Some other changes, however, were introduced by the Russian Parliament in 2013: a new concept of 'immovable aggregate' (*nedvizhimyĭ kompleks*) was added to Article 133.1 of the Civil Code. It is understood as totality of buildings and other things united by the sole purpose and connected inseparably physically or

[83] Russian Civil Code art 130.

[84] ibid; also, Federal'nyĭ Zakon RF ot 21 iiulia 1997 o Gosudarstvennoĭ Registratsii Prav na Nedvizhimoe Imushchestvo i Sdelok s Nim (Federal Law of the RF on State Registration of Immovable Property and Transactions with It) of 21 July 1997 no 122- ФЗ.

[85] Russian Civil Code art 130.

[86] RSPP, 'Zamechaniia i Predlozheniia k Proektu Federal'nogo Zakona no 474538-6/3 'O Vnesenii Izmeneniĭ v Chasti Pervuiu, Vtoruiu, Tret'iu i Chetvertuiu GK RF, a Takzhe v Otdel'nye Zakonodatel'nye Akty RF' (Russian Union of Industrialists and Entrepreneurs, 'Notes and Recommendations to the Bill No.47538-6/3 'On Introducing Changes to the Parts 1, 2, 3 and 4 of the Civil Code of the RF and Other Legislative Acts'), available at: media.rspp.ru/document/1/f/b/fbd85ae7eb0fd7b46fc029b58b98a1f1.pdf.

[87] Zakonoproekt no 474538-6/3 o Vnesenii Izmeneniĭ v Chasti Pervuiu, Vtoruiu, Tret'iu i Chetvertuiu GK RF, a Takzhe v Otdel'nye Zakonodatel'nye Akty RF' (Bill no 47538-6/3 on Introducing Changes to Subsection 3 of Section 1 of Part 1 of the Civil Code of the Russian Federation).

technologically or located on one land plot (such as a number of buildings with a sole purpose, or heating and sewerage systems, or power and communication lines). The reason for this amendment was that Russian courts categorised such complex objects in a diverging manner. This new addition clarified the issue.

In the EU, national laws of the Member States determine whether certain property is movable or immovable. For instance, in England, *lex situs* (the law of the place in which property is situated) determines 'whether particular property is a movable or an immovable', as explained by Russel J in *Re Berchtold.*[88] English common law tradition features the notions of personalty and realty, which almost entirely correspond to movable and immovable property. In most cases, the distinction is obvious: land is clearly immovable; a vehicle is clearly movable, etc. A couple of interesting points arise in connection with a mortgagee's interest to land, which in English law is considered as immovable.[89] Also, the proceeds of sale of 'settled land' in England are considered immovable.[90] The 'settled land' is understood as land allocated ahead of time for future generations of the family. This unique English understanding may cause some confusion. In its pure form, money is transferable and movable. However, when the money is obtained from sale of a 'settled land' or mortgage, it is immovable. Parties to international disputes need to bear this peculiarity in mind. English courts may legitimately assume jurisdiction in international cases relating to proceeds from a real estate sale. This concept is very different from the civil law approach, including that in the Russian Federation. No such provision exists in Russia, and introducing such a novel concept into the Russian understanding of real estate would be too radical and foreign to the historically formulated concept of immovable property.

iii. Scope of Disputes Relating to Immovable Property Subject to Exclusive Jurisdiction

As mentioned above, not all disputes relating to immovable property located in that state should be subject to the state's exclusive jurisdiction. The mandatory jurisdiction should not extend to any disputes mentioning immovable property located in that state.

This concept may be demonstrated by comparing approaches taken in the EU and Russia. The Brussels jurisdiction regime envisages exclusive jurisdiction in proceedings which have as their object rights *in rem* in immovable property or tenancies of immovable property. To clarify, 'actions for damages based on infringement of rights *in rem* or in damage to property in which rights *in rem* exist do not fall within the scope of [the Article]'.[91] In other words, personal

[88] *Re Berchtold* [1923] 1 Ch 192, 199.
[89] *In Re Hoyles* [1911] 1 Ch 179.
[90] *In Re Cutliffe's Will Trusts* [1940] Ch 565.
[91] Schlosser Report para 163.

claims connected in some way to land are not subject to exclusive jurisdiction by courts of a Member State where the immovable property is located. In contrast, claims that may fall under the exclusive jurisdiction relating to immovable property in Russia are understood rather broadly.[92] The range of actions relating to immovable property may include disputes over the status *in rem* in property or transactions connected with the property.[93] Claims may include, particularly, those for recovery of the property from unlawful possession, for elimination of violations not connected with dispossession of property, for establishment of easements (*servitut*), for separation of property from common possession (*razdel imushchestva*), for establishment of boundaries of land section (*zemelnyĭ uchastok*), and for release of property from seizure (*osvobozhdenie ot aresta*).[94] Also, such actions include any type of claim where their enforcement would entail the necessity of state registration of the occurrence, restriction, transfer or termination of rights to real estate, or would lead to making an entry in the Uniform State Register (*edinyĭ gosudarstvennyĭ reestr*) of rights in respect of transactions that are subject to state registration.[95]

In this regard, there is a risk that the approach by Russian courts is of an expansive rather than limited nature. There is a danger of excessive interference by the state into private affairs. State mandatory jurisdiction should only be allowed in cases directly related to – ie, having as their object – rights *in rem*. Mandatory allocation of any types of case mentioning immovable property to a certain forum is inconsistent with my view on jurisdiction, because it is too broad and places too much restriction on party autonomy. Cases involving rights to immovable property should be approached very carefully. In relation to Russian court practice, the judges should limit the application of this potentially exorbitant jurisdiction rule by requiring some other reasonable connection of the claim to Russia.

iv. Records in State and Land Registers

Closely related to the rule relating to immovable property, there is a rule concerning state registers. Brussels Ia envisages exclusive jurisdiction of EU Member State courts in proceedings which have as their object the validity of entries in public registers, if the register is kept in the Member State.[96] The rationale for this

[92] A Kopylov, 'Disputable Jurisdiction' (Спорная подсудность) (2010) 11 *EZh-Jurist* (*ЭЖ-Юрист*) 17.
[93] T Neshataeva, 'O Voprosakh Kompetentsii Arbitrazhnykh Sudov v Rossiĭskoĭ Federatsii po Rassmotreniiu Del s Uchastiem Inostrannykh Lits' ('On Issues of Competence of *Arbitrazh* Courts in the Russian Federation on Proceedings with Foreign Parties') (2004) *JURIT-Vestnik* 88.
[94] Postanovlenie Plenuma Vysshego Arbitrazhnogo Suda RF ot 12 oktiabria 2006 o Nekotorykh Voprosakh Podsudnosti Del po Iskam o Pravakh na Nedvizhimoe Imushchestvo (Resolution of the Plenum of the Supreme *Arbitrazh* Court of the RF on Certain Issues of Jurisdiction in Claims for the Rights for Immovable Property) of 12 October 2006 no 54, para 1.
[95] ibid.
[96] Art 24(3).

rule was to reflect what was already provided by the internal laws of the states-signatory to the Brussels Convention 1968. As the Jenard Report explained at the dawn of the uniform EU jurisdiction regime, this provision would cover, in particular, 'land registers, land changes registers and commercial registers'.[97]

Similarly, Russia establishes exclusive competence of Russian *arbitrazh* courts to hear disputes with a foreign element concerning declaration as invalid of records in state and land registers made in Russia.[98] State registers refer to, for example, federal and local immovable property registers and the uniform state register of legal entities. In addition, there are numerous other state registers in Russia (of pharmaceutical products, measuring equipment, etc). This particular exclusive jurisdiction rule does not seem to cause much controversy. Federal and local administration manage these registers; it is justified for the federal or local courts to adjudicate claims relating to making changes in the state registers. State interests in maintaining the uniformity and accuracy of these registers outweighs the opportunity for private parties to settle claims elsewhere at their convenience.

v. *Patents and Trademarks*

In Europe, in proceedings concerned with the registration or validity of patents, trademarks, designs, or other similar rights required to be deposited or registered, the courts of the Member State shall have exclusive jurisdiction, where the deposit or registration has been applied for, has taken place or is deemed to have taken place.[99] Notably, the proceedings must have as their object the registration or validity of the right for a trade mark or a patent. Simple actions for infringement or disputes relating to ownership do not fall under this rule.[100]

During the review of the Brussels I Regulation, the European Commission proposed a change to this rule, adding the phrase 'irrespective of whether the issue is raised by way of an action or as a defence'. The reasoning comes from the *GAT v LuK* case.[101] GAT, a company established in Germany and operating in the field of motor vehicle technology, brought a suit against its competitor LuK. In a plea in objection, LuK alleged that the spring (a tool) used by GAT infringed two French patents of which LuK was the proprietor. Upon appeal, the ECJ was asked whether the application of the provision on patents is limited solely to those cases when

[97] P Jenard (ed), 'Report on the Convention on Jurisdiction and Enforcement of Judgments in Civil and Commercial Matters' (1979) OJ C 59/1 (Jenard Report) 35.

[98] CAP art 248(4).

[99] Brussels I Recast art 24(4).

[100] A Briggs, *The Conflict of Laws*, 2nd edn (Clarendon, 2008) 68, referring to Case 288/82 *Duijnstee v Goderbauer* [1983] ECR 3663. Also, L Collins et al (eds), *Dicey, Morris & Collins: The Conflict of Laws*, 15th edn (Sweet & Maxwell, 2012) 524.

[101] Case C-4/03 *Gesellschaft fuer Antriebstechnik mbH & Co KG v Lamellen und Kupplungsbau Beteiligungs KG* [2008] ECR I-6509 (GAT v LuK).

the question of a patent's registration or validity is raised by way of an action. The ECJ decided that 'the rule of exclusive jurisdiction … concerns all proceedings … irrespective of whether the issue is raised by way of an action or a plea in objection'.[102] The decision, thus, resolved the controversy, providing equal protection of rights to patent holders. No matter whether the issue was brought by an action or as a defence, Article 22(4) applied. To clarify this issue, the Commission decided to adapt the text of the provision in Brussels I related to the patent's validity and insert the wording 'irrespective of whether the issue is raised by way of an action or as a defence'. The European Parliament and Council approved the new wording.

In addition, in 2014, the European legislators made further changes in the Brussels I Recast, in light of the so-called 'patent package' initiative, a background for uniform patent protection across the EU. One of the advantages of it is as a 'one-stop shop' basis for obtaining patents in the EU, and the immediate effect of a patent title in the EU countries. Other features of this initiative include transfer of jurisdiction from national courts to the Benelux Court of Justice and the Unified Patent Court. The initiative aims to ensure a coherent application of the Brussels jurisdiction regime, the 2012 Unified Patent Court Agreement and the 2012 Protocol to the Benelux Treaty setting up the Benelux Court of Justice.[103] It clarifies that within the meaning of Article 24(4) of the Brussels I Recast, the Unified Patent Court and the Benelux Court of Justice are courts that shall have jurisdiction in patents-related cases. The European Parliament and Council adopted Regulation 542/2014.

Similar to the EU, Russian *arbitrazh* courts have exclusive competence to hear and decide international disputes connected with registration or issuance of Russian patents, and certificates to inventions, trademarks, industrial designs, utility models or registration of the rights to other results of intellectual activity that require registration or issuance of a patent or a certificate in Russia.[104] Notably, a specialised single patent court started its operation in 2013 in Moscow. Based on the model of a patent court in Germany, this court was established in order to 'increase the efficiency of the system of protection of intellectual property rights in Russia taking into account international standards'.[105] The new court has exclusive jurisdiction in cases concerned with the validity of intellectual property rights as a court of first instance, except for copyright, neighbouring rights and circuit layout

[102] ibid.

[103] Regulation (EU) No 542/2014 of the European Parliament and of the Council of 15 May 2014 amending Regulation (EU) No 1215/2012 as regards the rules to be applied with respect to the Unified Patent Court and the Benelux Court of Justice (2014) OJ L 163/1.

[104] CAP art 248(3).

[105] 'GosDuma Rassmotrit Zakonoproekt o Sozdanii Patentnogo Suda' ('The Russian Duma (Parliament) Will Consider a Bill on Creation of Patent Court' (*Edinaya Rossiya News*, 26 September 2011), available at: er.ru/news/2011/9/26/gosduma-rassmotrit-zakonoproekt-o-sozdanii-patentnogo-suda, quoting Pavel Krashennikov, Head of Committee of Russian Duma on Civil, Criminal, *Arbitrazh* and Procedural Law.

rights; and as a cassation court in all other intellectual property-related cases.[106] *Arbitrazh* courts and courts of general jurisdiction will still assume jurisdiction in all other intellectual property rights cases.

Since the intellectual property instruments are issued and administered by state authorities, and their validity extends over territory of a particular state or polity, it is proper to adjudicate cases in state courts in that state or area. It preserves the existing structure of the intellectual property systems (which remains strictly territorial). Until the area undergoes significant changes – such as liberalisation or abolition of intellectual property rights as we know them – it is recommended that jurisdiction in claims over patents, trademarks, etc are adjudicated at the location of registration or issuance of the particular certificate.

vi. Claims Connected to Enforcement of Judgments

The last category of cases that does not raise much controversy includes proceedings concerned with the enforcement of judgments. The Brussels I Recast directs such claims to the exclusive jurisdiction of the courts in a Member State where a judgment has been or is to be enforced.[107] The Article is 'of narrow scope'.[108] Russian internal law does not envisage a similar rule of exclusive jurisdiction.

One may argue that the rule appears somewhat like stating the obvious. Of course, a judgment would have to be enforced where it needs to be enforced. If a judgment is due to be enforced in England, English courts shall have the jurisdiction to consider claims in relation to it. Where else would enforcement be reasonably sought? Upon further analysis of the Jenard Report, often used as guidance to the construction of the Brussels I Regulation, the meaning of the rule becomes a bit clearer. The rule relates to proceedings which can arise from recourse to force, constraint or distraint on movable or immovable property in order to ensure the effective implementation of judgments and authentic instruments.[109] Many EU Member States have internal law provisions designating such claims to the courts at the place of enforcement. Further guidance can be found in works by Lerebours-Pigeonnière and Loussouarn, who give examples of the relevant national law in France. There, courts have exclusive jurisdiction over

> measures for enforcement which is to take place in France (preventive measures, distress levied on a tenant's chattels, writs of attachment and applications for enforcement of a foreign judgment); over distraint levied on immovable or movable property, and over proceedings concerned with the validity of measures for enforcement.[110]

[106] P Savitsky, 'Protection of Product Appearance in Russia' (2013) 35 *European Intellectual Property Review* 143, 149.

[107] Brussels I Recast art 24(5).

[108] Briggs and Rees (n 56) para 2.74.

[109] Jenard Report, 36.

[110] ibid fn 2, referring to P Lerebours-Pigeonnière and Y Loussouarn, *Droit International Prive* (*Private International Law*), 7th edn (Dalloz, 1959) 9.

From this, one may understand that the creators of the Brussels Convention 1968 included this provision[111] to accommodate the internal exclusive jurisdiction rules in force in France – one of the original contracting states to the Brussels Convention. Then, the provision was adopted in the text of the Brussels I Regulation.

Another possible relevance of this rule might be connected to garnishee orders (now referred to as third-party debt orders). Suppose a debt is to be recovered from a debtor having bank accounts in England and elsewhere. When a person (judgment creditor) wants to obtain a court order to garnish the debt from a bank on behalf of the debtor (garnishee or a third party), he should do so in the courts of the state where the order is to be enforced. This rule is designed to prevent double liability of the bank in both those locations to cover the debt of the debtor.

For instance, this situation was brought up in *Société Eram Shipping Company v Hong Kong and Shanghai Banking Corporation*.[112] In that case, a question was raised whether the English court had the power to make a garnishee order. Société Eram, a Romanian shipping company obtained a judgment from a French court against Société Oceanlink and Mr Yoon Sei Wha Eram, resident in Hong Kong, to pay a debt. At the same time, the Hong Kong and Shanghai Banking Corporation, incorporated in Hong Kong and having a branch in London, had a debt due to Société Oceanlink on an account situated in Hong Kong and governed by the law of Hong Kong. The debtors failed to satisfy the French judgment. Then, Société Eram applied to an English court for a garnishee order, to recover the debt, due to them from Société Oceanlink, from the third party, the bank. The court decided it was not appropriate to make an order affecting the conduct of foreigners outside English jurisdiction. As Lord Bingham concluded, it is not acceptable for a court 'to make an order which, if made, would lack what has been legislatively stipulated to be a necessary consequence of such an order'.[113] By this, he meant that it is not practical to empower a court to make an order, where it appears that making of the order will not discharge the debt according to the law applicable to the debt. Moreover, as stated by Lord Hoffmann, it is generally inequitable to make the third-party debt order final 'if the garnishee [third party] would have to pay the debt twice over'.[114] For these main reasons, the application was dismissed. For the present discussion, the point of these proceedings is that a court shall not have jurisdiction in relation to suits, enforcement of which shall be most certainly done elsewhere; and a debt can only be discharged by the law of the place where it is recoverable.

A similar situation occurred in the *Kuwait Oil Tanker* case.[115] In that case, judgment creditors sought to enforce an English court judgment against money

[111] Brussels Convention art 16(5), later Brussels I Regulation art 22(5) and now Brussels I Recast art 24(5).

[112] *Société Eram Shipping Company Ltd v Hong Kong and Shanghai Banking Corporation Ltd* [2003] UKHL 30.

[113] ibid [26].

[114] ibid [53].

[115] *Kuwait Oil Tanker Co SAK and Another v Qabazard* [2003] UKHL 31.

allegedly held in the judgment debtor's accounts in Switzerland and England. The bank argued that the English court had no jurisdiction since the enforcement was sought in Switzerland pursuant to a provision identical to Article 22(5) of the Brussels I (Article 16(5) of the Lugano Convention 1988). The court upheld the *Société Eram Shipping* decision, and decided the exclusive jurisdiction belonged to the Swiss courts to make the garnishee order.

B. Exorbitant Exclusive Jurisdiction: Corporate Disputes and Transport Claims

In this subsection, I continue to discuss exclusive jurisdiction rules, focusing on the rules that appear excessive in light of the normative approach presented in this book. They include disputes connected with corporations and decisions of their main bodies and claims against transportation companies (in Russia).

i. Corporate Disputes

In particular, in the EU, in cases concerning the validity of the constitution, the nullity or the dissolution of legal persons, or the validity of the decisions of their organs, the courts of the Member States where the legal person has its seat shall have exclusive jurisdiction.[116] National law shall determine where the seat is located. In the UK, for example, a corporation is deemed to have its seat there if it has been incorporated by English law, or its central management is situated in the UK.[117]

The rationale behind this rule is the aspiration to avoid conflicting judgments regarding the existence of corporations, and the validity of decisions of their organs 'in the interest of legal certainty'.[118] Allocating jurisdiction to courts where the corporation has its seat is logical, simply because the most information can be found about the company in the state of its seat. This rule (as predicted by the Jenard Report) more often than not results in the application of the traditional principle of domicile – suing at the location of the defendant. It seems logical and appropriate to dispute a corporation's construction and organisation in a state where a corporation keeps its house and carries out its main business activity.

Application of this rule may be demonstrated by *Newtherapeutics v Katz*.[119] In that case, the proceedings concerned the legality of actions by directors of a company incorporated under the laws of England. Actions by the defendants in breach of the duties of fidelity and good faith resulted in considerable damages

[116] Brussels I Recast art 24(2).

[117] Civil Jurisdiction and Judgments Act 1982, s 43; Civil Jurisdiction and Judgment Order 2001, s 43 (UK).

[118] Jenard Report, 35.

[119] *Newtherapeutics v Katz and Another* [1990] 3 WLR 1183 (Newtherapeutics v Katz).

sustained by the plaintiff. The court interpreted the rule of exclusive jurisdiction in the corporate disputes narrowly. The main issue was whether the directors acted negligently, and not whether the directors acted outside their powers. Article 22(2) would have applied, had the directors acted as a corporate body. This view was presented by the second defendant and supported by the contemporaneous academic opinion expressed by Kaye and the editors of Dicey's *Conflict of Laws*.[120] Overall, the case presented an exception to the rule, showing when it should *not* apply.

The scope of the rule was further defined in an interesting debate between a global banking institution, JP Morgan, and a German public institution, Berliner Verkehrsbetriebe (BVG).[121] JP Morgan requested that BVG pay money under a credit swap agreement. The agreement contained a choice of English law and jurisdiction. The defendant argued that the English court had no jurisdiction because the proceedings had as their object the validity of the decision of the organ of a legal person, and, pursuant to rule in the Brussels I Regulation, Germany would be the appropriate forum to decide the claim. The English court retained jurisdiction because the proceedings did not principally concern the issue falling under the scope of rule, ie, the subject matter was the claim by JP Morgan to enforce a commercial agreement.

BVG lodged parallel proceedings in Germany. The Kammergericht Berlin (Berlin Appeal Court) asked the ECJ whether the German court had jurisdiction under the Brussels jurisdiction regime because the dispute involved, inter alia, the issue of validity of decisions made by the organs of a company whose seat was in Germany. The ECJ ruled that Article 22(2) should not extend to proceedings in which a company raised an objection because the decision of corporate bodies was supposedly invalid on account of infringement of company statutes.[122] Thus, the ECJ drew narrow limits of the rule. Both the English proceedings and the ECJ decision led to the same conclusion. The underlying objective of the exclusive jurisdiction rule would be avoiding the risk of conflicting decisions.

A similar rationale applied in *Hassett v South Eastern Health Board*[123] and *Calyon v Swidnik*.[124] The first case concerned the manner of exercising power by a company pursuant to the company's articles of association. The dispute did not constitute an instance of validity of a decision of a corporate body. The second case also confirmed that the rule should be read 'narrowly' and 'by reference to its central objective which is one of centralising jurisdiction in order to avoid

[120] Kaye (n 13) and L Collins et al (eds), *Dicey Morris & Collins: The Conflict of Laws*, 11th edn (Sweet & Maxwell, 1987) 366.

[121] *JP Morgan Chase Bank NA and another v Berliner Verkehrsbetriebe (BVG)* [2009] EWHC 1627 (Comm).

[122] Case C-144/10 *Berliner Verkehrsbetriebe (BVG), Anstalt des offentlichen Rechts v JP Morgan Chase Bank NA, Frankfurt Branch* [2011] ECR I-3961.

[123] Case C-372/07 *Hassett v South Eastern Health Board* [2008] ECR I-7403.

[124] *Calyon v Wytwornia Sprzetu Komunikacynego PZL Swidnik SA* [2009] 2 All ER (Comm) 603.

conflicting judgments being given as regards the existence of a company or validity of decisions of its organs'.[125]

The rule on exclusive jurisdiction in corporate disputes must be given an interpretation no broader than that required by its objective (avoiding the risk of conflicting decisions). Otherwise, the extensive application of the rule acquires unwarranted and excessive scope, as becomes evident in the Russian regime. In particular, Russian *arbitrazh* courts have exclusive competence to hear international claims connected with establishment, dissolution or registration of legal entities at the territory of the Russian Federation and claims disputing decisions of organs of such entities.[126] This provision on international jurisdiction concisely mentions the matters of establishment and liquidation of legal entities and disputing the decisions of corporate bodies. However, in addition to this rule, there is also a domestic jurisdiction rule, which directs commercial claims connected with internal corporate disputes to an *arbitrazh* court at the location of the legal entity in question.[127] For the purpose of this domestic rule, the Code of *Arbitrazh* Procedure specifies that 'corporate disputes' mean disputes connected with establishment, management and ownership of legal entities, including those claims relating to the attribution of shares of a corporation, management of a company, complaints regarding decisions of corporate bodies, issuing of securities, and other disputes.[128] Therefore, this domestic jurisdiction rule covers a broad range of corporate disputes, which must be subject to exclusive jurisdiction of courts at the location of the legal entity. The risk of the duality of the rule on exclusive jurisdiction in disputes connected with corporations is that courts may apply the broad 'corporate disputes' definition to international jurisdiction as well. Then, the majority of corporate disputes involving Russian companies become subject to the exclusive jurisdiction of Russian courts.

An example of such broad interpretation of the rule can be found in a case involving Fringilla, a Cypriot company, and Rubprominvest, a Russian corporation. A valid Cypriot court order[129] was unenforceable in Russia, because the Russian courts interpreted that the case was subject to the exclusive jurisdiction of the Russian courts.[130] The Cypriot decision concerned a corporate decision of

[125] ibid [93].

[126] CAP art 248(5). The wording of Art 248(5) appears to contain a technical mistake that needs to be corrected. It mentions 'establishment, liquidation and registration', and I think the legislator meant 'reorganisation' instead of 'registration'. Because 'establishment' and 'registration' are closely related terms, they could be covered by a single word 'establishment'. Furthermore, while establishment, reorganisation and liquidation concepts represent stages in the life of a corporate entity, registration refers to an official procedure of applying to the state organs and obtaining a certificate of state registration. Thus, 'registration' is from an absolutely different 'kettle of fish'. To align Art 248(5) with the general understanding of legal concepts, Russian legislators should substitute the word 'reorganisation' for 'registration'.

[127] CAP art 38(4.1).

[128] CAP art 225.1.

[129] Decision of the District Court of Limassol of 7 July 2011, no 4019/2010.

[130] Opredelenie Arbitrazhnogo Suda Goroda Sankt-Peterburga i Leningradskoĭ Oblasti ot 22 noiabria 2011 g (Decision of the *Arbitrazh* Court of Saint Petersburg and Leningrad region) of 22 November

a Russian company and thus infringed the 'Russian sovereignty' by adjudicating over matter subject to Russian exclusive jurisdiction. It violated the Russian public order, by endeavouring to apply Cypriot law to transactions which were to be regulated by Russian law. Unlike the EU, where validity of decisions of corporate bodies, and not the content or fairness of these decisions fall under the exclusive jurisdiction rule,[131] Russian courts interpreted the rule in a broader sense. Such interference with the exclusive jurisdiction of Russian courts and violation of the Russian procedural rules on jurisdiction prevented recognition and enforcement of the foreign judgment.

The case demonstrated a conflict of party autonomy to choose a forum and state sovereignty principles placing limits on party autonomy. It was an example where the state intervened to protect its public order rules – a set of laws of high importance to state sovereignty. The problem is that 'public order' is so abstract, that the risk exists to classify many state laws as fundamental for such purposes. Where to draw the line? The scope of such state sovereignty interests should be very narrow. Only a few instances should fall under exclusive jurisdiction, such as cases relating to the establishment and dissolution of corporations, and validity of decisions of their bodies. Subjecting a wide range of corporate matters relating to Russian corporations to be settled exclusively by Russian courts is excessive. To avoid the undesirable perception of Russia as a forum extending its exorbitant jurisdiction over disputes involving Russian corporations, a more careful and narrower interpretation of the rule is recommended for Russian courts.

ii. Claims Against Transport Companies

Another excessive rule of exclusive jurisdiction in Russia concerns claims involving transport companies. In particular, suits connected with the carriage of goods and passengers, and actions against a carrier arising out of a contract for carriage of goods, passengers, or their baggage must be filed in a court at the location of the carrier in Russia.[132] This rule grants the carriers the convenience of being sued exclusively at their place of business. The rationale for this rule comes from the times when major (few) companies providing public transportation services were owned by the state. In some sense, those companies represented national interests. They were very important to the state economy. To streamline the potential claims against them, the legislators provided for this exclusive jurisdiction rule.

2011 no A56-49591/2011; Postanovlenie Federal'nogo Arbotrazhnogo Suda Severo-Zapadnogo Okruga ot 6 marta 2012 g (Decision of the Federal *Arbitrazh* Court of the Northwestern Circuit) of 6 March 2012 no A56-49591; Postanovlenie Presidiuma Vysshego Arbitrazhnogo Suda Rossiĭskoĭ Federatsii ot 23 oktiabria 2012 g (Resolution of the Presidium of the Highest *Arbitrazh* Court) of 23 October 2012 no 7805/12.

[131] *Newtherapeutics v Katz* [1992] Ch 226, 228 (Knox J) and also subsequently reflected in the revised Brussels I Regulation text.

[132] CCP arts 403(2), 30(3); CAP art 38(3).

However, with societal and economic development throughout the twentieth century, privatisation of the interests in these companies, the rule seems outdated. Moreover, it contradicts the fundamental principle of equality of the parties. This excessive preferential treatment of transportation corporations needs to be revised, and suits against the carriers should be filed in accordance with the general rules: either in a forum parties agree on, or at the location of a weaker party (where applicable).

In this regard, an interesting case was considered by the Supreme Constitutional Court of Russia. Mr Belyaev filed a claim against the Russian Railway Company for recovery of non-pecuniary damages. The complaint was brought at the place of residence of Mr Belyaev, the consumer.[133] The court dismissed the claim. It referred to the exclusive jurisdiction rule mentioned above: that claims arising out of transport contracts can only be filed at the location of the transport company. Mr Belyaev was not happy with this provision and appealed to the Constitutional Court of the Russian Federation, arguing that this provision limited his constitutional right to effective judicial protection. He stated that this exception rendered it difficult for consumers to protect their rights in disputes with transportation companies. The Constitutional Court denied consideration of Belyaev's claim seeking the recognition of violation of his constitutional rights. It did not find the necessary grounds for the action.[134] In particular, the Constitutional Court noted that:

> Article 30 of the Code of Civil Procedure prescribes exclusive jurisdiction for certain categories of cases, which, in itself, is designed to provide the best conditions for proper and prompt consideration of cases, specific features of which make it difficult to consider them in other places. Therefore, this rule cannot be seen as violating Mr Belyaev's constitutional rights.[135]

Therefore, the Court explained that the rule works not to spite Mr Belyaev personally, but in the view of the overall administration of justice. Nevertheless, the Court clarified correlation of exclusive jurisdiction in transportation suits at the location of the carrier, and the rights of the consumer to bring claims at the place of his residence. The decision further read that the rule, if interpreted in the current legal context, does not preclude individuals from bringing claims protecting their

[133] Opredelenie Zheleznodorozhnogo Suda g Ekaterinburga Sverdlovskoĭ Oblasti ot 21 noiiabria 2003 g (Decision of the Railway Regional Court of Ekaterinburg City, Sverdlovskaia District) of 21 November 2003.

[134] Opredelenie Konstitutsionnogo Suda RF ot 20 iiunia 200 g no 170-O ob Otkaze v Priniatii k Rassmotreniiu Zhaloby Grazhdanina Beliaeva Sergeya Ivanovicha na Narushenie Ego Konstitutsionnykh Prav Chast'iu Tret'eĭ Stat'I 30 Grazhdanskogo Pretsessual'nogo Kodeksa RF (Decision of the Constitutional Court of the Russian Federation, Resolution of 20 June 2006 no 170-O on Denial of Acceptance for Consideration of Claim by Belyaev Sergey Ivanovich about Violation of His Constitutional Rights by Article 30(3) of the Code of Civil Procedure of the Russian Federation) (2005) *Vestnik Konstitutsionnogo Suda* RF, no 6.

[135] ibid para 2.

consumer rights, at the place of their domicile or at the place of execution of the contract.[136] Thus, Mr Belyaev had the right idea about the excessiveness of the Russian exclusive jurisdiction rule in favour of the carriers.

III. Conclusion

In these two chapters, I aimed to determine to what extent states need to safeguard their sovereign interests to maintain their integrity in allocation of jurisdiction in private international matters. I considered the interests of the state as a sovereign entity in the international arena. Then, I outlined the significance of home state sovereignty and continued to look for the state's role in protecting the general well-being of its citizens. I have concluded that some fundamental considerations of state sovereignty and the general public interest may, in certain cases, limit party autonomy to choose a forum to settle disputes.

First, some general principles of public international law delimit jurisdiction of states.[137] Although states should considerably reduce sovereign powers in jurisdiction, there is still some place for certain dimensions of their sovereignty. In particular, it is important to preserve the way states conduct foreign affairs and cooperate with other states for the sake of the integrity of international relations. Where certain cases are to be adjudicated, they may be beyond party autonomy to choose venue simply because courts may refuse jurisdiction based on the act of state doctrine, or because international standards of exorbitance of jurisdiction (the *Lotus* case) dictate so. In such cases, I concede to such limitations imposed by public international law that private parties have little control over.

However, where it comes to a state's home sovereignty, ie, its power on its territory, such sovereignty's role in civil jurisdiction should be revisited. I have considered the relevant interests from the perspective of states and private actors in international law and touched upon the academic points of controversy in private international law theory. I have determined that preservation of state sovereignty and territorial integrity represents the most important state interests. According to this traditional approach, in both the EU and Russia, there is a foundational rule that individuals domiciled or resident in a state shall be sued in that state. I have argued that it should matter little for private international disputes, as adjudicating cross-border claims does not infringe the state's territory. I proposed revising the rationale for the rule of suing at the defendant's domicile. Thus, in cases of absence of clear choice of forum by the parties, an ideal jurisdiction system would provide a fall-back rule of suing at the domicile of the defendant, but the rationale for that would be different. It would rather be based on suiting the interests of the parties

[136] ibid para 2.2.

[137] A Dutta, 'Jurisdiction of Domestic Courts (Public International Law)' in J Basedow, K Hopt and R Zimmermann (eds), *The Max Planck Encyclopaedia of European Private Law* (Oxford University Press, 2012).

(fairness to the defendant, predictability for both, practicality in general). In terms of reconceptualising the approach to jurisdiction in civil and commercial matters, Russia presents the example of one of the most traditional outlooks on state sovereignty and territoriality in jurisdiction. Although it recognises party autonomy (as demonstrated in my earlier chapters), the overall concept of jurisdiction is still viewed in the sense of power of the state over its citizens, property located on its territory, etc. Persuading Russian legislators to reassess their approach may be the hardest.

In chapter eight, I demonstrated how the revised approach to the role of sovereignty in jurisdiction can influence the jurisdiction rules in practice. I have analysed the existing rules of (a) suing at the location of the defendant in the EU and Russia and (b) exclusive (mandatory) rules on jurisdiction. I have suggested that the EU is in need of a harmonised solution regarding domicile of an individual for the purpose of jurisdiction, such as one based on a person's habitual residence for a certain time. Russia also needs to adjust its understanding of the residence of an individual, relaxing its strict understanding of an actual place of registration. Further liberalisation of the location of legal entities in Russia is also needed.

In terms of state mandatory jurisdiction, I have emphasised the exceptional character of these rules, and the need to narrow the scope of their interpretation, especially in respect of the Russian view on exclusive jurisdiction over corporate disputes of Russian companies and jurisdiction in transport claims. Both these categories need to be revised in view of their excessive state interference in private affairs.

9

Overall Conclusions and Recommendations

In this book, I offer a normative basis for judicial jurisdiction. In addition, I show that in at least two examined legal regimes, my ideal model of jurisdiction already has a strong hold in law and judicial practice.

I re-evaluate the set of values that should determine jurisdiction in private international law. Instead of the traditionally predominant view based on state sovereignty and territoriality, I advocate for a system that has party autonomy at its foundation. Every legal system may interpret party autonomy in its own way, conditioned by cultural and historical predispositions (some variations of understanding were offered). Notwithstanding these differences, it can be universally accepted that party autonomy represents the expression of the will and interests of private parties. In jurisdiction, party autonomy manifests itself in agreements in jurisdiction. I argue that the general and fundamental rule of jurisdiction should be giving effect to the parties' express choice of jurisdiction – by jurisdiction agreement and voluntary submission.

I offer justification for autonomy to be a proper foundation for jurisdiction. Having traced the history of recognition of party autonomy in the regimes that I focus my analysis on, I show how the national rules on jurisdiction have developed over the years to enforce the parties' choice of forum in domestic civil procedure. It occurred in Germany, for example, because of the influence of the French revolutionary awakening, recognising men as free and equal in their rights. It was also supported by the development of enlightenment thought. In Russia, recognition of party autonomy to choose forum first developed in the commercial sphere, because there were only a few commercial courts in major cities across its vast territory. To provide access to justice in commercial cases, parties were allowed to prorogate jurisdiction rules in favour of a local civil (non-commercial) court. Eventually, such recognition of party autonomy transpired to all civil transactions. It was further supported by the development of legal scholarship, influenced by the German and French thinkers, putting the freedom of will of the parties at the forefront. In England, with the development of the principle of autonomy in contract (in general), forum selection clauses (as terms of a contract) began to be recognised in the case law. Notably, this recognition of party autonomy to choose forum first developed in arbitration and then migrated to curial agreements. In addition, enforcement of the parties' choice of forum was justified by one of the main principles in English law that a party should be held to its word.

The arguments supporting my claim for party autonomy as the foundation for jurisdiction included growing recognition of party autonomy in terms of applicable law and the idea that party autonomy to choose forum facilitates better flow of international commerce. Furthermore, I have provided support of the overall shift of power to private parties (from the state) and discussed why sovereignty no longer should be at the basis of jurisdiction in civil and commercial matters. I have provided support for the growing role of individual actors in international law, as opposed to the previously accepted theory that only states and state-like formations are actors in international relations. All these factors, taken together, suggest that it is time to reconceptualise sovereignty as the foundation of jurisdiction and accept party autonomy as the main driving force behind the jurisdiction rules.

My argument is not monist. I have contended that party autonomy should not be absolute and cannot provide answers to all the questions. Where the choice of forum does not express the meaningful consent of both parties and abrogates the right of access to justice of some categories of weaker parties, it should be limited. Party equality plays the role of restoring the balance of interests of both parties. The principle of party equality should limit party autonomy in certain cases involving weaker parties. The principle of equality of the parties, supported by a vast literature in civil procedure and in private law, represents one of the other main values in a jurisdictional regime. It is closely connected with fairness in judicial process. Sometimes, to offset the drastic inequality of power between private parties, allocation of jurisdiction by the parties' agreement needs to be supplemented by the possibility of the weaker party being able to bring suit at his location. Having such a rule favourable to the weaker party may be justified by the absence of full and meaningful consent in contracts of adhesion, which usually feature non-negotiated standard jurisdiction clauses. I have shown the difference between asymmetric jurisdiction clauses – favourable to one party and not the other – in the commercial sphere and in transactions involving weaker parties. The necessity to compromise in commercial dealing may reasonably explain the willingness of the weaker party to sign a forum selection clause. As long as it is based on full and informed consent, such dealing is fair. In consumer transactions, however, clicking 'I agree' on a website can be equated, at best, to blanket assent. In such situations, to ensure the consumers' (the weaker parties') access to court, party autonomy, as the fundamental principle of an ideal jurisdiction regime, may be limited, in light of categorical equality. The state, as a fiduciary of the weaker parties, should be entrusted with enforcing such limitations, by providing access to state courts in certain cases to certain categories of weaker parties in spite of the existence of forum selection clauses.

The last part of my argument is that sovereignty may further limit party autonomy, when so required to preserve the integrity of the state. I have traced the meaning of sovereignty in jurisdiction in the conflict of laws scholarship. I have shown the main problem with sovereignty forming the basis of jurisdiction: lack of account of specific private interests. However, although globalisation, development of the open society and the new world order have facilitated a global decline in the role of the state in private international law, the future does hold some, although limited, role for states. In order to protect a state's integrity as a sovereign and uphold the interests of general will (the national public interest), I concede to limiting jurisdiction by the parties' agreement by mandatory rules. Thus, rather than conceiving jurisdiction as granted by the power of the state to private parties, based on state sovereignty and power, I reverse the power to private parties, so that it is initially an entitlement of parties to choose a forum and for the sovereign interests of the states to come in only in exceptional cases. I have discussed the potential state interests involved: the desire to maintain territorial integrity; pursuit of maintaining integrity of its internal structure and institutions; making itself be seen as an attractive forum to settle disputes (the 'open forum' policy); and protection of the general will and interests of its citizens and corporations. In some limited circumstances, justified by the overall preservation of states' internal integrity, exclusive jurisdiction rules may override other rules (in cases concerning rights *in rem*, the values in state registers, etc). Such mandatory state jurisdiction rules, however, must remain exceptional and should not become exorbitant.

Therefore, I have argued that private actors should drive and shape the order of prescribing the adjudicative jurisdiction of courts in international civil and commercial matters. Party autonomy, reasonably limited by categorical equality and state sovereignty, should be the values of the reconceptualised jurisdiction regime. When following the revised hierarchy of values – starting with party autonomy allowing certain exceptions in consideration of equality and some state sovereign interests – parties may be left with several jurisdictional options. In case of conflict of jurisdictions, the principle of practicality can provide guidance on narrowing down the choice among competent jurisdictions. Practicality may provide additional guidance for asserting jurisdiction by a state court. It may direct to the place of the location of evidence in a tort claim connected with several jurisdictions. More importantly, it may serve as an additional balancing consideration for a court when ascertaining jurisdiction in all other cases.

In addition to the proposed revisited mechanism of values behind civil jurisdiction, this book offers a comparative analysis of the existing law on civil jurisdiction in the EU and Russia. With a thorough understanding of the historical and cultural background of the EU and Russian regimes, and analysis of the rules in light of my proposed approach, I also offer a number of recommendations to improve the existing rules on jurisdiction in civil and commercial matters in the EU and Russia.

This book aims to contribute to the existing scholarship on jurisdiction and invoke further discussion on the topic and eventual change of how we view jurisdiction in private international law. The view presented in this body of work may hold answers to the few problems remaining after the review of the Brussels I Regulation. The recommendations proposed in relation to the Russian regime may be found useful during the current review of Russia civil procedural rules.

I. Jurisdiction by Parties' Agreement *ex ante*

First, although as a result of the most recent reform of the Brussels jurisdiction regime, it was ultimately decided to exclude all arbitration-related issues from the scope of the Brussels I Recast, problems in the areas of juxtaposition of arbitration and litigation remain. To avoid continuing *West Tankers* problems, it is recommended that where litigation and arbitration intersect, a unified EU approach is adopted, which should be grounded on the prima facie recognition of the parties' will.

To further enhance the effectiveness of jurisdiction agreements in Russia, the existing strict written form needs to be relaxed, and alternative forms (facsimile, electronic communications) need to be recognised as well.

Finally, in part relating to enforcement of choice-of-court agreements in Russia, correlation of the *lis pendens* rule and party autonomy in jurisdiction needs to be revised. Similar to the current EU rule, a court first seized of the matter should yield to the power of the court chosen by the parties.

II. Jurisdiction by Parties' Agreement *ex post*

The rule on submission to jurisdiction is given necessary priority over other rules in the EU. However, the underlying attitude should be reformed: the overall jurisdiction of EU courts should not be based on the 'imperialism' of the EU jurisdiction regime stretching over EU territory, but, rather, on the subjective will of individuals and companies consenting to the jurisdiction via submission (after commencement of proceedings) to the EU courts.

To enhance the enforcement of private parties' autonomy, a rule on silent acceptance should be introduced into the Russian Codes of Civil and *Arbitrazh* Procedure (or, the Unified Code of civil procedure, which is projected to combine the two codes in the next few years).

III. Jurisdiction Protecting Categorical Equality

A general suggestion for EU protective jurisdiction is to streamline its consumer protection in jurisdiction with other areas of law dedicated to consumer protection, to ensure consistency throughout EU policies.

In Russia, court practice currently lacks uniformity; further clarification and guidance is needed from the Russian Supreme Court in interpreting the law in this area.

IV. Jurisdiction in the Absence of Forum Selection (Tort)

The place where the harmful event occurred, location of the victim (in personal injury cases), place of damage to reputation (in defamation) all represent established and adequate places for jurisdiction in torts. Re-evaluation of the reasons why courts shall adjudicate tort claims is needed both in the EU and Russia. Rather than originating from the power of the state over events happening on its territory, it should be justified from the perspective of private parties' interests. Balancing the interests of the defendant (to reasonably expect being sued at his location) and the plaintiff (to sue at his domicile to compensate for the fact of being a victim of an accident) need to be considered.

In this regard, a 'place where a harmful event might occur' in the Russian rule on jurisdiction in torts should be added to account for potential torts before they occur, to coordinate with the existing rules on preventive measures.

V. Jurisdiction in the Absence of Forum Selection (Contract)

First, giving effect to party autonomy in cases arising out of contracts with no forum selection clause means allowing them to be filed in accordance with the default rules. In situations where such forum selection is made indirectly – by specifying the place of performance of contract – the rule of special jurisdiction at such place of performance will give effect to party autonomy.

The strict requirement of the Russian jurisdiction regime of specifying the place of performance of contract in the contract in order to allow subsequent filing at that place needs to be relaxed. Place of performance of contract can be determined from the general meaning of the contract and narrowed down from potential places in favour of the place of performance of the main obligation in question.

VI. Jurisdiction in the Absence of Forum Selection (Other)

First, across the EU, a harmonised understanding of domicile of individuals for the purpose of jurisdiction should be adopted. A definition based on the individual's habitual residence for a certain time would be an optimal solution, as has been previously recommended by the Heidelberg Report.

Secondly, in Russia, the strict understanding of residence of individuals for the purpose of jurisdiction at the place of their *registratsiia* (state registration) should be supplemented by the substantial connection of the individual to that place. The English case law provides helpful suggestions on which factors should be taken into account when establishing the substantial connection.

In addition, the Russian understanding of the location of legal entities for the purpose of jurisdiction should be broader than the current strict definition of 'place of state registration'. It needs to be supplemented by the entity's principal place of business and place of its central management.

VII. Limited Exclusive Jurisdiction Overriding Party Autonomy to Maintain Sovereignty

In terms of jurisdiction in proceedings which have as their object rights *in rem* in immovable property, the EU rule does not raise much concern. However, the equivalent Russian rule is currently interpreted in an expansive, rather than limited nature. Not all claims mentioning immovable property need to be considered at the location of the immovable property, but only those which concern the rights *in rem* in immovable property. Furthermore, some ambiguities in understanding of immovable property (objects 'firmly connected with land') need to be eliminated.

Jurisdiction in claims over patents, trademarks and other intellectual property instruments should continue to be allocated at the place of their registration, unless and until intellectual property as an area of law undergoes significant changes.

The rule on exclusive jurisdiction in corporate disputes must be given a limited scope of interpretation. Only a few instances should fall under this rule, such as cases relating to the establishment and dissolution of corporations, and the validity of decisions of their bodies. Accordingly, the wide range of corporate matters relating to Russian corporations that are currently to be settled exclusively by Russian courts is excessive and needs to be reformed.

Another peculiar rule of exclusive jurisdiction that the Russian legislators need to revisit is exclusive jurisdiction in claims against transport companies, which are currently to be filed exclusively at the location of the carriers. The rule has outlived its time; transport companies are no longer exclusively state-owned enterprises with strategic state interests. Private transport companies do not need this extra protection and preferential treatment. Claims should be filed in accordance with general rules.

BIBLIOGRAPHY

Books, Articles and Chapters

'Service by Alternative Method' (2000) 19 *Civil Justice Quarterly* 211.
Akehurst, M, 'Jurisdiction in International Law' (1972–03) 46 *British Yearbook of International Law* 151.
Anisimov, A, 'Podsudnost' Dela: Pravila Chasti 4 stat'I 36 APK RF dlia Podachi Iska' ('Jurisdiction of a Case: Rules of Article 36(4) of CAP RF for Filing a Claim') (2011) *EZh-Jurist* 22.
Atiyah, PS, *The Rise and Fall of the Freedom of Contract* (Clarendon Press, 1979).
—— 'Consideration: A Restatement' in PS Atiyah, *Essays on Contract* (Clarendon Press, 1990).
Babie, P, 'Sovereignty as Governance: An Organising Theme for Australian Property Law' (2013) 36 *University of New South Wales (UNSW) Law Journal* 1075.
Baelz, K and Baldwin, T, 'The End of the Real Seat Theory (*Sitztheorie*): The European Court of Justice Decision in *Ueberseering* of 5 November 2002 and its impact on German and European Company Law' (2002) 3 *German Law Journal* 85.
Barnett, R, 'A Consent Theory of Contract' (1986) 86 *Columbia Law Review* 269.
—— 'Contract is not Promise, Contract is Consent' (2012) 45 *Suffolk University Law Review* 647.
Basedow, J, *The Law of Open Societies: Private Ordering and Public Regulation of International Relations* (Recueil des cours 360, Martinus Nijhoff Publishers, 2013).
Beale, J, *A Treatise on the Conflict of Laws* (Baker, Voorhis & Co, 1935).
Beard, C, *The Idea of National Interest* (Macmillan, 1934 and 1966).
Beaumont, P and Yüksel, B, 'The Validity of Choice of Court Agreements under the Brussels I Regulation and the Hague Choice of Court Agreements Convention' in K Boele-Woelki, T Einhorn, D Girsberger and S Symeonides (eds), *Convergence and Divergence in Private International Law: Liber Amicorum Kurt Siehr* (Eleven International Publishing, 2010).
Bergson, H, *The Two Sources of Morality and Religion* (1932).
Blume, W, 'Place of Trial of Civil Cases: Early English and Modern Federal' (1949) 48 *Michigan Law Review* 11.
Boguslavskiĭ, M, *Mezhdunarodnoe Chastnoe Pravo* (*Private International Law*), 5th edn (Iurist, 2005).
Bomhoff, J, 'The Confluence of Private and Public International Law: Justice, Pluralism and Subsidiarity in the International Constitutional Ordering of Private Law by Alex Mills' (2011) 60 *International & Comparative Law Quarterly* 822.
Borchers, P, 'J McIntyre Machinery, Goodyear, and the Incoherence of the Minimum Contacts Test' (2011) 44 *Creighton Law Review* 1268.
Brand, R, 'Balancing Sovereignty and Party Autonomy in Private International Law' in J Erauw, V Tomljenovic and P Volken, *Liber Memorialis Petar Sarcevic: Universalism, Tradition and the Individual* (Sellier European Law Publishers, 2006).
—— 'Jurisdictional Developments and The New Hague Judgments Project' in *A Commitment to Private International Law: Essays in Honour of Hans van Loon* (Intersentia, 2013).
Briggs, A, *Agreements on Jurisdiction and Choice of Law* (Oxford University Press, 2008).
—— *Civil Jurisdiction and Judgments* (Oxford University Press, 2008).
—— *The Conflict of Laws*, 2nd edn (Clarendon Press, 2008).
—— 'Recognition of Foreign Judgments: A Matter of Obligation' (2013) 129 *Law Quarterly Review* 87.
Briggs, A and Rees, P (eds), *Civil Jurisdiction and Judgments*, 5th and 6th edns (Proforma, 2009, 2015).
Brilmayer, L et al, 'A General Look at General Jurisdiction' (1988) 66 *Texas Law Review* 721.
Buchanan, A, *Justice, Legitimacy and Self-Determination* (Oxford University Press, 2007).

Bugaevskiĭ, A, 'Dogovornaya Podsudnost' ('Jurisdiction by Agreement') in V Tadevosyan and F Nabok (eds), *Sbornik Stateĭ i Materialov po Grazhdanskomu Protsessu za 1922-1924 gg.* (*Collection of Essays and Materials on Civil Procedure for 1922–24*) (Iuridicheskoe Izdatelstvo Narodnogo Komissariata Iustitsii RSFSR, 1925).

Bulgakov, D, 'Spornaia Podsudnost' ('Disputable Jurisdiction') (2010) 10 *EZh-Jurist* 6.

Bull, H, The Anarchical Society: A Study of Order in World Politics (Columbia University Press, 1977).

Burchill, S, *The National Interest in International Relations Theory* (Palgrave MacMillan, 2005).

Burchill, S et al (eds), *Theories of International Relations*, 2nd edn (Palgrave Macmillan, 2001).

Camilleri, SP, 'Article 23: Formal Validity, Material Validity or Both?' (2011) 7 *Journal of Private International Law* 297.

—— 'Recital 12 of the Recast Regulation: A New Hope?' (2013) 62 *International & Comparative Law Quarterly* 899.

Cappalli, R, 'Locke as the Key: a Unifying and Coherent Theory of in Personam Jurisdiction' (1992) 43 *Case Western Reserve Law Review* 97.

Carmody, C, Garsia, F and Linarelli, J (eds), *Global Justice and International Economic Law* (Cambridge University Press, 2012).

Castro, S, 'The Morality of Unequal Autonomy: Revising Kant's Concept of Status for Shareholders' (2014) 121 *Journal of Business Ethics* 593.

Cavers, D, 'A Critique of the Choice-of-Law Problem' (1933) 47 *Harvard Law Review* 173.

Charvet, J and Kaczynska-Nay, E, *The Liberal Project and Human Rights* (Cambridge University Press, 2008).

Chervoniuk, V (ed), *Elementarnie Nachala Obshcheĭ Teorii Prava* (*Elementary Foundations of Jurisprudence*) (KolosS, 2003).

Collins, L et al (eds), *Dicey, Morris & Collins: The Conflict of Laws*, 11th, 14th and 15th edns (Sweet & Maxwell, 1987, 2006, 2012).

Conlon, B, 'Dostoevsky v the Judicial Reforms of 1864: How and Why One of Nineteenth-Century Russia's Greatest Writers Criticised the Nation's Most Successful Reform' (2014) 2(4) *Russian Law Journal* 7.

Currie, B, *Selected Essays on the Conflict of Laws* (Duke University Press, 1963).

Dickinson, A, 'Surveying the Proposed Brussels I *bis* Regulation: Solid Foundations but Renovation Needed' in A Bonomi and GP Romano (eds), *Yearbook of Private International Law Vol XII* (De Gruyter, 2010).

Dmitrieva, G, *Mezhdunarodnoe Chastnoe Pravo* (*Private International Law*), 1st and 2nd edns (Prospekt, 2001, 2009).

Drury, R, 'The Regulation and Recognition of Foreign Corporations: Responses to the "Delaware Syndrome"' (1998) 57 *Cambridge Law Journal* 165.

Dupuy, P-M, *Droit International Public*, 2nd edn (Broché, 1993).

Dutta, A, 'Jurisdiction of Domestic Courts (Public International Law)' in J Basedow, K Hopt and R Zimmermann (eds), *The Max Planck Encyclopaedia of European Private Law* (Oxford University Press, 2012).

Eisenberg, T and Miller, G, 'The Flight to New York: An Empirical Study of Choice of Law and Choice of Forum Clauses in Publicly-Held Companies' Contracts' (2009) 30 *Cardozo Law Review* 1475.

Eliseev, N, 'Dogovornaia Podsudnost' – Kakoĭ eĭ byt v Edinom Protsessual'nom Kodekse RF?' ('Jurisdiction by Agreement – What it Should be Like in the Single Civil Procedural Code of the RF') (2015) 12 *Zakon* 191.

Eng, E, 'A New Paradigm: Domicile as the Exclusive Basis for the Exercise of General Jurisdiction Over Individual Defendants' (2012) 32 *Cardozo Law Review* 849.

Fawcett, J, Carruthers, J and North, P, *Cheshire, North and Fawcett: Private International Law*, 14th edn (Oxford University Press, 2008).

Feldbrugge, F, *Law in Medieval Russia* (Martinus Nijhoff Publishers, 2009).

Fentiman R, 'Unilateral Jurisdiction Agreements in Europe' (2013) 72 *Cambridge Law Journal* 24.

Fox-Decent, E, *Sovereignty's Promise: The State as Fiduciary* (Oxford University Press, 2011).

Frankel, J, *National Interest* (Macmillan, 1970).

Fukiyama, Y, *The End of History and the Last Man* (Free Press, 1992).
Garnett, R, 'Coexisting and Conflicting Jurisdiction and Arbitration Clauses' (2013) 9 *Journal of Private International Law* 361.
Garnett, R and Richardson, M, 'Libel Tourism or Just Redress?' (2009) 5 *Journal of Private International Law* 471.
George, A and Keohane, R, 'The Concept of National Interests: Uses and Limitations' in A George, *Presidential Decision-making in Foreign Policy: The Effective Use of Information and Advice* (Westviewpress, 1980).
Gilles, L, 'Clarifying the "Philosophy of Article 15" in the Brussels I Regulation: C-585/08 *Peter v Reeder Karl Schluter GmbH and Co and C-144/09 Hotel Alpenhof Gesmbh v Oliver Heller*' (2011) 60 *International & Comparative Law Quarterly* 557.
Glanert S, 'Method?' in P Monateri (ed), *Methods of Comparative Law* (Edward Elgar Publishing, 2012).
Goldberg, J and Zipursky, B, 'Unrealised Torts' (2002) 88 *Virginia Law Review* 1625.
Gordley, J, *The Philosophical Origins of Modern Contract Doctrine* (Clarendon Press, 1993).
Goren, S (tr), *The Code of Civil Procedure Rules of the Federal Republic of Germany* (F Rothman & Co, 1990).
Guzman, A, 'Choice of Law: New Foundations' (2002) 90 *Georgetown Law Journal* 883.
Harding, C, 'Statist Assumptions, Normative Individualism and New Forms of Personality: Evolving a Philosophy of International Law for the Twenty First Century' (2001) 1 *Non-State Actors and International Law* 107.
Hartley, T, *International Commercial Litigation: Texts, Cases and Materials on Private International Law* (Cambridge University Press, 2009).
—— 'Libel Tourism" and Conflict of Laws' (2010) 59 *International & Comparative Law Quarterly* 25.
Henderson, J, 'Entrepreneurs and Consumers as Subjects of Civil Law' in W Simons (ed), *Private and Civil Law in the Russian Federation. Essays in Honor of FJM Feldbrugge* (Martinus Nijhoff Publishers, 2009).
Hess, B, *Private–Public Divide in International Dispute Resolution* (Recueil des cours, 2017).
Hill, J, *Cross-Border Consumer Contracts* (Oxford University Press, 2008).
Hook, M, 'The Choice of Law Agreement as a Reason for Exercising Jurisdiction' (2014) 63 *International & Comparative Law Quarterly* 963.
Iakovlev, V, 'The *Arbitrazh* Courts and the New Civil Code' in W Simons (ed), *Private and Civil Law in the Russian Federation. Essays in Honor of FJM Feldbrugge* (Martinus Nijhoff, Publishers, 2009).
Ibbetson, D, Book Review: '*Van Caenegem's An Historical Introduction to Private Law*' (1992) 41 *International & Comparative Law Quarterly* 958.
Ip, E, 'Globalization and the Future of the Law of the Sovereign State' (2010) 8 *International Journal of Constitutional Law* 636.
Ipsen, K, *Völkerrecht*, 5th edn (CH Beck, 2004).
Ivanov, N, *Osnovaniia Chastnoĭ Mezhdunarodnoĭ Iurisdiktsii* (*Foundations of Private International Jurisdiction*) (Scientific Papers of Kazan University, 1865).
Kant, I, *Groundwork of the Metaphysics of Morals: A German–English Edition* (M Gregor and J Timmermann eds, trs, Cambridge University Press, 2012).
Karapetyan, D, 'Jurisdiction, Recognition, and Enforcement of Court Judgments and Arbitral Awards: Analyses and Recommendations to Improve Armenian and Russian Legislation' (2002–03) 28 *Review of Central and East European Law* 211.
Karayanidi, M, 'Adjudicative Jurisdiction in Civil and Commercial Matters in Russia: Analysis and Commentary' (2016) 64 *American Journal of Comparative Law* 981.
Kaye, P, *Civil Jurisdiction and Enforcement of Foreign Judgments* (Professional Books Ltd, 1987).
Kazanskiĭ, P, *Vvedenie v Kurs Mezhdunarodnogo Prava* (*Introduction to the Course on International Law*) (Ekonomicheskaia, 1901).
Kelly, JM, *A Short History of Western Legal Thought* (Clarendon Press, 1992).
Kenny, D and Heffernan, L, 'Defamation and Privacy and the Rome II Regulation' in P Stone and Y Farah (eds), *Research Handbook on EU Private International Law* (Edward Elgar Publishing, 2015).

Keyes, M and Marshall, BA, 'Optional Jurisdiction Agreements' (2015) 11 *Journal of Private International Law* 345.

Khodykin, R, 'Prorogatsionnye Usloviia Vneshneekonomicheskikh Sdelok' ('Prorogation Conditions of Foreign Economic Transactions') (2002) 6 *Vestnik Vysshego Arbitrazhnogo Suda RF* 133.

Khrebtukova, A, 'A Call to Freedom: Towards a Philosophy of International Law in an Era of Fragmentation' (2008) 4 *Journal of International Law and International Relations* 51.

Komaritsky, S, 'Dogovornaya Podsudnost – Est N'iuansi' ('Contractual Jurisdiction – There are Nuances') (2003) 11 *Arbitrazh and Civil Procedure Journal* 18.

Komarov, A, 'The Role and Significance of international Arbitration in the Formation of a Modern Legal System in Russia' in W Simons (ed), *Private and Civil Law in the Russian Federation. Essays in Honor of FJM Feldbrugge* (Martinus Nijhoff Publishers, 2009).

Kopylov, A, 'Disputable Jurisdiction' (Спорная подсудность) (2010) 11 *EZh-Jurist* 17.

Kostin, A, 'Voprosy Deĭstvitelnosti Soglasheniia o Mezhdunarodnoĭ Podsudnosti na Etape Priznaniya i Privedeniya v Ispolnenie Inostrannogo Sudebnogo Resheniia' ('Issues of Validity of International Jurisdiction Agreements at the Stage of Recognition and Enforcement of a Foreign Judgment') (2014) 5 *Arbitrazhnyĭ I Grazhdanskiĭ Protsess* 49.

Krasavchikov, O, '*Dispozitivnost' v Grazhdansko-Pravovom Regulirovanii*' ('Principle of Free Exercise of Material and Procedural Rights by the Parties in Civil Law') (1970) 1 *Sovetskoe Gosudarstvo i Pravo* 41.

Krasheninnikov, P, *Postateinyĭ Kommentariĭ k Arbitrazhnomu Protsessual'nomu Kodeksu* (*Article-by-Article Commentary on Code of Arbitrazh Procedure*) (Statut, 2007).

Kraus, J, 'Personal Sovereignty and Normative Power Skepticism' (2009) 109 *Columbia Law Review Sidebar* 126.

Krylov, S, *Mezhdunarodnoe Chastnoe Pravo: Posobie k Lektsiiam* (*Private International Law: Textbook for Lectures*) (Priboĭ, 1930).

Kurochkin, S, 'Soglasheniia v Tsivilisticheskom Protsesse' ('Agreements in Civil Procedure') (2012) *Vestnik Grazhdanskogo Protsessa* 3.

Kuznetsov, S, *Sudebnie Obespechitelnie Sredstva v Rossiĭskom Grazhdanskom Prave* (*Legal Enforcement Remedies in Russian Civil Law*) (Wolters Kluwer, 2008).

Lauterpacht, H, *International Law and Human Rights* (Garland Publishing, 1973).

Layton, A and Mercer, H, *European Civil Practice*, 2nd edn (Sweet & Maxwell, 2004).

Legkiĭ, D, *Dmitry Vasil'evich Stasov: Sudebnaia Reforma 1864 g* (*Dmitry Stasov: Judicial Reform of 1864*) (Dmitry Bulanin, 2011).

Legrand, P, 'Beyond Method: Comparative Law as a Perspective' (1988) 36 *American Journal of Comparative Law* 788.

—— 'European Legal Systems Are Not Converging' (1996) 45 *International & Comparative Law Quarterly* 52.

Lehmann, M, 'Liberating the Individual from Battles between States: Justifying Party Autonomy in Conflict of Laws' (2008) 41 *Vanderbilt Journal of Transnational Law* 381.

Llewellyn, K, *The Common Law Tradition: Deciding Appeals* (Quid Pro Books, 1960).

Lunts, L, *Mezhdunarodnoe Chastnoe Pravo* (*Private International Law*), 3rd edn (Iuridicheskaia Literatura, 1973).

Lunts, L and Marysheva, N, *Kurs Mezhdunarodnogo Chastnogo Prava* (*Course on Private International Law*) (Iurid Lit, 1976).

Magnus, U and Mankowski, P (eds), *European Commentaries on Private International Law: Brussels I Regulation*, 2nd edn (Sellier European Law Publishers, 2012).

Maier, H and McCoy, T, 'A Unifying Theory for Judicial Jurisdiction and Choice of Law' (1991) 39 *American Journal of Comparative Law* 249.

Makarov, A, *Osnovnye Nachala Mezhdunarodnogo Chastnogo Prava* (*Fundamentals of Private International Law*) (IurIzdat NarkomIusta RSFSR, 1924).

Maleshin, D, 'Vmesto Predisloviya: "Pradedy" i "Pravnuki" Sudebnoĭ Reformy 1864' ('In Lieu of Introduction: "Great Grandfathers" and "Great Grandchildren" of the Judicial Reform 1864') in

Sudebnye Ustavy Rossiĭskoi Imperii 1984 goda (*Judicial Codes of the Russian Empire 1864*) (Statut, 2014).
Mance, L, 'In a Manner of Speaking: How Do Common, Civil and European Law Compare?' (2014) 78 *Rabel Zeitschrift für Ausländisches und Internationales Privatrecht* 231.
Mann FA, *The Doctrine of Jurisdiction in International Law* (Martinus Nijhoff Publishers, 1964).
—— *The Doctrine of International Jurisdiction Revisited After Twenty Years* (Martinus Nijhoff Publishers, 1984).
—— *Foreign Affairs in English Courts* (Oxford University Press, 1986).
Markovits, D and Schwartz, A, 'The Myth of Efficient Breach: New Defences of the Expectation Interest' (2011) 97 *Virginia Law Review* 1939.
Merrett, L, 'Article 23 of the Brussels I Regulation: A Comprehensive Code for Jurisdiction Agreements?' (2009) 58 *International & Comparative Law Quarterly* 545.
Michaels, R, 'Two Paradigms of Jurisdiction' (2006) 27 *Michigan Journal of International Law* 1003.
Michaels, R and Jansen, N, 'Private Law beyond the State? Europeanization, Globalization, Privatization' (2006) 54 *American Journal of Comparative Law* 843.
Micklitz, H-W, 'On the Intellectual History of Freedom of Contract and Regulation' (2015) 4 *Penn State Journal of Law & International Affairs* 1.
Miller, P, 'Principles of Public Fiduciary Administration' in A Scolnicov and T Kahana (eds), *Boundaries of State, Boundaries of Rights* (Cambridge University Press, 2016).
Mill, JS, *On Liberty* (Longman, Roberts, & Green Co, 1859/1975).
Mills, A, 'The Private History of International Law' (2006) 55 *International & Comparative Law Quarterly* 1.
—— 'Dimensions of Public Policy in Private International Law' (2008) 4 *Journal of Private International Law* 201.
—— *The Confluence of Private and Public International Law: Justice, Pluralism and Subsidiarity in the International Constitutional Ordering of Private Law* (Cambridge University Press, 2009).
—— 'The Identities of Private International Law: Lessons from the US and EU Revolutions' (2013) 23 *Duke Journal of Comparative and International Law* 445.
—— 'Rethinking Jurisdiction in International Law' (2014) 84 *British Yearbook of International Law* 187.
—— *Party Autonomy in Private International Law* (Cambridge University Press, 2018).
Mitina, M, 'O Ponimanii Sushchnosti Regulirovaniia Mezhdunarodnoĭ Podsudnosti: Sovremennye Tendentsii' ('On Understanding the Substance of Regulation of International Jurisdiction: Contemporary Tendencies') (2010) 4 *Izvestiia VUZov Pravovedenie* 229.
Morris, JHC, *Dicey's Conflict of Laws*, 6th edn (Stevens & Son Ltd, 1949).
Morris, JHC et al, *Dicey and Morris on the Conflict of Laws*, 9th edn (Stevens & Sons Ltd, 1973).
Muir Watt, H, 'Private International Law Beyond the Schism' (2011) 2 *Transnational Legal Theory* 347.
Myers, B, *Milton's Theology of Freedom* (De Gruyter, 2006).
Nefed'ev, E, *Osnovnye Nachala Grazhdanskogo Sudoproizvodstva* (*Fundamental Principles of Civil Procedure*) (Kazan, 1895).
Nelson, C, 'State and Federal Models of the Interaction between Statutes and Unwritten Law' (2013) 80 *University of Chicago Law Review* 657.
Neshataeva, T, 'International Civil Procedure in the Russian Federation: Sources and Issues' (2003) 28(2) *Review of Central and East European Law* 161.
—— 'O Voprosakh Kompetentsii Arbitrazhnykh Sudov v Rossiĭskoĭ Federatsii po Rassmotreniiu Del s Uchastiem Inostrannykh Lits' ('On Issues of Competence of *Arbitrazh* Courts in the Russian Federation on Proceedings with Foreign Parties') (2004) *JURIT-Vestnik* 88.
Nielsen, P, 'Jurisdiction over Consumer Contracts' in U Magnus P and Mankowski (eds), *European Commentaries on Private International Law: Brussels I Regulation*, 2nd edn (Sellier European Law Publishers, 2012).
Nokhrin, D, 'Russian National Report: Goals of Civil Justice' in D Maleshin (ed), *Civil Procedure in Cross-Cultural Dialogue: Eurasia Context* (Statut, 2012).
Nygh, P, *Autonomy in International Contracts* (Oxford University Press, 1999).

O'Brien, J, *Conflict of Laws* (Cavendish Publishing Limited, 1999).
O'Hara, E and Ribstein, L, 'From Politics to Efficiency in Choice of Law' (2000) 67 *University of Chicago Law Review* 1151.
Oman, N, 'Unity and Pluralism in Contract Law' (2005) 103 *Michigan Law Review* 1483.
Opalev, R and Rebrova, E, 'Rassmotrenie Spora po Mestu Ispolneniia Dogovora' ('Adjudication at the Place of Performance of Contract') (2011) 10 *EZh-Jurist* 3.
Oren, J, 'International Jurisdiction over Consumer Contracts in e-Europe' (2003) 52 *International & Comparative Law Quarterly* 676.
Pagden, A, *The Enlightenment: And Why it Still Matters* (Random House, 2013).
Peari, S, 'Savigny's Theory of Choice-of-Law as a Principle of "Voluntary Submission"' (2014) 64 *University of Toronto Law Journal* 106.
Pereterskiĭ, I, *Ocherki Mezhdunarodnogo Chastnogo Prava* (*Essays on Private International Law*) (Gosud Izdatelstvo, 1924).
Pereterskiĭ, I and Krylov, S, *Mezhdunarodnoe Chastnoe Pravo* (*Private International Law*) (IuridIz NKIu SSSR 1940).
Phillips, T, 'The Constitutional Right to a Remedy' (2003) 78 *New York University Law Review* 1309.
Pollock, F and Maitland, FM, *The History of English Law*, 2nd edn (Cambridge University Press, 1911).
Popper, K, *The Open Society and its Enemies*, 1st and 2nd vols, (Routledge, 1945).
Pryles, M, 'The Basis of Adjudicatory Competence in Private International Law' (1972) 21 *International & Comparative Law Quarterly* 61.
Ratković, T and Zgrabljić Rotar, D, 'Choice-of-Court Agreements under the Brussels I Regulation (Recast)' (2013) 9 *Journal of Private International Law* 245.
Rawls, J, *A Theory of Justice* (Clarendon Press, 1972 and rev edn, Oxford University Press, 1999).
Robb, R, 'Moral Theory, Autonomy, and Collective Rights: A Response to Dwight Newman' (2012) 25 *Canadian Journal of Law and Jurisprudence* 483.
Rolph, D, 'Splendid Isolation? Australia as a Destination for "Libel Tourism"' (2012) 19 *Australian International Law Journal* 79.
Rosenblum, D, 'How Firms and Nations Compete Through Intellectual Property Law' in H Muir Watt et al (eds), *Global Private International Law: Adjudication without Frontiers* (Edward Elgar Publishing, 2019).
Rousseau, J-J, 'The Social Contract' in E Barker, *Social Contract: Essays by Locke, Hume, and Rousseau* (Oxford University Press, 1960).
Rozhkova, M, 'Teoriya protsessual'nogo dogovora v sootnoshenii s kontseptsieĭ sdelok, napravlennyh na zashchitu prav' ('Theory of Procedural Agreement in Relation to the Concept of Transactions Aimed at Protection of Rights') (2007) 6 *Rossiĭskiĭ Ezhegodnik Grazhdanskogo i Arbitrazhnogo Protsessa* 184.
Rozhkova, M et al, *Dogovornoe Pravo: Soglasheniya o Podsudnosti, Mezhdunarodnoĭ Podsudnosti, Primiritel'noĭ Protsedure, Arbitrazhnoe (Treteĭskoe) i Mirovie Soglasheniia* (*Contract Law: Agreements on Jurisdiction, International Jurisdiction Agreements, Conciliation Agreements, Arbitration Agreements, Settlement Agreements*) (Statut, 2008).
Rühl, G, 'The Protection of Weaker Parties in the Private International Law of the European Union: A Portrait of Inconsistency and Conceptual Truancy' (2014) 10 *Journal of Private International Law* 335.
Ryngaert, C, *Jurisdiction in International Law* (Oxford University Press, 2008).
Sakhnova, T, *Tsivilisticheskiĭ Protsess* (*Civil Procedure*) (Prospect, 2014).
Sandel, MJ (ed), *Justice: A Reader* (Oxford University Press, 2007).
Savitsky, P, 'Protection of Product Appearance in Russia' (2013) 35 *European Intellectual Property Review* 143.
Schiff Berman, P, 'The Globalization of Jurisdiction' (2002) 151 *University of Pennsylvania Law Review* 311.
—— 'Choice of Law and Jurisdiction on the Internet: Towards a Cosmopolitan Vision on Conflict-of-Laws: Redefining Governmental Interests in a Global Era' (2005) 153 *University of Pennsylvania Law Review* 1819.

Sime, S, *A Practical Approach to Civil Procedure*, 10th edn (Oxford University Press, 2007).
Slaughter, A-M, *A New World Order* (Princeton University Press, 2004).
Smith R, *Conflict of Laws* (Cavendish Publishing Limited 1993)
Smith, S, *Contract Theory* (Oxford University Press, 2004).
Snijders, W, 'The Civil Codes of the Russian Federation and The Netherlands: Similarities and Contrasts' in W Simons (ed), *Private and Civil Law in the Russian Federation. Essays in Honor of FJM Feldbrugge* (Martinus Nijhoff Publishers, 2009).
Somek, A, 'German Legal Philosophy and Theory in the Nineteenth and Twentieth Centuries' in D Patterson (ed), *A Companion to Philosophy of Law and Legal Theory* (Blackwell Publishing Ltd, 1996).
Sorabji, J, 'Service where the Defendant is Outside the Jurisdiction' (2007) 26 *Civil Justice Quarterly* 279.
Steinle, J and Vasiliades, E, 'The Enforcement of Jurisdiction Agreements under the Brussels I Regulation: Reconsidering the Principle of Party Autonomy' (2010) 6 *Journal of Private International Law* 565.
Stevens, R, 'The Conflict of Rights' in A Robertson and HW Tang (eds), *The Goals of Private Law* (Hart Publishing, 2009).
Sultanov, A, 'Chelovek protiv Gosudarstva, Mezhdunarodnye Organy, Rossiia' ('Individual against the State, International Authorities, Russia') [2008] *Gosudarstvennaya Vlast I Samoupravlenie* 1.
Symeonides, S, *The American Choice-of-Law Revolution in the Courts: Today and Tomorrow* (Martinus Nijhoff Publishers 2003).
Tang, ZS, 'Exclusive Choice of Forum Clauses and Consumer Contracts in E-Commerce' (2005) 1 *Journal of Private International Law* 237.
—— 'Private International Law in Consumer Contracts: A European Perspective' (2010) 6 *Journal of Private International Law* 225.
—— 'Consumer Collective Redress in European Private International Law' (2011) 7 *Journal of Private International Law* 101.
Tesón F, 'The Kantian Theory of International Law' (1992) 92 *Columbia Law Review* 53.
Timohov, I, *Inostrannoe Pravo v Sudebnoi Praktike* (*Foreign Law in Judicial Practice*) (Wolters Kluwer, 2004).
Tomsinov, V, 'Russkiĭ Zakonoiskusnik Zakhar Anikeevich Goriushkin (1748–1821)' ('The Russian Jurist Zakhar Anikeevich Goriushkin (1748–1821)') (2009) 6 *Zakon* 287.
Toussaint, *Beck'scher Online Kommentar (OK)* ZPO (Beck-online, 15th edn, as of 1 January 2015) § 38.
Trapeznikov, V, 'Dopustima li Dogovornaya Podsudnost' Iskov?' ('Is Jurisdiction by Agreement Permissible?') (1924) 33 *Ezhenedelnik Sovetskoi Iustitsii* 770.
Twigg-Flesner, C (ed), *The Cambridge Companion to European Union Private Law* (Cambridge University Press, 2010).
Twitchell, M, 'The Myth of General Jurisdiction' (1988) 101 *Harvard Law Review* 610.
van Caenegem, RC, *An Historical Introduction to Private Law* (Cambridge University Press, 1988).
van Calster, G, *European Private International Law* (Hart Publishing, 2013).
van Rhee CH, 'The Influence of the French Code de Procédure Civile (1806) in 19th Century Europe' in L Cadiet and G Canivet (eds), *De la Commémoration d'un Code à l'Autre: 200 Ans de Procedure Civile en France* (*On Commemoration of the Code of Others: 200 Years Anniversary of Civil Procedure in France*) (LexisNexis/Litec, 2008).
Vasiljeva, K, '1968 Brussels Convention and EU Council Regulation No 44/2001: Jurisdiction in Consumer Contract Concluded Online' (2004) 10 *European Law Journal* 123.
Vershinina, E and Stakheeva, I, 'Usloviia Deĭstvitelnosti Sdelki v Rossii i Frantsii: Sravnitelno-Pravovoi Analiz' ('Conditions for Validity of Transaction in Russia and France: Comparative Analysis') (2013) 32(5) *Vestnik* 197.
Vinnichenko, O, Marochkin, S and Racheva, S 'Internal and External Law of Medieval Russia: A Look from the Current West' (2014) 2(3) *Russian Law Journal* 141.
von Mehren A, *Adjudicatory Authority in Private International Law* (Martinus Nijhoff Publishers, 2007).

von Mehren, A and Murray, P, *Law in the United States* (Cambridge University Press, 2007).
von Mehren, A and Trautman, D, 'Jurisdiction to Adjudicate: A Suggested Analysis' (1966) 79 *Harvard Law Review* 1121.
von Savigny, FK, *Of the Vocation of Our Age for Legislation and Jurisprudence* (Abraham Hayward tr, Littlewood & Co Old Bailey, 1831).
—— *A Treatise on Conflict of Laws, and the Limits of Their Operation in Respect of Place and Time* (William Guthrie tr, T&T Clark 1880).
Vorobieva, O, *Private International Law in Russia* (Kluwer Law International BV, 2012).
Waddams, S, 'Private Right and Public Interest' in M Bryan (ed), *Private Law in Theory and Practice* (Routledge-Cavendish, 2007).
Wai, R, 'Transnational Private litigation and Transnational Governance' in M Lederer and P Müller, *Criticizing Global Governance* (Palgrave Macmillan, 2005).
Waltz, K, *Theory of International Politics* (Waveland Press, 2010).
Wardhaugh, B, 'Bogeymen, Lunatics and Fanatics: Collective Actions and the Private Enforcement of European Competition Law' (2014) 34 *Legal Studies* 1.
Wass, J, 'The Court's *In Personam* Jurisdiction in Cases Involving Foreign Land' (2014) 63 *International & Comparative Law Quarterly* 103.
Weinrib, E, *The Idea of Private Law* (Oxford University Press, 2012).
Whincop, M and Keyes, M, *Policy and Pragmatism in the Conflict of Laws* (Ashgate, 2001).
Wood, D, 'The Structure of Sovereignty' (2014) 18 *Lewis & Clark Law Review* 215.
Yablochkov, T, *Kurs Mezhdunarodnogo Protsessualnogo Prava* (*The Course of International Procedural Law*) (Tipografiia Gubernskogo Pravleniia, 1909).
Yarkov, V, *Juridicheskie Fakty v Mekhanizme Realisatsii Norm Grazhdanskogo Protsessualnogo Prava* (*Legal Facts in the Mechanism of Application of Rules of Civil Procedure*) (SYuI, 1992).
—— 'Access to Justice: Foreign Persons and Russia's New Arbitration Procedure Code (Part I)' (2007) 32 *Review of Central and East European Law* 121.
—— (ed), *Arbitrazhnyĭ Protsess: Uchebnik* (*Arbitrazh Procedure: Textbook*), 4th edn (Infotropic Media, 2010).
Zhuikov, V, *Sudebnaia Reforma: Problemy Dostupa k Pravosudiiu* (*Judicial Reform: Problems of Access to Justice*) (Statut, 2006.)
—— 'The Supreme Court and the New Civil Code of the Russian Federation' in W Simons (ed), *Private and Civil Law in the Russian Federation. Essays in Honor of FJM Feldbrugge* (Martinus Nijhoff Publishers, 2009).
Zile, Z (ed), *Ideas and Forces in Soviet Legal History: A Reader on the Soviet State and Law* (Oxford University Press, 1992).
Zvekov, V, *Mezhdunarodnoe Chastnoe Pravo* (*Private International Law*) (NORMA, 2000).

Other Secondary Sources

'The Shareholders of AB Lietuvos Dujos Approved the Initiation of Arbitration Proceedings against OAO Gazprom' (Ministry of Energy of the Republic of Lithuania Newsletter, 30 January 2014), available at: enmin.lrv.lt/en/news/the-shareholders-of-ab-lietuvos-dujos-approved-the-initiation-of-arbitration-proceedings-against-oao-gazprom.
'GosDuma Rassmotrit Zakonoproekt o Sozdanii Patentnogo Suda' ('The Russian Duma (Parliament) Will Consider a Bill on Creation of Patent Court' (*Edinaya Rossiya News*, 26 September 2011), available at: er.ru/news/2011/9/26/gosduma-rassmotrit-zakonoproekt-o-sozdanii-patentnogo-suda.
American Law Institute (ALI)/UNIDROIT 'Principles of Transnational Civil Procedure' (2004) 9 *Uniform Law Review* 758.
Briggs, A, 'The Impact of Recent Judgments of the European Court on English Procedural Law and Practice' (2006) University of Oxford, Faculty of Law Legal Studies Research Paper Series, Working Paper No 11/2006.
—— 'Which Law Governs Forum Selection Clauses' (Paper for ASIL Webinar 'The Nature of Natures of Agreement Relating to Jurisdiction to Governing Law', 2 March 2016).

Cuniberti, G and Requejo, M, 'Damages for Breach of a Choice-of-Court Agreement' (2010) *ERA Forum* 7.

Dergachev, S, '"Dogovornaia Podsudnost" v Grazhdanskom i Arbitrazhnom Processe Rossii' ('"Jurisdiction" by Agreement in Civil and Commercial Procedure in Russia') (PhD, Russian Academy of Justice affiliated with the Supreme Court of the Russian Federation, 2011) (on file with author).

—— Assistant Professor, Chair of Civil, *Arbitrazh* and Administrative Procedural Law, Russian Academy of Justice (Dublin, Ireland–Moscow, Russia (skype interview) 20 April 2015).

Dickinson, A, 'The Proposal for a Regulation of the European Parliament and of the Council on Jurisdiction and the Recognition and Enforcement of Judgments in Civil and Commercial Matters (Recast)' (Note, European Parliament, Directorate General for Internal Policies, PE 453.200, Brussels 2011).

EU Commission, 'Common European Sales Law Proposals to be Replaced as New Consultation is Opened on Online Sales Barriers', June 2015, available at: www.out-law.com/en/articles/2015/june/common-european-sales-law-proposals-to-be-replaced-as-new-consultation-is-opened-on-online-sales-barriers.

European Commission for the Efficiency of Justice (CEPEJ), *European Judicial Systems – Edition 2014 (2012 data): Efficiency and Quality of Justice*, available at: www.coe.int/t/dghl/cooperation/cepej/evaluation/2014/Rapport_2014_en.pdf.

European Commission, 'Consumer Attitude towards Cross-Border Trade and Consumer Protection' (Flash Eurobarometer 358 Report 2013), available at: ec.europa.eu/public_opinion/flash/fl_358_en.pdf.

Giuliano, M and Lagarde, P, 'Report on the Convention on the Law Applicable to Contractual Obligations' (1980) OJ C 282/1.

Gulotta, C, 'L'Estensione Della Giurisdizione Nei Confronti Dei Datori di Lavoro Domiciliati All'estero: il Caso Mahamdia e il Nuovo Regime del Regolamento Bruxelles I-bis' ('The Extension of Jurisdiction over Employers Domiciled Abroad: The Mahamdia Case and the New Regime under the Brussels I-bis Regulation') (2013) 49 *Rivista di diritto internazionale privato e processuale* 619, summary by Francesca Villata in Conflict of Laws.net, available at: conflictoflaws.net/2014/third-issue-of-2013s-rivista-di-diritto-internazionale-privato-e-processuale.

Hague Conference on Private International Law (HCCH), 'The Judgments Project' (Overview by the HCCH), available at: www.hcch.net/en/projects/legislative-projects/judgments.

—— 'Conclusions and Recommendations of the Special Commission on the Practical Operation of the Hague Apostille, Service, Taking the Evidence and Access to Justice Conventions' (Permanent Bureau, 2–9 February 2009), available at: www.hcch.net/upload/wop/jac_concl_e.pdf.

—— 'Letter to Mr Lobach, Deputy Director, Ministry of Foreign Affairs' (The Hague, 7 July 2011, on file with author).

—— Russian Federation-Central Authority & Practical Information, available at: www.hcch.net/index_en.php?act=authorities.details&aid=699.

Heinze, C, 'Choice of Court Agreements, Coordination of Proceedings and Provisional Measures in the Reform of the Brussels I Regulation' (2011) Max Planck Private Law Research Paper no 11/5.

Hess, B, 'Should Arbitration and European Procedural Law be Separated or Coordinated?' (Conflict of Laws.net, Guest Editorial, 14 February 2010), available at: conflictoflaws.net/2010/guest-editorial-hess-should-arbitration-and-european-procedural-law-be-separated-or-coordinated.

Hess, B, Pfeiffer, T and Schlosser, P, 'Report on the Application of Regulation Brussels I in the Member States' (Institute for International and Private International Law, Ruprecht-Karls-University Heidelberg, Study JLS/C4/2005/03, Final Version, September 2007).

International Law Association (ILA), 'International Civil Litigation for Human Rights Violations' (C Kessedjian, E Ho and J van de Velden (eds), ILA Sofia Conference Final Report, 2012).

Jenard, P (ed), 'Report on the Convention on Jurisdiction and Enforcement of Judgments in Civil and Commercial Matters' (1979) OJ C 59/1.

John, Mark and Abboud, Leila, 'Far-right National Front Stuns French Elite with EU "Earthquake"' *Reuters* (Paris, 25 May 2014), available at: www.reuters.com/article/2014/05/25/us-eu-election-france-idUSBREA4O0CP20140525.

Kawohl, F, 'Commentary on the Copyright Provisions in the Baden Statute Book of 1809' in L Bently and M Kretschmer (eds), *Primary Sources on Copyright (1450–1900)*, available at: www.copyrighthistory.org.

Krasheninnikov P, Opening Statement to the Framework for the Consolidated Code of Civil Procedure of 8 December 2014 no 124(1).

Kucher, A, Yadykin, A and Asoskov, A, 'Are Asymmetric Jurisdiction Clauses Valid According to the Russian Law Following the Supreme *Arbitrazh* Court Decree in Sony Ericsson Case?' (Debevoise & Plimpton Client Update, 28 November 2012), available at: documents.lexology.com/ba1a3296-1ef5-489a-8c48-a7b06dac2125.pdf.

—— 'Entry into Law of Bundle of Amendments to Russian Civil Code – Section on Private International Law' (Debevoise & Plimpton Client Update, 18 October 2013).

Loboda, A, 'Sovremennye Teorii Mezhdunarodnogo Chastnogo Prava v Svete Podhodov Traditsyĭ Kontinentalnogo i Obshego Prava' ('Contemporary Theories of Private International Law in Light of the Traditions of Continental and Common Law') (Lecture, Private International and Civil Law, MGIMO).

Markovits, D, 'Sharing Ex Ante and Sharing Ex Post: The Non-Contractual Basis of Fiduciary Relations' (Max Planck Institute for Comparative and International Private law, Aktuelle Stunde (weekly discussions on comparative law), Hamburg, Germany, July 2014).

Miller, P, 'Dimensions of Fiduciary Loyalty' (Private Law Workshop at Harvard Law School Working Paper, Fall 2015, on file with author).

Nuyts, A, 'General Report on Study on Residual Jurisdiction (Review of the Member States' Rules concerning the "Residual Jurisdiction" of their courts in Civil and Commercial Matters pursuant to the Brussels I and II Regulations)' (3 September 2007, 3rd version), available at: ec.europa.eu/civiljustice/news/docs/study_residual_jurisdiction_en.pdf.

Obzor Sudebnoĭ Praktiki Verkhovnogo Suda RF 'Nekotorye Vorporsy Sudebnoĭ Praktiki po Grazhdanskim Delam' (Review of Court Practice by the Supreme Court of the RF, 'Certain Issues of Court Practice in Civil Cases' (1998) 10 *Bulletin of the Supreme Court of the RF* 22.

Pertegás, M and Dogauchi, M, 'Introducing the 2005 Hague Convention on Choice of Court Agreements' (Conference on International Litigation in the Asia Pacific Region, Wuhan, People's Republic of China, 23 September 2013).

Pocar, F, 'Explanatory Report on the Convention on Jurisdiction and the Recognition and Enforcement of Judgments in Civil and Commercial Matters, signed in Lugano on 30 October 2007' OJ C 319/1

Prihod'ko, I, 'Dostupnost' Pravosudiia v Arbitrazhnom i Grazhdanskom Protsesse: Osnovnye Problemy' ('Access to Justice in Arbitrazh and Civil Procedure: Main Issues') (speech at the All-Russian Research and Practice Conference on Access to Justice, Moscow, January–February 2001), available at: www.legist.ru/conf.html.

Raoul-Duval, P and Stoyanov, M, 'Comparative Study of "Residual Jurisdiction" in Civil and Commercial Disputes in the EU. National Report for: France' (National Report on Residual Jurisdiction, France, for The General Report: Study on Residual Jurisdiction edited by Arnaud Nuyts, 3 September 2007), available at: ec.europa.eu/civiljustice/news/docs/study_resid_jurisd_france_en.pdf.

Relevant Media LLC, 'How to Find an Address of a Person' (*KakProsto*) (online magazine) 2012.

Requelo, Marta, 'Is the Shevill Doctrine Still Up to Date? Some Further Thoughts on CJEU's Judgment in Hejduk (Case C-441/13)' (*ConflictofLaws*.net, 24 January 2015), available at: conflictoflaws.net/2015/is-the-shevill-doctrine-still-up-to-date-some-further-thoughts-on-cjeus-judgment-in-hejduk-c-44113.

RosPotrebNadzor, 'O Postanovlenii Plenuma Verkhovnogo Suda RF ot 28 iiunia 2012 g no 17 o Rassmotrnii Sudami Grazhdanskikh Del po Sporam o Zashchite Prav Potrebiteleĭ' (Federal Service for Supervision in the Area of Consumer Protection and Human Well-Being, On Resolution by the Supreme Court of the Russian Federation of 28 June 2012 no 17 'On Court Practice in Cases Protecting the Rights of Consumers') of 23 July 2012 no 01/8179-12-32.

RSPP, 'Zamechaniia i Predlozheniia k Proektu Federal'nogo Zakona no 474538-6/3 'O Vnesenii Izmenenii v Chasti Pervuiu, Vtoruiu, Tret'iu i Chetvertuiu GK RF, a Takzhe v Otdel'nye Zakonodatel'nye Akty RF' (Russian Union of Industrialists and Entrepreneurs, 'Notes and Recommendations to the Bill No.47538-6/3 'On Introducing Changes to the Parts 1, 2, 3 and 4 of the Civil Code of the RF and Other Legislative Acts'), available at: media.rspp.ru/document/1/f/b/fbd85ae7eb0fd7b46fc029b58b98a1f1.pdf.

Schlosser, P (ed), 'Report on the Convention on the Association of the Kingdom of Denmark, Ireland and the United Kingdom of Great Britain and Northern Ireland to the Convention on jurisdiction and the enforcement of judgments in civil and commercial matters and to the Protocol on its interpretation by the Court of Justice' (1979) OJ C 59/71.

UK Border Agency, 'Nationality Instructions: Registering British nationals (nationality instructions)' (29 November 2013), available at: www.gov.uk/government/publications/chapter-12-registering-british-nationals-nationality-instructions.

Vick, D and Campbell K, 'Public Protests, Private Lawsuits, and the Market: The Investor Response to the McLibel Case' (2001) 28 *Journal of Law and Society* 2, 204.

—— 'McLibel: Longest Case in English History' (*BBC News*, 15 February 2005), available at: news.bbc.co.uk/2/hi/uk_news/4266741.stm.

Woodruff, C and Reed, K, 'Comparative Study of "Residual Jurisdiction" in Civil and Commercial Disputes in the EU: National Report for England' (National Report on Residual Jurisdiction, England, for The General Report: Study on Residual Jurisdiction edited by Arnaud Nuyts, 3 September 2007), available at: ec.europa.eu/civiljustice/news/docs/study_resid_jurisd_england_en.pdf.

Zhilin, G, 'Tseli Grazhdanskogo Sudoproizvodstva i Ikh Realizatsiia v Sude Pervoi Instantsii' ('Goals of Civil Procedure and Their Realisation in a Court of First Instance') (LLD Book, Institute of Law and Comparative Law adjunct to the Government of Russia 2000).

INDEX

www.ingramcontent.com/pod-product-compliance
Ingram Content Group UK Ltd.
Pitfield, Milton Keynes, MK11 3LW, UK
UKHW021908150926
475560UK00003B/260